Publication Number 27

Duke University Commonwealth-Studies Center

*The International Law Standard and
Commonwealth Developments*

Duke University Commonwealth-Studies Center Publications

* Program in Comparative Studies on Southern Asia publication.

The International Law Standard and Commonwealth Developments

Robert R. Wilson   Robert E. Clute

John M. Howell   Herman Walker

Don C. Piper

Edited by

Robert R. Wilson

Published for the

Duke University Commonwealth-Studies Center

Duke University Press, Durham, N. C.

1966

Printed in the United States of America
by Kingsport Press, Inc., Kingsport, Tenn.

Preface

Legal devices have served various purposes in the life of the Commonwealth. The role which public international law has had would seem to invite particular attention by reason of the varied contexts in which it is discernible. Some of these are obvious. The very concept of statehood is one, since independence is meaningless except in terms of relations between separate entities. Aside from this, however, are broad areas in which the law's applicability may find demonstration, although it may not be the major factor in all of these areas.

The initial chapter of the present volume deals selectively with notions of statehood as advanced by men politically minded and prominent in the old Commonwealth. Their ideas are perhaps deserving of re-examination in light of the direction of development in the more than three decades since the attainment by the dominions of full independence. This new status was not to be attended by the complete and immediate dissolution of all the pre-existing ties with Great Britain. Retention of such ties was, however, to be at the will of each of the associated states. In this respect any ties which the new states chose to have continued were consistent with international law.

The emergence, in the fifth, sixth, and seventh decades of the twentieth century of additional independent states within the Commonwealth association heralded the advent of a new type of nationalism which in the present volume has been called "neonationalism" to distinguish it from the type familiar in the period of the old Commonwealth. A distinguishing characteristic of a number of these new states has been their disposition not to renounce international law, but to interpret it so as to combat what

has been called colonialism and fascism. Such parts of international law as those touching state succession and prescription,
as also the standard of responsibility for the treatment of resident
aliens and alien-owned property, have come into question in this
connection. Views on these subjects have found expression through
international organization as well as in ordinary diplomatic exchanges. Illustrative instances have been noted in the second
chapter of the present volume.

Chapter 3 considers the manner in which official representation
has developed as a means of cohesion and cooperation between
Commonwealth members as well as for purposes of international
law generally. Types of public agents functioned for the purpose
of facilitating business between Great Britain and her colonies
long before the latter became fully independent. Later came association of dominion representatives with British missions at international conferences as well as at such capitals as Washington. A
distinctive development both throughout this period and later was
that of the office of high commissioner. In the 1960's the United
Kingdom's merging of its Foreign Office representation abroad
with Commonwealth Relations Officer personnel overseas (but
with no immediate amalgamation of these two offices in London)
affected the traditional distinction which had been preserved between British representation in its former colonies and that in
"foreign" states. There followed the institution in 1965 of a mixed-
manned secretariat of the Commonwealth, the law involved being
rather adjective than substantive in character.

The fourth chapter reviews in a brief manner the transfer of law
to British colonies. More particularly, it considers the claimed ingredient of international law in the common law. Holdings of
national courts concerning the authority of international law,
provisions in written constitutions as to the relationship of international law to municipal law, and positions taken in diplomatic
correspondence as well as in national legislative bodies have
thrown light on Commonwealth states' positions as to the reality
and applicability of international law. Concession of reality and
applicability has not, of course, precluded differences of opinion
as to the interpretation of pre-existing law or as to the relative

utility of particular parts of it. Asian and African states that are members of the Commonwealth have found opportunity, sometimes in cooperation with other states, to express views with respect to existing law in connection with recent efforts for codification. Forums of international organizations have provided still other opportunities for individual Commonwealth states' representatives to make their views known on legal as well as on political matters.

In realization of the rather broad range of the inquiry, it seemed appropriate that the present volume should take the form of a symposium rather than a monograph. Chapters 5 through 9 comprise analyses of problems that involve inherent questions of international law. In his chapter on citizenship and nationality, as well as in that on extradition and in the Appendix, which deals with naturalization and registration, Professor Robert E. Clute (of the Department of Political Science, University of Georgia) has considered rights and practice with respect to individuals under both international law and the municipal law of Commonwealth states. Professor Herman Walker (of the Department of History and Political Science, State University College, New Paltz, New York), a former specialist on commercial policy in the United States Department of State, who has in the past several years conducted independent research in the General Agreement on Tariffs and Trade, has presented in Chapter 7 an analysis of Commonwealth states' situation with relation to international trade and particularly the European Common Market; in this connection he has had occasion to consider international law principally in conventional form. Professor John M. Howell (Chairman of the Department of Political Science, East Carolina College, Greenville, N. C.), who in previous publications has dealt with the concept of domestic jurisdiction in general and with delimitation of the concept, has in Chapter 8 of the present volume directed attention especially to what Commonwealth states have advocated concerning domestic jurisdiction and concerning the emergent doctrine of international concern. Professor Don C. Piper (of the Department of Government and Politics at the University of Maryland), whose earlier published studies have examined some Canadian and Canadian-

American positions concerning the law of nations, has in Chapter 9 shown the extent to which, and the manner in which, Commonwealth states have cooperated in the recognition and enforcement of each other's court judgments.

Chapter 10 is not designed as a "conclusion" of the traditional type or as a mere summary. It seeks, rather, to weigh factors which, as brought out in earlier chapters, have seemed to affect Commonwealth states' adherence to and application of international law. That this law has assumed relative importance in the relations of states that are Commonwealth members would seem to be indicated, at least illustratively, by the evidence which the preceding chapters have endeavored to present.

The rapidity of change in the Commonwealth makes it difficult to be completely up to date in any volume dealing with Commonwealth developments. In the present symposium there has been an effort to note selected phenomena up to the middle of 1965. This leaves out of consideration such subsequent events as Rhodesia's unilateral declaration of independence and the detachment of Singapore from Malaysia. The objective throughout the symposium has been to discern situations in which the fact of international law has, in some manner appearing to be significant, affected the Commonwealth story.

The design for the present volume grew out of periods of study and observation in a number of states of the Commonwealth. For courtesies shown them, the authors are indebted to scholars at various universities of the Commonwealth, and also to parliamentary librarians and govermental officials who have made useful suggestions concerning materials. I personally am particularly indebted for courtesies extended at the Canadian Archives in Ottawa, at the Institute of Commonwealth Studies at the University of London, at the Institute for Advanced Legal Studies at the same University, at Chatham House, and at the Library of the Royal Commonwealth Society in London. The personnel of the Duke University Library and of the Duke Law School Library have with their unfailing courtesy given valuable assistance.

To my fellow contributors to the volume, Professors Clute,

Howell, Walker, and Piper, I express my thanks for what has been for me a most pleasant association. My special thanks are due to Professor David R. Deener of Tulane University, well known for his own published work in the field of international law and of Commonwealth relations, for his technical editing of the present volume, and for his many helpful suggestions for its improvement. Officers of the Duke University Press, which has now published more than twenty-five volumes in its Commonwealth-Studies Center series, have shown characteristic courtesy in connection with the present volume. Mrs. C. W. Ralston has rendered assistance of great value in the preparation of manuscripts, in the checking of proofs, and in the decision of various questions concerning the form and arrangement of materials.

Inclusion of the volume in the Duke University Commonwealth-Studies Center series was made possible by grants from the Carnegie Corporation to the Duke University Commonwealth-Studies Center: for opinions expressed or conclusions reached, however, the respective authors alone are responsible.

ROBERT R. WILSON

Durham, North Carolina
June 15, 1966

Contents

Contents

The International Law Standard and
Commonwealth Developments

1

Concepts of Statehood, 1917–1939

Robert R. Wilson*

"Status," wrote Loring Christie in 1926, "is no mere matter of window-dressing. It is a highly practical conception, as all our law, both international and private, shows." The Canadian legalist, who was later to be his country's chief of mission to the United States, added that "we have to tackle the legalities—as decently as possible but to whatever extent is necessary to put us right."[1]

The former British "dominions" (a term that came into regular use after 1907) have long since become full members of the world family of nations. They have in the course of the twentieth century assumed all rights and responsibilities in the international-law sense. Newer members of the Commonwealth, which are also full states for the purposes of international law, have had no quite comparable earlier experience as entities with qualified international status. The process through which the old members of the Commonwealth became fully independent was naturally the subject of considerable discussion by leaders of the respective countries. The manner in which both types of Commonwealth members have subsequently interpreted and applied international law has not been dissociated from this earlier thinking. Effects of a common heritage, some disposition to act along parallel lines in dealing with problems that are international in the broadest sense, and a continuing disinclination of these states to treat each other as wholly foreign have continued to be in

* James B. Duke Professor of Political Science, Duke University.
1. Borden Papers (Canadian Archives), folder 59, pp. 148301, 148303 (letter to Philip Kerr, March 15, 1926).

evidence. These considerations give point to an inquiry into the collective effect that Commonwealth countries have had or may have upon the understanding and development of the law of nations. Their very acquisition of national status provides instructive example.

In the course of the dominions' progress toward statehood there was not at all times primary emphasis upon international legal factors. It would probably be unrealistic to ascribe major importance in the progress of the dominions toward independence to international legal considerations. Yet in the total process such considerations, both in customary and conventional contexts, had a part. For statehood, attained as it was through the process of claiming and exercising rights and acknowledging duties, could not have been completely meaningful except against a background of an international legal system. In the British tradition, it was hardly conceivable that the process could have gone on without a considerable ingredient of legalism with respect to external as well as internal relations.

For the present purpose, states of the "old" Commonwealth are therefore to receive attention before the newer Commonwealth members. The manner in which the former moved toward the assumption of full international status was affected by (a) the implications in the thoughts of representative political leaders concerning self-government, (b) changing power alignments in the period under consideration, and (c) local situations that made the transition slower in some of the dominions than in others.

1. Implications of Dominion Self-Government

It is common knowledge that a relatively small number of men who were willing to tackle the legalities as well as face political and economic problems had a preponderant part in guiding the dominions toward the assumption of full statehood. The communities in which they were active had already had considerable experience in self-government. It was natural that there should be a growing desire for self-determination in the field of external affairs. On the other hand, moves toward autonomy in such affairs seemed to some, at least, to presage a disruption of the British Empire and the values which it represented. Fears of this development tended to be a brake on any rapid movement toward full independence and encouraged dreams of a type of imperial federation, which involved proposals alternative to those looking to complete control by each dominion of its foreign relations.

The change from dominion to full international status came more gradually than might have been the case had there been revolutionary, rather than evolutionary, effort. The statesmanship of Mackenzie King is too well known an example to require extended mention here. Also associated with evolutionary change are the names of Robert Borden, Newton D. Rowell, Loring Christie, and John W. Dafoe in Canada; General Jan Smuts in South Africa; and, to a lesser extent, William M. Hughes of Australia and William F. Massey of New Zealand. In the case of Massey the influence tended to be a moderating rather than an accelerating one. Without following either a chronological or a rigid topical arrangement one can discern in the words of these men the type of thinking that looked to statehood as a goal rather than to some form of imperial federation of the self-governing communities.

For the present purpose the names of Borden and Smuts are most prominent in the list. The former, when Canadian prime minister, had been invited by Asquith in 1915 to attend British Cabinet meetings. Later in the course of World War I (in 1917) Borden offered in the Imperial War Conference a resolution (IX) which was to be invoked rather frequently in the ensuing decade. The resolution, which the conference adopted, contained the following:

The Imperial War Conference are of opinion that the readjustment of the constitutional relations of the component parts of the Empire is too important and intricate a subject to be dealt with during the War and that it should form the subject of a special Imperial Conference to be summoned as soon as possible after the cessation of hostilities.

They deem it their duty, however, to place on record their view that any such readjustment, while thoroughly preserving all existing powers of self-government and complete control of domestic affairs, should be based upon a full recognition of the Dominions as autonomous nations of an Imperial Commonwealth, and of India as an important portion of the same, should recognise the right of the Dominions and India to an adequate voice in foreign policy and in foreign relations, and should provide effective arrangements for continuous consultation in all important matters of common Imperial concern, and for such necessary concerted action, founded on consultation, as the several Governments may determine.[2]

The conclusion of the war and the making of the peace treaty with Germany provided occasion for some practical application of the ideas which the resolution had set forth. There was some anticipation on the part of the dominion representatives at Paris that Allied Powers not familiar with the "family" relationships existing between the different British communities would question the enlargement of the British Empire delegation at the conference so that each dominion might be given a spokesman. Borden's view was that it was for the empire to define the rights and duties of the "component nations." Foreign nations, he thought, had no right to question that definition.[3]

As Dafoe reported, after the matter was presented to the other Allied Powers, the point concerning the dominions was "handsomely conceded" by them and the matter was settled as the dominions desired.[4] The outcome was a departure from precedent in that at Paris the dominions were to have a direct voice in political and diplomatic discussions—a distinct advance over the system that had previously permitted them to have some voice in their own external affairs mainly insofar as commercial policy was involved.[5] Press reaction emphasized the novelty of this. In a speech at London, as reported in *The Times* (London) of May 17, 1919, Borden said:

2. See M. Ollivier, *Colonial and Imperial Conferences*, vol. 11, *Imperial Conferences*, pt. 1 (1954), p. 175. For an earlier (French-Canadian) view as to status, see Henri Bourassa, *Independence or Imperial Partnership* (1916), especially at p. 62.
3. Borden Papers (Canadian Archives), RLB 8 (2), p. 87080.
4. *Ibid.*, p. 49932 (telegram of Dafoe to Nicholls, Jan. 14, 1919).
5. For discussion concerning commercial policy and the dominions, see Robert E. Clute and Robert R. Wilson, "The Commonwealth and Favored-Nation Usage," 52 *Am. J. Int'l L.* 455 (1958).

Two years ago we met in the Imperial War Conference, in the summer of 1917, and, without attempting to lay down very definite terms as to what the future relations of the parts of the Empire should be, we did reach the unanimous conclusion—accepted at that time without the slightest hesitation by the Government of the United Kingdom—that the future of the Empire must be based on one great principle alone—and that is: equality of nations within the British Empire.

. . . Equal nationhood within the British Empire—that has been carried out in Paris; in the first place, by affording the representatives of the great Dominions of the Empire a place at the council table, just as they had a place in the battlefield. If they have one place, why should they not have the other?

There are those in certain quarters who have been disturbed by this, because they believe that the equality of nationhood as applied in the proceedings of the Peace Conference tends towards the disintegration of the British Empire. I know something of the ideas and aspirations of one British Dominion, and I venture to quiet any such alarm by saying that, so long as that principle is observed, there is not the slightest ground for apprehension; but there would be grave danger indeed if there should be the least attempt to depart from it.

A new precedent had indeed been set. Yet this did not necessarily mean that the new method of transacting diplomatic business affecting the external relations of the dominions would quickly become normal. Developments relating to the Washington Conference on the Limitation of Naval Armament, 1921–1922, were soon to emphasize this fact. Invitations to the conference did not go to the dominion governments. As Borden said in a speech at New Haven, there was in at least one dominion expression of regret that "the status of self-governing Dominions had not received due consideration."[6] General Smuts also felt that a protest was in order and wrote that he "never dreamt that any other course than the Paris precedent would be followed." After first declining to have South Africa represented at the conference, he later requested that full powers in respect of that dominion be issued to Mr. Balfour, who eventually signed the treaties as delegate for the Union of South Africa as well as delegate for the

6. Borden Papers (Canadian Archives), folder 70, p. 149437. In referring to the point, Borden noted that Italy separately invited Canada to an economic and financial conference in 1922 and that the United States had invited Canada to a conference on revision of a convention on industrial property.

United Kingdom. Writing to Borden under date of April 26, 1922, Smuts said that it was he and Borden who had been "mostly responsible for that recasting of the British Empire which is perhaps the most solid fact that has emerged from the Great War. A great world group of states bound together in some indefinable organic union is quite a new constitutional category in the historical evolution of the world." He went on to say that, "unless we hold firmly to this principle of Dominion equality of Status, republican and separatist movements will begin in the Great Dominions which it would be difficult to deal with."[7]

On January 9, 1923, Borden wrote to Smuts that their commonly held idea was a means of preserving unity. "Like you," he added, "I am sometimes charged with carrying the principle of equal nationhood so far as to endanger the unity of the Commonwealth. With you, I am firmly convinced that the full application of this principle offers the only means of preserving that unity which after all is of the spirit and not of statute or parchment."[8]

The Lausanne peace settlement with Turkey and the making of the Locarno agreements provided further occasion for reflection upon the status which the dominions appeared to have attained. Concerning a Borden memorandum on the first of these developments, Loring Christie wrote from London to express his hope that in further discussions at Ottawa "legal niceties" might be avoided and thought given to the "realities of the idea of cooperation" and to the "relation of that idea to the substance of foreign policy." He suggested that the dominions should exert a voice against entry into guaranties and alliances on the Continent without the understanding and support of the dominions and without the United States' also going along. He took the occasion to describe the dominions as "the only western countries where the answer to these fundamental questions of national life and status were not settled and taken universally for granted."[9]

By the ninth article of the principal treaty signed at Lausanne, the treaty was not to impose any obligations upon India or the

7. *Ibid.*, folder 69, pp. 149189, 149190.
8. *Ibid.*, p. 149196.
9. *Ibid.*, folder 58, p. 148084.

dominions without their acceptance. This still did not allay concern in all quarters over the general direction of the development with reference to the dominions' control of their own foreign policies. Under date of December 23, 1925, General Smuts wrote to Borden that Locarno had accomplished the desirable object of getting Germany into the League of Nations. He observed, however, that from the point of view of the empire an "evil" precedent had been set: the British Empire seemed to have been divided and the united front broken. On the issue of whether the latter would ever be restored, Smuts said that there was great apathy in South Africa. He considered that such a development held "the seed of future decay and dissolution for the Empire."[10]

To Austin Chamberlain, British foreign minister, Borden wrote on January 30, 1926, that he had been "rather disturbed by the recession from the method and spirit of negotiation in which all the nations of the Commonwealth took part," a method which, he thought, had "worked admirably both at Paris and at Washington," and was a means by which, at conferences where treaties or conventions were under consideration, the spirit of the resolution of the Imperial War Conference (i.e., the resolution of 1917) could be "carried into practical effect." He noted that the question of consultation during intervals between such conference discussions as those referred to was "much more difficult." He pointed out that there was, especially in South Africa and in Canada, a certain indifference to responsibilities that accompanied the statehood which the dominions claimed and "which they must assume if the Commonwealth is to endure."[11]

Writing to Borden under date of February 27, 1926, Chamberlain referred to the "highest point of cooperation" that up to that time had been reached. He said, on the subject of nomenclature, that while the term "Imperial Cabinet" had at first seemed acceptable in connection with co-operation, there had later been objection by the dominions to the term "Cabinet" as implying "too intimate a responsibility." He further said that "by the wish of

10. *Ibid.*, folder 71, p. 149711.
11. *Ibid.*, folder 9, p. 148239.

Dominion statesmanship" there had been reversion to the term "Conference." Chamberlain thought this a matter for regret, since it seemed to him to "cover what is really the big issue." He mentioned his own practice, since he had been foreign secretary, of sending, for communication to the dominion prime ministers, "practically everything on foreign affairs . . . thought to be of sufficient consequence to be circulated to the Cabinet at home." While this covered the *information* aspects of the problem, it left what he described as "the most difficult" side, namely, the absence of a dominion representative with whom the foreign secretary would be authorized to discuss confidentially such problems and who would be in position to give the foreign secretary advice on what he and his government were thinking on such problems.[12]

In London, Loring Christie (who had been legal adviser to the Ministry of External Affairs at Ottawa from 1913 to 1923) continued to reflect upon the legal and political aspects of the dominions' (and particularly Canada's) changing situation. Speculating upon how Canada might move in the light of her widening responsibilities, he raised (in a communication dated February 25, 1926) certain questions concerning the logical next steps. One question was the practicability of Canada's assuming "complete sovereignty under the Crown," his idea being that Great Britain and foreign states might formally recognize the new arrangement. He also suggested the possibility of a loose federation with Great Britain: Canada might have direct representation through diplomatic and consular officers in some countries, while in others there would be representation for Canada through the British diplomatic service. Christie envisaged "many consequential questions concerning citizenship and so on." He thought that the head of the Canadian state might have the title of Governor-General and be elected by the Dominion Senate and House of Commons, or perhaps by provincial delegates.[13] In a communi-

12. *Ibid.*, folder 71, p. 149723. Chamberlain in the same letter pointed out that he could not communicate through their representative as he would through the ambassador of a foreign country, a fact which he thought would not matter so much if time were not of the essence of successful diplomacy.
13. *Ibid.*, folder 59, p. 148282.

cation dated June 4 of the same year Christie envisaged within
the existing imperial legal structure "a project compatible with
real Canadian national responsibilities" and with Canada's "inescapable position on the map."[14]

Commonwealth statesmen disagreed as to the necessity or
desirability of spelling out in legal terms the precise position of a
dominion in relation to the United Kingdom. On the question of
action by Canada herself along the line suggested, Newton D.
Rowell had written in 1922, "If we can define our own status then
we have no constitution which governs the action of our Federal
Parliament."[15] However, that the problem required legal definition and arrangement rather than merely drifting into a new state
of things seems to have been strongly felt by Christie. Writing to
Kerr in March, 1926, he spoke of "completing our present
international status."[16] Writing to Christie in the following month,
Borden observed that the principle of consultation had never
received a fair trial. He submitted that it could not receive a fair
trial until the dominions took the initiative. Describing the
dominions as "proud and happy to regard themselves as Nations,"
he went on to say that if they were to make their voices and
influence felt they must take such steps as were necessary to that
end.[17]

The principal proponents of full statehood as a goal for the
dominions appear to have been aware that to the "plain man" this
meant disunity of the empire. Borden's view, on the other hand,
was that the alternative to such statehood, i.e., imperial federation, was not a matter of "practical politics."[18] His thought was
undoubtedly directed primarily to Canada's immediate problems,
but he looked to a solution of those problems through the
acquisition of an independent status that would permit co-operative arrangements with other self-governing dominions. His idea
of internationalism embraced more than mere constitutional

14. *Ibid.*, folder 70, p. 148376. In this same letter Christie wrote that "the
executive act and stroke of pen that put Canada in a state of war continue to
reside here" (i.e., in London).
15. *Ibid.*, p. 149418 (letter of Dec. 5, 1922).
16. *Ibid.*, folder 59, p. 148304 (letter of March 15, 1926).
17. *Ibid.*, p. 148361 (letter of April 16, 1926).
18. *Ibid.*, p. 148247.

arrangements. As early as 1922, speaking at New Haven, he seemed to be referring to legalism when, in words attributed to Gladstone, he said that the world's unity for peace "must be found in realization of public right and international justice."[19]

It is perhaps true, as Balfour suggested, that the novel character of the British Empire after World War I was a favorite theme for statesmen and professors,[20] although, as an authoritative writer has pointed out, the foreign policies of the Commonwealth members for the most part lacked dramatic interest until 1939.[21] Before that date, however, there had come to be a strong note of idealism in expressions of some of the leading Commonwealth spokesmen. Thus Dafoe, in 1927, referred to an "implication" which he said had become established, "that in Canadian matters the crown of England could be advised exclusively by Canadian ministers." He regarded the winning of responsible government as the great step toward attainment of independence and thought that the enlargement of self-governing power rose naturally out of the operation of responsible government. The "new theory of Empire" he conceived simply as the non-subordination of any part to any other part.[22]

The concept of nationhood thus was founded in a theory of both constitutionalism and internationalism. As has been seen, progress toward actual independence, whatever the theory of continuing unity under a single crown, seemed to some to foreshadow a disunity few would have desired. There continued to be suggestions of South Africa's becoming a republic. There does not seem to have been general agreement upon the possibility of the Union's taking this step without its implying a complete

19. *Ibid.*, folder 70, p. 149449. He concluded the address with these words: "In the world community and in each national sphere peace and good government rest ultimately upon enlightened and active public opinion upholding ordered justice and restraining lawless violence." Cf. Newton Rowell's quotation of Gladstone in his reference to "enthronement of public right as the governing idea of European policy" and as "the common and precious heritage of all lands." Rowell Papers (Canadian Archives), folder 42, p. 6815.
20. Nicholas Mansergh, *Survey of British Commonwealth Affairs: Problems of External Policy, 1931–1939* (1952), p. 4.
21. *Ibid.*, Introduction, p. xvii.
22. John W. Dafoe, "The Problems of Canada," in *Great Britain and the Dominions* ("Lectures on the Harris Foundation 1927") (1928), pp. 192, 194, 197.

severance of the ties holding the dominions to each other. For all
the dominions there was, with the contemplated loosening of
imperial ties and the implications of such actual independence as
they had attained, a very practical consideration. This was the
matter of defense. The dominions faced the prospect of having to
choose the course that would be consistent with their protection
while asserting in foreign as well as domestic relations the right to
responsible government. Power alignments had to be taken into
account in dominion thinking.

2. Effects of Changing Power Alignments

During the third and fourth decades of the twentieth century,
as the dominions progressed toward the status of fully independent states in the international-law sense, their leaders could not be
indifferent to what was happening in the new era when international responsibility was proclaimed—even if collective security
was not also attained. It was to be expected that self-interest
would impel the former British colonies toward common positions
in international politics, but there was no clear acceptance of an
obligation for the emerging communities to take uniform action in
specific situations. Problems of the peace settlement after World
War I gave point to the concern of dominion statesmen concerning police action or other enforcement measures, as, for example,
action to be taken in Europe. Early in the history of the League of
Nations, Canada's move to secure an interpretation of Covenant
article 10 seemed to reflect this concern. By a limitative interpretation of article 10 (which interpretation was not formally
adopted because of one adverse vote in a situation where
unanimity was required, but which seems actually to have
attained some importance as a guide to practice), geographical
propinquity would have become a factor when there was a
question of deciding which League members would have been
called upon to assist with enforcement action in the territory of
another state.

The Chanak incident in 1923, Washington and London conference decisions concerning limitation of armament, and the termination of the Anglo-Japanese Alliance were developments to which dominions could hardly be indifferent. Dominion statesmen had to consider the possibility of armed conflict in which their respective countries might be called upon to assist, but in which they might feel that they had no very direct stake.

The always-present question of whether a dominion could be brought into a legal state of war by reason of Great Britain's declaring war was not to be settled until 1939, and events of the immediately preceding decade were to affect the decision. Each of the dominions accepted for itself, and not simply by virtue of Great Britain's acceptance, the Paris Pact for the Renunciation of War as an Instrument of National Policy. A few years earlier (in 1923) had come a situation in which a precedent was set for a new procedure in bilateral treaty-making by a dominion. Arranging with the United States for regulation of halibut fishing off the Pacific coast, Canada had (and apparently welcomed, the British government being acquiescent) an opportunity to make a treaty that was signed by a Canadian official and a United States secretary of state, but not by an official of Great Britain. A United States Senate reservation, had it been adopted, would have had the effect of making the treaty rules effective for all British subjects (not merely those in Canada), but this was not acceptable to the Canadians, not desired by the American executive, and not insisted upon by the United States Senate.[23]

Several dominions accepted responsibilities for mandated areas under the League of Nations. One of these areas, South-West Africa, was later to become the subject of considerable discussion and controversy. Such South African leaders as John Xavier Merryman apparently looked to its annexation by the Union of South Africa. While this did not occur after the demise of the League, South Africa stood on firm legal ground in claiming that she was not obligated to convert the mandate into a United Nations trust territory after the termination of World War II, and

23. See R. MacGregor Dawson, *William Lyon Mackenzie King, A Political Biography* (1958), pp. 430–436; U. S., *For. Rel.*, 1924, I, pp. 338–341.

the International Court of Justice sustained the South African position on this point.

While Australia continued to rely heavily upon British sea power in an insecure world, Canada was soon to become increasingly closer, in the matter of defense planning, to the United States. In the Union of South Africa there continued to be a considerable amount of sentiment for withdrawing from the imperial system. New Zealand, being much more inclined to stay within the British fold, felt no special need for changing dominion and imperial relationships.[24]

Questions of German rearmament and default on German reparations marked the period, and in the mid-thirties Mussolini's adventure in Ethiopia brought the states of the Commonwealth, with other League states, into a situation wherein they were called upon to approve economic sanctions against Italy. No interruption in Commonwealth ties resulted from these developments. Throughout the remainder of the decade, except for Ireland's disaffection, the dominions did not change their formal legal relations with Great Britain, although they moved toward more completely separate handling of their own affairs. In this connection there were some developments in the matter of channels for representation, but in this matter, as in various others, the pace of advance was by no means the same in all of the states.

3. Unevenness in Transition

In light of the differences in their geographical, political, and defense situations, it was hardly to be expected that the "old" Commonwealth members would react with precisely the same alacrity to proposals that they assume a greater measure of self-direction of their own external relations. Assumption of status as fully independent states in this sense could have its disadvantages. The kind of statehood which Borden and others envisaged

24. See below, this chap., pp. 17–18.

could conceivably mean, as more conservative Commonwealth people thought, the breakup of that unity in general objectives, as well as in public policy, that had fortunately obtained. On the other hand, some, if not all, advocates of a fairly rapid movement toward autonomy in the matter of foreign as well as domestic affairs seem to have considered this the only real way to conserve unity in the fuller sense of the word—a unity resting upon bonds that transcended the merely legal ones.

In any case, there was considerable variance, both as to the basic theory advanced and the actual courses pursued. The Irish Free State, in the strict legal sense a product of a "treaty" (or, as the British apparently preferred to call it, a "charter of liberty") between the Irish and the British governments, became what one observer has described as a dominion in name but not in spirit.[25] The situation of South Africa remained a special one, General Herzog's disposition in the mid-twenties apparently being to proceed toward withdrawal unless the redefinition of the relationships could be effected along lines which he desired.[26] Canada as a League member gave evidence of her spirit of independence of outside control, as, for example, in regard to such matters as the position of Albania in the League and with respect to a report on a minorities treaty.[27]

On matters that were more intrafamily in nature, such as the settlement of disputes between members of the Commonwealth, there seemed to be no special disagreement. Australia, for example, took the position that the settlement of such disputes was a domestic matter. The means might not be exactly determined, but the disputes stopped short of being "international" within the ordinary meaning of that word. It was considered quite natural that the boundary dispute between Britain and the Irish Free State should be referred to the Judicial Committee of the Privy Council. On relations with outside states in general, concern was expressed, not for the "barren right to enter into separate relations with foreign powers" but for "assurance that the whole weight of

25. Mansergh, *op. cit. supra* note 20, at p. 10.
26. *Ibid.*, p. 11.
27. C. A. W. Manning, *The Policies of the British Dominions in the League of Nations* (1932), pp. 65, 69–72.

British diplomacy" should be on Australia's side, "whether the matter arises within or without the League of Nations."[28]

New Zealand's conservatism on the question of whether the dominions had assumed the prerogative of independent states in relation to Great Britain found expression in parliamentary debates at Wellington on the work of the Washington Conference on the Limitation of Naval Armament. As to the significance of the arrangements and proceedings at that conference, New Zealand's delegate to the conference (Salmond) stated that the dominions had in fact become recognized, for international purposes, as independent states. They had been given, he said, a voice in the handling of the British Empire's external affairs, the empire remaining a single, undivided unity. He emphasized that the empire had exclusive control of the foreign relations and pointed out that the dominions did not vote separately in respect of their affairs qua separate entities. The report on the conference submitted that a particular dominion's failure to sign a treaty in behalf of that dominion would have no effect upon the international application of the treaty terms; any difficulties resulting from such failure would present intra-empire problems and would not affect external relations of the empire with other contracting parties.[29]

That the same view prevailed in New Zealand for some years after that particular conference is indicated in the public discussion that followed the signing of the Locarno treaties in 1925. In the course of this discussion Minister of Finance Stewart denied that the dominions had acquired a new status and asserted that the supposed equality of the entities that made up the empire never had been real. "Generally speaking," an authoritative

28. W. Harrison Moore, "The Imperial and Foreign Relations of Australia," in *loc. cit. supra* note 22, at p. 346.

29. New Zealand, *Appendix to the Journals, House of Representatives,* 1922, vol. 1, Appendix A5, p. 16.

In the course of parliamentary discussion of Salmond's report, Prime Minister Massey said that he had "never liked the arrangement which was made in connection with the League of Nations. There was one dangerous feature in it." He further emphasized that he "did not agree with everything that had been said, that in signing the Peace Treaty we became independent nations. That is absolute nonsense, and the wish of the people who so expressed themselves was in many ways father to the thought." New Zealand, *Parl. Deb.,* vol. 196 (Aug. 3—Sept. 13, 1922), pp. 480–481.

observer wrote in 1927, "New Zealand writers and statesmen incline to the view that the less written about an imperial constitution or imperial relationships the better."[30]

On the other hand, there was assertion elsewhere of any dominion's right to move toward autonomy (within the constitutional forms of the Crown and advisers for each dominion) on matters relating to that dominion, whatever other dominions might do. As a Canadian spokesman put it in 1927, "If New Zealand desires to remain, in practice, subordinate, leaving all her international functions to be exercised by the British government, it is her right to take this course; but the progress of other dominions is not hereafter to be limited by her reluctance to undertake responsibilities to which, at the present time, she does not feel equal."[31]

The precedent set when Canada signed the Halibut Treaty with the United States in 1923 (without there being any signer for the British government) apparently evoked some adverse reaction from those who favored less rapid progress toward complete separateness (under the Crown) in foreign policy. The subject matter of that treaty made a convenient one on which advocates of greater separateness could make a case, for neither the empire as a whole nor any dominion other than Canada could argue very persuasively that interests involved were those of any part of the empire other than Canada. Robert Borden himself did not attach great constitutional significance to Canada's signing without the British ambassador's signing. He pointed out that Canada's right to sign a treaty affecting only Canadian interests had not for some time been denied.[32]

In the Declaration of 1926 were assertions which appeared to cover essential relationships between states of the British family, although some questions of international relations of Common-

---

30. J. B. Condliffe, "The Attitude of New Zealand on Imperial and Foreign Affairs," in *loc. cit. supra* note 22, at pp. 379–380. The same writer noted that the advent of the Labour party marked the introduction of an anti-imperialistic view, one which tended to parallel the Canadian and South African view. This, however, had apparently not gained great support by 1927. *Ibid.*, pp. 380–381.

31. John W. Dafoe, in *loc. cit. supra* note 22, at p. 199.

32. Borden Papers (Canadian Archives), Post-1921, folder 71 (letter to Smuts, May 26, 1927).

wealth members, such as the possibility of a member's being a neutral when Great Britain was at war, still remained open. There was, of course, room for difference of opinion as to the effect of what had taken place up to a particular time. It is not surprising that there were gradations of view with regard to the point which the dominions as a group, or any one of them, had reached by the end of the thirties in their advance toward full and complete statehood in the international-law sense. Definitions, or attempts at definition, did not necessarily provide velocity. There had been significant formal steps, as in 1926 and 1931. Yet, as one analyst noted years later, developments which had been regarded at short range as "great landmarks" had by the mid-century "almost disappeared from view."[33] A Commonwealth prime minister could observe, concerning the Commonwealth, "It would be the tragedy of our history if what began as a splendid achievement and grew into a proud brotherhood should end up as a lawyer's exercise."[34]

The very unevenness of the development in the several dominions was in a sense indicative of a spirit of independence. The clear disinclination of any one of the dominions to be controlled by the actions or the theories of others needs to be taken into account in estimating the actual movement that took place in the period between World Wars I and II. Theories of empire and of commonwealth tended to precede formal constitutional arrangements. With the gradual attainment of full statehood, the implications for public law and particularly for formal relations of the new entities were to receive deserved attention. The status which the dominions sought and obtained was one that rested squarely upon international law. Rules which the members elected to accept *inter se* were to prove useful for a limited time. However, neither these rules nor retained imperial standards were to be the bases for the long-range development.

33. Mansergh, *op. cit. supra* note 20 at p. 9.
34. Robert Gordon Menzies, *Speech Is of Time* (1958), p. 17.

2

Neo-nationalism

Robert R. Wilson

The full assumption of international rights and duties came in the "old" Commonwealth through an evolutionary process. There had been a prior period of dominion status and of self-government in internal affairs. In contrast, within less than two decades after the cessation of fighting in World War II a group of states reached full stature in the international legal sense and full association in the Commonwealth through what was in some cases a somewhat abrupt transition. The circumstances of their emergence varied from state to state, but in keeping with Commonwealth traditions they attained standing in the unique association on a basis of substantial equality, so far as essential legalities were concerned, with the "old" Commonwealth members. For the international lawyer the development affords not merely examples of the manner in which communities become entitled to rights and subject to duties in the full international sense but also of some techniques that are peculiar to the Commonwealth. In the process questions have arisen of state succession, citizenship, and the adaptation of governmental systems (including judicial machinery) to the new status of independence, to the relationships which attend Commonwealth ties, and to movements looking to federalism.

Few generalizations concerning the states that in the post-1945 period have joined the Commonwealth could apply equally to all. Nor does a mechanical classification into republics and monarchies go beyond the obvious. So far as the United Kingdom is concerned, there has been developed a set of formulas, now commonly used in statutes, concerning the applicability or non-applicability after independence of legislation such as that touching appeals from judicial decisions in the former colonies or trust territories, the applicability of legislation concerning diplomatic privileges and immunities, and the provision of choices as to citizenship. For the purpose of discerning what Commonwealth membership does or does not mean it might in some cases be instructive to note for the purpose of comparison the situation of some states, such as Eire and Burma, which are not now members of the rapidly changing Commonwealth. For the present purpose, however, it is proposed to restrict attention to (a) the varying circumstances under which the states came to full stature as independent entities, (b) some international legal implications of the transition, and (c) questions of federation and of status in international public organizations.

1. Varying Circumstances of Emergence

In the course of parliamentary debate concerning the postwar status of Burma, the secretary of state for that country referred to possible "Commonwealth status" for that country, not as "independence minus something, but as independence plus the rights and privileges and practical advantages accruing from association with a world-wide free partnership."[1] While Burma elected not to assume this membership, others exercising their freedom of choice did so elect. India, with more than two decades of membership in the League of Nations, apparently found it

1. From debate on a Burma White Paper of May, 1945 (remarks of Mr. Amery, secretary of state for Burma), as quoted by Marjorie M. Whiteman, *Digest of International Law* (1963) I, 524. The speaker added that such "was the status of Britain herself." In a comment in the House of Lords on the freely made decision, the then secretary of state for Burma said in part: "We here do not regard membership of the Commonwealth as something to be thrust by force upon a reluctant people, but as a priceless privilege granted only to those who deeply desire it and are conscious of its obligations as well as its advantages. The essence of the Commonwealth relationship is that it is a free association of nations with a common purpose, who belong together because they have decided of their own volition to give and to take their fair share in a world-wide partnership." See Nicholas Mansergh, *Documents and Speeches on British Commonwealth Affairs, 1931–1952* (1953), p. 789.

natural as an independent state to continue in the Commonwealth. When Pakistan became a separate state in 1947, United
Kingdom legislation provided that no law or provision of any law
of Pakistan (or of India) would be void on the ground that it was
repugnant to the law of England or any existing or future act of
Parliament. By the same legislation the government in the United
Kingdom was to have after independence "no responsibility as
respects the government of any of the territories which, immediately before that day, were included in British India."[2]

For a time the people of what had been British India were to
remain under a common allegiance (with Britain) to the Sovereign, but when there was later a choice of republican government
this occasioned no such problem as had arisen over Eire's
becoming a republic.[3] For India the Sovereign was to remain the
unifying symbol of Commonwealth association but not of common allegiance. In the case of Pakistan, an official statement by
the Conference of Prime Ministers at their meeting in London in
February, 1955, on the continued membership of Pakistan (upon
its becoming a republic) in the Commonwealth of Nations was
ratified by a constituent assembly of Pakistan in March of the
following year. That membership of a state did not commit it to
acquiesce in decisions which other Commonwealth states might
make in general foreign policy is suggested by a remark of Prime
Minister Nehru in the upper house of the Indian Parliament,
December 2, 1956, at the time of the Suez crisis. "The Commonwealth," he observed, is "no tying up of any kind."[4] Ceylon's
emergence in 1948 as an independent state in the Commonwealth
furnished occasion for further generalization as to what the
Commonwealth had become. An External Affairs Agreement
concluded with the United Kingdom referred to Ceylon's having
reached in her constitutional development the stage when she was
ready to assume her new status, "in no way subordinate in any
aspect of domestic or external affairs, freely associated and united

2. 10 & 11 Geo. 6, c. 30.
3. Cf. A. G. Donaldson, *Some Comparative Aspects of Irish Law* (1957), pp.
156–163.
4. *Keesing's Contemporary Archives*, June 5–12, 1957, p. 15310.

by common allegiance to the Crown."[5] There was a further statement to the effect that Ceylon and the United Kingdom in their relations would "observe the principles and practices . . . observed by the Members of the Commonwealth." That the expression "dominion status" had by this time fallen into disuse is indicated by the fact that the words do not appear in any of the documents relating to Ceylon's new situation.[6] A new era in the evolution of the Commonwealth had begun. The freedom of any of the associated states to change from a monarchical to a republican form of government was reiterated by the Conference of Prime Ministers when Ceylon later brought up the question of a possible change to that form.[7]

In the case of Nigeria, a prelude to independence was the federation of that country under constitutional arrangements which provided for some exclusively federal powers, some concurrent ones, and still others exercisable exclusively by the regions. To allow sufficient time for completing preparations, Nigeria's independence finally came on October 1, 1960, the United Kingdom legislation making provision for "responsible status" for the new member of the family of nations having become effective in the previous July. Even before this date (on May 9 of the same year) there had been agreement by the Conference of Prime Ministers of the Commonwealth that upon attaining its independence Nigeria would be received into Commonwealth membership.

Connected with the advent of Cyprus were special factors which make the early experience of that country in relation to the Commonwealth unique. The very geographical location of the island, on the "eastern flank" of NATO, affected the final arrangements with reference to status. Years of bitter tension as well as outside pressure from directly interested countries, continuing effort looking to action by the United Nations bodies, and acts of

5. Cmd. No. 7257 (1947); 86 U.N.T.S. 26–29.
6. Sir W. I. Jennings, *The Constitution of Ceylon* (1949), p. 25, as quoted in Whiteman, *op. cit. supra* note 1, at p. 524.
7. Australia, Dep't of External Affairs, *Current Notes on International Affairs*, vol. 27 (1956), p. 10.

terrorism on the island itself[8] marked the years from 1955 to August 16, 1960, the date of Cypriot independence. When the new status finally came, it meant denial of union with Greece, which had been the objective of the EOKA. The Constitution of Cyprus (based on the Zurich and London agreements) was not drafted by a constitutional convention of the ordinary kind, but rather by the interested outside powers, Greece, Turkey, and the United Kingdom. The constitution was in a sense given to Cyprus, and independence was the means of bringing about some kind of peace on the island. The frank recognition of the two "communities" and the provision for communal rule in each of the five principal cities, along with the fixing of a 70–30 ratio for civil servants and the giving of a veto on vital legislation to the Turkish-Cypriot vice-president (as well as to the Greek-Cypriot president), were part of the constitutional plan. Cyprus was at first independent without being a member of the Commonwealth, although the delay of about six months in its becoming a member of the association was apparently due to the decision of the Cypriots themselves and not to that of members of the Commonwealth.

The outlook of Cyprus is (for such purposes as possible entry into the Common Market on some basis) rather European, as contrasted with that of the Commonwealth members of Asia or those in the Antipodes. That in some sense the Commonwealth may be a convenient agency for supplying judicial skill to the island is suggested by the fact that when, in 1963, the German member resigned from the Supreme Constitutional Court of the Republic, an effort was reportedly begun to find his successor (who by the constitution could not be a citizen of Turkey, Greece, or the United Kingdom) in a Commonwealth country. In 1962 a Canadian jurist became a judge of the High Court of Justice of Cyprus, which by the constitutional arrangement was to consist of two members whose ethnic background was Greek, one whose ethnic background was Turkish, and one from a country other than Greece, Turkey, or the United Kingdom.

At a reception in Nicosia in June, 1963, to celebrate the

8. Charles Foley, *Island in Revolt* (1962), *passim.*

birthday of the Queen, Head of the Commonwealth, President Makarios expressed his belief "that the Commonwealth has a great role to play in international affairs and generally in the future shaping of the world."[9] As one of the guarantor states committed by treaty to seeing that the agreements on constitutional arrangements for Cyprus are observed, the United Kingdom is in a somewhat different legal position from that which it occupies in relation to any other Commonwealth member. The utility of the constitution in the matter of communal divisions and guaranteed rights of the ethnic minority in the island have become a matter of concern to Great Britain as well as to Cypriots.[10] The resumption of communal strife late in 1963 and the subsequent sending of a United Nations peace force to Cyprus meant continued uncertainty as to the island's future.

A constitutional novelty within the Commonwealth resulted from formal steps taken with respect to what came to be the Federation of Malaya, the latter being an elective monarchy. United Kingdom legislation of 1957 authorized the conclusion with the "Rulers of the Malay States" of agreements which appeared to be expedient for the establishment of the Federation as "an independent sovereign country within the Commonwealth."[11] There followed in 1961 steps looking to a new federation of Malaysia, to include the Federation of Malaya, Singapore, North Borneo, Sarawak, and Brunei. In the new Malaysia federation the Federation of Malaya was to have responsibility for defense, external affairs, and security, while Singapore was to retain some local autonomy, as in matters of labor and education. The new federal arrangements became effective in 1963. A sequel was the Indonesian challenge of the whole new Malaysian design as a British imperialist device. In 1965 Singapore became a separate state.

9. Cyprus *Mail,* June 9, 1963, p. 1.

10. The case for constitutional rearrangements that would, from the point of view of the Greek ethnic community, seem to make the constitution more workable is set forth in a reported interview with Flafcos Clerides, president of the Cyprus House of Representatives, in the Cyprus *Mail,* June 11, 1963, pp. 2–3. An opposing view, reportedly taken by the Turkish press, was that there should be a period of years under the constitution which would demonstrate its utility or inutility.

11. 5 & 6 Eliz. 2, c. 60.

Ghana joined the Commonwealth following the enactment by the Parliament of the United Kingdom in 1957 of legislation whereby the Gold Coast would attain "fully responsible status within the British Commonwealth of Nations."[12] An order in council originally contained the Gold Coast Constitution; another such order was made in advance of Ghana's independence day to regularize the new situation. Three years later voters in a plebiscite approved a republican form of government. Ghana then ceased to be a monarchy but remained within the Commonwealth. Prior to Ghanaian independence the people of Togoland under British administration expressed the desire to unite with Ghana; this union occurred in 1959.[13]

Sierra Leone's acceptance into the Commonwealth followed action by the Commonwealth prime ministers' conference of 1961 after the government of Sierra Leone had asked the government of the United Kingdom to support Sierra Leone's desire for such acceptance. The conference extended a welcome to that country as a member "on the completion of the necessary constitutional processes."[14] The new state comprised the Sierra Leone Colony and the Sierra Leone Protectorate, and passage of the Sierra Leone Independence Act was followed by an order in council which brought the new Constitution of Sierra Leone into force on the date of the country's independence.[15]

The expression "fully responsible status within the Commonwealth" appeared again in the legislation of the United Kingdom which comprised the Uganda Independence Act, 1962,[16] and Uganda became independent on October 9 of the same year. A Uganda Constitutional Conference of 1961 reached provisional agreement that the country should attain its independence on October 9, 1962.[17] The Constitutional Conference of 1962 confirmed this. All of the Uganda representatives joined in expressing the wish that, on attaining independence, Uganda should be

12. *Ibid.*, c. 6.
13. For an opinion that the Ghana-Guinea Union, effective May 1, 1959, was not thought to have affected Ghana's relationship to the Commonwealth, see Whiteman, *op. cit. supra* note 1, at p. 523.
14. Communique of Commonwealth prime ministers' conference issued on March 16, 1961; cited in *ibid.*, p. 532.
15. *Stat. Instr.*, 1961, No. 741.
16. 10 & 11 Eliz. 2, c. 57.
17. Cmnd. No. 1778, at para. 12 (1961).

accepted as a member country of the Commonwealth, and that Uganda should be under the sovereignty of Her Majesty the Queen as Queen of Uganda. The United Kingdom delegation at the conference supported, with the other Commonwealth members, Uganda's application for acceptance as a fellow member.[18] The fact that Uganda had been a protectorate did not seem to occasion substantial variance from the procedure for establishing independence; the United Kingdom legislation included such provisions as that the Colonial Laws Validity Act, 1865 (mentioned in Schedule 1 of the act), should not apply to any law made by any legislature established for Uganda or any part thereof.

Some variance from the formulas employed in independence acts and constitutional arrangements that have been noted above is found in connection with Tanganyika's becoming an independent state on December 9, 1961. This may have been due in part to the fact that Tanganyika had been a mandate and later a trust territory, and not a colony. The basic act of the United Kingdom was entitled "An Act to Make Provision for, and in Connection with, the Attainment by Tanganyika of Fully Responsible Status within the Commonwealth."[19] At the very first Tanganyika did not elect to have a republican form of government, but the legislative body soon voted for such a form. As set forth in an official statement:

On the 9th December, 1961, we became—suddenly—a monarchy. By deciding to remain in the Commonwealth, without making immediate provision for introducing a republican form of government at independence, we automatically followed the precedent set by the other non-republican countries of the Commonwealth. The Queen, who is the head of the Commonwealth and Sovereign of several of the member countries, became our Sovereign. . . .

. . . For Tanganyika . . . the British Monarchy has always been a foreign institution.[20]

In the case of the two states of the West Indies that have

18. *Ibid.*, para. 13.
19. 10 & 11 Eliz. 2, c. 1.
20. Tanganyika, Gov't. Paper No. 1 (1962), "Proposals of the Tanganyika Government for a Republic." See also Tanganyika, Constituent Assembly, Act No. 2 (1962), "An Act to Make Provision, Consequential upon Tanganyika's Becoming a Republic and for Matters Incidental thereto, and to Repeal and Amend Certain Laws."

become members of the Commonwealth, Jamaica and the State of Trinidad and Tobago, admission came after several years of experimentation under a plan of federation with other governments in the region. This plan had come into effect in January, 1958, although the possible advantages of federation had been discussed earlier, particularly since the time of a conference at Montego Bay in 1947. The British secretary of state for the colonies had invited to this conference the governments of the region which were under British rule. To these governments the secretary made, as spokesman for the United Kingdom, an offer of independence for the British West Indies if and when the governments concerned could work out constitutional arrangements for a federal government in the region. Later conferences at London (in 1953, 1955, and 1956) provided opportunity for discussion of the division of power between the federation and its member states. By 1960, however, growing sentiment in Jamaica against continuance of the federation led to the Jamaican government's holding a referendum on that state's continuing in the regional arrangement. The dissolution of the federation was followed by the application of Jamaica as well as by that of Trinidad and Tobago for admission to the Commonwealth. In the case of both of these new Commonwealth members there was the expressed desire of the people to retain their allegiance to the Queen.

The attainment of statehood by other new members of the Commonwealth was not marked by any very novel procedures, although there was in the case of two, Tanganyika and Zanzibar, almost immediately after the latter state's attainment of independence, a union to form the new state of Tanzania. The Zambia Independence Act, 1964, provided termination of Her Majesty's jurisdiction in Northern Rhodesia on October 24 of that year and removed Northern Rhodesia from the list of countries that had been protectorates under the British Nationality Acts. The Malta independence constitution (July, 1964) had provisions concerning Commonwealth citizens and dual citizenship.

The Commonwealth prime ministers' (and presidents') conference at London in July, 1964, was the occasion for the first participation in such a conference by some new members. Malawi attained statehood on the eve of the conference. Southern Rhodesia did not inherit (from the former Federation of Rhodesia and Nyasaland) the right to be represented, and Southern Rhodesia's claimed right to declare its own independence did not win approval at the meeting. At the conference there was indication of the expected emergence of still other independent states as Commonwealth members. Within a few months after the conference Zambia, Malta, and Gambia had attained this status.

2. International Legal Implications of New Status

The striking fact is that in the decade ending in 1963 the number of Commonwealth members doubled, although South Africa had in the meantime ceased to be a member. If it be true, as was said by one British observer at the time of the South African withdrawal, that the Commonwealth is not a club which one may join but a family in which one grows up, the process of coming of age in this period has proceeded at a pace that could hardly have been anticipated at mid-century. (Implications of the development from the point of view of citizenship of the peoples concerned are to receive separate attention.[21]) Effects from the point of view of international responsibility, succession to rights and duties, diplomatic intercourse, and to some extent the relationship between national and international law[22] present rather obvious questions for the newcomers to the Commonwealth since they are also newcomers to the family of nations. It is not surprising that the new nations do not take immediate positions on these questions, but do so gradually as need arises in specific cases.

Practice rather than a hypothetical approach is likely to assume importance. As in the case of some of the older nations, the taking of positions even on some fundamental matters involving interna-

21. See chap. 5, *infra.*
22. For detailed discussion of Commonwealth practice regarding the relationship between international and municipal law, see chap. 4, *infra.*

tional law may come only in the course of considerable time, as necessity arises for executive action or judicial decision. Experience shows that codification, in which the new states as well as older ones have had some part, will not quickly nor easily produce very complete formulations that are universally acceptable.

In the matter of state responsibility it seems likely that at least some of the new states may find attractive the idea that upon becoming independent a new member is not *ipso facto* bound by the body of rules that was evolved through practice before the new states came to full stature. A sounder position would seem to be that a newcomer is bound by such rules, but that the latter are not static and should, if they are to have real utility, be responsive to the developing and newly realized needs of the international community as a whole. The newest members of the Commonwealth have come of age at a time, for example, when there is some challenge of the principle that private property of aliens may not, consistently with international law, be taken for public use without just, adequate, and effective compensation. That there is difficulty in phrasing or securing universal assent to this principle is borne out by the discussions in the International Law Commission. The need on the part of the new states for capital investments by foreigners may affect the positions they will ultimately take concerning this subject, and the British tradition of due process and regard for private property seems likely to influence ultimate positions. In the meantime public aid from the metropolitan countries may have special attention.

Legal instruments in the form of British statutes and agreements between the United Kingdom and the respective new states seem well designed to make clear the complete legislative separateness of the latter from the former, whether the people of a particular new Commonwealth state choose to remain under a monarchical form of government or to have a republican form. The matter of state succession to treaties made by the United Kingdom with third states and previously applicable to one or more of the comunities which have become independent can apparently not be decided by the mere will of the United

Kingdom government and the government of such a new state, but only in light of third states' rights and by application of international law. There naturally has been speculation as to the manner in which the previously made treaties can become applicable to the new states or can be terminated by them. The United Kingdom has made so-called devolution agreements with a number of the new states, and opinion has been advanced by one publicist that the applicable instruments could devolve upon the latter, but that no rule of universal succession applies.[23] It is of course possible to have a situation in which a metropolitan state exercising protection over another state (as was formerly the case, for example, with France in respect to Tunis) may permit the latter to exercise within limits the power to make treaties. If, however, a community has not, prior to its independence, exercised such power (as would appear to be the case with several of the new Commonwealth members, such as Ghana, Cyprus, Nigeria, and the two West Indian members), nor has it previously been an international person with even qualified status, there might be a stronger argument for novation.

Perhaps the most striking statement concerning the whole question of succession to treaties was that issued by Uganda in 1963. This declared that when the state became independent it "fell to the Government" of Uganda to decide what attitude should be taken as to treaties applicable to the protectorate prior

---

23. A. P. Lester, "State Succession to Treaties in the Commonwealth," 12 *Int'l & Comp. L. Q.* 475 (1963). This writer noted that Tanganyika had refused to conclude a devolution agreement with the United Kingdom. Before its union with Zanzibar to form Tanzania, Tanganyika found some pre-existing British agreements touching Tanganyikan territory unacceptable, as, for example, agreements with Belgium in consideration of payment of one Belgian franc annually to have lease of sites in Tanganyikan ports.

For a discussion of Jamaican policy, particularly in the light of the dissolution of the Federation of the West Indies and the independence of Trinidad and Tobago, see L. R. Francis, "Jamaica Assumes Treaty Rights and Obligations: Some Aspects of Foreign Policy," 14 *Int'l & Comp. L. Q.* 612–627 (1965). The writer observes that the continued application of such treaties as those under consideration is not necessarily automatic once a self-governing state has attained independence. He points out, however, that Jamaica agreed, as a matter of policy, to assume all treaty obligations and rights relating to Jamaica and entered into in its behalf prior to independence by the British government and the government of the Federation of the West Indies (Cmnd. No. 1638).

By an exchange of letters, Trinidad and Tobago concluded a similar undertaking with Great Britain in Feb., 1963 (Cmnd. No. 1919).

to independence. The decision was "(a) that as far as possible treaty relationships should be preserved and . . . obligations to other countries should be honoured; (b) that a firm and binding decision upon each individual treaty must await thorough examination of the terms of the treaty . . . [such examination] now being made by the Department of External Affairs in collaboration with the Ministry of Justice; (c) that pending the outcome of this examination of individual treaties suitable interim arrangements should be made to preserve our international relationships." In line with this decision Prime Minister Obote, in his capacity as the minister responsible for external affairs, addressed a letter to the secretary-general of the United Nations which contained the following:

2. In respect of all treaties validly concluded by the United Kingdom on behalf of the Uganda Protectorate, or validly applied or extended by the former to the latter, before the 9th October, 1962, the Government of Uganda will continue on a basis of reciprocity to apply the terms of such treaties from the time of its independence, that is to say, 8th October, 1962, until the 31st December, 1963, unless such treaties are abrogated, or modified by agreement with the other high contracting parties before the 31st December, 1963. At the expiry of this period, or of any subsequent extension of this period which may be notified in like manner, the Government of Uganda will regard such treaties, *unless they must by the application of the rules of customary international law be regarded as otherwise surviving,* as having terminated.

3. The declaration in the previous paragraph extends to multilateral treaties; and during this period of review any party to a multilateral treaty which was validly applied or extended to Uganda before the 9th October, 1962, may on a basis of reciprocity as indicated above, rely on the terms of such treaty as against the Government of Uganda.

4. It is the earnest hope of the Government of Uganda that during the aforementioned period, the normal processes of diplomatic negotiations will enable it to reach satisfactory accord with the States concerned upon the possibility of the continuance of modification of such treaties. In the case of multilateral treaties, the Government of Uganda intends, before the 31st December, 1963, or such later date as may be subsequently notified in like manner, to indicate to the depositary in each case the steps it wishes to take, whether by way of

confirmation of termination, or confirmation of succession or accession, in regard to each such instrument.

5. It would be appreciated if Your Excellency would arrange for the text of this declaration to be circulated to all Members of the United Nations.[24]

With its saving clause concerning the continued applicability of customary international law, the statement would seem to provide a desirable model which might well be utilized by other new states in the regularization of their treaty relations.

The matter of diplomatic relations for the very new members of the Commonwealth is to some extent facilitated by the applicability, now regularly made effective by express language in United Kingdom legislation when a new state emerges in a region formerly under British sovereignty or control, of full privileges and immunities to diplomatic representatives such as high commissioners from the newly admitted Commonwealth states. In the bicommunal state of Cyprus there has been a practice of having the high commissioner in London selected from the community that is in the majority and the deputy high commissioner from the same Commonwealth state chosen from the minority community. The expense of maintaining missions in a great number of states has apparently been too great for some of the new states. Other means of conducting business abroad have been utilized. Cyprus, for example, has made use of honorary consuls in a number of cities in Europe.[25]

An advantage accrues to citizens of Commonwealth states in the matter of diplomatic relations from the fact that individuals may find convenient the interest or good offices of other Commonwealth states. This was the case in an incident involving procedure against the captain of an Indian-registry ship who allegedly failed to fly a flag of the port state as well as the flag of the ship's registry when in a port of Pakistan;[26] in this instance the

24. Uganda, "Treaty Obligations," Sess. Paper No. 2 (1963); italics inserted.
25. A list is in the Cyprus *Mail*, June 19, 1963, p. 3.
26. This incident, which occurred in Dec., 1958, involved K. R. M. Kinnier, a United Kingdom citizen, who was captain of the Indian ship "Jalamani," which was owned by the Scindia Steam Navigation Company. The captain was fined. It is understood that the British High Commission did not organize the defense of the captain and did not intervene in the case but limited itself to following the

British High Commission at Karachi was in interest because of the captain's citizenship. Commonwealth states not having any official relations with one another may derive such advantage as a third Commonwealth state's High Commission may provide or the Commonwealth Relations Office in London may provide.

3. Federation and International Organizations

The matter of status for Commonwealth states, new or old, is necessarily affected, if not in a strictly international sense then certainly in a practical political one, by their internal composition, by their participation in movements for federal union, and by their assumption of place in international public organizations. The manner in which a state has emerged from a condition of dependence to one of independence, as well as its previous experience or relative inexperience in self-government, naturally assumes importance. Even the label of "state" may connote something that is artificial. Thus President Makarios has been reported to have said soon after Cyprus became independent that there had been created "a new state but not a new nation."[27] What has been labeled as "decolonisation" involves in some cases the transition to a Western type of system that includes a central government and a civil service from a kind of "cultural heterogeneity" based upon tribal groups.[28] Uganda has been used as a case in point; one critic, taking note also of the position in that country of the Kingdom of Buganda with its Kabaka and some three million people, has likened the new entity to a lion harnessed to twenty lambs.[29]

---

development in the manner considered appropriate in international as well as Commonwealth practice when the interest of a United Kingdom citizen was involved. The arrest and fining of the captain were reported in *The Times* (London) for Dec. 27, 1958, p. 5 and Dec. 30, 1958, p. 5. There are references to the case in various issues of *Dawn* (Karachi) between Dec. 27, 1958, and June 6, 1959.

27. For further discussion of developments in inter-Commonwealth relations and representation, see chap. 3, *infra*, pp. 53–65.

28. Audry Richards, "Constitutional Problems in Uganda," 33 *Pol. Q.* 360 at 361, 362 (1962).

29. *Ibid.*, p. 369.

Not merely the composition of the state with respect to tribal or other divisions, but also schemes of federation, either past or present, would seem to have some bearing upon the capacity of the new states to make the most of their new freedom and to live up to their new responsibilities. Thus the Federation of Rhodesia and Nyasaland, which came to an end in 1963, has been of more than passing importance in the history of the Commonwealth, the prime minister of the Federation having had place in the meetings of Commonwealth prime ministers although the government over which he presided did not assume full membership in the concert of other Commonwealth members. The membership of two West Indian communities, Jamaica, and Trinidad and Tobago, in the Commonwealth came as the sequel to the demise of the West Indian Federation, in which Jamaica had been the principal member.[30] The inclusion in a number of national constitutions, such as that of Ghana, of provisions looking to a United States of Africa could, if carried out, have significant effects upon continuance of the traditional co-operation of Commonwealth states. Although they had co-operated through their system of common services, the East African states failed to federate before the individual states became independent members of the Commonwealth.[31] There has been in this area a problem of designing federal arrangements that would be most useful as well as acceptable for newly independent states that are in different stages of political and cultural development.

Each individual state's maintenance of even minimal diplomatic relations with many other states presents a considerable financial problem which federation might help to solve. Federation would presumably affect markets; a recent study has noted the "striking and curious parallel between East Africa's pause at the threshold of functional economic integration before deciding whether to pursue political federation and the present pattern of

30. An Economic Survey Mission to Tanganyika, organized by the International Bank for Reconstruction and Development, reported that minimum diplomatic establishments in London and Washington and to the United Nations could cost Tanganyika £ 200,000 a year. *The Economic Development of Tanganyika* (1961), p. 57.
31. On legal aspects involved, see generally, Thomas M. Franck, *East African Unity Through Law* (1964).

the European Common Market."[32] A new federation including some states that are now members of the Commonwealth and some entities that are not such members might raise questions of the former states' continuance in the traditional Commonwealth relationship. There was no new "person" in the ordinary international-law sense by reason of the establishment of the East African Common Services Organization.[33] Some African states that are now full members of the Commonwealth might, upon becoming members of a new political federation, come to have what has been described as "semi-diplomatic" representation in foreign states (including those that are Commonwealth members), as have some regions in Nigeria.[34]

Upon assumption of their role as members of international public organizations newly independent states in the Commonwealth have had the advantage of instruction and training in association with older Commonwealth members. Representatives from new states to the United Nations have had meetings with delegates from older Commonwealth members during sessions of the General Assembly.[35] The position of at least one of the new states, Cyprus, in the principal world organization apparently is unique, since the United Nations had the question of Cyprus before it for some years prior to the island's independence, and subsequently communal strife in Cyprus has led to United Nations peace-keeping actions.

In forums of the specialized agencies as well as in the central world organization African members of the Commonwealth have

32. Carl G. Rosberg, Jr. and Aaron Segal, "An East African Federation," No. 543 *Int'l Conc.* 71 (1963).

33. *Ibid.*, pp. 68–69. Cf. Thomas M. Franck, *op. cit. supra* note 31, at p. 165, on the point that the East African Common Services Organization was not a federation. There was a "working party" (authorized by the Nairobi "Declaration of Federation by the Governments of East Africa" in June, 1963), but one of the things upon which this working party was unable to agree was the status of East Africa in international law. *Ibid.*, pp. 156, 161.

34. Three regions of Nigeria have agents-general in the United Kingdom; see *Nigeria Yearbook* (1961). Agent representation in London by constituent members of federations was first developed by the older members of the Commonwealth; the practice dates from the latter half of the nineteenth century; see chap. 3, *infra*, p. 55.

35. Thomas B. Millar, "The Commonwealth and the United Nations," 16 *Int'l Org.* 736 at 740–741 (1962). Cf. Catherine Hoskyns, "The African States and the United Nations, 1958–1964," 40 *Int'l Aff.* 466 (1964).

played a prominent role in denouncing racial policies of a former Commonwealth member, the Republic of South Africa. For example, at the forty-seventh Conference of the International Labor Organization, Tanganyika's minister of labor said concerning South African (and Portuguese) policies with respect to the "African brothers" that the "time has come for this body to present an ultimatum to these countries and to fix a definite time limit for them to choose between expunging their offensive legislation or being expelled from our midst."[36] It was from this conference that thirty-one African states withdrew in protest against the presence of a South African delegation; the Nigerian federal minister of labor resigned from the conference presidency.

Questions of international organization, federation, and Commonwealth relations arose for certain Commonwealth states in connection with the greater Malaysian federation in 1963. The secretary-general of the United Nations was willing to test sentiment for the federation in Sarawak and Borneo only with the consent of Great Britain and on condition that his report would be agreed to in advance by all parties concerned. For Malaya the agreement to seek federation was a major step in the country's foreign policy after the very brief period of more limited federation. From Australia, New Zealand, and Pakistan, as well as the United Kingdom, there was reported concern as to the possible effect of the new arrangement upon SEATO and, specifically, upon the right to have forces of SEATO members in Singapore.

It has become commonplace to note that Commonwealth membership does not bind a state to adjust its foreign policies to bring them into accord with those of other members. It is understandable that, in a country such as Canada, at periodic meetings of high commissioners accredited to Canada the Kashmir question might not be an appropriate one for general discussion. At conferences of Commonwealth prime ministers the

36. Quoted in Cyprus *Mail*, June 10, 1963, p. 3. On the position of new African states with respect to international organization in general, see symposium, "Africa Speaks to the United Nations," 16 *Int'l Org.* 310 (1962), especially at pp. 316–319 (remarks of the president of Ghana) and pp. 327–330 (remarks of the prime minister of Nigeria).

subject of defense apparently does not come under discussion by all representatives sitting together. The Suez crisis found members on different sides on a major question of policy; yet the sequel to this crisis demonstrated the convenience and usefulness of Commonwealth ties, Australia being allowed to have one of its nationals join the diplomatic mission of Canada in Cairo for the purpose of handling certain questions concerning Australian property in Egypt.[37]

The consistency of the foreign policies of some of the African members of the Commonwealth with the internal policies of these states (or at least some of them) has occasioned some discussion. In this connection there has been the suggestion that leaders in at least one of these states south of the Sahara may have been more concerned about freedom from foreign domination for themselves and others than about the liberty of individuals in their own midst.[38]

The very new members of the Commonwealth have had but a short period of independence in which to demonstrate that they can make a significant change in the total impact of the Commonwealth upon the wider community of states. While the fact of serious internal problems that differ from state to state makes difficult any broad generalization that would be very accurate, it is obvious that a new type of nationalism finds frequent expression in Afro-Asian states of the Commonwealth. Kenya and Tanzania are among the states to find expression of goals through the Organization of African Unity, which purposes (as set out in article 2, paragraph 1 of its charter): "(a) to promote the unity and solidarity of the African States; (b) to co-ordinate and intensify their co-operation and efforts to achieve a better life for the peoples of Africa; (c) to defend their sovereignty, their territorial integrity and independence; (d) to eradicate all forms

37. Australia, Dep't of External Affairs, "Australian Affairs in Egypt," *Current Notes on International Affairs*, vol. 29 (1958), p. 432, where it was reported that the "Canadian Government with the concurrence of the Egyptian Government have agreed to the attachment of an Australian official to the Canadian Embassy in Cairo which is in charge of Australian interests in Egypt." The arrangement was designed to assist the transfer to Australian owners of properties in Egypt which were sequestrated but were later desequestrated.

38. See M. J. Bonn, "The Commonwealth: Parting of the Continents," *Year Book of World Affairs, 1962* (1962), pp. 12–22.

of colonialism from Africa; and (e) to promote international co-operation, having due regard to the Charter of the United Nations and the Universal Declaration of Human Rights."

The possible implications of "colonialism" in this declaration of purposes necessarily touch international legal relations. There have, in any case, been strong expressions of a desire to harmonize policies and to work out co-operative measures.[39] Whatever political and constitutional objectives may be achieved, it would seem to be inevitable that a large element of universalism will subsist in the legal relations between these new states and other members of the family of nations. Afro-Asian nationalism is a very new force. If effectively tempered by ideals of individual liberty and free government, with loyal oppositions operating through parliamentary forms inherited or copied from Great Britain, this nationalism may conceivably assist the further universalization of the values which, for its older members, the Commonwealth has traditionally symbolized.[40] Since regard for law in general has been an important part of the Commonwealth heritage, legality at the international level finds logical inclusion. It is therefore appropriate to consider the manner in which the associated states, both new and old, have adhered to, made use of, and evinced willingness to make further use of law in their relations with one another and with non-Commonwealth states.

Newness does not imply absence of law. Neo-nationalism is not inherently opposed to traditional internationalism based on law. As illustrated in at least some of the new Commonwealth members, new nationalism has come to be associated with relative emphasis upon human rights, strong condemnation of racial discrimination, and to some extent a questioning of prescriptive rights over Asian or African territory. This type of nationalism has seemed to encourage re-examination of such rules as those pertaining to state succession and the responsibility of states in the matter of property rights of aliens.

39. Cf. Norman J. Padelford, "The Organization of African Unity," 18 *Int'l Org.* 521 at 540 (1964).
40. John Holmes, "The Impact on the Commonwealth of the Emergence in Africa," 16 *Int'l Org.* 291 (1962). Cf. Robert R. Wilson, "The Commonwealth as Symbol and as Instrument," 53 *Am. J. Int'l L.* 392 (1959).

Official Representation

Robert R. Wilson

The process through which the dominions came to assume positions as persons in international law involved not merely the development of a concept but also the devising of means of official communication. The former colonies had of course had occasion to be acquainted with the forms and practices associated with exercise of the *ius legationis,* but experience peculiar to these British communities figured importantly in the process of assuming full exercise of the right. Since a mere chronological account of what the dominions did would hardly be adequate, it may be useful to note, instead, some occasions that particularly affected thought concerning representation and the considerations that seemed to make a more regularized system desirable and ultimately necessary. In this matter the experience of the "old" Commonwealth has been shared only to a limited extent by the new Afro-Asian states that have come to be parts of the concert. Usage as well as law requires attention in this general field of inquiry. It is appropriate to note (*a*) practice with respect to certain international conferences, (*b*) arrangements that Commonwealth members had with non-Commonwealth states, (*c*) the development of the office of high commissioner, and (*d*) some recent trends in relations between the United Kingdom and other Commonwealth states.

1. International Conferences

In the early post-World War I period there was abundant opportunity to raise questions concerning the position of the dominions with respect to official participation in international discussions. The British Empire delegation's role at the Paris Peace Conference of 1919 provided special occasion. Having made substantial contributions in men and treasure to the achievement of victory in the war, the dominions were unenthusiastic about any arrangements that would seem to equate them with some of the smaller states of Europe. Robert Borden, who in the Imperial War Cabinet in 1917 had done what he could to assure the dominions of something besides a passive role in the making of policy vitally affecting them, found in the preparations for the Paris Peace Conference and in the conference itself opportunity to press for wider acceptance of the principle. The time was ripe for allowing the dominions a greater voice on basic policy matters. The fact that this marked a considerable departure from past practice was not lost upon contemporary observers. Thus one observer could write:

Less than a dozen years ago the British Government gave as their reason for not consulting the Dominion of Canada on a question intimately associated with its welfare the fact that Canada had had no place in the drafting of the treaty which it was proposed to abrogate. Nor have ten years passed since Mr. Asquith, then Prime Minister, and Viscount Grey of Falloden, then Foreign Secretary, declared in the most emphatic terms that in the domain of foreign policy the Imperial Government could not admit the Dominions to any share of responsibility. All these old ideas have gone by the board. The impossible has happened.[1]

In a telegram of January 13, 1919, Borden said, concerning the decision to give special representation to the dominions, "this enlarged representation means no predominance in actual strength since decisions of conference will be determined not by voting power but by agreement." In a communication of the following day, John W. Dafoe informed Nicholls at Ottawa that the Dominion representation was in substantial agreement with the proposition submitted on their behalf by Borden to the Imperial War Cabinet in London. Dafoe, noting that Lloyd George had strongly advocated the dominions' right to special and direct representation at the conference, reported that "Antic-

1. Borden Papers (Canadian Archives), O. C. 578, p. 63395.

ipation that some of the allied powers not familiar with family relationships of British nations would question proposed arrangement as undue enlargement of British representation was verified; but after presentation of the British case point was handsomely conceded and matter settled in keeping with wishes of Dominions."[2]

In a memorandum dated January 15, Borden recorded that President Wilson, while speaking with great respect for the dominions and their war effort, said that if the plan desired by the dominions should be adopted, the result would be that the British Empire would get five chief delegates who would sit at each meeting of the conference and twelve from the dominions, making seventeen in all. To Mr. Lansing's question of why Canada should be concerned in the settlement of European affairs, Lloyd George replied that the dominions believed themselves to have that right because some hundreds of thousands of persons from the dominions had died for the vindication of public right in Europe. Clemenceau being sympathetic toward the dominions' attitude, Lloyd George declined to withdraw his proposal.[3]

After the dominions became separate members of the League of Nations, there soon arose another occasion to decide upon status for the purpose of international conference discussions—this time not under League auspices. The occasion was the Washington Conference on the Limitation of Naval Armament, 1921–1922. To this the dominions received no separate invitations —an omission which Newton D. Rowell attributed to the fact that Mr. Harding in his successful campaign for the American presidency in 1920 had opposed dominion representation in the League.[4] The withholding of separate invitations was not over-

2. *Ibid.*, O. C. 476 (1), p. 49932.
3. *Ibid.*, O.C.A. 198, pp. 81559, 81560 (General Memorandum No. 2).
Hughes of Australia, along with Botha and Smuts, had also pressed for dominion representation at the peace conference. The biographer of Hughes notes that this was a rather severe jolt for the Foreign Office but that Lloyd George was won over. Acting Prime Minister Watt of Australia was reported as having cabled Hughes that advocacy of separate representation of the dominions at the peace conference was "not reasonable." W. Farmer Whyte, *William Morris Hughes: His Life and Times* (1957), p. 279.
4. Borden Papers (Canadian Archives), Post-1921, folder 71, p. 149680 (letter of Rowell to Borden, Oct. 26, 1921).

looked by the leaders in the dominions who had already advocated so strongly the new position of the dominions for the
purpose of international conference discussions. In the end,
however, the dominions were represented by plenipotentiaries
nominated on their behalf and to whom full powers were issued
under substantially the same plan that had been used at Paris in
1919; Balfour represented both the United Kingdom and the
Union of South Africa. At the conference the delegates were
seated alphabetically and not as parts of a united British delegation.

It was, of course, true at this time as well as in later years that
not all of the dominion statesmen were eager to have these states
move forward rapidly toward complete management of their
foreign affairs. General Smuts, for example, considered the role of
Australia and that of New Zealand to be a passive one, but he
seemed to feel that there was every reason for the dominions to
be represented at the Paris Peace Conference.[5] With this may be
compared a subsequently expressed New Zealand view that "in
most contexts" it was a mistake to invite comparison of New
Zealand's position and action with Canada's or South Africa's.[6]

It was inevitable that the question of dominion representation
in public international discussions would arise when the matter of
membership in the League of Nations was to be decided. When,
in the early postwar period, there was the possibility that the
United States might join the League, dominion status became a
matter of concern to American, United Kingdom, and dominion
statesmen. In the United Kingdom the problem did not appear to
be considered as one of great difficulty. Thus in the House of
Commons on June 3, 1919, when asked whether in the constitution of the League it was the intention of the British government

5. *Ibid.*, For. Pap., Post-1921, folder 69, pp. 149189, 149190 (letter of Smuts to
Borden, April 26, 1922).
6. F. L. W. Wood, *The New Zealand People at War: Political and External
Affairs* (1958), p. 18. This author felt that leaders such as Bell, Ward, Massey,
Forbes, and Coates were true interpreters of New Zealand and were staunch
imperial statesmen. They did not, the author submits, regard dominion status as an
"empty concept" and "their loyalty to British leadership was neither blind nor
dumb." He felt that New Zealand had made clear that she intended to
participate when it suited her in the privilege of dominion status and that this
position had been recognized both in Wellington and in London.

that representation of the self-governing dominions would be as full as that of the smaller sovereign nations, and whether a representative of the dominions would be eligible for membership on the League Council, Prime Minister Bonar Law replied: "The answer to both parts of the question is in the affirmative. As regards the second part, the Dominions will be eligible for appointment to the Council on exactly the same terms as the other members of the League not permanently represented on it."[7]

The effect of the League Covenant arrangements would thus apparently be to consolidate the gains which the dominions had already made toward establishing themselves as separate nations. One observer suggested that the movement for recognition of dominion status had "few greater victories than that on which the Covenant was drafted."[8] An American newspaper editorial was entitled "The League within the League—Persia Will Make It Seven," and a legal authority in England (Sir Frederick Pollock) was quoted as saying that "The States of the Empire stand on an equal footing, except that the Government of one of these represents all the rest in the community of nations, and is gracefully permitted, in consequence, to undertake and to pay for maritime defence."[9]

The "six to one" argument had its effect. There was introduced in the United States Senate a proposed American reservation to United States acceptance of the Covenant, with wording to the effect that the United States as a member would be entitled to a number of votes equal to that of any other member of the League and its self-governing dominions, colonies, and parts of empire. The matter became one of great concern for American, British, and dominion friends of the League. Ex-President William Howard Taft, for example, seems to have thought that unless Canada were to leave the League, she would probably have to accept such an amendment.[10] Loring Christie perceived the danger in Canadian assent to a situation in which she could participate in the

7. 116 *H. C. Deb.* (5th ser.) (1919).
8. Geoffrey Butler, *A Handbook to the League of Nations* (1926), p. 49.
9. New York *Sun*, Oct. 8, 1919.
10. Rowell Papers (Canadian Archives), folder 38, p. 5654 (copy of letter of Taft to George W. Wrong, Toronto, Feb. 7, 1920).

choice of a British Empire spokesman in the councils of the League and also have separate representation. Under Covenant article 4(5) Canada had the right to have a Canadian representative present when the League Council discussed matters in which Canada had an interest. By joining in the choice of an imperial representative, Canada might imperil the basis for dominion representation and membership. It would be difficult, Christie thought, for Canada to be "riding two horses or one according as it suits our interests at the moment."[11]

The outcome of this—the fact that the dominions did become separate members of the League and were eligible for non-permanent membership in the League Council—did not settle all questions of status with respect to diplomatic relations generally. Practice in the transaction of business in the new international organization did not necessarily establish the right of entering into direct discussions with foreign states on international matters in general.[12] Nor was there automatic approval by outside governments of the new type of British representation at international conferences. It was reported, for example, that the French government opposed the idea of separate representation of the dominions at the Lausanne Conference. The French were willing to approve on the condition that French non-self-governing colonies and protectorates (Algeria, West Africa, and Tunisia) should be represented on the same basis as the dominions. Apparently the British government transmitted this word confidentially to the Canadian government as the reason for the British government's not insisting upon individual dominion representation at Lausanne.[13]

While India as a member of the League had direct relations with such bodies as the International Labor Office and the Committee for International Cooperation in Science and Culture, Indian delegates were apparently responsible to the British Cabinet and not to the Indian legislature.[14]

11. *Ibid.*, pp. 5656, 5657 (memorandum of Feb. 9, 1920).
12. See A. B. Keith, *The Dominions as Sovereign States* (1938), pp. 37–46.
13. Arnold J. Toynbee, *The Conduct of British Empire Foreign Relations since the Peace Settlement* (1928), p. 86. See also Cmd. No. 2146 (1924).
14. P. N. Banerjee and N. C. Roy, "India and International Affairs," 1 *Indian Yb. of Int'l Aff.* 166 (1952).

By the time of the Locarno discussions in the mid-twenties, some substantial precedents had been set with respect to dominion representation at international meetings, but these did not necessarily control subsequent British policy. To the two most ardent advocates of separate dominion voices, the matter seemed to be one of some seriousness. As has been seen, there was fear on Smuts's part that the effect of what had been done at the Locarno Conference might be to depart from the previously established plan of representation through the British Empire delegation.[15]

Apparently Borden took a view similar to that of Smuts, but did not ascribe all of the fault to the British. He took the position that there was, especially in Canada and in South Africa, a certain indifference to responsibilities that of necessity accompanied the status of nationhood, responsibilities which they must assume if the Commonwealth was to endure. Noting that some people felt the pathway to nationhood meant a tendency to disruption, he expressed his own judgment that this was a wholly mistaken view. The spirit of nationhood, he said, had been growing since he entered public life (in 1896) and he was "wholly confident that in the Resolution [of 1917] the basis and hope of imperial unity was to be found."[16]

It had been less than two decades since the Colonial Conference of 1907, at which the United Kingdom leadership had for the first time taken the communities called "dominions" into its confidence concerning the state of international relations.[17] The dominions had, in the meantime, gone far toward making their respective voices felt in the councils of the empire. They had, in

15. See chap. 1, *supra*, p. 9.
16. Borden Papers (Canadian Archives), folder 59, p. 148239. With this statement of Borden's may be compared some observations of Loring Christie in a letter to Borden less than five months later. Under date of June 4, 1926, Christie wrote: "I could see the case for a waiting policy if anyone would outline within the four corners of the present Imperial legal structure a project compatible with real Canadian national responsibility and with our inescapable position on the map. . . . I feel also that if Canada is to hold together Canadians will be driven in this last ditch, as their fathers always were in other ditches, to the simplest elements of political science, and will find that responsibility for their region of North America and for its repercussions on others in a new age must somehow be faced by them before the world—that responsibility must rest where interest and knowledge rest." *Ibid.*, p. 148376.
17. Geoffrey Sawer, *Australian Federal Politics and Law, 1901–1929* (1956), I, 78.

addition, become separate members of the most important international public organization of the time. Full stature involved for them, however, separate official relations with other entities than the British government at London and the League of Nations.

2. Arrangements with Non-Commonwealth Countries

It was logical for the self-governing dominions, after they had attained place in international organizations and had come to have separate voice from Great Britain's in certain international conferences, to seek separate representation in non-Commonwealth countries. The process was in fact a gradual one. At the outset it was a matter of supplementing (rather than in any sense replacing) British representation in such a country as the United States. In international practice there was some precedent for having component parts of an empire represented at foreign capitals where the empire as such was also represented. On this point, Loring Christie drew attention to the fact that such entities as Bavaria and Saxony had had representation at foreign capitals where the German Empire had ambassadors. Usage did not seem to impose excessively rigid limitations upon what could be done. In the working out of plans for representation of the dominions there was apparently some tendency at times to superimpose new duties upon agents whose previous functions had not been essentially diplomatic ones.

Canada took the lead when she moved to establish diplomatic channels with the United States. The creation of such agencies went beyond, but was more natural in the light of, previous Canadian-American arrangements. There existed, under the Boundary Waters Treaty of 1909, the International Joint Commission, which had considerable authority. While this commission fell far short of being a diplomatic creature of the ordinary type, as a quasi-judicial agency it could consider matters (if the two governments should agree to refer them) other than those relating to boundary waters.

Canadian diplomatic representation at Washington dates from 1920. By the arrangement of that year the appointee was to join the British mission in the United States. The Canadian prime minister explained the plan to the House of Commons at Ottawa as follows:

As a result of recent discussions an arrangement has been concluded between the British and Canadian Governments to provide more complete representation at Washington of Canadian interests than has hitherto existed. Accordingly, it has been agreed that His Majesty, on advice of his Canadian Ministers, shall appoint a Minister Plenipotentiary who will have charge of Candian affairs and will at all times be the ordinary channel of communication with the United States Government in matters of purely Canadian concern, acting upon instructions from and reporting directly to the Canadian Government. In the absence of the Ambassador the Canadian minister will take charge of the whole Embassy and of the representation of Imperial as well as Canadian interests. He will be accredited by His Majesty to the President with the necessary powers for the purpose.

This new arrangement will not denote any departure either on the part of the British Government or of the Canadian Government from the principle of the diplomatic unity of the Empire.[18]

Four years later, on October 7, 1924, a diplomat from the Irish Free State, Timothy A. Smiddy, presented his credentials as Minister to the President of the United States. On November 5, 1926, a communication from the Canadian prime minister advised the British Foreign Office that Canada wished to name, as her envoy extraordinary and minister plenipotentiary in the United States, a representative who would not, as had been contemplated under the 1920 arrangement, be a member of the British Embassy at Washington. After this change had been made there was the possibility of overlapping interests. On this subject, in the Canadian Parliament on May 28, 1928, Prime Minister Mackenzie King said:

The representatives of Canada to other countries are appointed in reference to the domestic and external affairs of Canada, and they

18. 143 *H. C. Deb.* 2178 (1920). On the Canadian War Mission to the United States as a step toward the establishment of diplomatic representation, see H. Gordon Skilling, *Canadian Representation Abroad: From Agency to Embassy* (1945), pp. 196 ff.

have to deal only with matters in respect of which we are primarily concerned. At these legations they meet, in the same capitals, the representatives of the British government, who are similarly charged with the responsibility of representing the British government in regard to its domestic and foreign affairs, wherever those domestic and foreign affairs come to be a matter of international interest and concern. It is conceivable that in some cases the foreign affairs of one part of the empire will intersect the arc which relates to the foreign affairs of another part of the empire. In that event one would assume that the obligations with reference to what is held in common would be a joint obligation and that the two representatives, or more if there are such, would carry out their trusteeship in co-operation with each other after consultation. Possibly there may be some who will object that there is always the possibility of difference arising. . . .[19]

The Prime Minister went on to say that should there be differences of the kind which he had suggested, they would be dealt with as they had in the past when there had been differences between parts of the empire.

When Canada proposed to have a minister at Washington who would be a member of the British Embassy, there was some thought that this would be a special situation, due "exclusively" to Canada's contiguity to the United States, and that it was highly unlikely that any other dominion's desire to send a diplomatic representative to Washington would meet with a favorable response.[20] As late as 1927 there were those who viewed the dominions as states, but "not exactly independent states," since they were "states in such intimate relations with another long-recognized member of the family of nations that a classification of them as states does not precisely fit the situation."[21] At about the same time an Australian publicist probably reflected realistic thinking, certainly that in his own country, when he said that the concern of Australia was "not the barren right to enter into relations with foreign powers, but an assurance that the whole

19. 179 *H. C. Deb.* 3466–3467 (1928). See also Skilling, *op. cit. supra* note 18, at pp. 212–213 and documents there cited.

20. Nathan Manfred, "Dominion Status," 7 *Transact. Grot. Soc'y.* 117 at 128 (1922). However, as has been seen, a diplomatic representative of the Irish Free State was accredited to Washington in 1924.

21. V. Kenneth Johnston, "Dominion Status in International Law," 21 *Am. J. Int'l L.* 481 at 485 (1927).

weight of British diplomacy" would be on her side, "whether the matter arises within or without the League of Nations."[22]

The fact that through the thirties the dominions' reliance for defense continued to be upon the empire and that no dominion had really accepted the responsibility of maintaining armament sufficient for its own defense needed to be taken into consideration in assessing the separateness of the dominions in more than a superficial sense.[23] Further clarifications, in a formal sense, of the status of the "autonomous" units were to be sought through the Imperial Conference declaration of 1926 and the Statute of Westminster, 1931. Even in the period of transition, however, a case could be made for the establishment of more adequate channels of communication between individual Commonwealth states and countries that were outside of the Commonwealth. Nor was the limited volume of relations involved necessarily a justification for delaying the creation of direct channels. As late as 1950 Foreign Minister Spender of Australia suggested the justification for general Commonwealth representation:

Although the main burden of British Commonwealth policy in relation to European affairs falls not unnaturally upon the United Kingdom, it is necessary for the Commonwealth as a whole to make its presence and strength felt in Europe as well as in Asia. It is therefore essential for us, along with other Commonwealth countries, to maintain direct diplomatic relations with the leading countries of Western Europe so as to be fully informed of events, and to adjust our policies in accordance with such events.[24]

The eventual establishment by the dominions of diplomatic missions in various states of the world came about in some cases after an intermediate period when there were officers in a quasi-diplomatic role. This finds illustration with respect to the representation at Washington of Australia and of India. In the case of the former state, developments between 1920 and 1929 gave rise

22. W. Harrison Moore, "The Imperial and Foreign Relations of Australia," in *Great Britain and the Dominions* ("Lectures on the Harris Foundation 1927") (1928), p. 338.
23. Cf. C. A. W. Manning, *The Policies of the British Dominions in the League of Nations* (1932), p. 59.
24. Australia, Dep't of External Affairs, *Current Notes on International Affairs*, vol. 21 (1950), p. 167.

to certain questions concerning the role of trade commissioners. As early as February, 1920, there was a question of the status for the purpose of customs facilities of the commissioner of the Commonwealth of Australia to the United States, who seems to have had credentials not addressed to anyone but signed by the governor-general of Australia.[25] In January of 1922 the American consul-general at Melbourne reported to the Department of State the establishment of an Australian Department of External Affairs, described as "tantamount to a Foreign Office," to be directly under the jurisdiction of the prime minister's department. (Some two decades earlier the Commonwealth government had inaugurated a department similar to this, but after a time, the consul-general reported, it was "considered unnecessary."[26]) In 1926 Sir Hugh Denison, a two-year appointee as commissioner to the United States, bore a commission signed by the deputy governor-general of Australia. During Denison's incumbency, the legal adviser of the Department of State had occasion to write, concerning the commissioner:

He is not to be regarded as a diplomatic officer nor is he a consular officer. His mission is one pertaining to trade and commerce. He belongs to that class of officers designated as Trade Commissioners as distinguished from Commissioners whose missions are for political purposes and whose status is analogous to that of a minister. Several of the British Dominions, Australia, Canada and South Africa, have had Commissioners in the United States and this Government has similar arrangements in foreign countries, including British Dominions. Those on the part of the United States are appointed by the Secretary of Commerce.[27]

To the inquiry of an American firm, the Department of State replied that the Australian commissioner was merely an official of the Australian government, not accredited to the government of the United States and having no official relations therewith. "All formal relations relative to Australia," the letter said, "are conducted by the Department through the British Embassy in Washington."[28] Apparently the incumbent himself, at least on the

25. U. S. Dep't of State file (National Archives), 847.01 B 11/50.
26. *Ibid.*, 847.01 B 11/47.
27. *Ibid.*, 847.01 B 11/45.
28. *Ibid.*

eve of his departure for the United States in 1926, had thought that the scope of his work might be broader than that of his predecessors in the office of Trade Commissioner and had felt that it might be imperative that he have something of a quasi-diplomatic status.

At the time of the resignation of Denison, it was reported from Melbourne that Australian Prime Minister Bruce had in mind the creation of an office the holder of which would "partake of the nature of a 'liaison officer,' the exact nature of the position still being undetermined." The social prestige and recognition of his office had been a matter of concern to the retiring commissioner; he was, according to the report, hindered in his work because he could not deal directly with American government officials. Former holders of the commissioner's post confirmed what had been said concerning official contact, but said that the effectiveness of a commissioner's work depended upon the individual holding the office.[29]

At the time of the appointment of Sir Herbert Brooks as Commissioner of Australia to the United States (1929), the Consultate-General again referred to the feeling with respect to the nature of the position. It reported that "in the minds of the Australian people" the importance of the office and its incumbent was comparable to that of the British ambassador to the United States, but the new appointee said, "I am not an ambassador."[30]

In the case of India, the fact that the country's independence did not come until 1947 and that it consequently depended upon British personnel for such formal relations as there were for India until the period of World War II greatly influenced the nature and pace of the process of establishing officers in other countries. One feature of this was the maintenance of buffer states around India and the creation of consular posts, the latter being largely manned by British officers of the Indian Political Service.[31] In the full diplomatic sense, India as such had no representation before World War II in any foreign country.

29. *Ibid.*, 847.01 B 11/50.
30. *Ibid.*, 847.01 B 11/45.
31. Hashishura Dayal, "The Genesis and Organization of the Indian Foreign Service," 1 *Indian Yb. of Int'l Aff.* 26 (1952).

In 1941 a distinguished Indian civil servant was appointed to represent the government of India in Washington, with the title of Agent-General.[32] He was to act in association with the British ambassador to the United States. There was a similar arrangement for India's representation in Nationalist China. In the fifteen years just prior to Indian independence, the country had trade commissioners in such foreign states as Italy, Germany, and Japan. By the early fifties, India had come to have twenty embassies, seven legations, and two "special missions" abroad, aside from her representation in other countries of the Commonwealth and in British colonial territories.[33] India as an independent state has in a number of cases followed the practice of various other countries (presumably for reasons of economy) in accrediting some of her envoys to more than one foreign capital.

Within a relatively short period from the time when there began to be discussion of the utility and desirability of having dominion government representatives attached to United Kingdom missions in such countries as the United States, the members of the Commonwealth came to have full diplomatic relations with foreign states generally. Yet dominion relations with other Commonwealth states have followed a somewhat different pattern in the matters of titles, channels of communication, and scope of functions.

3. Development of the High Commissionership

Even before any dominion had received a "high commissioner" from any other dominion in the presently accepted diplomatic sense of the term, there were in England official representatives of British colonial territories. After confederation, for example, Canada had emigration officers there; their function was to encourage the migration to Canada of such persons as farmers with capital and agricultural laborers.[34] As has been seen, there were also in various foreign countries trade commissioners from

32. U. S., 5 *Dep't State Bull.* 74 (1941).
33. Dayal, *loc. cit. supra* note 31, at pp. 28, 31.
34. Skilling, *op. cit. supra* note 18, at p. 14.

dominions before the latter began to send diplomatic agents.

In the 1870's a member of the British House of Commons, Edward Jenkins, was named General Resident Agent in London and also Superintendent of Emigration. His duties were in fact somewhat more than those of an emigration commissioner, for he was to give attention to "Canadian gentlemen calling in London" and he might be entrusted by the Canadian government with what were described as political missions to the British government.[35] He was not, however, a diplomatic agent and, by the very fact of his membership in the British Parliament, he could hardly be assimilated to an ambassador from Canada.

When there arose in 1879 the question of Canada's having permanent representation in London with quasi-diplomatic status, there was disagreement on the title that such a representative should have. The Canadian government proposed that it be "Resident Minister," but the British government apparently preferred "Dominion Commissioner" or "Canadian Commissioner."[36] Something more than mere title seems to have been in mind, conceivably Canada's desire not merely to make her own engagements but also to consult on the making of British treaties with foreign states in general. On this latter point, Lord Salisbury (foreign secretary) said in a letter of August 8, 1880, to the colonial secretary (Hicks-Beach):

> In any treaty we make with foreign States, in which Canada is interested, it is our influence that gets the treaty made, it is our strength that has to enforce it, it is we who must bear the brunt if Canada breaks it on her side. That in addition she should ask to have machinery constructed to enable her to decide on its terms, is a little too much. . . .[37]

In a communication to the Foreign Office Hicks-Beach had previously suggested that the title of "High Commissioner" did

35. *Ibid.*, p. 86.
36. Lady Victoria Alexandrina Hicks-Beach, *Life of Sir Michael Hicks-Beach* (1932), p. 68. It was explained that since the appointee would not be a minister from a foreign court, his relations with the British government would not be correctly defined as of a diplomatic character; he would communicate primarily with the Colonial Office, and the Foreign Office would decide as to the manner in which his services might be rendered in special circumstances.
37. *Ibid.*, p. 67.

not seem to be very appropriate, and he suggested, instead, "Resident Envoy for Canada in London." He also noted the effect of talk concerning titles upon other colonies; Sir Julian Vogel, he said, on hearing that there might be a "Resident Minister" from Canada, had at once suggested to his government in New Zealand that the latter should also have a Resident Minister in London.[38]

By the agreement finally reached between the Canadian and British governments, the title became "High Commissioner of Canada in London." The Foreign Office had considered that it was not qualified to express an opinion on the title, so long as no interference with the precedence of the Foreign Office was contemplated.[39] The first incumbent of the new office was Sir Charles Tupper, who had been a member of the Canadian Cabinet. Some doubt has been expressed about whether he was pleased with the idea of being "relegated" to the high commissionership.[40]

Not until 1912 did all other members of the "old" Commonwealth, following Canada's example, have high commissioners in London. There were, for a considerable time, agents-general in London, some of them representing component units (provinces and states) within dominions. Canada herself had agents-general from her provinces, but after the close of the nineteenth century these were apparently not accredited to or officially received by the government of the empire. In view of the different constitutional position of the states in Australia, agents of these states seem to have occupied a more representative position in England than did agents of the Canadian provinces.[41]

With the development of dominion representation at London there came eventually a change in administrative arrangements in the British government for the purpose of handling the work involved. In response to the expressed desire of a number of Commonwealth spokesmen, Great Britain established in 1907 a Dominions Division in the Colonial Office. In 1925 this division

38. C. O., 42/765 (P. R. O., London), p. 27.
39. *Ibid.*, p. 29.
40. J. W. Longley, *The Makers of Canada Series* (1926), VIII, 188.
41. Skilling, *op. cit. supra* note 18, at pp. 107, 108.

became a Dominions Office headed by a secretary of state (although from 1925 to 1930 and for short periods subsequently the Secretary of State for the Colonies was also the Secretary of State for Dominions Affairs). This was to be followed by the creation in 1947 of the Commonwealth Relations Office. The latter had, in addition to handling relations with the Commonwealth members and Ireland, responsibility for the administration of Bechuanaland, Basutoland, and Swaziland. This latter responsibility was discharged through the British High Commissioner to the Union of South Africa (who, as governor, worked through deputies in each of these protectorates) until South Africa became a republic in 1961, after which time the newly accredited British ambassador to South Africa succeeded to the responsibility.[42] The Commonwealth Relations Office also had responsibilities relating to the Federation of Rhodesia and Nyasaland (later to Southern Rhodesia) and the Maldive Islands.

During the period when Great Britain in effect conducted the foreign relations of the dominions, there arose certain legal questions concerning representation of foreign states in the dominions. As early as the Imperial Conference of 1911, Sir Wilfrid Laurier raised a question of a possible quasi-diplomatic status for consuls-general or consuls sent by major foreign states to function within the jurisdiction of dominions. Apparently nothing was done, however, to give such individuals any type of immunities other than those to which they would be entitled in the British Isles. To one individual, who was serving as a consular officer in Australia when he was assigned to a South American country as a minister plenipotentiary, was accorded in Australia (after such assignment) the status of a diplomatic envoy en route through a third state.[43]

Not until the interwar period of the twentieth century did Great Britain send a high commissioner to any of the dominions. Appointment in 1928 of a British high commissioner to Ottawa

42. See, generally, J. D. B. Miller, "The C.R.O. and Commonwealth Relations," 2 *Int'l Studies* 42–59 (1960).
43. H. Charteris, "The Position of Consuls in Australia," *Proc. of the Australian and New Zealand Society of Int'l Law* (1935), I, 78, 79.

marked the beginning of a new phase in Commonwealth representation.

Before World War I, there were, as a matter of actual practice, various types of communication that were essentially Commonwealth related. These included direct communications between prime ministers on matters of high importance, communications between the Dominions Office at London and the Department of External Affairs at Ottawa, formal communications between British and dominion representatives at international conferences, and (for British-Canadian relations) personal communications between the Canadian high commissioner at London and the Dominion secretary of state and between the British high commissioner at Ottawa and the Department of External Affairs there.[44]

In the period of World War II, Canada sent high commissioners to other Commonwealth countries and received high commissioners from those states. The position of Eire is unique in that, while sending agents who fall within the familiar classifications of diplomatic representatives, it accredits its envoy to London through the Commonwealth Relations Office rather than through the Foreign Office. The advantages of this arrangement are apparently recognized by the governments of both Eire and Great Britain.[45] Some difficulty in accrediting a diplomatic representative from Great Britain to Ireland arose out of the fact that the Irish constitution in its second article states that "the national territory consists of the whole island of Ireland." Since letters of credence were customarily signed by the sovereign as Queen of the United Kingdom *and Northern Ireland,* there was need for some compromise that would not throw doubt upon Her Majes-

---

44. Skilling, *op. cit. supra* note 18, at p. 174.

45. Miller, *loc. cit. supra* note 42, at pp. 58–59. See also *Commonwealth Relations Office, Third Report from the Select Committee on Estimates,* Sess. 1958–1959 (1959). In hearings conducted by this committee, a witness (from the Commonwealth Relations Office) said: "Confusion can be caused by the fact that the Commonwealth Relations Office deals with the Irish Republic but we do not take them into the intimate exchange of confidential and other information as we should with Canada, Australia or Ghana, but naturally, because of trading and political considerations, there is quite a lot of correspondence with the Irish Republic through the identical diplomatic channel." *Ibid.,* p. 10.

ty's title. It took shape in a form of address which directed the credentials to the President of Ireland personally rather than in his official capacity.[46]

After World War II one of the steps taken to assure that official relations between Commonwealth states would be on as high a plane as any diplomatic relations under international law and usage was that of granting to high commissioners privileges and immunities that would be no less than those granted to any ambassador. This step was not deterred by some suggestion that the effect might seem to make more formal the arrangements that had theretofore existed on the basis of family-like ties. Another move was to put any high commissioner whom a Commonwealth state might receive in as favorable a position, with respect to precedence in the diplomatic corps in the capital of the receiving state, as any diplomatic agent received by that state.[47] This is not hindered by the practice followed in the actual accrediting of high commissioners. The Commonwealth states that are still kingdoms do not send to each other commissioners accredited by the head of state, for in such a case accreditation would have to be by Her Majesty to Her Majesty; accrediting is, therefore, from government to government. This problem does not arise when the high commissioner goes from a republic in the Commonwealth to a kingdom in the Commonwealth; the President of India, the President of Pakistan, or the Yang di-Pertuan Agong of Malaysia would normally accredit a high commissioner to the head of state of another Commonwealth country.

46. Robert R. Wilson, "Some Questions of Legal Relations between Commonwealth Members," 51 *Am. J. Int'l L.* 611 at 617 (1957).

47. Illustrated in a notice published in New Zealand in 1954. By this an existing rule, to the effect that the position of Dean of the Diplomatic Corps at Wellington should be held by the senior foreign ambassador, was "amended to the extent that, in the light of constitutional developments in the Commonwealth, the New Zealand Government considers that it would be appropriate in future for a High Commissioner who is resident in New Zealand to be eligible, on a basis of seniority, to assume the position of Dean of the Diplomatic Corps in Wellington. The Amendment has received the approval of Her Majesty the Queen." *New Zealand Gazette*, No. 67 (Nov. 4, 1954), p. 1739.

It may also be noted that the Vienna Convention on Diplomatic Relations, 1961 (*U. N. Doc.* No. A/CONF. 20/13 [April 16, 1961]), makes provision for high commissioners although not by that name. Art. 14 of the convention enumerates three classes of heads of mission, the first being, "that of ambassadors or nuncios accredited to Heads of State, and other heads of mission of equivalent rank." The category last designated would include high commissioners.

In recent years, there has been maintained the usage whereby high commissioners in London are in a more favorable position than are ordinary diplomatic agents accredited there (with the possible exception of the representative of the United States of America). This is because the high commissioners have direct access to the British prime minister and access to other agencies of the British government besides the Commonwealth Relations Office.[48]

Early developments which had been considered highly significant no longer claim major attention.[49] In the matter of representation the Commonwealth members, given their divergent practices, as in accrediting through queen, prime minister, or president (and with some arrangements taking into account the peculiar situation of Eire, which is not a Commonwealth state but is treated much as if it were one), have at length assumed full rights of states under international law. Efforts to keep the whole system of representation in the Commonwealth abreast of rapidly changing conditions are apparent in recent reorganization moves in Great Britain and in recent conference developments.

4. Recent Trends

The evolution toward normal and ordinary diplomatic relations within the Commonwealth has not yet proceeded to the point where each Commonwealth state has with every other Commonwealth state arrangements identical with those which such a state has with any other member of the family of nations. The difference is not merely one of nomenclature. Smuts's thesis—that the sum is greater than the parts—is, as one Commonwealth statesman has

48. *Report* cited *supra* note 45, at p. 56. A memorandum submitted on behalf of the Secretary of State for Commonwealth Relations contained the statement that: "A point of particular note is that the U. K. High Commissioner has closer and more frequent contact with the Prime Minister of the Commonwealth country in which he is serving than is the case with foreign heads of missions. Practice on the point naturally varies, but in Australia, for example, on all important matters and whenever a formal approach is called for, the High Commissioner deals directly with the Prime Minister."

49. Nicholas Mansergh, *Survey of British Commonwealth Affairs: Problems of External Policy, 1931–1939* (1952), p. 8.

suggested, proved by the Commonwealth itself.[50] There is room within the framework of general international law for varying degrees of affinity and for the operation of a system which, without being an alliance, involves preferential treatment of representatives. That this is so was emphasized by two developments in 1964. The first was the appearance of the Plowden Report; the second was the meeting in London of the Commonwealth prime ministers' conference.

The Plowden Report indicated the background as follows:

. . . there has been a major change in the nature of the Commonwealth. Before the war, the relationship of Britain to other Commonwealth countries was still largely a maternal one in the sense that British Ambassadors in foreign countries normally looked after the interests of the Dominions as well. Only Canada then had a Foreign Service of any size. Commonwealth countries commonly looked first to Great Britain in all circumstances, irrespective of their geographical position. This is no longer true. The "Old Dominions" are now involved in political and military relationships in their own parts of the world and have their own regional interests to safeguard. . . . This does not mean that everything has changed or that nothing of the old exclusive relationship has survived or can survive. . . . But it does mean that new interests have come in as well and made the relationship more complicated. The "Old Dominions" will pursue their own regional objectives, although they will continue to be influenced by their close ties of culture and sentiment with Britain, by the still wide areas of common interest, including trade, and by the habit of intimate conversation. Although there are wide areas of common interest with the new Commonwealth countries, our link with them is of a different character. Like other newly independent countries, these Commonwealth countries have an acutely developed sense of national consciousness and are anxious to develop links with countries other than Britain.

The report continued by referring to the Commonwealth link as a "bridge" between the continents of the world. Without weakening this bridge, it was submitted that the effort should be to continue the cultivation of Commonwealth countries "on as deep a level as possible"; British diplomacy, however, "must

50. Robert Menzies in his Smuts Lecture at Cambridge University, May 16, 1960; reproduced in Australia, Dep't of External Affairs, *Current Notes on International Affairs,* vol. 31 (1960), pp. 255–263; see remarks at p. 256.

recognize the maturity of Commonwealth countries and their determination to play their part as individuals in regional and world affairs."[51] The report noted that there were on the staff of the United Kingdom Commonwealth Service 1,059 officers serving in London and 2,422 officers overseas. Thirteen heads of mission (high commissioners) in Commonwealth countries were Commonwealth Service Officers; the remaining high commissionerships had been filled from outside the Commonwealth Service.[52]

The Plowden committee considered, among other matters, the need which United Kingdom citizens in other Commonwealth countries might have for formal consular services and pointed out that, traditionally, such persons had not been regarded as "foreigners" and that they could rely upon the normal facilities available in the country where they happened to be. "This concept," the committee pointed out, was "no longer realistic." The report continued:

In Commonwealth countries as in others problems are bound to arise for United Kingdom citizens in which they need the help of properly equipped officials from their own country. The principle that consular work on behalf of United Kingdom citizens in Commonwealth countries is unnecessary has often had to be breached already. Consular services in the Commonwealth have had to be provided on an ad hoc basis by officials who do not enjoy normal consular facilities or recognition. Often Information Officers and Trade Commissioners have had to do the job. There is a real need in many places in the Commonwealth to face the fact that open and formal British consular facilities are needed to enable consular help and protection to be given to United Kingdom citizens. This need not mean that United Kingdom citizens in Commonwealth countries should cease to avail themselves of the special facilities which other Commonwealth countries continue to make available to nationals of Commonwealth countries. Commonwealth countries took part in the negotiations which resulted in the drawing up of the Vienna Convention on Consular Relations in 1963. This should lead to greater standardisation of consular practices and privileges throughout the world, including the Commonwealth. Thus,

51. *Report of the Committee on Representational Services Overseas, Appointed by the Prime Minister under the Chairmanship of Lord Plowden, 1962–63,* Cmnd. No. 2276 at pp. 3, 4 (1964).
52. *Ibid.,* p. 25.

the time is ripe for placing consular representation in Commonwealth countries on a more regular basis.[53]

Some of the problems to which the Plowden committee referred in its report had to do with administrative organization. It was pointed out, for example, that there might be more than one British representative in important Commonwealth cities (in separate offices) without any clear chain of command except that all were subordinate to the high commissioner in the particular country. The committee recommended that British representation in Commonwealth countries be unified "to correspond to present-day needs."[54] It found that no members of the Commonwealth Relations legal staff (who are consulted upon, *inter alia,* interpretation of agreements between Commonwealth countries) were posted abroad on a resident basis and that there had not been enough staff to meet demands for sending persons to conferences. Recommending a unified legal element in the Diplomatic Service and foreseeing no serious problem that would attend adoption of the plan for such a unified legal service, the committee envisaged, rather, a "continued requirement for specialized advice on Commonwealth questions in which detailed knowledge of Commonwealth law will be valuable." In general, however, it was felt that "the questions to be dealt with by legal staff are closely akin, whether they arise in Commonwealth or in foreign countries." Senior legal staff in the Commonwealth Relations Office would need at least for some time to be chosen, the committee concluded, "from those with special experience of the legal problems special to the Commonwealth."[55]

A sequel to the acceptance of the Plowden committee's report has been the merging of the Foreign and the Commonwealth Services of the United Kingdom. While there is still a Commonwealth Relations Office separate from the Foreign Ministry (the Plowden Report not having urged the immediate creation of a single ministry), a move in that direction appears to have been made; the new arrangement became effective on January 1, 1965.

53. *Ibid.*, p. 73.
54. *Ibid.*, p. 74.
55. *Ibid.*, p. 78.

Should the further step be taken of amalgamating the two ministries, this would seem to have the effect of putting the diplomatic relations of Great Britain with Commonwealth states on substantially the same basis which exists between foreign states.

The extent of the present representation of foreign states in Great Britain and of the resulting commitment of the United Kingdom to accord privileges and immunities according to international law is indicated in a statement submitted to the House of Commons shortly before the appearance of the Plowden Report. According to this statement there were 6,235 persons in foreign and Commonwealth missions resident in Great Britain (including 1,873 wives) to whom were accorded full diplomatic immunities. There were in the country, in foreign missions, 386 persons entitled to immunities restricted to their official acts. Consular officers and employees, having immunities that were restricted to their official acts, numbered 709. Of the persons in the United Kingdom who were connected with international organizations, 7 were reported to be entitled to full immunity, 19 reported to be entitled to immunity in respect of their official acts and from detention and arrest in respect of acts done in their official capacities, and 217 entitled to immunity from legal process in respect of official acts only.[56]

A different type of representation, but one of major importance to the Commonwealth's functioning, is that at the highest level meetings, i.e., the conferences of prime ministers and presidents. The conference at London in July, 1964, while perhaps less widely heralded than the conference of 1961 (the year in which South Africa left the Commonwealth), provided occasion for emphasis upon the changing nature of the Commonwealth and for re-examination of Great Britain's role in it. Four years earlier a statesman from the "old" Commonwealth had said that, "When we [the prime ministers] meet, we have no set agenda. We move no resolutions and we have never cast votes. But we learn a great deal about the world's problems and our relations to them. . . .

56. 684 *H. C. Deb.* (5th. ser.) 29 (Nov. 18, 1963). Cf. editorial, "Far Too Much Privilege," *The Times* (London), July 6, 1964, p. 11.

We do not meet as a tribunal to sit in judgment upon each other or to ventilate and pass upon intra-Commonwealth issues. We are not a superstate."[57] While the basic theory of the conferences seemed to be maintained as late as the conference of 1964, the situation with respect to Southern Rhodesia appeared to put some strain upon the traditional planning and presumably upon control by Great Britain of arrangements for and general direction of the conferences. There was, of course, opportunity for the prime ministers of other Commonwealth countries to express their views concerning Southern Rhodesia. On this subject, the text of the final communiqué issued at the close of the conference simply recorded that:

The Prime Minister of Great Britain said that he would give careful consideration to all the views expressed by other Commonwealth Prime Ministers. At the same time he emphasized that the Government of Southern Rhodesia was constitutionally responsible for the internal affairs of that territory and that the question of the granting of independence was a matter for decision by the British Parliament.[58]

The racial composition of the 1964 Conference emphasized the changing character of the association with respect to representation at the highest level. Of the eighteen Commonwealth states participating, only five were represented by white spokesmen. There were seven Africans, two West Indians, and four Asians.

Perhaps even more significant than the changing character of the representation at the periodic conferences has been the establishment of a Secretariat for the Commonwealth. In January, 1965, talks began in London on this subject, pursuant to a plan that had been envisaged at the Conference of Prime Ministers and Presidents in the previous July. Since Commonwealth states generally have now developed diplomatic representation with many countries outside the Commonwealth, as well as between themselves, establishment of a multinational administrative machinery for the Commonwealth seems to be more feasible than at

57. Robert Menzies, *loc. cit. supra* note 50, at p. 260.
58. Text of Final Communique Issued at the Close of the Commonwealth Prime Ministers Meeting Held in London, July 8–15 (issued by British Information Services, New York, July 16, 1964), at p. 6.

any time in the past. At the 1964 conference at London, Trinidad and Tobago along with three African states reportedly took the initiative for talks looking to such construction.[59] It was anticipated that preliminary discussion might lead to action at a future conference of prime ministers and presidents that would supply a type of machinery which the Commonwealth had not previously had. Such action came at the 1965 prime ministers' conference. Depending upon the extent of authority or planning entrusted to such a secretariat, this move could conceivably produce for the associated states a device that would bring their plan of co-operation much closer to becoming an international public organization—of the type with which the Commonwealth has in the past been more frequently contrasted than compared.

The changed and still changing situation in the composition and methods of the Commonwealth perhaps gives added justification for inquiry into what the associated states individually and collectively have done and have proposed to do concerning public international law. Their reception of that law, the relative importance assigned to it in their respective governmental systems, and their apparent influence upon its development are to be considered in the following chapter.

59. "Commonwealth Change," *The Economist,* Jan. 9, 1965, pp. 97, 98.
The United Kingdom government's position in 1964 and 1965 in withholding independence from Southern Rhodesia was apparently regarded by representatives of the established government there as detrimentally affecting its representation in the United Kingdom. In a talk at London on April 1, 1965, the High Commissioner for Rhodesia in London, Mr. Evan Campbell, is reported to have said that "Forty years ago my High Commission was one of five in London. Today it is one of 20—and it is being given second-class status." The High Commissioner also referred to the "humiliating rebuff" in that his prime minister had been excluded from the last prime ministers' conference and was not to receive an invitation to the next one. 8 *Commonwealth J.* 116 (June, 1965).

Reception of Norms

Robert R. Wilson

International law applies between states despite differences in municipal law systems. Courts within states vary in their organization, their relation to executive and legislative branches of government, and their authorization to apply international law. Where such courts have substantial independence of other branches of government their rulings on points of international law may derive wider significance than they otherwise would. If the law of nations is a part of the "law of the land," executive action may also be influenced by this fact. In the case of the Commonwealth, evidences of the reception of international law include constitutional provisions, judicial decisions, occasional executive pronouncements, and records of positions taken when there has been codification effort. The very quantity of this evidence seems to justify restriction, for the present purpose, to illustrative situations that indicate the place of international law in municipal law systems.[1]

Communities that prior to their becoming independent states have been under a common political authority will presumably reflect in their legal arrangements the common inheritance, unless there has been transformation of social and ethical standards in

---

1. Among recent studies on the subject are: D. P. O'Connell, "The Relationship between International Law and Municipal Law," 48 *Geo. L. J.* 431 (1960); I. Seidl-Hohenveldern, "Transformation or Adoption of International Law into Municipal Law," 12 *Int'l & Comp. L. Q.* (4th ser.) 88 (1963); and L. Erades and W. L. Gould, *The Relationships between International Law and Municipal Law in the Netherlands and in the United States* (1961). On one aspect of the general subject which would appear to be relatively important, see Richard A. Falk, *The Role of Municipal Courts in the International Legal Order* (1964).

the course of revolution. It is natural that a part of that heritage should fall within the range of ideas touching international law. This does not mean that all the new states will with the same degree of emphasis adhere to this standard or that they will assign identical roles concerning it to municipal courts. In any event, if statehood comes not through transforming revolution but after a period of tutelage,[2] evidences of previously accepted ideas as to the relationship between municipal law and international law may reasonably be expected. Traditionalism of the kind suggested does not, of course, preclude innovation, the re-interpretation of familiar rules, or the adaptation of the latter to changing conditions.

In the early evolution of the Commonwealth its member states depended upon constitutional arrangements that were distinctively British. In the course of the twentieth century, however, they have not all adhered in every respect to British models.[3] Some of the newer states have preferred republican to monarchical forms and have drawn to some extent from constitutional systems other than the British. The suitability or efficiency of these for dealing with legal questions that touch foreign relations is not the principal subject of the present inquiry. It has been seen that the older members of the Commonwealth came to political maturity through a process not bringing about any great changes in their systems of jurisprudence when they became independent states. Conceivably, newer members may have come to regard their common heritage differently from the way in which the older members regard it. This possible difference in viewpoint is one of the factors which lend incentive to an examination of the manner in which the international law standard now has place in the jurisprudence of the Commonwealth states.

At least in internal legal relations, perhaps the factor which has

2. See statement to the effect that "if there is one lesson to be drawn from human experience it is that empires always die. Previously the process has been one of violence, fragmentation and confusion. We have sought a new and more constructive concept and tried by the orderly processes of evolution to establish communities in a new relationship with each other." From address by Lord Home (later Sir Alec Douglas Home), "The Commonwealth as a World Force," in 6 *Commonwealth J.* 149 (1963).

3. See, generally, S. A. de Smith, *The New Commonwealth and Its Constitutions* (1964).

received most attention from analysts of practice in the states of
the Commonwealth has been the common law, usually identified
as the English common law. In this context it is convenient to
consider (*a*) the effect of this common-law heritage upon attitudes toward (or authoritative character assigned to) international law, (*b*) the judicial role in interpretation and application,
(*c*) specific provisions in Commonwealth states' constitutions
concerning customary international law, and (*d*) some illustrative instances of Commonwealth states' participation in efforts
looking to the further development of international law.

1. Incidence of Common-Law Heritage

British subjects settling in a previously uninhabited country, it
has been said, "must carry with them English law as in force at
the time of settlement, otherwise they have no law at all."[4] The
statement does not preclude variation in light of the factual
situation in each territory. More than half a century earlier
another writer had observed, "As regards a settled colony, the
principle is well established that an Englishman carries with him
English law and liberties into any unoccupied country where he
settles so far as they are applicable to the situation having regard
to all the circumstances."[5] A broad general statement to this effect
does not, however, settle all the practical questions that may
arise. To say, as did the Court of Chancery in 1722, that "if there
be a new and uninhabited country found out by *English* subjects,
as the law is the birthright of every subject, so, wherever they go
they carry their laws with them," and that "such new-found
country is to be governed by the laws of England,"[6] is not to
discover what the law is at a particular time. Nor, if there be
uncertainty, does it explain how such uncertainty is to be
resolved. The English law was not static but was constantly being

4. Sir Kenneth Roberts-Wray, in J. N. D. Anderson, ed., *Changing Law in Developing Countries* (1963), p. 16.
5. Sir Henry Jenkyns, *British Rule and Jurisdiction beyond the Seas* (1902),
p. 5.
6. Anonymous (Case 15), 2 P. Wms. 75 (1722); cited after Charles J. Tarring,
Chapters on the Law Relating to the Colonies (4th ed., 1913), p. 5.

supplemented or altered by fresh enactments. Some of these were enactments by colonial legislatures. Later acts of Parliament, i.e., measures passed after the original extension of a body of law to the colony, might or might not be intended to apply in the colony. In 1769, for example, Lord Mansfield observed that "No Act of Parliament made after a colony is planted, is construed to extend to it, without express words shewing the intention of the Legislature 'that it should.' "[7] A later expression of judicial opinion emphasized that, as to a particular colony, "English settlers carried with them all the immunities and privileges and laws of England," and that Englishmen in a province that had been settled "were as free Englishmen, with as much privilege as those that remained in England." Furthermore, since the law in question was the law of England as it was at the time of settlement, subsequent legislation in England altering the law did not affect colonists' rights unless it was expressly made to extend to the province or the colony.[8]

For the purpose of determining what law applied, there was a distinction between a "new and uninhabited country" and one which had previously been under some other sovereign authority. In a conquered or ceded area there appears to have been application of a general rule that the law existing before the cession or conquest was presumed to continue in force until the law was altered. Pre-existing legal arrangements were necessarily affected, however, by the law of the conqueror with respect to some matters of administration of appellate jurisdiction and of "universal" policy such as that touching navigation.[9]

As has been noted above, the situation with respect to extension of the common law to the colonies was affected by the establishment of colonial legislatures. After these bodies came into being the Crown was apparently in much the same position with respect to the colonial legislatures as it was to the Parliament in England. There was judicial holding to the effect that the Crown must

7. R. v. Vaughan, 4 Burr. 2494 at 2500, 98 Eng. Rep. 308 (1769).
8. Per Lord Blackburn, The Lauderdale Peerage, 10 App. Cas. 692 at 745 (1885); see also Tarring, *op. cit. supra* note 6, at p. 6.
9. Jenkyns, *op. cit. supra* note 5, at p. 6. Treaties of cession, such as the Treaty of Paris, 1763, sometimes expressly provided for the continued application of some pre-existing private law.

follow English law and could not authorize procedure unknown to that law.[10]

Treaties that Great Britain had made prior to the acquisition of new territories also had to be taken into account. Here the intention of the treaty-making states became relevant to determining the relations of the newly acquired regions with the outside world. An early twentieth-century treatise refers to the British practice of excluding self-governing British colonies from the areas to which treaties that would affect the colonies' internal law might otherwise have applied—although there could be inclusion if the colonial governments so desired. Even then Great Britain commonly retained the right to denounce the treaties for each colony separately. The policy of non-application to colonies was sometimes maintained in the face of demands from foreign states for enforcement in colonial possessions of rules included in treaties which these states had made with Great Britain.[11] Directly related to external affairs of the colonies was their involvement in a war in which Great Britain was a belligerent. For the British government, aid from the colonies involved not merely questions of legality but also of political expediency, so long as the colonies had no direct voice in decisions on questions of peace and war.[12] General imperial policy on a matter such as the slave trade found application in the colonies as well as in the British Isles. Of practical importance from the point of view of adherence to international law was the functioning of prize courts in the colonies. In 1894 the British Parliament conferred upon the Crown power to issue "dormant" commissions whereby courts sitting in prize with British commissions could exercise jurisdiction in prize cases by reason of a British vice-admiral's proclamation that war had broken out. Thereafter, when functioning, these tribunals were regarded as imperial courts; appeals could be taken from them to the King in Council.[13]

10. In re Lord Bishop of Natal, 3 Moor. P. C. (n.s.) 155 (1864).
11. Jenkyns, *op. cit. supra* note 5, at p. 24. Examples cited were China's complaints against Chinese exclusion laws in New South Wales and in Victoria and Japanese reaction to legislation of British Columbia for exclusion of Japanese from that province.
12. *Ibid.*, pp. 25, 26.
13. 53 & 54 Vict., c. 27, § 6.

From the point of view of more purely private law, it was possible to speak with some accuracy of unwritten constitutional custom in the colonies; moreover, extension of the common law to the colonies did not preclude the later passage by colonial legislatures of some law that was at variance with the common law, and in this respect there was considerable leeway for local legislative policy.[14] There were, of course, territorial limits to the application of colonial laws. Thus when the legislature of New Zealand in its Foreign Offenders Apprehension Act, 1863, authorized deportation of persons charged with indictable misdemeanors in other colonies, the Supreme Court of New Zealand held that the act was beyond the proper powers of the legislature because it authorized detention of persons on the high seas. The legislature, said the court, could enact for peace, order, and good government, but only within the limits of the colony.[15]

Invocation and application of international law, for example in relations between metropolitan states and protected or "semi-sovereign states," gave rise to practical questions particularly in the nineteenth century when there were extensive claims by European states to overseas territories. In this connection the earlier British experience in India apparently had considerable influence upon the steps taken by other countries. Thus Bismarck in his planning for German protectorates in Africa was apparently much influenced by British experience and particularly by the role of the East India Company.[16] For the present purpose, however, the substantive content of the law which Great Britain made operative in her overseas territories assumes primary importance.

The actual extension of the common law of England to these territories was naturally affected by the peculiar needs of particular colonies, the varying circumstances under which the British authority had been established, and the type of colonists who

14. Jenkyns, *op. cit. supra* note 5, at p. 72. The relevance of the Colonial Laws Validity Act to the general subject does not seem to require extended comment.

15. In re Gleich, O. B. & F. (S. C.) 39 (1880). Cf. statement by Sir Kenneth Roberts-Wray, *loc. cit. supra* note 4, at pp. 26–27, that "the Queen can make a law for two or more territories which could not be made by any one of them because it would then purport to act extra-territorially."

16. Hans Spellmeyer, *Deutsche Koloniz Politik im Reichstag* (1932), p. 15.

were involved. Where, in acquired territory, there was already in existence another system of private law based upon code rather than custom or where there were native customs which continued to have utility, complete replacement was obviously not in the general interest. In other situations, where colonists were predominantly British, there was less justification for non-extension or non-application of the common law. Thus in 1774 the Continental Congress in North America declared that the colonists were entitled to this law, which afforded them protection against arbitrary processes and assured them the traditional safeguards of Englishmen.[17] Potentially at least, the fact of the common law's being established had significance also in situations involving elements of the law of nations as, for example, where ships under foreign flags or diplomatic agents claimed rights under that law.

In any case the question of whether there had in fact been extension of the common law and, if so, the exact date on which it became effective in each particular colony was apparently regarded as having considerable practical importance. In what is now the most populous of the Commonwealth states, the common law has had an impressive history. As an observer in that country has put it:

We, in India . . . have a very long legal tradition. The Indian legal system which is based on the Common Law began to function in India certainly as far back as 1726. Thereafter followed through the years the making of the Indian codes . . . of civil and criminal law. In these Codes is embodied the major part of the law in force in India today. They are based mainly on the principles underlying the English Common Law and Statute Law.[18]

The exact dates for extension of the common law are recorded, although in some cases there was some uncertainty during particular periods. This was the case, for example, in the colony

17. *Journals of the American Congress from 1774 to 1788* (1823), I, 21.
18. Remarks of M. C. Setalvad, *Record of the Second Commonwealth and Empire Law Conference, Ottawa, April 14–21, 1960* (1962), pp. 45–46. Cf. reference by the Federal Attorney General and Minister of Justice for Nigeria to the interpenetration of laws as having "gone on to an extent which is making erratic and isolated developments in individual colonies more and more unlikely." T. O. Elias, *British Colonial Law: A Comparative Study of the Interaction between English and Local Laws in British Dependencies* (1962), p. 286.

of Jamaica, where the situation was eventually clarified by the British Parliament's confirming that the laws of England applied there.[19] In other areas common-law rules were applicable in civil but not in criminal matters, e.g., in the Gold Coast, to which Parliament extended the common law as it existed on July 24, 1874, although the Criminal Code of 1892 excluded the common law.[20] In Nigeria, the common law as it existed in England on January 1, 1900, was made applicable *inter alia*, although native custom was to apply to proceedings between natives.[21] Before Trinidad and Tobago were united by the Order in Council of November 17, 1888,[22] the common law of England had applied in Tobago along with local ordinances, some of which are said to have introduced English statute law. Prior to Great Britain's acquiring Trinidad the Spanish law had applied there. It was gradually replaced by local enactments said to have been shaped along the lines of English law; as late as the beginning of the twentieth century, however, certain private-law relationships continued to be governed by the older, Spanish, law.[23]

After its occupancy by the British, Sierra Leone had "plantation" status; the common law was in effect, along with statute law including measures of general application in force in England on January 1, 1880. Roman-Dutch law that was in force in the maritime provinces of Ceylon (before Holland ceded the territory to Britain in the early nineteenth century) came to be modified by local enactments, as affected by judicial decisions that are said to have followed in certain instances rules of English law; in the field of personal relations rulings apparently reflected

19. Bryan Edwards, *The History, Civil and Commercial, of the British Colonies in the West Indies* (3d ed., 1801), I, 215–220.
20. William Burge, *Colonial Laws and Courts, With a Sketch of the Legal Systems of the World and Tables of Conditions of Appeal to the Privy Council*, A. W. Renton and G. G. Phillimore, eds. (1907), p. 264; reprinted from *Burge's Commentaries on Colonial and Foreign Laws*, Renton and Phillimore, eds. (1907).
21. *Ibid.*, p. 268.
22. This was pursuant to the Trinidad and Tobago Act, 1887 (50 & 51 Vict., c. 44), which repealed, insofar as it related to Tobago, 39 & 40 Vict., c. 47.
23. Burge, *op. cit. supra* note 20, at pp. 247, 248. On some aspects of the continuation of laws, see Eric Williams, *History of The People of Trinidad and Tobago* (1962), pp. 69–75.

the earlier legal system.[24] Even in areas where the civil law prevailed prior to English rule, the influence of the common law has been felt.[25] Zambia and Malawi have systems based on English law.[26]

Some of the regions mentioned in the preceding paragraph have become states and have assumed places in the "new" Commonwealth.[27] As independent entities they stand in relation to international law on the same basis as all other members of the family of nations and not merely as heirs of Great Britain. Yet their common-law heritage can conceivably affect their outlook upon the rules which compose the law of nations and their potential for promoting the rule of law on a basis that is wider than a merely national one. To a considerable extent courts of the respective Commonwealth countries have an opportunity to contribute to this development.

24. Burge, *op. cit. supra* note 20, at p. 273, citing Ordinance No. 14 of 1904.
25. Elias, *op. cit. supra* note 18, *passim*.
26. As Elias points out, in Uganda, Ghana, and Nigeria, "the English common law is the basic or residual law, whereas in South Africa, the High Commission Territories and at least Southern Rhodesia, the Roman-Dutch Law is 'the common law.' This cleavage reflects a certain divergence of attitude towards customary law, which enjoys a scope and prestige wider and greater in the English common law areas than in the 'civil law' ones." *Ibid.*, p. 132.
27. The parts of the Commonwealth that have been specifically referred to do not include all to which the common law has been extended. There was extension to the Federation of Nigeria as of Jan. 1, 1900, to Uganda on Aug. 11, 1902, to Tanganyika on July 22, 1920, and to Cyprus on Sept. 3, 1953.
Dates for extension to other parts of the empire are indicated in the following list: Aden Colony, April 1, 1937; Bahamas, Dec. 2, 1799; Bermuda, July 11, 1612; North Borneo, Dec. 1, 1951; British Guiana, Jan. 1, 1917; Northern Rhodesia, Aug. 17, 1911; British Honduras, Jan. 1, 1899; British Solomon Islands, March 15, 1893; Brunei, April 25, 1951; Falkland Islands, May 22, 1900; Fiji, Nov. 2, 1875; Gambia, Nov. 1, 1888; Gibraltar, Dec. 31, 1883; Gilbert and Ellice Islands, March 15, 1893; Grenada, Dec. 19, 1764; Hong Kong, April 5, 1843; Kenya, Aug. 12, 1897; Nyasaland, Aug. 11, 1902; St. Helena, May 10, 1895; Sarawak, Dec. 12, 1849; Singapore, Nov. 26, 1826; Somaliland, March 16, 1900; Turks and Caicos, Dec. 2, 1799.
In the case of Malaysia, while it is settled that the law of England was introduced into the Straits Settlements, "it is not settled, and may never fall to be decided in view of modern legislation, what was the operative date of its introduction." L. A. Sheridan, *Malaya and Singapore: The Borneo Territories* (1961), p. 14. For purposes of the law the question of how Malacca was acquired (by cession or conquest) and of how the British acquired Penang and Singapore (by cession or settlement) are apparently of historical interest only. *Ibid.*, p. 15. The same author, referring to justification for judicial modification of English law, points out that the royal charters themselves were regarded as authorizing modification, although these charters themselves "do not . . . give any guide as to what modifications there should be or how they should be made." *Ibid.*, p. 17.

2. Judicial Role

The term "common law" might be given various meanings as applied to the various regions formerly under British rule and now independent members of the Commonwealth. Reconciliation of local customary law with the standards of English law provided opportunity for judicial statesmanship in practical situations, both in courts of first instance and in appellate tribunals. One view of the practical problem involved sees in it the judicial dilemma of striking "a nice balance between what is reasonably tolerable and what is essentially below the minimum standard of civilised values in the contemporary world."[28] While in the process of adjudication there might be some element of law-giving (*ius dare*) rather than law-declaring (*ius dicere*), a prime objective in any case presumably would be to avoid mere arbitrary rulings. In this process the raising of questions involving traditional international law would, in all likelihood, be relatively infrequent. Questions concerning the treatment of ordinary aliens and of alien-owned property (particularly after a state succession), navigation rights, and coastal fisheries, the status with respect to taxation of property owned by foreign states, the force and effect of the "act of state" doctrine, and the jurisdictional immunities of public agents would normally be among the types of questions that might arise. To these might conceivably be added, as the body of rules composing international law develops, human rights and fundamental freedoms of persons, even persons who are nationals of the forum state. With the extension of the range of international law, the greater mobility of people, and the growth of commerce, occasions will naturally increase for national courts to pass upon what are essentially international legal rights.

It is in connection with questions such as those suggested that the doctrine of Blackstone concerning English municipal law and the law of nations becomes relevant. The doctrine is that the generally accepted rules of international law are a part of the

28. Elias, *op. cit. supra* note 18, at p. 104.

common law of England.[29] The proposition, which is still challenged by some legalists, would appear to provide judges with a basis for upholding international law in the event it is invoked in actual litigation. It would not seem to place serious inhibitions upon law-making authorities, as statute law might take precedence over common-law rules, but if there was utilization of statutes for that purpose, the intent of the legislature would presumably have to be clear. The suggestion that a national court give effect to international law even when there is a statute contrary to the international-law rule has been opposed because of the supposed weakness in international law itself. This quality, it has been argued, would make it undesirable to put limitations upon legislative bodies in situations wherein the law of nations was invoked. "An implied limitation of this sort" (i.e., upon the enactment of statutes contrary to international law), as one publicist puts it, "is really out of the question, for the single reason that international law is too ill-defined to act as a criterion, and . . . no case has yet been decided on the basis suggested, while the duty of the British courts to give effect to British legislation despite objections on the score of international law is unquestioned."[30] Even if this argument were valid, however, the doctrine itself would not be useless. For there would still be the possibility that, in the absence of statute law on a given subject, a court, if given evidence of the existence and applicability of a rule of international law, might apply that rule in actual litigation. Established international custom would presumably guide decision-makers. If Commonwealth states were involved, there might naturally be regard for judicial precedents in holdings of the Judicial Committee of the Privy Council. This would be true, even if decisions of the latter tribunal no longer had legally

29. *Commentaries on the Law of England* (1876 ed., Philadelphia), bk. 4, chap. 5, p. 67.

30. A. B. Keith, *The Dominions as Sovereign States* (1938), p. 341. Among other cases, the author cites Mortensen v. Peters, 14 Scots L.T.R. 227 (1906), and Re Arrow River & Tributaries Slide & Boom Co., Ltd., [1932] 2 D.L.R. 250.

Cf. the Australian High Court's decision to the effect that the drafting of aliens was contrary to international law but the national court could not disregard the statute which authorized such drafting; Polites v. The Commonwealth and Another; Kandiliotes v. The Commonwealth and Another, 70 Commw. L. R. 60 (1945).

controlling force in the country where the judicial precedent was invoked. That the abolition of appeals from some Commonwealth states to the Privy Council has not destroyed the value and influence of its past decisions is suggested in an opinion given in 1956 by Chief Justice Munir of the Pakistan Supreme Court. He said in part:

> I agree that decisions of the Privy Council are no longer binding on us now, but being expositions of the law by one of the highest judicial tribunals in the world composed of distinguished men who had special knowledge of our public law, they are entitled to the greatest respect and we are not to disregard them merely on the ground of changed conditions because the recognition of any such grounds for departure from well-settled and fundamental principles would be tantamount to imputing judicial dishonesty to that Tribunal.[31]

Whether the rule to be applied in a decision is derived from precedent or through inquiry into what the international law is on a particular subject, the actual or potential importance of the Blackstone doctrine is apparent. As a leading scholar pointed out, even before there were very many independent states of the Commonwealth for which the question might arise,[32] the effect would be twofold. In its construction of a statute a court having before it two possible interpretations of a statute, one consistent with what the court found to be existing international law and the

---

31. Noorul Hassan v. Federation of Pakistan, [1956] 1 P.L.D. 331 at 359 (Sup. Ct., Pak.). This was not a case directly involving a *ratio decidendi* touching international law, although the facts giving rise to the case involved the partition of Pakistan from India and the claimed tenure in Pakistan of persons who had been in public employment under Indian rule.

32. H. Lauterpacht, "Is International Law a Part of the Law of England?" 25 *Transact. Grot. Soc'y.* 51 at 57–59 (1939). From the affirmative answer to the question raised in the title of the above article there is dissent at least in part by W. S. Holdsworth, "The Relation of English Law to International Law," 26 *Minn. L. Rev.* 141 at 151 (1941); the author refers to international law as a source, rather than a part, of the common law. On the relationship in Canada, see D. C. Vanek, "Is International Law Part of the Law of Canada?" 8 *U. Toronto L. J.* 251 (1950).

On the broad question of the relationship of international law to municipal law, see also J. E. S. Fawcett, *The British Commonwealth and International Law* (1963). This study submits (p. 18) that in the United Kingdom and the legal systems derived from it there has been no general adoption or incorporation of international law, although there has been observance and application of particular customary or conventional rules of the law. See also the same author's discussion (with illustrations in three fields) of the reception of customary international law (pp. 35–55).

other not consistent with that law, would presumably apply the former. As a matter of evidence this rule of international law, not being "foreign" law, would not have to be proved as would foreign law.[33]

A finding that international law had come to be part of municipal law as an element of common law (as, for example, in a case involving an alien's access to municipal courts[34]) might have, from the point of view of strengthening the body of rules composing the law of nations, but temporary utility, for variance from the international legal standard in municipal courts could be achieved by the simple passage of legislation that would authorize or direct enforcement of a rule not consistent with customary international law. A foreign state whose nationals were concerned might of course bring a claim diplomatically or in an international forum against the state whose courts had applied such legislation.

The mere fact of international law's being regarded as an element of the common law might, however, have broader significance. Recourse to a common law to which international law could be subsumed may be useful in promoting a regard for law in general. It has been said that in India "the common law tradition found a natural ally in the Indian judiciary which preserves well established rules of international law, in so far as they are not inconsistent with the constitution."[35] In South Africa after World War II there was occasion for judicial reference to the law of nations, and to common law other than English common law, in the treason trial of a German who was never naturalized in South Africa but owed allegiance there by reason of his residence and was charged with having aided the Germans after having been captured by them. There was apparent deference to the law of nations, although this did not save the defendant in the particular case. The tribunal observed that no question of international law or of the comity of nations required

33. See generally, on the manner of such proof, Otto C. Sommerich and Benjamin Busch, *Foreign Law: A Guide to Pleading and Proof* (1959).

34. On the question of whether there is a rule of international law by which aliens must be accorded access to courts, see Robert R. Wilson, *United States Commercial Treaties and International Law* (1960), chap. 8.

35. C. H. Alexander, "International Law in India," 1 *Int'l & Comp. L. Q.* (4th ser.) 289 at 300 (1952).

a state to refrain from punishing a person accused of having committed treasonable acts against it while in another state. It is proper, the court said, "in ascertaining the extent of our common law conception of high treason to have some regard to the principles of the law of nations." After referring to the Joyce trial in England the tribunal observed that, in Roman-Dutch law, high treason committed outside of the Union was as much punishable as was Joyce's offense under English common law.[36]

Perhaps the most frequently cited English decision on the subject of customary international rules that may become binding even without the passage of (declaratory) statutes is the *Barbuit* case (1737).[37] Thirty-seven years later Lord Mansfield referred to the declaratory nature of the enactment in 7 Anne, c.12.[38] With the modern practice of setting forth in considerable detail the international law concerning jurisdictional immunities of diplomatic agents and diplomatic establishments, as illustrated in the Vienna Convention of 1961, there presumably will be less room for differences in the implementation of statutes on this subject. Another jurisdictional matter which has provided occasion for pronouncements by Commonwealth state courts (as, for example, in Canada[39]) concerns the jurisdictional immunities of visiting friendly foreign armed forces. In connection with this there has been a considerable development in the international law that is

36. Rex v. Neumann, [1949] 3 So. Afr. L. R. 1238 at 1248–1249.
37. Buvot v. Barbuit, Cas. t. Talbot 281, 25 Eng. Rep. 777 (1737).
38. Triquet v. Bath, 3 Burr. 1478, 97 Eng. Rep. 936 (1764). Commenting on this case, Fawcett, *op. cit. supra* note 32, at p. 36 n., points out that there was doubt as to the criminality of the law's infraction. Another investigator considers entirely unsound Lord Mansfield's statement in *Triquet* v. *Bath* (in which case Blackstone was counsel for the plaintiff) to the effect (*a*) that the act of 7 Anne, c. 12, was occasioned by doubt as to whether the law of nations (as applicable to public ministers) was part of the law of England, and (*b*) that the infraction of the minister's rights was criminal. The same investigator submits that before 1700 violation of ambassadorial immunities was not criminal, punishment for such violation being a matter for prerogative action; his conclusion is that before 1709 this part, at any rate, of the law of nations was not part of the common law. Edward Robert Adair, *The Exterritoriality of Ambassadors in the Sixteenth and Seventeenth Centuries* (1929), p. 241; see further reference (at p. 242) to the "old cliché that international law is necessarily part of the common law of England."
39. See Reference re Exemption of U. S. Forces from Canadian Criminal Law, [1943] 4 D.L.R. 11, and notes in J. G. Castel, ed., *International Law Chiefly as Interpreted and Applied in Canada* (1965), pp. 788–789. On earlier decisions concerning immunities of foreign-owned public property in Canada, see Norman McKenzie and Lionel H. Laing, *Canada and the Law of Nations* (1938).

applicable since the ruling of the United States Supreme Court in *Schooner Exchange* v. *McFaddon*.[40] On another subject (that of restrictive covenants) a Canadian appellate court had occasion to consider the effect of Canada's becoming a party to the Atlantic Charter and the United Nations Charter. It found that legislation would be necessary in order to incorporate the racial non-discrimination provisions into applicable municipal law.[41] Given the strong feeling in states of the new Commonwealth against such discrimination, it might be expected that courts in those states would be more likely to utilize such international instruments as were unsuccessfully invoked in this case.

British colonial law comprises various elements. It is presumably the task of the courts to apply the law, whether public or private, in such a manner that there will be conformity to modern standards of civilized values.[42] While the role of the courts has been primarily in the application of private law, the generalization would seem to apply with equal force to matters that fall within the scope of public international law. With the transition from colonial to independent status there has been in the Commonwealth no abrupt change in the task of the judiciary. The record in general seems to involve what has been described as "the almost adulatory regard justifiably paid by the ordinary people to English law and British justice."[43] In the handling of actual litigation, where "positive law, custom, and equitable analogies based upon proved custom cannot be traced," there has been occasion, and continues to be occasion, to consult a wider range of sources.[44] In the total process invocation of the law of nations has been associated with the English common law, and there has come to be a practice of looking to what custom has established on such matters as privileges and immunities of diplomatic agents.

Not all of the states that are now full members of the Commonwealth have seen fit merely to leave to courts the finding

40. 7 Cr. 116 (1812).
41. Re Noble and Wolf, [1948] 4 D.L.R. 123.
42. Cf. Elias, *op. cit. supra* note 18, at pp. 293–299.
43. *Ibid.*, p. 141.
44. See Duncan H. Derrett, in Anderson, ed., *op. cit. supra* note 4, at pp. 150–151.

of international law in custom. Some of them have elected to spell out in their respective constitutions the nature of the relationship between municipal law and international law, or at least some parts of international law.

3. Written Constitutions

Legal status and capacity as an international person may accrue to a community through the very fact of its becoming independent and being so recognized by already existing members of the family of nations. In the case of a community formerly under another sovereignty, it is not necessary that there be a formal conveyance of such authority.[45] In the case of the emergent states of the new Commonwealth, however, it has become customary for the United Kingdom and the state concerned to set dates for independence. Written constitutions have set forth in considerable detail the organization and powers of government. Some of the new states, but not all, have in their constitutions also set forth in express wording the intended relationship between the national law and the law of nations. There is no common pattern in these constitutional clauses.

The development which has occurred raises the question of monism and dualism in the Commonwealth, which is essentially the question of whether international law is part of municipal law or is a separate system, no less binding upon the state in its external affairs, but not comprising a set of instructions to municipal courts. So far as the Commonwealth has been concerned, the utilization of written constitutions to make specific references to international law began before the mid-twentieth century. The 1937 Constitution of Eire, in its article 29, made "the

45. See Stampfer v. Atty. Gen., [1956] Int'l L.R. 284. The Supreme Court of Israel, sitting as a Court of Criminal Appeals, said that Israel's declaration of independence gave the state access to international laws and customs; there was no longer need, said the court, "to obtain those principles second-hand."

On the question of Southern Rhodesia's claim of the right to declare its own independence, see chap. 3, note 58, p. 64, and Robert R. Wilson, "Commonwealth Prime Ministers' Conference of 1964," 59 *AM. J. Int'l L.* 570–573 (1965).

generally recognized principles of international law" the state's "rule of conduct in its relations with other States." There was in clause 5 a more specific provision concerning the legal force and effect of international agreements to which the state might become a party. Judicial interpretation and application did not soon set at rest all questions concerning the effect of these parts of Eire's basic law.[46] Nor has experimentation in other states of the Commonwealth (or, for that matter, in states outside of this group) provided complete clarification.

If, through incorporation by reference, the whole body of customary international law can be made an element of the state's municipal law, it is still doubtful that such incorporation can provide answers for all questions. There is, for example, the effect of a changing international custom upon statute law that may have been enacted in reliance upon such custom as it existed prior to the change. The idea of "transformation" of international law into municipal law has received deserved attention from publicists, and questions have been raised as to whether petrification of rules grounded in custom might result from such transformation.[47] The fact that a state does not have in its written constitution express wording concerning this matter does not necessarily mean that there is no recognition by the state of the authority of international law. It could mean (a) that there was no ground for doubting such authority or (b) that the state's adherence to the law was regarded by it more as a matter for diplomacy than as one for municipal courts.

In states of the "old" Commonwealth there has apparently been little incentive for inclusion, in the constitutional law of the respective states, of directives making specific mention of international law. There had been occasional opportunity for courts to

46. See A. G. Donaldson, *Some Comparative Aspects of Irish Law* (1957), pp. 103–107. A possibly indirect reference to international law appears in sec. 75 (ii) of the Australian Constitution Act, 1900, which confers on the High Court original jurisdiction in "all matters" affecting consuls or other representatives of other countries.

47. See Erades and Gould, *op. cit. supra* note 1, and Seidl-Hohenveldern, *loc. cit. supra* note 1. On recently published discussions of theories as to the relationship of the two kinds of law, see also M. P. Tandon, *Public International Law* (8th ed., 1961), pp. 78–84, and J. G. Starke, *An Introduction to International Law* (5th ed., 1963), pp. 16–20, 66–86.

address themselves, sometimes in dicta, to the relationship between two forms of law. An Australian observer writing in 1956
noted that the interaction of municipal and international law had
not been necessarily involved in any case before the High Court
of his country. He pointed out, however, that there had been a
few occasions when it had been considered. One of these was the
case of *Zachariassen* v. *The Commonwealth of Australia.*[48] It
involved an action for damages brought by the foreign owner of a
foreign-registry ship against the Commonwealth of Australia for
refusal of clearance. The case was decided on demurrer, it being
held that an action had been taken by the Australian government
in exercise of belligerent powers in time of war.[49] In the much-
publicized case of *Croft* v. *Dunphy* the question was raised of
whether Canada was restrained by international law from enacting legislation applicable in a contiguous zone off the Canadian
coast. The Privy Council's dictum, which has called forth considerable discussion, included the following statement:

Legislation of the Imperial Parliament even in contravention of
generally acknowledged principles of international law, is binding
upon and must be enforced by the Courts of this country, for in these
Courts the legislation of the Imperial Parliament cannot be challenged
as ultra vires. . . . It may be that legislation of the Dominion
Parliament may be challenged as ultra vires on the ground that it is
contrary to the principles of international law, but that must be
because it must be assumed that the British North America Act has not
conferred power on the Dominion Parliament to legislate contrary to
these principles. In the present case . . . there is no question of
international law involved, for legislation of the kind here challenged
is recognized as legitimate by international law. . . .[50]

The levying of rates on foreign legations and on high commissioners' residences provided occasion for the Supreme Court of
Canada to consider the source of rules that were involved.

48. 24 Commw. L.R. 166 (1917).
49. See comment on this and other dicta in Anstey Wynes, *Legislative,
Executive and Judicial Powers in Australia* (2d ed., 1956), pp. 111–114.
50. [1933] A.C. 156 at 164. See comment by Herbert Evatt, in 1 *Proc. of the
Australian and New Zealand Soc'y of Int'l L.* 27 at 48–53 (1935); see also G. V.
La Forest, "May the Provinces Legislate in Violation of International Law?" 39
Can. B. Rev. 78 (1961).

Concerning the rule that property of a foreign state is exempt from local property taxation, Chief Justice Duff said in part:

I think . . . that the proper conclusion from the legislation of the Imperial Parliament, particularly in the eighteenth century, in force, as some of the statutes were, when the common law was formally introduced into Upper Canada, from the decisions and judgments I have cited, and from the text-writers, is that this rule, recognized by France, is also implicit in the principle of international law recognized by the law of England; and consequently by the law of Ontario.[51]

Six years after the holding in *Croft* v. *Dunphy*, a case arising in New Zealand provided an opportunity for a New Zealand court to discern a source of power of that state not identifiable with Great Britain. With respect to a mandate from the League of Nations Council the court held that New Zealand had authority, not indirectly or derivatively from the King in Council, but within the power of a "sovereign" state.[52]

With respect to the basis for determining the jurisdictional status of foreign troops visiting a friendly state, the chief justice of the Supreme Court of Canada had occasion to say that if such visiting troops were exempt from the jurisdiction of Canada, the exemption would derive its validity solely from international law. He noted that at the time neither England nor Canada had ever recognized any rule of international law by which this exemption could be established.[53]

From the illustrative cases that have been mentioned above it will appear that in the states of the "old" Commonwealth courts have taken a position which in their respective jurisdictions is similar to that of the English courts as to principles and conventions that are established. More recent decisions have supplied additional statement on the point.[54] Some new Commonwealth

51. Reference re Tax on Foreign Legations, [1943] 2 D.L.R. 481 at 501.
52. In re Tamasese, a Prisoner, [1929] N.Z.L.R. 209. Cf., on the legislative power over Samoa, Nelson v. Braisby, [1934] N.Z.L.R. 228.
53. C. J. Duff, in *Reference Re Exemption of U. S. Forces from Canadian Criminal Law*, cited in note 39 *supra*. The Chief Justice observed that he found no exemption for land forces such as were involved in this instance, but he noted that Canadian courts did not as a rule interfere unless a Canadian was concerned. On the general subject, see Roland J. Stanger, "The Status of Forces," in Richard A. Falk *et al.*, *Essays on International Jurisdiction* (1961), pp. 75–94.
54. Cf. In re Heyting, [1928] N.Z.L.R. 233, and In re Scholer, [1955] N.Z.L.R. 1190.

states, however, have elected to include in their constitutions more specific provisions concerning adherence to international law. Others have been explicit on the power of public bodies to implement decisions of public international organizations or on the force and effect of the law of nations in relation to the municipal law of the state. There is considerable variance in the wording of the relevant clauses. The language may take the form of a general directive rather than an "incorporative" clause; it may be "hortatory."[55] With full realization of the inadequacy of mere textual commentaries in light of the fact that these constitutions are very new, it is relevant to consider some of the new wording as it pertains to customary international law and treaty law.

Perhaps the constitution which has received most attention in this connection is that of India. By its article 51(c) the state is to "foster respect for international law and treaty obligations." The opinion has been expressed that the directive of 51(c) applied not to the judiciary of India, but to the government and Parliament. Furthermore, this part of the constitution, it has been suggested, has little significance for Indian judges who tend to accept the same interrelationship between international law and muincipal law that already prevails in English law, i.e., that based upon the doctrine of Blackstone.[56] It is of course possible for municipal courts to have regard for customary international law even without a specific directive to that effect. In New Zealand, practice appears to follow that of the High Court of Justice in England.[57]

If a constitution contains no general statement as to the relationship between international law and municipal law, there

55. The descriptive word has come to be used with reference to provisions indicating general respect for international law or observance of it without more specific wording to the effect that the courts will apply it; see D. R. Deener, "International Law Provisions in Post-World War II Constitutions," 36 *Cornell L. Q.* 505 (1951).

56. M. Alexandrowicz, *Constitutional Developments in India* (1957), p. 215. Cf. M. K. Nawaz, in *Proc. Am. Soc'y Int'l L.* 1963, pp. 275–290. Cf. also the view that the provisions of art. 51(c) are only hortatory, a political directive, neither providing a legal guide for the judiciary in the latter's application of international law nor imposing a legal check upon the legislatures of India. Fawcett, *op. cit. supra* note 32, at p. 27.

57. See cases cited in note 54, *supra*.

may still be mention of the former as it concerns specific subjects. In the constitutional arrangements for Cyprus, for example, there is reference to the republic's regulating by law matters concerning aliens "in accordance with International Law."[58] Perhaps relevant in this connection is a reference in the Sierra Leone Constitution to rights and freedoms in terms of "any" person;[59] this would presumably include aliens.

The Constitution of Pakistan contains provisions whereby the parliament may punish "offenses against the law of nations,"[60] this wording being comparable to that in article 1, section 8, paragraph 10 of the United States Constitution.[61] The 1960 Constitution of Nigeria, article 76(1)(a), provided for legislative power to implement the decisions of any international organization of which Nigeria was a member; the 1963 constitution of the same state also refers (article 74) to the implementing of a "decision of an international organization." There is comparable language in the Constitution of Malaysia (article 132 and Third Schedule).

In general, the new constitutions of Commonwealth states commonly assign legislative powers for the regulation of "external affairs," and executive powers to appoint diplomatic representatives; the existence of such affairs and of such representatives would seem to presuppose the applicability of international law.[62] Aside from clauses of this type and those which define aliens (and distinguish citizens of other Commonwealth states from other aliens) there is little in the wording of the new constitutions that commits the new states to a particular position concerning international law. In a general commentary (not singling out international law) one observer has noted that "valiant attempts to crystallize specific conventions in the form of

58. Cmnd. No. 1093 at p. 105 (1960).
59. Art. 170, paras. 1 and 2.
60. Art. 131 (b) and Third Schedule.
61. The Supreme Court of the United States found in this part of the United States Constitution support sufficient to uphold federal legislation making it punishable to counterfeit the securities of a foreign state. United States v. Arjona, 120 U. S. 479 (1887).
62. In an address before the American Society of International Law, an ambassador of the Soviet Union to the United States (Troyanovsky) once said that "an Ambassador is a personification of the consistency and of the universality, and to some extent a proof of the existence of international law." *Proc. Am. Soc'y Int'l L.* 1934, p. 195.

strict rules of law are to be found in the constitutions of Nigeria, Sierra Leone, Jamaica, Trinidad, and Uganda, and . . . nearly all the constitutional instruments made during the last few years have broken away from antiquated institutions."[63]

There exists no general practice of making treaties a part of the "supreme law of the land." In general Commonwealth practice, formal agreements with foreign states do not fall within the category of rules having binding force as municipal law without implementation through parliamentary acts. This is in contrast to the basic law of the United States, where the constitution includes as part of the "supreme law" treaties made or which shall be made under the authority of the United States. It is true that the distinction which has developed in American constitutional law between "self-executing" and "non-self-executing" treaties (the courts being competent to determine classification) has to some extent limited operation of the broad rule of article 6, paragraph 2 of the constitution.[64]

In the case of Canada even before it became fully independent the British North America Act provided in section 132 that "The Parliament and Government of Canada shall have all powers necessary and proper for performing the Obligations of Canada or of any province there, as Part of the British Empire, towards Foreign Countries arising under Treaties between the Empire and such Foreign Countries." There has been judicial holding that in Canada (as in Great Britain) treaties do not confer rights as between the state and the subject, or as between subjects. Such rights can only be conferred by the common law or by legislative enactments.[65] Since what has been called the "labour conventions experience" (in reference to the Judicial Committee's decision in *Attorney General for Canada* v. *Attorney General for Ontario* ([1937] A.C. 326 [Can.]), there has been some hesitancy by the central government to sign treaties unless the proposed agree-

63. De Smith, *op. cit. supra* note 3, at p. 79.
64. See, generally, Alona E. Evans, "Self-Executing Treaties in the United States," 30 *Brit. Yb. Int'l L.* 178 (1953).
65. R. St. John MacDonald, "Public International Law Problems Arising in Canadian Courts," 11 *U. Toronto L. J.* 224 (1956). This writer referred (at p. 247) to the "general judicial attitude indicative of the declining strength international law enjoys as a superior legal order."

ments deal with matters that are clearly within the central government's powers. The situation has led one observer to suggest that the practicing lawyer faced with a question on which there is (for reasons of law or policy) no governing agreement must of necessity fall back upon the rules of customary international law.[66] In contrast to what the same writer has described as the "inadequacy" of the British North America Act and the "laconic generality" of the Australian constitution,[67] some of the new Commonwealth states have included in their constitutions broad language on treaty implementation as, for example, article 253 of the Indian constitution, article 108 of the Constitution of 1956 of Pakistan (which has now been replaced by the Constitution of 1962), and article 169(b) of the Malaysian constitution. This language would seem to envisage the exercise by parliaments of extensive powers in international community interest.[68]

In the case of Cyprus, a treaty made by that state has the force

66. Fawcett, *op. cit. supra* note 32, at p. 28.
67. *Ibid.*
68. Wording of relevant parts of the 1956 Constitution of Pakistan elicited discussion, *inter alia,* of the effect of legislative powers as limited by international law and the extent to which Islamic thought influenced the principles set forth in the constitution. A legal scholar in Pakistan has submitted that the constitution imported adherence to the law of nations. He points out that the constitution provision giving legislative competence as to all persons (foreigners not excluded) was interpreted as being subject to the ordinary rules of public and private international law concerning diplomatic and consular immunities. Furthermore, the rule of construction which English courts had evolved—to the effect that, in the case of crimes committed abroad, a state exercises jurisdiction only as to its own citizens—was thought to make the broad wording in the constitution inapplicable to acts committed by foreigners outside the state. He referred in this connection to The Queen v. Jamison, [1895] 2 Q. B. 425, which held that the rule rests upon international law that binds a sovereign to respect the rights and the subjects of other sovereign powers outside his territory. With respect to the same (1956) constitution the commentator considered a report which had asserted that "no rule of international law and no provision in any convention or treaty to which Pakistan is a party which is contrary to the Quran and Sunnah shall be binding on any Muslim in Pakistan" and pointed out that this was not reflected in the constitution itself and that to the extent, at any rate, the constitution could not be called "Islamic." A. K. Brohi, *Fundamental Law of Pakistan* (1958), pp. 221, 745.
Cf. remarks of Mohammad Zafrulla Khan concerning Islam as being not only a religion in the ordinary sense, but a way of life which seeks to regulate all aspects of man's life, religious, social, economic, individual, national, and international— although it does not seek to impose its own system upon other communities. *Pakistan Constitutional Debates,* vol. 11, no. 6 (April 17, 1952).
See also, in this connection, wording of art. 76 (2) of the Constitution of Malaysia.

of municipal law if it can be shown that there is reciprocity on the part of the other party to the agreement—a rule that has come to be familiar under the most recent constitution of France, as also in some states that were formerly members of the French Union.[69] The absence of a rule concerning reciprocity or of a rule that a treaty is part of the supreme law of a particular Commonwealth state would not, of course, change the fact that a treaty would be binding upon the state in the international sense. In general, however, in the period since Commonwealth states have become completely independent there has apparently been no discernible trend away from the traditional rule in England that a treaty is not self-executing for purposes of municipal courts and therefore is not enforceable in such courts without implementing legislation.[70]

4. Development of Rules

The part which Commonwealth states have essayed in the actual shaping of, or giving direction to, rules of international law in the period since the mid-fifties (selected here because most of the present members of the Commonwealth have emerged as independent states in this period) appears from both unilateral

69. See comment by Robert R. Wilson, "International Law in New National Constitutions," 58 *Am. J. Int'l L.* 432 (1964). On Commonwealth states' practice, see also David R. Deener, "Treaties, Constitutions and Judicial Review," in 4 *Va. J. Int'l L.* 7–33 (1964) and the same author's "Some Post World War II Trends in the Relationships of Municipal Law to Treaty Law," 5 *Indian J. Int'l L.* 267 (1965).

70. Among various judicial pronouncements that might be cited in support of this would be those in the Canadian case of *Re Noble and Wolf*, cited in note 41 *supra*, and the Indian case, Birna v. State of Rajasthan, [1951] All India Rep. 127 (Rajasthan). In the former the court said that if "the obligations arising under the Charter of the United Nations are in conflict with the international law of a signatory power, it has evidently not yet been determined by agreement of the nations concerned that the internal laws should be overborne by the provisions of the Charter." In the *Birna* case the court said that "mere execution of a treaty for extradition cannot by itself be treated as equivalent to enacting law carrying it into effect. Treaties which are part of international law do not form part of the law of the land unless expressly made so by the legislature. . . . In the present case the treaty remained a treaty and no action was taken to incorporate it into a law of the Dholpur State." A note added that it might not be necessary to incorporate *all* treaties into the statute books, but treaties affecting private rights of citizens must be made binding "by express legislation."

and joint effort. This has found expression in parliamentary bodies in the course of efforts for new treaty commitments designed to modernize certain parts of the law. It is also discernible in what is said in forums of public international organizations and in reactions to the work of the principal body which is presently engaged in the effort to restate international law and influence its development, i.e., the International Law Commission of the United Nations.

Before consideration of more specific provisions it may be appropriate to note the fact of a growing emphasis, especially since South Africa's withdrawal in 1961, upon the idea of racial non-discrimination and the obligation of states to pursue internal policies consistent with the principle of racial equality.[71] It is natural that individual and collective action by Commonwealth states in matters of public international law as well as in other matters would be advocated. In the forums of international public organizations new Commonwealth states have tried to exclude or to penalize states accused of discrimination.[72] While this whole general area may seem to involve international politics rather than international law, there has been anticipation of the effects of anti-colonialism upon such parts of international law as relate to aggression and intervention. A spokesman for India, for example, has phrased and emphasized a concept of "permanent aggression."[73]

Less emotional but of great practical importance to various Commonwealth states have been customary and treaty rules relating to the law of the sea. The role of Commonwealth states which were participants in the codification conference under auspices of the League of Nations in 1930 contrasts strongly to that of Commonwealth states at the Conference on the Law of the Sea which was sponsored by the United Nations in 1958. Whereas at the former conference the dominions tended to follow the British lead, at the 1958 conference Commonwealth spokesmen showed

71. Fawcett, *op. cit. supra* note 32, at p. 87.
72. See chap. 2, p. 37.
73. See section, "Amending the Law of Nations," in Ali A. Mazrui, "The United Nations and Some African Political Attitudes," 18 *Int'l Org.* 499–520 (1964).

much greater independence in dissenting from views of United Kingdom representatives.[74] British policy as to reshaping legal commitments was naturally influenced by geographical considerations. At the 1960 conference on the same subject the great majority of represented states supported Canada's proposal for a "six-plus-six" formula—the limit of territorial waters to be six miles from low-water mark, with the shore state having a right to control fisheries out to a distance of six additional miles. Subsequently, the United Kingdom has concluded with her principal neighbors in interest a multilateral treaty[75] which has already influenced or seems likely to influence the traditional international law based upon custom.

Another jurisdictional subject in which certain Commonwealth states have strong interest relates to polar areas. The position of Canada with respect to application of the sector principle in the Arctic region is well known; a leading Canadian publicist sees the theory involved as triumphing, "if not as a matter of formal

74. Mirza H. Hamid Kizilbash, "Commonwealth States and International Conferences on the Law of the Sea" (Master's thesis, Duke University, 1962).

75. The extent of the problem which it has sought to handle was indicated by facts presented to Parliament on Nov. 10, 1963, showing the number of foreign vessels prosecuted for fishing in waters that were regarded as exclusively British and a list of British vessels prosecuted by foreign states claimed by the other (foreign) states to be within their exclusive jurisdiction, 613 *H. C. Deb.* (5th ser.) 39 (1963).

By the treaty, to which fifteen states were signatory (Austria, Belgium, Denmark, France, Federal Republic of Germany, Iceland, Italy, Luxembourg, the Netherlands, Norway, Portugal, Spain, Sweden, Switzerland, and the United Kingdom) and which became effective on Sept. 30, 1964, the shore state is to have exclusive fishing rights and jurisdiction over a belt of six miles measured from the baseline of its territorial sea. Within the belt between six and twelve miles measured from the baseline of the territory only the coastal state and states that have habitually fished there between Jan. 1, 1953, and Dec. 31, 1962, have fishing rights for their vessels; the foreign states which received benefits under this rule may not shift their fishing areas, *Final Act of the European Fisheries Conference, London, Dec. 3, 1963–March 2, 1964, with Fisheries Convention, Protocol of Provisional Application and Agreements as to Transitional Rights.* Cmnd. No. 2355 (1964).

In Canada, Prime Minister Pearson explained in June, 1963, that the government had decided to establish a twelve-mile exclusive fisheries zone along the whole of Canada's coast line (effective May, 1964) and to implement the straight baseline system at the same time as the basis from which Canada's territorial sea and exclusive fisheries zone would be measured. Under this headland-to-headland theory, the statement indicates, the Hudson Bay and the Gulf of St. Lawrence are territorial waters if the line encloses them. Canada, *Parl. Deb.* (Commons), Sess. 1963, p. 621.

acceptance by non-sector Arctic states, then at least because of the facts of geography and administration."[76] Some five years earlier Mr. Pearson had said, "The sector theory is not enough, it must be followed by rights based on discovery and effective occupation."[77] For the region of the Antarctic there has been achieved a treaty arrangement in which three Commonwealth members have participated. The 1959 treaty concerning Antarctica and the agreement looking to measures to make it effective[78] comprise what the President of the United States, in a special report to Congress, described as an outstanding example of cooperation between nations.[79]

In the field of judicial assistance, and specifically the extradition of accused persons from one Commonwealth state to another, there has been some progress toward abandonment of the system based upon the Fugitive Offenders Act, 1881[80] (which made no exception for political crimes in the process of extradition), and substitution of procedure under the rules of ordinary international law for the *inter se* rule.[81] Experience in connection with the *Enahoro* case between Nigeria and the United Kingdom[82] may have had some influence.

The matter of legal rules and machinery for the protection of

76. Maxwell Cohen, "Some Main Directions of International Law: A Canadian Perspective," 1 *Can. Yb. Int'l L.* 15 at 23 (1963). The author points out the contrasting attitudes of Canada and the Soviet Union toward the "open waters" of the Arctic and the Arctic icepack.

77. Canada, *Parl. Deb.* (Commons), Sess. 1958, p. 3512. On an earlier occasion, when asked specifically whether the Canadian government subscribed to the sector theory, the government spokesman (Fleming) had replied, "We subscribe to the Canadian theory of sovereignty." *Ibid.*, Sess. 1960, p. 577.

78. 402 U.N.T.S. 71, T.I.A.S. No. 5274.

79. New York *Times*, Sept. 3, 1964, p. 9.

80. 44 & 45 Vict., c. 69; see also, *infra*, chap. 8, pp. 227–228.

81. In a case involving a petitioner from Ceylon who, having committed an extradictable offense in Ceylon, escaped to India, the Madras court held that the Fugitive Offenders Act was no longer applicable, but the Indian Extradition Act, 1903, was applicable, having been continued by art. 372 of the Constitution of India. The emergence of a new state or a change of sovereign, the court said, did not bring about a break or interruption in law. In re Chockalingan Chettier, 47 All India Rep. 548 (1960) (Madras). By a 1962 decision, however, a political opponent of the party in power in Cyprus was extradited to that state under the Fugitive Offenders Act. Zacharia v. Republic of Cyprus, [1962] 2 All E. R. 438.

82. See Robert R. Wilson, "Some Questions of International Law in Commonwealth Relations," in W. B. Hamilton, K. C. Robinson, and C. D. W. Goodwin, eds., *A Decade of the Commonwealth, 1955–1964* (1966), chap. 8; also, *infra*, chap 8, pp. 224–225.

human rights has been the subject of consideration on various occasions. On one such occasion, when a proposed human rights covenant and court were under discussion in the British Parliament, there was a government spokesman's expression of the view that "the strength of the Commonwealth association is in great part due to the absence of this type of formal, institutional machinery."[83]

Commonwealth members as well as other states in the United Nations have had the opportunity to express themselves on various questions of international law as these questions have come under discussion by the International Law Commission of the United Nations. The commission in 1964 included in its membership a person from each of three Commonwealth states— Canada, Nigeria, and the United Kingdom. Expressions of opinion on the commission's drafts may be by agencies of a group of states as well as by individual states. One such agency is the Asian Legal Consultative Commission. Burma, Ceylon, India, Indonesia, Iraq, Japan, and Syria co-operated in the creation of this body of legal specialists, their function being to consider problems referred to them and to exchange views and information on matters of common interest. In 1959 the participating states changed the name of this agency to Asian African Legal Consultative Committee. By the time of the committee's sixth session (1964) Ghana, Pakistan, Thailand, and the United Arab Republic had joined; to the sixth session, Lebanon, Liberia, Mali, Nigeria, and the Arab League sent observers.

In its annual meetings the committee has considered questions that have been under consideration by the International Law Commission. The third session of the committee, for example, provided occasion for the several Commonwealth states' representatives to express opinions on some broad questions. The Indian government spokesman submitted a memorandum on the relationship between international law and municipal law and on the nature and content of the law on the subject of diplomatic

83. 621 *H. C. Deb.* (5th ser.) 564–565 (April 7, 1960).
    For a discussion of a particular Commonwealth state's role in relation to international law and organization, see Mohammed Ahsen Chaudhri, *Growth of International Law and Pakistan* (1965), chap. 5.

immunities. In the course of the discussion representatives of Ceylon and Pakistan, respectively, presented their views.

The Indian memorandum proceeded from the position that international law as such was not binding upon municipal courts, the law being regarded, so far as such courts were concerned, as the body of doctrines concerning international rights and duties of states as adopted and made a part of the law of the land. In the case of a newly independent state, the memorandum suggested, it might be doubtful whether the common law of the land could be said to contain within it the principles of international law relating to diplomatic immunities. It was noted that in the older Commonwealth countries the rules of international law on the subject apparently were recognized as a part of the common law of the land.[84] In some states of the Commonwealth, the memorandum stated, the basis for diplomatic immunities (immunities that were in fact accorded) was not so apparent, no declarations on such basis being available in the pronouncements of the courts or in executive statements.[85]

As to the precise scope of the immunities, there was apparently some difference of opinion in the Consultative Committee. Discussion touched upon immunity for private acts of an accredited diplomat, the status of the subordinate staff with respect to immunities, and the manner of claiming diplomatic immunities in national courts. There was also discussion of the principle of reciprocity, the Indian spokesman taking the position that reciprocity should be a condition, while the representative of Ceylon thought it should be so in certain matters but not for the minimal immunities proposed for listing in articles of agreement. The Pakistan member, while in his individual capacity endorsing the committee's recommendations, indicated that his government had not had sufficient time for consideration of the matter.

There was some reference in the discussion to practice of states outside of the regional group represented. With respect to immunities of states for their commercial transactions, it was

84. Statement by the secretary of the committee, *Asian African Legal Consultative Committee, Report of the Third Session, Colombo, 1960* (1960), pp. 18–19.

85. *Ibid.*, p. 20.

noted that the recommendations of the Consultative Committee seemed to be in line with practice of western European states and of the United States of America. Ceylon's representative mentioned that there had been no cases in municipal courts of his country on this particular point, while an Indian spokesman drew attention to an Indian court case in 1955;[86] both of these speakers thought that for the time being a qualified immunity should be accorded to states engaging in commercial transactions. They further agreed that the subject matter should not be outside the jurisdiction of local courts and that it should make no difference whether the transactions were actually entered into in the name of a state trading organization or of the government itself. There was suggestion that for a private trading organization taken over by a government there should be no immunity as to transactions before or after the taking.[87]

Another subject which has apparently been one of special interest to member states of the "new" Commonwealth is that of a state's responsibility for the treatment of aliens within its territory. An introductory note in the Consultative Committee's report of its third session related to the status of aliens. The "minimum standard" of treatment as developed in the nineteenth century— to the effect that under international law a state would be held responsible for treatment falling below this minimum—was referred to as "somewhat outmoded" if it meant that a state was held to accord the treatment without reference to how it treated its own nationals. There appeared to be agreement in the committee that there should be national treatment of foreigners as to freedom from arbitrary arrest, the practice of religion, and freedom of speech. It was stated that in the Indian constitution there were no safeguards against arbitrary, harsh, and unjustified expulsion of aliens and that by the law of Ceylon an alien could be expelled from that state for reasons of public security.[88]

The Consultative Committee also gave attention to international rights and duties concerning the extradition of fugitives, a

86. *Ibid.*, p. 72. The speaker did not, so far as the *Report* indicates, identify the particular case.
87. Statement by the secretary of the committee, *ibid.*, pp. 72, 76.
88. *Ibid.*, pp. 150, 152.

form of judicial assistance which traditionally has been handled in the Commonwealth on the basis of statutory rules which members have applied *inter se*. The Indian spokesman did not feel that there was justification for a state's refusing to surrender its own nationals (a matter which, under international law, is left for each state to settle for itself when it concludes extradition conventions). Spokesmen for Pakistan, Ceylon, and India, respectively, indicated willingness to accept the rule which was incorporated in the committee's report to the effect that there should not be extradition of persons charged with political offenses unless there should be treaty commitments to this effect.[89]

At the committee's fifth session (1962) the concept of nationality received special attention. Problems relating to dual or multiple status, nationality of married women, determination of "real" and "effective" nationality, and compulsory military service by non-nationals were among those presented. In the "Memorandum and Comments of the Government of Ceylon," for example, there was reference to solution of certain problems (military service by aliens, protection, and determination of nationality by a third state) as having been indicated "in accordance with principles generally accepted by nations."[90] At the fifth session the committee also authorized the Secretariat to submit to the participating governments a draft "Report on Legality of Nuclear Tests." On the subject of arbitral procedure, there was discussion of the Model Rules prepared by the International Law Commission (e.g., the principle of non-frustration) but disagreement as to whether the rules set forth views consistent with existing international law. The subject was not carried over as an agenda item.[91]

At its sixth session (1964) the main subjects with which the committee concerned itself were the legality of nuclear tests, dual nationality, and the United Nations Charter from the point of view of the Asian and African countries. On the last-mentioned subject, the committee in a resolution noted with satisfaction the adoption by the United Nations General Assembly on December

89. *Ibid.*, p. 216. On this point as it had been raised in connection with the extradition of Chief Enahoro from England to Nigeria in 1963, see discussion referred to in note 82, *supra*. On other aspects of the case, see p. 215, n. 31 *infra*.
90. *Report of the Fifth Session* (1962), p. 142.
91. *Ibid.*, pp. 184–188.

17, 1963, of a resolution (No. 1691, Eighteenth Assembly) on equitable representation on the Security Council and the Economic and Social Council.[92]

A phase of the subject of responsibility of states which has had much attention in the twentieth century relates to compensation for alien-owned property that has been taken for public use. On this matter the United States in its commercial treaty policy (in relation to Commonwealth and other states) has taken a consistently strong position that there is an obligation for states to make just, prompt, and effective compensation for property thus taken, without restriction to what policy the taking state follows with reference to property of its own nationals.[93] In the absence, however, of general acceptance by all other states of the standard which it proclaims in this connection, the United States has initiated a practice of concluding bilateral agreements with other states for government guarantee of investments abroad by its nationals and companies. Commonwealth states which have entered into such agreements with the United States include Trinidad and Tobago, Jamaica, Nigeria, and Cyprus.[94] The conclusion of such agreements would not seem to prejudice the views of the parties thereto with respect to what the international law standard is on this subject.

Whether regarded as a part of the legal heritage from Great Britain, or as incident to the very fact of independence,[95] interna-

92. Report by Jiménez de Arachaca to the International Law Commission on the Sixth Session of the Asian African Committee, *U. N. Doc.* No. A/CONF. 4/172 (May 11, 1964).

93. Robert R. Wilson, *op. cit. supra* note 34, at chap. 4.

94. U.N.T.S. Nos. 5237, 5270, 5278, and 5364.

95. The usual procedure incident to the emergence of new states which become members of the Commonwealth has involved a decision by the United Kingdom on the date for independence of each newly emerging entity. That this may not be the only manner in which additional members of the new Commonwealth may emerge was suggested by press reports that Southern Rhodesia might not wait for action in London but might declare its own independence if it could not reach agreement with London. On the discussions concerning the conditions of the British government for granting independence to Southern Rhodesia, see *The Economist*, Aug. 15, 1964, p. 634, and *The Times* (London), Sept. 12, 1964, p. 8.

With the reported view of the United Kingdom government may be compared the position of a spokesman for Ceylon (Malalasekere) in the United Nations General Assembly in 1962. After noting that when the question of non-self-governing territories had been under discussion a number of delegations had continued to record reservations on the basis of "treaty claims dating back for a century or more," the speaker invoked art. 103 of the Charter and submitted that

tional law inevitably conditions the life of Commonwealth states, as of all states. Whether made effective through judicial interpretations of customary rules (along with executive and diplomatic application), incorporated in "law-making" treaties, or emphasized through the provisions of written constitutions, the law is not static, and forces such as those in Commonwealth relationships may influence its development. While the international law standard tends to supplant the system of rules developed by the former dominions in their relations *inter se*, it does not preclude preferential relations between its member states. Nor is it inconsistent with multilateral (less than universal) arrangements on such subjects as fisheries or jurisdiction in polar areas. Some of its member states have evinced special interest in the reshaping of rules believed by them to be associated with "colonialism" as well as rules pertaining to resident aliens and alien-owned property.

Since the Commonwealth is not a legal entity, but rather a device for co-operation, it is possible in a measure to discern its significance for the law of nations through the practice of its member states individually or collectively. The foregoing summary examination of the manner in which these states have received, interpreted, and applied the law of nations has been brief and necessarily selective. It has not undertaken to discern the effects upon Commonwealth members and their uses of law of the part which these states have had (especially through interna-

---

in the event of a conflict of obligations the Charter should prevail. Making specific application, he said that the criteria of whether Southern Rohodesia is or is not a self-governing territory must stem from the Charter and not from the Constitution of 1923. He further suggested that, if the General Assembly should accept the claim (in the draft resolution under reference) that Southern Rhodesia was a non-self-governing territory within the meaning of chap. 11 of the Charter, the decision would be morally binding upon the United Kingdom to apply the same principle for all of its "forty-odd" territories that were non-self-governing. *U.N. Gen. Ass. Off. Rec.* 16th Sess., vol. 2, pt. 3, p. 1437 (1962).

Later in the same year the status of Uganda was referred to in the following statement by a spokesman (Swai) of Tanganyika:

"We rejoice to witness the recovery of full sovereignty by Uganda. I have deliberately used the phrase 'recovery of sovereignty,' rather than 'attainment of sovereignty,' for Uganda was never conquered, nor was it ever a colony. For about sixty-eight years Uganda was a protectorate under the United Kingdom. Its rulers entered into treaties with the United Kingdom. To take but two examples, the Kingdoms of Buganda and Bunyoro had been highly organized societies, long before the acceptance of a protectorate status from the United Kingdom. Mountains of the Moon, known since the time of Ptolemy in the second century, and the source of the Nile River have long haunted the imagination of man outside Africa." *Ibid.* 17th Sess. vol. 2, p. 574 (1962).

tional public organizations) in shaping such a concept as that of domestic jurisdiction.[96] Nor has it tried to assess the significance for Commonwealth states of proposed British participation in the European Common Market. It has omitted a detailed examination of the international legal aspects of citizenship in the Commonwealth and has touched but briefly on judicial assistance between its members. These matters are to receive attention in the chapters which follow.

96. Aside from the principle of domestic jurisdiction, other matters relating in some way to general international law have, with relative frequency, been the subjects of remarks by Commonwealth states' spokesmen in the forums of public international organizations. This is illustrated in positions recently taken by representatives in the United Nations General Assembly on such subjects as the law of the Charter and, particularly, the claimed legal effect upon it of the resolution concerning colonialism, Gen. Assembly Res. 1514 (XV). Quaison-Sackey, as spokesman for Ghana, submitted that this pronouncement by the General Assembly "must be regarded as amending" chaps. 11 and 12 of the Charter "in spirit and intent." As far as Ghana is concerned, he submitted, "after 31 December 1967, all colonial Powers which have not granted independence to non-independent countries in Africa will be regarded as aggressors who are disturbing the peace of the world." *U. N. Gen. Ass. Off. Rec.*, 17th Sess., vol. 3, pp. 930, 933 (1962). With this may be compared the view of an Australian spokesman, earlier in the discussions, to the effect that the declaration was not able to override the Charter. *Ibid.* 15th Sess., vol. 2, pt. 2, p. 1090 (1960). In an earlier discussion, a Ceylonese representative (Perera) said, on the subject of colonialism, the trusteeship system, and non-self-governing territories, that he would "like to regard the draft resolution . . . submitted as coming in the long line of various declarations which have become international law." He added that it was not a question of "a pure juridical concept or the creation of law," but, on the contrary, a question of "trying to find the proper place in the development of human rights for the particular measure." *Ibid.*, p. 1002 (1960). At the Fifteenth Assembly Mr. Perera observed that the United Nations Charter was "not only a Charter which contains political principles and high social and economic principles" but also "a document which enshrines the highest concept of law." He continued by observing that the Charter "gives body and currency to the whole idea of international law." *Ibid.*, p. 1327 (1960).

That Commonwealth states' representatives have supported the effort for developing law for outer space is illustrated in positions taken by Canada and by Pakistan respectively. A spokesman for the former state (Green) pointed out in 1961 that, unless there is a body of law, outer space could be exploited for aggressive purposes with greatly increased danger for all nations. *Ibid.* 16th Sess., vol. 2, pt. 1, p. 200 (1961). Two years earlier Mr. Qadir of Pakistan had urged the desirability of establishing, from the very beginning of the space age, basic legal norms relating to the nature and the use of such space; he shared the view that the principles of classical international law concerning territory, sovereignty, and occupation could not be regarded as applicable to outer space and celestial bodies. *Ibid.* 14th Sess., vol. 2, p. 179 (1959). In 1960 Mr. Diefenbaker for Canada had expressed the views that no celestial body should be considered capable of appropriation by any state, that space vehicles should be identified by a system of registration of launchings, call signs, and other characteristics, and that frequencies for communications should be allocated on a rational and agreed basis. *Ibid.* 15th Sess., vol. 2, pt. 1, p. 111 (1960). The General Assembly's Resolution 1721 of Dec. 20, 1961, was in harmony with the views of the Commonwealth spokesmen mentioned.

· 5 ·

Nationality and Citizenship

*Robert E. Clute**

The development of the British Empire into the Commonwealth of Nations has greatly affected the relationships of the
inhabitants of the former empire with respect to their nationality.
Natural persons in the Commonwealth have preserved some legal
arrangements as a heritage from the time when there was a
common allegiance for all of the empire. Such arrangements
display a considerable inventiveness which accords legal rights to
or imposes legal obligations on the people of non-Commonwealth
countries. Prior to the end of World War II there was only one
category of persons owing allegiance to the Crown, i.e., British
subjects. When the self-governing dominions began to develop
into separate international entities it became desirable to distinguish a separate nationality—for the purpose, for example, of
appointing judges under the Statute of the Permanent Court of
International Justice. There was, however, no departure from the
common code until after World War II.

1. Common Status[1]

The passage of the Canadian Citizenship Act of 1946[2] heralded
the demise of the common code on nationality. At the same time

* Department of Political Science, University of Georgia.
1. For a detailed study of common status, see Robert R. Wilson and Robert E.
Clute, "Commonwealth Citizenship and Common Status," 57 *Am. J. Int'l L.* 566
(1963); reprinted in Duke University Commonwealth-Studies Center, Reprint
Series, No. 10.
2. The Canadian Citizenship Act of 1946, as amended. sec. 23. 10 Geo. 6, c. 15.
The Canadian act was subsequently amended by 13 Geo. 6, c. 6 (1949); 14 Geo.
6, c. 29 (1950), and 15 Geo. 6, c. 12 (1951). The act and amendments were

it contained the embryo of a new but looser common status more in keeping with the changed constitutional status and international position of the Commonwealth countries. The Canadian act created a new status of citizen of Canada but also recognized that all persons who were British subjects under the law of any Commonwealth country would be recognized as such in Canada. The following year a Commonwealth Conference held in London formulated the general plan for common status that was embodied in the British Nationality Act of 1948.[3]

British subject or Commonwealth citizen. The British act of 1948 declared that anyone who was a citizen of the United Kingdom and Colonies, a Commonwealth country, Singapore, or the Federation of Rhodesia and Nyasaland should have the status of a British subject—or Commonwealth citizen, which should have the same meaning. Any citizen of Eire on the effective date of the act who gave notice of intent to retain such status was also a British subject.[4]

consolidated in R.S.C. c. 33 (1952) and further amended by 1 & 2 Eliz. 2, c. 23 (1953), 2 & 3 Eliz. 2, c. 34 (1954), 4 & 5 Eliz. 2, c. 6 (1956), and 7 Eliz. 2, c. 24 (1958). The act as amended will hereafter be cited as the Canadian Citizenship Act.

3. Cmd. No. 7326 (1947–48). Common status was to apply not only to persons, but also to merchant ships. See The British Commonwealth Merchant Shipping Agreement, Dec. 10, 1931, pt. I, art. 2, 129 L.N.T.S. 177.

4. The British Nationality Act of 1948, 11 & 12 Geo. 6, c. 56, as amended by the British Nationality Act of 1958, 6 & 7 Eliz. 2, c. 10; and the British Nationality Act of 1964, 12 & 13 Eliz. 2, c. 22. This act as amended will hereafter be cited as the British Nationality Act. The operation of the principal act in regard to protectorates, protected states, trusteeships, and protected persons has been given effect by orders in council. The operation of the act for communities not electing to join the Commonwealth, members leaving the Commonwealth, newly emerged Commonwealth countries, and certain self-governing units is effectuated by the Burma Independence Act, 1947, 11 Geo. 6, c. 3; Ireland Act, 1949, 12 & 13 Geo. 6, c. 41; Ghana Independence Act, 1957, 5 & 6 Eliz. 2, c. 6; Federation of Malaya Independence Act, 1957, 5 & 6 Eliz. 2, c. 60; Nigeria Independence Act, 1960, 8 & 9 Eliz. 2, c. 55; Cyprus Act, 1960, 8 & 9 Eliz. 2, c. 52; British Nationality (Cyprus) Order, 1960, *Stat. Instr.*, 1960, No. 2215; Sierra Leone Independence Act, 1961, 9 & 10 Eliz. 2, c. 16; Republic of South Africa (Temporary Provisions) Act, 1961, 9 & 10 Eliz. 2, c. 23; Tanganyika Independence Act, South Africa Act, Jamaica Independence Act, Trinidad and Tobago Independence Act, Uganda Independence Act, of 1962, in 10 & 11 Eliz. 2, cs. 1, 23, 40, 54, and 57, respectively; Malaysia Act, Kenya Independence Act and Zanzibar Act, of 1963, in 11 & 12 Eliz. 2, cs. 35, 54, and 55, respectively; Malawi Independence Act, 1964, 12 & 13 Eliz. 2, c. 46; and the British Nationality Act, 1958 (Commencement) Order, 1958, *Stat. Instr.*, 1958, No. 327, which brought sec. 1 of the British Nationality Act of 1958 into operation on March 31, 1958. The nationality of adopted children is treated in the Adoption Act, 1960, 8 & 9 Eliz. 2, c. 59.

Although not all Commonwealth states adopted the "common clause," no Commonwealth country considers British subjects or citizens of other Commonwealth entities to be "aliens" in the full sense of the word. Neither Pakistan, Ceylon, nor the Union of South Africa adopted the common clause although it would appear that the legislation of each of these countries accomplished substantially the same purpose. India recognizes that a citizen of another Commonwealth country has the status of a Commonwealth citizen in India.[5] Pakistan and Ceylon[6] define an alien as anyone who is not a British subject, and the latter term is to have the same meaning as it has in the British Nationality Act. South Africa, prior to the time it left the Commonwealth, defined an alien as anyone who was not a citizen of the Union, a Commonwealth country, or Eire.[7]

5. Citizenship Act No. 57 of 1955, sec. 11, India, Ministry of Law, *Acts of Parliament, 1955,* p. 307, as amended by the Citizenship (Amendment) Act. No. 65 of 1957, *ibid., 1957,* p. 492, hereafter cited as the Indian Citizenship Act. Citizenship is also covered by the Constitution of India, 1949, pt. II, arts. 1–11. The fact that the Indian act does not confer the status of a Commonwealth citizen or British subject on the citizens of India would appear to have little effect within the Commonwealth as long as the laws of the other Commonwealth countries recognize a citizen of India as a British subject. For example, in the New Zealand case of *Bava Bhaga* v. *Parbhu,* the defendant contended that he was a citizen of India and not a British subject. The court found that he was a British subject and that a writ could be served in India against him. [1954] N.Z.L.R. 1039.

6. Pakistan Citizenship Act, 1951, *The Central Acts and Ordinances of Pakistan, 1951,* Act No. 2; as amended by Pakistan Citizenship (Amendment) Act, 1952, *ibid., 1952,* Act No. 5, hereafter cited as Pakistan Citizenship Act. Ceylon Citizenship Act of 1948, *The Acts of Ceylon, 1948,* Act No. 18, as amended by Citizenship Amendment Act of 1950, *ibid., 1950,* Act No. 40, and Citizenship Act of 1955, *ibid., 1955,* Act No. 13, hereafter cited as the Ceylon Citizenship Act.

7. South African Citizenship Act of 1949, sec. 1, *Statutes of the Union of South Africa, 1949,* Act No. 44, as revised by the South African Citizenship Amendment Act, 1961, *ibid., 1961,* Act No. 64, and the Commonwealth Relations Act of 1962, Republic of South Africa, *Government Gazette* (June 20, 1962), vol. 4, No. 264, pp. 31 ff. South Africa's failure to encourage dual citizenship has been attested by non-recognition of nationality *jure soli* in the case of a person whose father was a prohibited immigrant and by her rule that a South African of full age acquiring the citizenship of the United Kingdom by registration would forfeit his South African citizenship. See Clive Parry, "Plural Nationality and Citizenship with Particular Reference to the Commonwealth," 30 *Brit. Yb. Int'l L.* 279 (1953).

The British Nationality Act of 1948 having defined "British subject" as anyone who is a citizen of named countries (without any specific mention of the Commonwealth), the rule continued to apply to South African citizens even after their state left the Commonwealth. The precedent of Eire and certain wording in the United Kingdom-Burma Treaty of Oct. 17, 1947 (70 U.N.T.S. 183), did not, however, control British policy. The South African Act, 1962, 10 & 11 Eliz 2, c. 23, amended earlier legislation on nationality by providing that at the end of a "stand still" period (May 31, 1962) South Africans who were British subjects only by virtue of their South African citizenship would become aliens; until the end of

British subject without citizenship. In addition to distinguish-ing the British subject or Commonwealth citizen the British Nationality Act provided for a transitional status of British subjects without citizenship. The latter were persons who would not attain citizenship under the laws of any Commonwealth country or would have become stateless but for this provision. Such persons who had been British subjects on the effective date of the act and who gave proper notification of their intent to remain so were to have temporarily many of the privileges they enjoyed under pre-1948 legislation. They were to be treated as British subjects until their country of residence enacted a citizen-ship law. If that country did not grant them citizenship and they had not previously become United Kingdom citizens, aliens, or citizens of Eire, such persons became United Kingdom citizens on the effective date of the citizenship act of their country of residence.[8] New Zealand and Australia adopted similar provi-

---

1965, however, certain categories of South African citizens could become United Kingdom citizens by registering instead of going through the naturalization process, and South African citizens employed in Great Britain in positions not open to aliens might, until the end of 1965, choose between applying for United Kingdom citizenship and abandoning such positions.

New Zealand took a similar action by providing that as of Jan. 1, 1963, South Africans who had been British subjects by virtue of their South African citizenship ceased to be British subjects. However, such a person applying for New Zealand citizenship prior to Jan. 1, 1964, was to be processed as if he were a British subject for purposes of citizenship. *N.Z.L.J.* (Dec. 18, 1962), p. 552.

In South Africa, the Commonwealth Relations (Temporary Provision) Act, 1961, provided that South African laws containing references to the Common-wealth or to a particular Commonwealth country should not be affected by the fact that the Republic was not a member of the Commonwealth. If, however, a Commonwealth country should exclude the Republic from the benefits enjoyed by other Commonwealth countries, the Republic might do likewise. *Statutes of the Union of South Africa, 1961,* p. 486. However, by sec. 18 of the Commonwealth Relations Act of 1962, cited above, the word "alien" in the South African Citizenship Act was re-defined to mean "a person who is not a South African citizen." Thus, a Commonwealth citizen or British subject who is not a citizen of the Republic of South Africa is now an alien in South Africa.

8. British Nationality Act of 1948, sec. 13. The constitutions of Jamaica, Nigeria, Sierra Leone, Trinidad and Tobago, and Uganda, for example, provide that persons who are British subjects without citizenship under the British Nationality Act shall have the status of Commonwealth citizens in their respective countries. See the Jamaica (Constitution) Order in Council of 1962, sec. 9(2), *Jamaica Gazette Supplement* (Aug. 11, 1962), vol. 85, No. 76; Constitution of the Federation of Nigeria, 1963, sec. 14(1), *Supplement to the Official Gazette Extraordinary* (Sept. 19, 1963), vol. 50, No. 71, Act 20; Sierra Leone (Constitution) Order in Council, 1961, sec. 7(2), *Stat. Instr.,* 1962, No. 741; Trinidad and Tobago (Constitution) Order in Council, 1962, sec. 15(2), *Stat. Instr.,* 1962, No. 1875; and the Constitution of Uganda, sec. 13(2).

sions,[9] and South Africa, although it did not use the term "British subject without citizenship," appeared to regard such persons as citizens of a Commonwealth country. Legislation in some of the other Commonwealth countries omits reference to British subjects without citizenship, but since such persons are eligible to enjoy the rights of ordinary British subjects through United Kingdom legislation, they are not aliens in such countries.

British protected person.   British law has long used the term "British protected persons" to refer to certain protégés (inhabitants of protectorates, protected states, and mandates or trusteeships), but this category apparently received statutory definition for the first time in the British Nationality Act.[10] Orders in council provide that certain persons are to enjoy this status and lay down regulations for the acquisition and transmission of such status in much the same manner as the British Nationality Act regulates status for citizens of the United Kingdom.[11] As the term indicates, British protected persons enjoy the Crown's protection in the

9. Australian Nationality and Citizenship Act of 1948, *Commonwealth Acts, 1948,* Act No. 83, as amended by Nationality and Citizenship (Amendment) Act of 1950, *ibid., 1950,* Act No. 58; Nationality and Citizenship (Amendment) Act of 1952, *ibid., 1952,* Act No. 70; Nationality and Citizenship Act of 1953, *ibid., 1953,* Act No. 85; Nationality and Citizenship Act of 1955, *ibid., 1955,* p. 321; Nationality and Citizenship Act of 1958, *ibid., 1958,* Act No. 63; Nationality and Citizenship (Amendment) Act of 1959, *ibid., 1959,* Act No. 79; Nationality and Citizenship (Amendment) Act of 1960, *ibid., 1960,* Act No. 82. The Nationality and Citizenship Act as amended will hereafter be cited as the Australian Citizenship Act. For special provisions regarding Burma, see Nationality and Citizenship (Burmese) Act, *ibid., 1950,* Act No. 12.

British Nationality and New Zealand Citizenship Act, *New Zealand Statutes, 1948,* Act No. 15, as amended by the British Nationality and New Zealand Citizenship (Amendment) Act, *ibid., 1959,* Act No. 38, as amended by the British Nationality and New Zealand Citizenship (Amendment) Act, *ibid., 1959,* Act No. 38; the British Nationality and New Zealand Citizenship Amendment Act, 1962, as cited in note 7, *supra,* hereafter cited as the New Zealand Citizenship Act. For citizenship of adopted children in New Zealand, see sec. 16 (2)(e) of the act to consolidate and amend certain enactments of the general assembly relating to the adoption of children, Act No. 93 of 1955, *ibid., 1955.*

10. See J. Mervyn Jones, *British Nationality Law* (rev. ed., 1956), p. 186, and the same, "Who Are British Protected Persons?" 22 *Brit. Yb. Int'l L.* 122 (1945); S. A. de Smith, *The Vocabulary of Commonwealth Relations,* Commonwealth Papers, No. 1 (1954), p. 21. Sec. 32 (1) of the British Nationality Act defines a British protected person as a "person who is a member of a class of persons declared by Order in Council made in relation to any protectorate, protected state, mandated territory or trust territory to be for the purpose of this Act British protected persons by virtue of their connexion with that protectorate, state or territory."

11. See note 4, *supra.*

international-law sense. They may be represented in a foreign country by a member of the Commonwealth of Nations and for the purposes of the law concerning international responsibility they are considered to be British subjects.[12] Although the laws of most Commonwealth countries recognize this category of persons, the laws of Canada, Ceylon, and Malaysia are silent on the matter.

Gradations in status. The practical effect of the legislation discussed above is to accord a multiple status to nationals of the Commonwealth of Nations. All citizens of individual Commonwealth countries are also known as either British subjects or Commonwealth citizens. British subjects without citizenship and British protected persons are not citizens of individual Commonwealth countries and have a distinctly different status despite the fact that they enjoy substantial benefits and many of the rights of citizens. That such gradations in status are not new is illustrated by the legal position of the American Indians in the United States prior to the time when they became citizens in the full sense of the word.[13] This multiple status, however, does not preclude discrimination in the policies followed by Commonwealth countries in their *inter se* relations.

Discrimination against persons having common status. The holder of common status may find that such status gives him more benefits outside of the Commonwealth of Nations than in it. Within some Commonwealth countries the non-citizen who has the status of British subject, British subject without citizenship, or British protected person may find that his legal disabilities are as great, if not greater, than those of an alien. Rights of British subjects throughout the Commonwealth and empire are dependent on local laws which vary considerably from one Commonwealth

12. See J. Mervyn Jones, *op. cit. supra* note 10, at pp. 185, 195; Clive Parry, *Nationality and Citizenship Laws of the Commonwealth and of the Republic of Ireland* (1957), p. 116; Oppenheim, *International Law* (8th ed., Lauterpacht, 1955) I, 646, n. 3; for an excellent discussion of the status of protected persons see, Parry, *op. cit.*, chap. 7.

13. D. O. McGovney's essay on non-citizen nationals in Max Radin and A. M. Kidd, eds., *Legal Essays* (1935), pp. 323–374; Robert R. Wilson, "Gradations of Citizenship and International Reclamations," 33 *Am. J. Int'l L.* 146 (1939).

country to another. Within the diverse legal systems of the Commonwealth, the law of domicile or the place of birth often becomes a substitute for nationality law in determining the legal rights or obligations of subjects within the separate entities.[14]

A British subject may encounter legal barriers which prevent his migration to another Commonwealth entity or, once he has gained entry for residence, he may be discriminated against on the basis of ethnic origin. The United Kingdom permitted unrestricted migration from all parts of the Commonwealth until the passage of the Commonwealth Immigrants Act of 1962. The latter act placed quotas on immigrants who were Commonwealth citizens (except for Irish immigrants and bona fide students) who did not have employment, did not have special skills, or were unable to support themselves without working.[15]

14. See the case of Johnson *in re* Roberts v. Attorney General, [1903] 1 Ch. 821.

Professor Gey van Pittius noted the effectiveness of nationality as an indication of status within the empire and Commonwealth. He directed attention to the tendency to stress the place of a person's habitual residence. The concept of domicile was found to follow the inhabitant of the empire "like a shadow" and to make it possible to keep separate legal entities of the empire intact by classifying British subjects according to the part of the empire to which they were deemed to belong by residence.

A good example of the use of domicile as a substitute for citizenship is to be found in the Constitution of British Guiana which did not provide for the status of a citizen of British Guiana. However, it skilfully limited some rights, such as the protection of freedom of movement, to British subjects having a close connection with that country; such persons must have been born in Guiana of parents who were ordinarily resident or were naturalized in Guiana as British subjects or such persons must have seven years of residence in British Guiana. In order to hold office in the Legislative Assembly or Senate a person must be a British subject who has been resident the previous two years or is domiciled in British Guiana. The British Guiana (Constitution) Order in Council, 1961, secs. 10, 49, and 51, *Stat. Instr.*, 1961, No. 1188. The Constitution of Aden likewise does not provide for the status of a citizen of Aden, but members of the Legislative Council must either be British subjects born in Aden or have resided in Aden seven out of the previous ten years prior to nomination. The Aden (Constitution) Order in Council, 1962, *Stat. Instr.*, 1962, No. 2177.

15. 10 & 11 Eliz. 2, c. 21. The Leader of the Opposition in the House of Commons said, "It is a plain anti-Commonwealth Measure in theory and it is a plain anti-colour Measure in practice." He concluded, "I beg the Government now, at this last shameful moment to drop this miserable, shameful and shabby Bill. Let them think, consult and inquire before they deal another deadly blow to the Commonwealth." 693 *H. C. Deb.* (5th ser.), cols. 799, 803 (1962). *The Times* (London) called the Bill "bad" and editorialized that it "strikes at the very roots of British tradition and Commonwealth links" (Nov. 19, 1961, p. 11). Alastair Buchan noted that the act "drives a long nail into the coffin of the Old Commonwealth." *The Observer* (London), July 15, 1962, p. 18. The immigration restrictions of the 1962 act were extended to Dec. 31, 1965, by the Expiring Laws Continuance Act 1964, 12 & 13 Eliz. 2, c. 94.

The "old" Commonwealth had long carried out a white immigration policy which excluded migrants from Africa, Asia, and the West Indies. Canada softened this policy in 1956 and 1958 by arrangements with India, Pakistan, and Ceylon, respectively, which permitted a yearly token quota of citizens from these states to enter as migrants.[16] Ceylon has greatly restricted immigration in an attempt to stem the tide of Indian migrants. Pakistan and India have tightened immigration controls in order to prevent the migration of Hindus and Moslems across their respective frontiers. Malaysia has also adopted restrictive policies to maintain the balance between people of Malay, Indian, and Chinese origin within its borders. Cyprus has likewise attempted to restrict migration to maintain the Turkish-Greek population ratio at a constant level.[17]

A British subject who had attained residence or citizenship in a Commonwealth country other than that of his origin might still face numerous and burdensome restrictions based on ethnic origin rather than nationality. In parts of Canada, for example, a native-born British subject or Canadian citizen of oriental descent could not be licensed for certain types of work, could not work underground in the mines, could not employ white women in his place of business, and could not cut timber on Crown lands. Chinese, Japanese, and Indians may also be prohibited from being

16. 284 U.N.T.S. 90, 96, 102 and 316 U.N.T.S. 376.

17. For examples of Commonwealth laws discriminating against Commonwealth immigrants, see: Canada, R.S.C. pp. 2121, 3134, 3162 (1952); South Africa, Immigration Regulation Act, 1913, as amended, *The Union Statutes, 1910–1947*, vol. 7, p. 221; New Zealand, Act No. 44 of 1919, *New Zealand Statutes*, 1955, p. 1677, and Act No. 23 of 1920, *ibid.*, p. 1681; Australia, *Commonwealth Acts, 1901–1950*, pp. 2003–2005; Pakistan, Control of Entry Act, 1952, *The Central Acts and Ordinances of Pakistan, 1952*, Act No. 15; India, Influx from Pakistan Control Act of 1949, [1949] All India Rep., Act No. 102 and [1952] All India Rep., Act No. 108.

In the case of Re Munshi Singh, [1914] B.C. 243, the Chief Justice in referring to immigration to Canada said, "in my opinion, the British subject has no higher right than an alien in coming to the shores of Canada." In the case of De Marigny v. Langlais [1947] K. B. 741, Justice Cassey held, "I take it to be established that the status of a British subject does not carry with it the right of free entry into any country of the Commonwealth, if a competent legislative authority has by positive law restricted or denied that right." The House of Lords reached a similar decision in the case of Thornton v. Police, [1963] A.C. 336, in which the Lords upheld a Fiji Immigration Ordinance of 1947 requiring any person entering the Islands to leave within four months. Thornton, a newspaper man, was ordered to leave despite the fact that he was a British subject. See also Appendix, *infra*, note 57.

placed on the voting register. Such disabilities are based on ethnic origin rather than citizenship. This is illustrated by a 1955 decision of the Canadian Supreme Court which found that natural-born British subjects of Trinidad, who were of Indian descent, were Asians, since they descended from an Asiatic ethnic group, and were liable to deportation.[18] As a matter of fact, non-Commonwealth citizens from Asia who are protected by treaty rights may be in a better position than a Commonwealth Asian. This is illustrated by the fact that Hindus in Canada complained to the Imperial Conference of 1911 that the Japanese and Chinese through treaty rights could enter Canada whereas British subjects of Asiatic origin could not.[19] South Africa has long discriminated against its own citizens and Commonwealth citizens of non-white ethnic origin. Such discrimination culminated in the Group Areas Act of 1950.[20] Australia and New Zealand have likewise practiced such discrimination.[21]

It was but natural that discrimination in countries of the "old" Commonwealth should be met with reactions from the African and Asian portions of the Commonwealth of Nations. Section 10 of the Constitution of Zambia grants non-citizen Commonwealth subjects all legal and constitutional rights on a reciprocal basis except the right of voting and holding office in the National Assembly; section 12 of the Indian Citizenship Act makes the granting of rights to non-citizen British subjects discretionary, but the central government has not passed any order conferring rights

18. Harry Narine-Singh and Mearl Indra Narine-Singh v. Attorney General of Canada, [1955] Can. Sup. Ct. 395.
19. Cd. 5746–1 (1911).
20. See Group Areas Act. Act No. 41 of 1950, as amended by Act No. 65 of 1952; Act No. 6 of 1955; Act No. 68 of 1955; Act No. 29 of 1956 and Act No. 57 of 1957. The amended acts were consolidated by Act No. 77 of 1957.
21. For disabilities of British subjects within the empire and Commonwealth, see Norman Mackenzie, ed., *The Legal Status of Aliens in Pacific Countries* (1937), chap. 1 on Canada, chaps. 2, 3, and 9 on Australia, Canada, and New Zealand, respectively; C. F. Fraser, *Control of Aliens in the British Commonwealth of Nations* (1940), *passim;* H. F. Angus, "The Legal Status in British Columbia of Residents of Oriental Race and Their Descendants," 9 *Can B. Rev.* 1 (1931); Jean Mercier, "Immigration and Provincial Rights," 22 *ibid.* 856 (1944); Paras Diwan, "Treatment of Indians and the Question of Apartheid in South Africa," 16 *Supreme Court Journal* (India) 135 (1953); Henry J. May, *The South African Constitution* (3d ed., 1955), chaps. 10 and 23; G. W. F. Gould and C. P. Joubert, *The British Commonwealth,* vol. 5: *The Union of South Africa* (1955), chap. 12.

on such persons. The courts of India have, therefore, found that "all that is guaranteed to non-citizens is protection of life and liberty in accordance with the law of the land."[22] Although the Pakistan Citizenship Act defines an alien as a person who is not a citizen of Pakistan or a Commonwealth citizen, a Pakistan court held that the Foreigners Act of 1946 and the Foreigners Order of 1951 were applicable to an Indian citizen who had been seized as a spy in Pakistan.[23] Sierra Leone appears to discriminate against its own citizens. A citizen of Negro descent must have resided in that country continuously for twenty-five years or have served in the civil service or armed forces of Sierra Leone continuously for twenty-five years in order to become a member of the House of Representatives.[24]

Legal effect of common status. Despite such discriminations, the status of British subject may endow the holder who is present in a Commonwealth country of which he is not a citizen with certain legal rights and duties. The idea of common status has helped to preserve the so-called *inter se* doctrine for such matters as the extradition of fugitives from justice, use of letters rogatory, and the recognition of foreign judgments. Such matters between

22. Noor Mahammed and Others v. The State, [1956] All India Rep., M.B., 211–214. The decision was upheld in Naziranbai v. The State, [1957] All India Rep., M.B., 1.

23. Mansab Ali v. N.W.F.P. Government, [1954] 2 All Pak. Leg. Dec., Peshawar, 84.

24. Sec. 2 of the Constitution (Amendment) Act No. 2 of 1962. The citizenship laws of Sierra Leone are to be found in the Sierra Leone (Constitution) Order in Council, 1961, *Stat. Instr.*, 1961, No. 741, as revised by the Constitution Amendment Acts Nos. 2, 10, 11, and 12 of 1962 in *Supplement to the Sierra Leone Gazette* (1962), vol. 93.

Provisions in the constitutions of a number of the new Commonwealth countries which forbid discrimination on the basis of race, place of origin, creed, color, and political opinion are weak. The constitutions of Uganda and Jamaica are illustrative. In these countries such protections of fundamental rights and freedoms do not apply to non-citizens and do not even apply to their own citizens in regard to many matters such as the appropriation of revenues or public funds and matters of personal law. In Uganda such protections do not apply to restrictions on the acquisition or use by any person of land or property in Uganda. See the Jamaica Constitution, 1960, sec. 24 and the Constitution of Uganda, 1962, sec. 29. Although the Constitution of Trinidad and Tobago forbids discrimination on the grounds of race, origin, color, religion, or sex, a bill passed by three-fifths of the members of both houses of the legislature may become law even though it violates these provisions. Such a bill must, however, be "reasonably justifiable in a society that has a proper respect for the rights and freedoms of the individual." Trinidad and Tobago Constitution, 1962, chap. 1.

Commonwealth countries in regard to Commonwealth citizens are handled on the basis of imperial acts and other legislation rather than under customary international law or under international treaties. These statutory arrangements have greatly facilitated and expedited justice within the Commonwealth, and those based on imperial acts continue in validity under the Statute of Westminster, 1931, until specifically repealed by a member state.[25] Thus, in some areas of Commonwealth law a Commonwealth citizen may continue to be governed by the same body of statutory law, despite the fact that he is not present in his own country, so long as he is still within the Commonwealth of Nations.

In some Commonwealth countries resident British subjects may register to vote and may have a duty to render services of the kind normally required of nationals. For instance, in the United Kingdom such persons may vote, hold office, or be conscripted into the armed forces. Australia likewise conscripts non-citizen, resident British subjects.[26] Section 24 of the Australian Citizenship Act defines a British subject as a person who prior to the effective date of the act was entitled in Australia to all political and "other rights, powers and privileges" of a native-born British subject. Irish citizens apparently continue to have such rights and obligations under the provisions of Australian law even though they have not elected to become British subjects or Commonwealth

25. On this doctrine and the decline of its importance, see J. E. S. Fawcett, *The Inter-Se Doctrine of Commonwealth Relations* (1958), *passim.* See also chap. 9 *infra.*

26. Practice in the Commonwealth indicates that British subjects are held liable to military service. The acquiesence of the state of which the individual is a citizen may be an important fact. See Nicholas Mansergh *et al., Commonwealth Perspectives* (1958), pp. 70–71; Clive Parry, "International Law and Conscription of Non-Nationals," 31 *Brit. Yb. Int'l L.* 437 (1954).

For examples of Commonwealth countries which have permitted British subjects or Commonwealth citizens to vote, see Nyasaland (Constitution) Order in Council, 1961, *Stat. Instr.*, 1961, No. 1189, sec. 23; Northern Rhodesia (Constitution) Order in Council, 1962, *Stat. Instr.*, 1962, No. 1874, sec. 36; Constitution of Trinidad and Tobago, 1962, sec. 34; Constitution of Jamaica, 1962, sec. 37; and note 14, *supra*. The Constitution of Malaysia provides in sec. 155 that where the law in force in any other part of the Commonwealth confers upon citizens of the Federation any right or privilege it shall be lawful notwithstanding anything in the Malaysian constitution to confer a similar right or privilege on citizens of that part of the Commonwealth. See also, Appendix, *infra,* pp. 287–288.

citizens. The High Court has thus held that such an Irish citizen is entitled to serve as a juror in Australia.[27]

The British subject may also at times be in a different position from an alien in that he may be subject to the jurisdiction of a Commonwealth country of which he is not a citizen for extra-territorial offenses. Some, but not all, of the Commonwealth citizenship laws contain specific provisions applicable to such situations. There is thus considerable variation in existing practice of Commonwealth countries in regard to jurisdictional arrangements applicable to persons having the common status. The United Kingdom law-makers envisaged the practical problem involved in such diversity.

The British Nationality Act of 1948 provides that citizens of other Commonwealth countries resident in the United Kingdom are not subject to the latter's jurisdiction to the same extent as would be United Kingdom citizens for acts committed outside of the United Kingdom's jurisdiction. Section 3(1) of the act declared that a Commonwealth citizen may not be punished for an offense occurring outside of the United Kingdom unless such an act would be punishable by the Commonwealth country of which the accused is a citizen if it were committed within a foreign country. In each case the United Kingdom court must therefore determine the extent of territorial jurisdiction exercised in the Commonwealth entity whose citizen is accused in order to determine whether or not the United Kingdom has jurisdiction.

The resultant variations are illustrated by the Indian legal system. Indian courts may in some instances exercise jurisdiction over an Indian citizen for an act or omission committed abroad.[28] A United Kingdom court which would not normally exercise jurisdiction over one of its own citizens for a crime committed abroad might under the act exercise jurisdiction over a citizen of India for the same kind of offense because such an offense would have been punishable in India if it had occurred in a foreign

27. Stapleton v. The Queen, 86 Commw. L. R. 358 at 377 (1952).
28. Central Bank of India, Ltd. v. Ram Narain, [1955] All India Rep., Supreme Court, 36.

country. Provisions similar to section 3(1) of the United Kingdom statute are in force in many Commonwealth countries.[29] Canada makes no specific reference to such a situation in its legislation, but under the Citizenship Act of Canada an alien is subject to the same jurisdiction as a native-born citizen. It therefore follows that in jurisdictional matters a Commonwealth citizen is in the same legal position as a citizen of Canada.

The legal advantages of common status are even more apparent in international legal transactions between Commonwealth countries and non-Commonwealth countries. Under the *inter se* doctrine the United Kingdom maintains that it may present the claim of any Commonwealth subject against an outside state and apparently takes the position that any other Commonwealth government may exercise the same right. In the matter of international reclamations the United Kingdom has at times in its post-World War II contractual agreements acted on behalf of the entire Commonwealth, has acted at other times on behalf of an individual Commonwealth entity, and on other occasions has confined the operation of such transactions to the United Kingdom and Colonies.[30] Commonwealth countries have also negotiated instruments with foreign states presenting their respective claims without assistance from the United Kingdom.[31] Presumably the United Kingdom ceased to present the claims of Irish citizens in its international transactions after the passage of the Ireland Act of 1949 whereby Ireland left the Commonwealth.[32]

29. Australian Citizenship Act, sec. 9; Jamaica Constitution, 1962, sec. 10; Nigeria Constitution, 1963, sec. 15; New Zealand Citizenship Act, sec. 5; Sierra Leone Constitution, sec. 8(1); Trinidad and Tobago Constitution, 1962, sec. 19 and the Uganda Constitution, 1962, sec. 14.

The Ghana Nationality and Citizenship Act of 1957, sec. 11, *Ordinances and Acts of Ghana, 1957,* Act No. 1, contained provisions similar to those of the British Nationality Act. The 1957 act was replaced by the Ghana Nationality Act of 1961, *ibid., 1961,* Act No. 62, which is silent on the matter.

30. See, for example, 99 U.N.T.S. 132; 146 *Brit. & For. State Papers* 552 (1946); 157 U.N.T.S. 104; 99 U.N.T.S. 150; 87 U.N.T.S. 3; 273 U.N.T.S. 121; 249 U.N.T.S. 20; Cmd. No. 7600 (1948–49). For discussion of these treaties and those cited in note 31, *infra,* see Wilson and Clute, *loc. cit. supra* note 1, at pp. 581 ff.

31. 80 U.N.T.S. 28; 161 U.N.T.S. 186. See note 30, *supra.*

32. In an agreement signed with Yugoslavia on Dec. 23, 1948, in regard to compensation for British property nationalized in Yugoslavia, no mention was made of Eire although Eire had formerly been covered by such agreements. Cmd. No. 7600 (1948–49). At that time Eire had already passed the Republic of Ireland Act, 1948.

In matters of international representation in general the United Kingdom has long maintained the right to represent any Commonwealth country or British subject and has frequently done so. In a very broad sense the United Kingdom represented the interests of the other Commonwealth countries in recent negotiations with European countries concerning Britain's entry into the Common Market. The failure of the United Kingdom to enter the Common Market was to a great extent owing to her lack of success in gaining desired concessions on behalf of the Commonwealth. Commonwealth countries have also maintained the right to represent other Commonwealth countries or the citizens thereof in their foreign embassies, ministries, or consulates. Thus there are still some areas in which a Commonwealth citizen who finds himself in a foreign country may be able to enjoy the good offices of a Commonwealth country of which he is not a citizen by reason of the fact that in the broad sense of the term he is still a British subject or Commonwealth citizen.

2. Transitional Provisions for Citizenship

The framers of the new citizenship laws were confronted with the problem of determining through transitional provisions which of their residents should become citizens by reason of their connection with the respective countries prior to the commencement of the citizenship enactments. The draftsmen also made the normal provisions for the acquisition of citizenship by future generations through a permanent law of citizenship. One is tempted to apply the traditional term "involuntary acquisition of citizenship" to these provisions, but it does not seem appropriate since such acquisition of citizenship is not, in all cases, involuntary. Although the permanent law of citizenship is not overly complicated, the rules governing the transitional provisions are extremely diverse.

The transitional provisions have been greatly influenced by demographic and political motivations. With the exception of the Union of South Africa, the "old" Commonwealth was comparatively free of unwanted or unassimilated groups. This was owing in part to the relatively long period of self-government in such countries during which they could exercise a strict control of entry to exclude unwanted classes. The desire of the same countries to increase their numbers by attracting Europeans also led them to develop lengthy transitional laws designed to make citizenship possible for individuals whose connections with the country were at times rather far removed. The United Kingdom, which traditionally kept its doors open to all peoples of the empire, was as the mother country motivated to the same end by a desire to maintain the former unity. Britain also accepted the responsibility of attempting to prevent statelessness throughout the Commonwealth which might otherwise have been widespread as a result of the new citizenship laws.

The motivations of the "new" Commonwealth countries were quite different. Rising nationalism was a common drive which tended toward exclusiveness. India and Pakistan each felt the need to form cohesive populations sympathetic toward the new governments despite the mixed religious and ethnic origins of the inhabitants. Ceylon and Malaysia, because of the large unassimilated groups within their borders, attempted to exclude non-indigenous peoples and as a result cut their transitional provisions to a minimum. Cyprus also designed her citizenship laws in such a manner as to maintain the existing balance between members of the Greek and Turkish communities. Citizenship laws of the new Commonwealth countries do not reveal any particular attempt to attract British subjects unless such persons have fairly deep roots in the country concerned.

Birth within territory. The transitional provisions of all Commonwealth citizenship laws granted citizenship to certain persons born within the designated territory prior to the commencement of the new citizenship enactments. However, their provisions varied greatly. Birth on a vessel registered in the Commonwealth country concerned is deemed to have been a birth within the territory of the registering country. The transitional provisions of Canada, India, Jamaica, Pakistan, and Trindad and Tobago utilize the principle of *jus soli* subject to certain conditions.[33] Ceylon and the African Commonwealth countries, with the exception of Zambia, do not grant citizenship by birth within their territories unless certain of the individual's antecedents were also born within the territory.[34] However, Sierra Leone limits natural-born citizenship to persons of "negro African descent" and thus becomes the first Commonwealth country to include a racial qualification in its nationality laws.[35] Cyprus requires that a citizen have certain residence requirements or antecedents.[36] The citizenship provisions of the Federation of Malaysia allow citizenship by birth under certain conditions. However, the Malaysian provisions are extremely complicated as they involve state succession in regard to the Malay States, the

33. Such an individual becomes a citizen of Canada if born before Jan. 1, 1947, and if not an alien on that date; Canadian Citizenship Act, secs. 4(1)(a) and 39(1). In India such a person must have domicile at the commencement date of the act and may not have voluntarily acquired citizenship in a foreign state; Constitution of India, arts. 5 and 9. In Jamaica or Trinidad and Tobago such a person must have been a citizen of the United Kingdom on the effective date; Constitution of Jamaica, 1962, sec. 3 and Constitution of Trinidad and Tobago, 1962, sec. 9(1). In Pakistan such a person must not have been permanently resident outside of Pakistan after Aug. 14, 1947; Pakistan Citizenship Act, sec. 3(a).

34. In the case of Ceylon an individual's father or his paternal grandfather and paternal great grandfather must have been born in Ceylon, but the maternal line may be substituted in the case of illegitimate children; Ceylon Citizenship Act, secs. 4(1) and 9(1). In Ghana and Nigeria all United Kingdom citizens or British protected persons born in the territory become citizens if any of the parents or grandparents were born in the respective country; Ghana Citizenship Act, 1957, sec. 4(1); Ghana Nationality Act, 1961, sec. 20 and the Constitution of Nigeria, 1963, sec. 7. In Uganda the provisions are the same as for Ghana except that one of the parents must have been born in Uganda; Constitution of Uganda, 1962, sec. 7(1).

35. Sierra Leone Constitutional Amendment No. 2, 1962, sec. 2. The amendment defines a person of "Negro African descent" to mean a person whose father and paternal grandfather were or are Negroes of African descent.

36. The British Nationality (Cyprus) Order, *Stat. Instr.*, 1960, p. 421, provides that any person born in Cyprus on or after Nov. 5, 1914, who has been ordinarily resident on the Island of Cyprus for five years shall become a citizen. Any citizen of the United Kingdom born between Aug. 16, 1960, and Feb. 16, 1961, becomes a citizen at the date of his birth if his father becomes a citizen of Cyprus under the provisions of sec. 2 of the order. Under the provisions of sec. 2 of Schedule D of the order, any person born in Cyprus and now resident in a Commonwealth country, Greece, or Turkey, or who does not so reside but would otherwise become stateless shall be entitled on application to be granted citizenship of the Republic of Cyprus. The number of such applications to be granted is based on a yearly quota which admits four times as many persons to the Greek community as are admitted to the Turkish community. However, a person born in Cyprus who was resident in Cyprus the twenty years immediately before Feb. 16, 1961, or the wife of such a person, is exempt from the quota provisions.

Federation of Malaya, Singapore, and the Borneo States.[37] The
Union of South Africa granted citizenship by birth only to
persons born within its territory who were Union nationals or
certain persons who were deemed to be Union nationals at the
commencement date of the act.[38] Australia, the United Kingdom,
and New Zealand grant citizenship to all persons born in their
territories who were British subjects prior to the commencement
of the acts.[39] The provisions of the latter countries and a number

37. Citizenship in the Federation of Malaya was originally regulated by the
Federation of Malaya Agreement 1948, *Stat. Instr.*, 1948, p. 1231 as amended by
the Federation of Malaya Agreement (Amendment), 1952, Malaya, *Federal
Ordinances*, 1952, No. 23 of 1952. The Federation of Malaya Agreement provided
that any citizen of the United Kingdom and Colonies born in the Federation
before the prescribed date of the agreement would be a citizen if one of the
parents of such an individual had also been born in the Federation. Any subject of
the ruler of a Malay State within the Federation became a citizen of the
Federation if under the laws he became a subject of such a state by birth.
    After Aug. 31, 1957, citizenship in the Federation of Malaya was governed by
the Constitution of Malaya, 1957, *Stat. Instr.*, 1957, p. 832. Art. 14(1) of the 1957
constitution provided that any person who had become a citizen of the Federation
under the Federation of Malaya Agreement, 1948, prior to Aug. 31, 1957,
continued to be a citizen of the Federation. For documents and commentary on
the acquisition of citizenship in the states of the Federation of Malaya prior to
Aug. 31, 1957, see Parry, *op. cit. supra* note 12, at chap. 8; F. G. Carnell,
"Malayan Citizenship Legislation," 11 *Int'l & Comp. L. Q.* 504 (1952).
    By the Constitution of the Federation of Malaysia, 1963, as amended up to
March 31, 1964, all persons who had become citizens of Malaya under the
Federation of Malaya Agreement of 1948 were citizens of Malaysia. Citizens of
Singapore likewise became citizens of Malaysia. All persons, other than Singapore
citizens, born within the Federation of Malaysia after Aug. 31, 1957, and before
Oct. 1, 1962, became citizens. Every person born in the Federation after Sept. 30,
1962, and before Sept. 16, 1963, became a citizen if either parent was at the time
of the birth a citizen of the Federation but not a citizen of Singapore, or a
permanent resident of the Federation, or was not born a citizen of any other
country. A person born in a Borneo State or Brunei and resident therein as a
citizen of the United Kingdom and Colonies before Sept. 16, 1963, became a
citizen of the Federation. Singapore citizens had a dual citizenship in that all citizens of Singapore were also citizens of the Federation of Malaysia, but citizenship of Singapore was not severable from citizenship in the Federation. If a
person lost either one of the citizenships, he would also lose the other. A person
gained Singapore citizenship through the operation of Sinagpore law and thus
became a citizen of Malaysia. The Constitution of Malaysia granted citizenship
only to persons not citizens of Singapore except in the case of citizens of Singapore
who wished to drop their dual status and become citizens of Malaysia by
naturalization or enrolment.
    38. South African Citizenship Act, sec. 2.
    39. However, in Australia such a person must also be entitled to all political and
other rights of a natural-born British subject. In Australia an individual born in
New Guinea, and in New Zealand an individual born in Western Samoa may
become a citizen if he was a British subject prior to the commencement date of the
acts. The same is true in the United Kingdom of a person born in a protectorate,
protected state, or United Kingdom trust territory. See Australia Citizenship Act,
secs. 24, 25(a); United Kingdom Citizenship Act, secs. 12(1)(a) and 12(3);
New Zealand Citizenship Act. secs. 16(1)(a) and 16(3).

of the new African Commonwealth states concern the inhabitants of trust territories who have the status of British protected persons.

The requirements of Australia, New Zealand, and the United Kingdom that a person born within the territory must have been a British subject prior to the commencement of the acts in order to attain citizenship are somewhat deceptive in their simplicity. They are not easy requirements for persons born in trust territories. Section 1 of the British Nationality and Status of Aliens Act of 1914[40] made the acquisition of the status of a natural-born British subject by birth outside of His Majesty's Dominions and allegiance normally dependent on the fact that the individual's father was either a British subject or in the service of the Crown. Since the trusteeships were formally mandated territories, they fall outside of His Majesty's Domain. The indigenous population may therefore find it extremely difficult to meet the requirements that they be British subjects on the effective date of the commencement of the act in order to qualify as citizens.[41] The few cases which have come before the courts since the passage of the act indicate the extent of further disabilities which individuals born in trust territories may encounter.[42]

---

40. 4 & 5 Geo. 5, c. 17. For subsequent revisions of the British Nationality Act see 8 & 9 Geo. 5, c. 38; 12 & 13 Geo. 5, c. 44; 23 & 24; Geo. 5, c. 49; 6 & 7 Geo. 6, c.14.

41. The phrase "Dominions and allegiance" has been interpreted to exclude British-protected states, R. v. Graham Campbell, [1921] 2 K.B. 473; persons indigenous to the princely states of India, Mahomed and Minor Son v. Immigrants Appeal Board, 38 N.L.R. 7 (1918); or mandates of the League of Nations, Ffrost v. Stevenson, 58 Commw. L. R. 528 (1937), and R. v. Ketter, [1940] 1 K.B. 787. Individuals born in these areas will therefore find it difficult to meet the provisions that they be British subjects unless they are born of British parents or have been naturalized. See also D. P. O'Connell, "Nationality of Class 'C' Mandates," 31 *Brit. Yb. Int'l L.* 458 (1954).

42. The Australian courts have held that a person born in New Guinea on Jan. 15, 1916, of Chinese parents was not a British subject and could be deported under the Refugees Removal Act of 1949 as an alien. The court found that from Sept., 1914, until the creation of the mandate under the League of Nations on May 19, 1921, New Guinea was a German possession under military administration and noted that "while permanent acquisition by cession or otherwise may effect nationality, mere military conquest never does." Wong Man On v. The Commonwealth of Australia, 86 Commw. L. R. 125 (1952).

The case of Annandale v. Collector of Customs, [1955] N.Z.L.R. 168, indicates that an individual born in Western Samoa of native parents would stand little chance of becoming a New Zealand citizen even if he or his parents managed to become British subjects outside of New Zealand. Annandale was born in the

Ghana had a rather special problem since the state of Ghana included the Northern Territories of the Gold Coast and the Togoland trust territory, both of whose inhabitants were British protected persons. The United Kingdom was most desirous of maintaining the status of British protected person for any individual within Ghana who wished to retain such status. Thus section 4 (1) of the Ghana Citizenship Act of 1957 providing for citizenship by birth prior to the commencement of the act must be viewed in the light of certain United Kingdom legislation. The Ghana Independence Act of 1957 adjusted the British Nationality Act of 1948 to include Ghanaian citizenship. However, it also contained the proviso that the inhabitants of the two territories would not lose their status as British protected persons unless they became citizens of Ghana under any law of the parliament of Ghana providing for such citizenship.[43] The British Nationality Act of 1958 was formulated in part to deal with the fact that all citizens of Ghana had a dual status in that they were also citizens of the United Kingdom and Colonies. The 1958 act therefore provided that any person who was a citizen of Ghana and whose father or paternal grandfather was born in Ghana would cease to be a citizen of the United Kingdom. No individual was to cease to be a United Kingdom citizen if he or his father or paternal

mandate of Western Samoa of a Samoan mother and a father who was a natural-born British subject. The appellant was convicted in a lower court for residing in New Zealand on an expired permit in violation of sec. 5 of the Immigration Restriction Amendment Act of 1920 by which no person other than a person of British birth and parentage could enter New Zealand without a valid permit. Sec. 5(2) of the act stated: "A person shall not be deemed to be of British birth and parentage by reason that . . . he is an aboriginal Native or the descendant of an aboriginal Native of any dominion other than the Dominion of New Zealand or of any colony or other possessions or of any protectorate of His Majesty." The Supreme Court of New Zealand found that Annandale was of British birth and parentage regardless of the status of Samoa at the time of his birth since he did not have to base the claim on his Samoan mother but could, rather, on his British father. It appears that not only would Annandale have lost his case had he been born of Samoan parents but also that numerous British subjects of other parts of the Commonwealth of Nations would not qualify as citizens of New Zealand under sec. 5(2) of the 1920 act. The reference to the status of Samoa at the time of birth was presumably directed to the fact that Samoa was outside of the King's Domain, although the court did not speak directly to the matter.

43. Ghana Independence Act, 1957, sec. 2; Ghana Nationality Act, 1961, sec. 20. The independence acts of a number of other new Commonwealth countries including Jamaica, Kenya, Malaysia, Nigeria, Sierra Leone, Tanganyika, Trinidad and Tobago, and Uganda adopted the same formula in regard to British protected persons.

grandfather was born, naturalized, or registered as a citizen in the United Kingdom and Colonies, or if he became a British subject by the annexation of any territory included in the United Kingdom and Colonies. A person was not to cease to be a citizen of the United Kingdom and Colonies if he were born in a protectorate, protected state, or a United Kingdom trust territory, or if his father or his paternal grandfather was so born or was at any time a British subject.[44] The Ghanaian transitional provisions will therefore at times conflict with the provisions of the United Kingdom Act.

Members of Parliament in passing the 1958 act were especially concerned with protecting the status of British protected persons and were assured by the Joint Secretary of State for the Home Department at the time the bill was being discussed that such status had been preserved until a British protected person elected to become a Ghanaian citizen.[45] However, it must be admitted that if Ghana did not choose to allow the United Kingdom to act on behalf of British protected persons within the territory of the former, the latter would be in a very difficult position to give any practical effect to such status. This would be particularly true where many of the individuals concerned might have little or no knowledge of their rights as British protected persons. No special United Kingdom laws similar to the British Nationality Act of 1958 were passed in regard to other "new" Commonwealth countries. However, all such countries have used the same formula that was utilized in the Ghana Independence Act regarding British protected persons.

Birth abroad. Probably the most diverse and complicated portions of the citizenship enactments are the transitional provisions under which a person born abroad prior to the effective dates of the enactments acquires citizenship. The laws do not lend themselves to exhaustive comparison, but there are several unique provisions worthy of mention. The provisions of the United Kingdom are more inclusive than those of any other

44. British Nationality Act of 1958, sec. 2(1–3).
45. For discussion of the aims of the British Nationality Act of 1958 and the concern of the members of Parliament to extend the transitory provisions of the act, see 581 *H.C. Deb.* (5th ser.) cols. 281–299 (1958).

country. Australia, Canada, and New Zealand will permit certain British subjects or nationals born abroad prior to the commencement of their citizenship acts to become citizens if the father was a British subject who but for his death would have been a citizen of the Commonwealth country concerned or was naturalized or resident in such a country. Jamaica, Sierra Leone, and Trinidad and Tobago provide that a person born abroad will become a citizen if his father was or but for his death would have become a citizen of the particular country on the commencement date of the citizenship enactment. An individual born outside of the Union of South Africa prior to the commencement date of the act whose father was considered to be a British subject in the Union may become a citizen. However, the father of such a person had to be born in the Union, naturalized in the Union, have been in the service of the Union government at the time of the birth, have acquired British nationality by the annexation of territory, or have been domiciled in the Union or South-West Africa at the time of the birth.[46]

Ceylon granted citizenship to a person born abroad if either the father *and* the paternal grandfather or the paternal grandfather *and* paternal great grandfather were born in Ceylon.[47] A person who is domiciled in India on the commencement date and who has not acquired foreign citizenship may become a citizen of India on the commencement date of the act if either parent were born in India or if such a person had been ordinarily resident in India for five years prior to the commencement date. Pakistan granted citizenship to a person born abroad if the person was not permanently resident outside of Pakistan prior to August 14, 1947. However, such a person must have had domicile in Pakistan on the commencement date of the act and have had a parent or grandparent born in the territory of Pakistan or a parent or grandparent born in the India of March 31, 1947.[48]

46. Australian Citizenship Act, sec. 25(3, 5); Canadian Citizenship Act, sec. 4(1)(b); Jamaica Constitution, 1962, sec. 3(2); New Zealand Citizenship Act, sec. 16; Sierra Leone Constitution, 1961, sec. 5; South African Citizenship Act, sec. 5(1); Trinidad and Tobago Constitution, 1962, sec. 9(2).

47. Ceylon Citizenship Act, secs. 4(2) and 9(1).

48. Indian Constitution, arts. 5(b,c) and 9; Pakistan Citizenship Act, secs. 3 and 16.

Ghana, Malawi, Nigeria, Tanganyika, Uganda and Zambia permitted anyone born abroad who was a United Kingdom citizen or a British protected person on the commencement date of the act to become a citizen. However, the father, or in the case of Ghana one parent, must have been born in the respective country and have been or but for his death would have been a United Kingdom citizen or a British protected person. The Federation of Malaysia likewise permitted persons born abroad prior to September 16, 1963, to assume citizenship under certain conditions.[49] In Cyprus certain persons born abroad who are descendent in the male line from persons eligible for Cyprus citizenship become citizens of the Republic. A person of "Cypriot origin" born abroad may under certain conditions apply for citizenship.[50]

Migration. The residence, domicile, and migratory requirements of Pakistan and India are skilfully designed to exclude those who fled from India to Pakistan (and vice versa) for religious or ethnic reasons in the period of upheaval during and after partition, since such flight would ordinarily cast some doubt on their loyalty. Under the provisions of the Indian constitution any person who

49. Ghana Citizenship Act, 1957, sec. 5; Ghana Nationality Act, 1961, sec. 20; Constitution of Nigeria, 1963, sec. 7(2); Constitution of Uganda, 1962, sec. 7(2).

The Federation of Malaya Agreement, 1948, permitted a person born abroad to become a citizen if his father was born in a Malay State and was a citizen (or, but for his death, would have been a citizen) if the act had been in force at the time of the individual's birth abroad. A citizen of the United Kingdom born abroad prior to Feb. 1, 1948, could also become a citizen of the Federation if his father was born in either of the Settlements. Status thus gained was retained by the Constitution of the Federation of Malaya, 1957, art. 14, and the Constitution of the Federation of Malaysia, Second Schedule.

By the Constitution of the Federation of Malaysia, 1963, all citizens of Singapore are citizens of Malaysia. All persons other than citizens of Singapore born outside of the Federation on or after Aug. 31, 1957, and before Sept. 16, 1963, are citizens if the father was a citizen at the time of the birth and was either born in the Federation or was in the service of the government of the Federation at the time of the birth. If the father of such a person was a citizen other than by birth he could still become a citizen of the Federation if the birth was properly registered with the federal government within one year. All United Kingdom citizens normally resident in a state of Borneo or in Brunei prior to Sept. 16, 1963, also became citizens of the Federation of Malaysia. See note 37, *supra.*

50. The British Nationality (Cyprus) Order, 1960, sec. 2, 4. The Constitution of the Federation of Nigeria, sec. 7, provided that every person born outside of the territory of Nigeria, who was on Sept. 30, 1960, a United Kingdom subject or a British protected person, would become a citizen if his father was born in the territory of Nigeria and became (or but for his death would have become) a citizen of Nigeria on Oct. 1, 1960.

migrated to India from a territory of Pakistan is deemed a citizen on the commencement date of the constitution if either parent or any grandparent were born within India as defined by the India Act of 1935. However, such an individual must have migrated prior to July 19, 1948, and have since been resident in India. In the event that such an individual migrated to India on or after that date he must have been registered as a citizen by an officer of the government of the Dominion of India. Application to such officer must have been made prior to the commencement date of the constitution and after at least six months residence in India during the time immediately prior to the application.[51] Notwithstanding the aforementioned migratory provisions, a person who migrated after March 1, 1947, from India to Pakistan and returned to India under a permit for permanent return or settlement is deemed to have migrated prior to July 19, 1948.[52]

If a person migrated to Pakistan before the effective date of the Pakistan Citizenship Act from any territory in the Indo-Pakistan subcontinent with the intention of permanently residing in the territory of Pakistan, he is deemed to have been a citizen of Pakistan on the effective date of the act.[53] Anyone who was born, or who had parents or grandparents who were born, within the India of March, 1937, and has domicile within the meaning of part 2 of the Succession Act of 1925 (as in force at the commencement date of the act) in the territories of Pakistan is also deemed to be a citizen on the effective date of the act.[54]

The transitional provisions of Pakistan and India leave a rather serious "no man's land" in the citizenship law, for a person is not considered to be a citizen until he has actually migrated. Therefore an individual residing in the territory of one country after partition before migrating to the territory of the other experiences a period in which his status is akin to statelessness. The inadequacy of this arrangement was illustrated in the Indian courts. It was held that an individual who committed an offense in Pakistan before migrating to India could not be punished in India as the latter could only exercise extra-territorial jurisdiction

51. Constitution of India, art. 6.
52. *Ibid.*, art. 7.
53. Pakistan Citizenship Act, sec. 3(d).
54. *Ibid.*, sec. 3(b).

over its own citizens. The offender was not found to have become an Indian citizen until he actually entered India.[55]

Pakistan court decisions indicate that mere residence within the territory is not sufficient to establish domicile and that it is apparently easier for a Moslem to meet this requirement than for persons of non-Moslem origin.[56] Furthermore, mere possession of

55. Central Bank of India Ltd. v. Ram Narain, [1955] All India Rep., Supreme Court, 36. Another weakness of the migratory provisions of the Constitution of India is revealed by the case of *Supt. & Remr. of L.A., W. B.* v. *Rab Nawaz Khan.* Khan was born in India and had a place of business in that country when he went to Pakistan to visit a sick child. On his return to India, Khan accepted a temporary permit from the high commissioner for India in Pakistan in order to avoid difficulties on his return. His permit expired on March 7, 1949, but on Dec. 28, 1949, he received a certificate of registration as a citizen of India. He was arrested under the Influx from Pakistan Control Act of 1949, but the lower court held that he was a citizen by both arts. 5 and 6 of the constitution. However, the court held that since Khan was arrested on July 12, 1949, and the articles on which the respondent relied did not go into effect until Nov. 26, 1949, the constitution would not operate to protect him. Thus, although the respondent had received a certificate of registration as a citizen of India and had satisfied the provisions of art. 6 of the constitution governing the acquisition of citizenship by migrants, he was convicted. [1952] All India Rep., Calcutta, 838–840. The interpretation of the court leads to the rather fantastic conclusion that a citizen could acquire no status as a citizen under arts. 5 and 6 of the constitution until Nov. 26, 1949, since the articles merely provide that a person will be deemed a citizen as of the effective date of the constitution and have no retroactive effect. Thus another "no man's land" was created in India's citizenship law if the court's interpretation is accepted.

56. For instance, in the case of Carter v. Carter, [1958] All Pak. Leg. Dec. (W.P.), Lahore, 923, the appellant had been born in India, opted for Pakistan on partition, and settled in Pakistan where he married in 1948 and resided until the time of the trial. Appellant had applied under sec. 12 of the British Nationality Act of 1948 to be registered as a citizen of the United Kingdom and was so registered by the high commissioner for the United Kingdom in Pakistan. Although this would seem to have been sufficient to prove that Carter did not intend to reside in Pakistan permanently or to establish domicile, the judge said, in part: "In the case of a Muslim resident of India who opted for Pakistan the exercise of option would be presumptive, if not conclusive, proof that he intended henceforth to live in Pakistan, but the same can not be said of a person in the position of the appellant. His forefathers were, by domicile and nationality, English." The judge then went on to cite Vinans v. Attorney-General, [1904] A.C. 287 and concluded that "when a domicile of origin of a party is another country and a plea is taken that Pakistan was a domicile of choice, there is, according to the authorities, a heavy onus cast on the petitioner to prove by clear evidence the acquisition of Pakistani domicile." Carter was not found to be domiciled in Pakistan.

In the case of Palmer v. Palmer, [1958] All Pak. Leg. Dec. (W.P.), Lahore, 699, the judge even differentiated between different classes of persons of English descent. Justice Kayani noted that sec. 10 of the Succession Act declares that a man acquires a new domicile by taking up his fixed habitation in a country which is not his domicile of origin. The Justice, however, directed attention to the fact that a man had no fixed habitation in British India by reason of residing there in service or for similar reasons. The Justice declared, "It is obvious that this was intended to cover Europeans who came to India for the service or trade and had no intention of settling here. This cannot, however, apply to the class which came to be known as 'Anglo-Indian' and which settled here permanently." Appellant was therefore found to have established domicile in Pakistan.

a permit to re-enter India under the provisions on migration is far from being an assurance that the holder of the permit will gain citizenship. The courts have held that migration in the legal sense in which it is used in the citizenship law implies much more than migration in the ordinary sense of the word.[57] The courts will probably give great weight to the individual's actions as evidence of intent actually to migrate, and regulations permit the cancellation of a permit without giving the reasons for such cancellation.[58] The Indian Supreme Court has also held that article 7 overrides article 5 of the constitution.[59] Thus if an individual has domicile in India at the effective date of the constitution and has not acquired citizenship of a foreign state, he will be considered an Indian citizen under article 5. However, under article 7, if he migrates from India after March 1, 1947, and does not have a permanent permit to re-enter, or if such permit is cancelled, he will not be considered to be a citizen of India.

Some confusion has also existed in the matter of domicile of married women. The court of Allahabad held that minor, married

57. For a discussion of recent court interpretations of the term "migration" in India, see Nagendra Singh and M. K. Nawaz, "The Contemporary Practice of India in the Field of International Law," 1 *Int'l Studies* 184–187 (1959).

58. In the case of *Mohammad s/o Ibrahim & Others* v. *High Commissioner for India in Pakistan and Others*, a man and wife long resident in India took their son to Pakistan in Oct. 1948, and remained until April, 1949. Their permanent permit on which they re-entered was cancelled by the high commissioner for India in Pakistan on Dec. 12, 1949. The state held that applicants had disposed of much property in India and had returned only to dispose of the remainder. The court even noted that a granddaughter and a "number of their relations admittedly reside in Pakistan." The court therefore held that the inference to be drawn from the facts was that the couple had migrated after March, 1947, and had lost their citizenship. As to the cancelled permit, the court noted that whether a permit shall be granted or refused was entirely within the discretion of the high commissioner and cited Rule 29 of the Permit System Rules that "Every permit issued under these rules shall be liable to cancellation at any time, without reason being assigned by the issuing authority of the Central Government." [1951] All India Rep., Nagpur, 39–42. This case is illustrative of the rather grave risk involved for a Mohammedan with family connections in Pakistan to leave the country, as he may be hard put to prove that he did not migrate.

Evidently the courts have taken a somewhat different position in regard to Jammu and Kashmir owing to the rather unsettled conditions in that area. In a 1959 case the court held that a woman residing in the portion of Jammu and Kashmir occupied by India did not lose her status as a subject of the state despite the fact that her husband had left the area and was residing in a portion of the state under the occupation of Pakistan. [1959] All India Rep., Jammu and Kashmir, 32, as cited by M. K. Nawaz, "Public International Law," 9–10 *India Yb. Int'l Aff.* 333 (1960).

59. The State of Bihar v. Kumar Rani Saveeda Khatoon and Others, 18 *Supreme Court Journal* (India) 311 (1955).

(Mohammedan) girls who were taken from India to Pakistan by their parents in 1947, and whose husbands were Indian citizens residing in India, were not migrants and were themselves citizens of India by birth. The court found that so long as the marriage subsisted the women could not change their domicile at will and that during their minority the only persons who could decide such questions were their husbands.[60] However, in a later case the Supreme Court of India held that a female Indian citizen by birth who left India in July, 1948, and returned in December, 1948, under a temporary permit had become a migrant. She was therefore not deemed to be an Indian citizen although her Indian husband and three sons continued to reside in India during her absence.[61]

Miscellaneous. All of the Commonwealth countries have provisions whereby the wife of a person who becomes a citizen, or would have become a citizen on the effective date of the independence or citizenship act but for his death, may attain the citizenship of her husband. However, the mode of acquiring such citizenship and the type of citizenship acquired varies greatly. In all Commonwealth countries except Malaysia and Ceylon it is possible for a person who was naturalized under the laws of the territory concerned prior to the attainment of independence to become a citizen with relatively few restrictions. A number of the Commonwealth countries made citizenship available to certain individuals who had established residence or domicile in their territories prior to the commencement of their citizenship acts.[62] Australia, New Zealand, and the United Kingdom deem a person to have been a British subject immediately prior to the commencement of their respective citizenship acts if that person would have retained such status except for his failure to register a

60. Mst. Allah Bandi v. Government of Union of India, [1954] All India Rep., Allahabad, 456.
61. See case cited, note 59, *supra*.
62. See for example, Canadian Citizenship Act, secs. 9(1) and 39; Australian Citizenship Act, sec. 25; Constitution of India, art. 5; Constitution of Malaysia, Second Schedule; New Zealand Citizenship Act, sec. 16(1); South African Citizenship Act, sec. 5; Constitution of Trinidad and Tobago, 1962, sec. 10(1).

declaration of retention before becoming of age or after marrying an alien.[63]

The United Kingdom position. The United Kingdom transitional provisions are illustrative of the attempt of that country to retain individuals with former connections as citizens. This is especially true when such provisions are viewed alongside the extremely liberal registration provisions of the United Kingdom. The provisions of the British act which confer the status of British subjects on persons who would have had such status but for their omission to make a declaration of retention, provisions regarding naturalization, provisions for those born abroad, and the arrangements for married women, are all indications that the United Kingdom has in its transitional provisions sometimes accepted extremely tenuous connections as qualifications for citizenship. The British Nationality Act of 1964, section 2, even went so far as to provide that if a person made a declaration of renunciation of citizenship in the United Kingdom and Colonies in order to become a citizen of another country he would be deemed to have remained a United Kingdom citizen unless he gained citizenship of the other country within six months.

The United Kingdom provision regarding married women is especially illustrative of the fact that if a person is deemed to be a British subject under one of the transitional provisions of the acts, such status may have legal effect far beyond the acquisition of citizenship in the country concerned. Such a status also confers certain legal rights granted to British subjects by the laws of the Commonwealth countries, as is illustrated by the case *In re Veen* (*Deceased*). Gwendoline Veen was born in Surabaya, Netherlands East Indies, on September 10, 1903, of a father who was born in Singapore of British parents. She was a British subject but married a Dutch national. Her husband died and she asked for a British passport to return to New Zealand where she died leaving a will. The New Zealand court held that, although Mrs. Veen was not domiciled in New Zealand either at the time she made out the

63. Australian Citizenship Act, sec. 28; New Zealand Citizenship Act, sec. 17; British Nationality Act, sec. 15.

will or at the time of her death, the will could still be probated in New Zealand as she was deemed to be a British subject at the commencement of the act under section 14 of the British Nationality Act of 1948.[64] The case illustrates not only the length to which the transitional provisions have been stretched but also the benefits resultant therefrom even though the individual does not elect to become a citizen of the country which includes him in such a provision.

3. Permanent Arrangements for Citizenship

The provisions for the acquisition of citizenship on or after the commencement of the citizenship enactments, or in some cases on or after a specified date, are intended to provide the rules for acquisition of citizenship by future generations. They are called permanent provisions, although they may, of course, be changed by new enactments. Since the process of selection from among the inhabitants of the respective territories at the time of the effective date of the acts was accomplished by transitional provisions, the permanent provisions tend to be much less exclusive and much less complicated.

Birth within the territory. The generally accepted rules of international law applicable to *jus soli* are accepted in the case of the United Kingdom, Australia, New Zealand, India, Jamaica, and Pakistan.[65] However, Ceylon, Ghana, Malaysia, Malawi, Nigeria, Sierra Leone, Tanzania, Trinidad and Tobago, Uganda, and Zambia have qualified citizenship by birth within their territories by requiring that a parent of such an individual be a citizen at the time of the birth. Sierra Leone limits citizenship thus acquired to persons of "negro African descent."[66] In Canada the individual

64. [1957] N.Z.L.R. 351.
65. British Nationality Act, sec. 4; Australian Citizenship Act, sec. 10; Indian Citizenship Act, sec. 3; Jamaica Constitution, 1962, sec. 5; New Zealand Citizenship Act, sec. 3; Pakistan Citizenship Act, sec. 4.
66. Ceylon Citizenship Act, secs. 5(1) and 9(1); Ghana Citizenship Act, 1961, sec. 1; Constitution of Nigeria, 1963, sec. 11; Sierra Leone Constitution, Amendment No. 2, 1962, sec. 3; Trinidad and Tobago Constitution, sec. 12(1), and Constitution of Uganda, 1962, sec. 9.
A person born in the Federation of Malaysia after Sept. 16, 1963, but outside

will not become a citizen by birth within the territory if the father is an alien who has not been lawfully admitted to Canada for permanent residence; in South Africa an individual will not attain citizenship if either he or his father is deemed to be a prohibited immigrant under the immigration laws.[67]

All Commonwealth countries except Ceylon have provisions excluding the children of diplomats from the acquisition of citizenship by birth within the territory.[68] None of the enactments except that of Canada refers to ambassadors, ministers, or envoys; they generally refer to persons who would have such immunity from suit and legal process as would be accorded to such individuals. Thus the child of a high commissioner would fall under such provisions. Canada has gone further than the other Commonwealth countries in excluding the children of representatives of other governments from the operation of her citizenship laws.[69]

With the exception of Canada and Ceylon all countries which have enacted citizenship laws provide that an individual shall not be a citizen if the birth occurs at any place under enemy occupation at a time when the father is an enemy alien. Canada, Ceylon, and Malaysia have made specific provisions in their laws covering

---

Singapore becomes a citizen if either of his parents at the time of birth are permanently resident in or citizens of the Federation but are not citizens of Singapore. However, every person born within the Federation outside Singapore becomes a citizen if he would not otherwise become the citizen of any other country. The latter provision is a rather admirable innovation to prevent statelessness. A person born in Singapore of a parent who is a citizen of the Federation at the time of the birth but not a Singapore citizen, becomes a citizen of the Federation if he has not already gained citizenship by other provisions in the constitution. Constitution of Malaysia, Second Schedule. See note 37, *supra,* for citizenship by birth within the Federation of Malaya prior to Sept. 16, 1963.

67. Canadian Citizenship Act. sec. 5(1–2); South African Citizenship Act, sec. 3(1–2).

68. Probably such a provision was not deemed necessary in the citizenship act of Ceylon since birth within the territory does not bestow citizenship unless one of the parents is also a citizen.

69. Under sec. 5(1)(b) of the Canadian Citizenship Act, an individual born in Canada after Dec. 31, 1946, will not become a citizen if the responsible parent is:

"(i) A foreign diplomatic or consular officer of a representative of a foreign government accredited to Her Majesty;

(ii) An employee of a foreign government attached to or in the service of a foreign diplomatic mission or consulate in Canada, or

(iii) An employee in the service of a person referred to in subparagraph (i). . . ."

foundlings. A newly born deserted infant of unknown parentage found in these countries is deemed to have been born within the territory until the contrary is proved.[70] Birth on a registered vessel is tantamount to birth within the territory of the vessel's registration under the laws of all Commonwealth countries.

The passage of the Irish Nationality and Citizenship Act of 1956 created conflicting claims on the part of the United Kingdom and Eire over the inhabitants of Northern Ireland. Section 6 (1) of the 1956 act declares, "Every person born in Ireland is an Irish citizen by birth." However, section 7 states that, pending "the re-integration of the national territory," section 6 (1) will not apply to a person, not otherwise a citizen of Eire, who had been born in Northern Ireland on or after December 6, 1922, unless such individual or his parents or guardian filed a declaration that he was a citizen of Eire.[71]

The prime minister of Northern Ireland made the following motion before the House of Commons of Northern Ireland:

that this House, having taken notice of a measure passed by the Parliament of the Republic of Ireland . . . repudiates the gratuitous attempt therein to inflict unwanted Irish Republican nationality upon the people of Northern Ireland; proclaims the indivisible allegiance of its people to the British Crown; and rejects outright the unfounded claims of the Republican Parliament. . . .

The main objections to the act seemed to center around sections 6 (1) and 7. The motion was passed by both the House and the Senate.[72]

Birth abroad. A person born anywhere outside of India, New Zealand, Pakistan, or the United Kingdom after the commencement dates of the acts, or in the case of India after June 26, 1950, of a father who is a citizen other than by descent at the time of such birth becomes a citizen by descent. However, if such an

70. Canada Citizenship Act, sec. 7; Ceylon Citizenship Act, sec. 7; and the Constitution of Malaysia, Second Schedule. However, it is to be noted that most Commonwealth countries provide for the registration of any minor child as a citizen at the discretion of the minister. Presumably such registration would be used to cover foundlings.
71. *Acts of the Oireachtas, 1956*, Act No. 26.
72. 28 *J. of the Parliaments of the Commonwealth* 45–46 (1957).

individual's father was a citizen by descent, an individual born abroad will not become a citizen if the birth is not registered within a specified period of time or unless the father was in the service of the government concerned.[73] In New Zealand and the United Kingdom such an individual will become a citizen despite the fact that the father was a citizen by descent if either he or his father was born in a protectorate, protected state, mandate, trutseeship, or a place in a foreign country where His Majesty's government has or had jurisdiction by lawful means over British subjects. The United Kingdom grants citizenship to an individual born in any Commonwealth country whose father is a citizen of the United Kingdom by descent if a citizenship law has taken effect in such Commonwealth country and the individual does not thereby become a citizen at birth.[74]

Under the citizenship laws of Australia, Ceylon, Canada, New Zealand, and Sierra Leone a child born abroad after the effective date of the act (in the case of Canada after December 31, 1946) of a father who was a citizen at the time of the birth may become a citizen. However, in Australia such an individual does not become a citizen if born in another Commonwealth country where he becomes a citizen at birth if the parent through whom he claims status is not ordinarily resident in Australia or New Guinea. In Canada a person born abroad ceases to be a citizen within three years after he becomes twenty-one years of age unless he has filed a declaration of retention of citizenship or has his place of domicile in Canada by that date.[75]

The provisions of Ghana covering birth abroad after the effective date of the act are unique in that citizenship may be transmitted either through the mother or the father. However, in order to transmit such status the father must be a citizen of Ghana other than by descent or the mother must be a citizen by birth.

73. Indian Citizenship Act, sec. 4; New Zealand Citizenship Act, sec. 7; Pakistan Citizenship Act, sec. 5; British Nationality Act, sec. 5(1)(b,c).

74. New Zealand Citizenship Act, sec. 7; British Nationality Act, sec. 5(1)(a,c).

75. Australian Citizenship Act, sec. 11; Ceylon Citizenship Act, sec. 5(2); Canadian Citizenship Act, sec. 5(1)(b) and sec. 5(1)(b)(1A); New Zealand Citizenship Act, sec. 7(1)(b); Sierra Leone Constitutional Amendment, No. 10, 1962, sec. 3(2).

Thus the illegitimate child of such a mother would be qualified to attain citizenship. However, a child whose parents did not meet these qualifications could become a citizen of Ghana under the registration provisions if either parent were Ghanaian by descent.[76] In Malawi, Nigeria, Jamaica, Sierra Leone, Tanzania, Trinidad and Tobago, Uganda, or Zambia a person born abroad after the commencement date of the act becomes a citizen if at the time of the birth the father is a citizen of the particular country unless the father was also born abroad and had become a citizen by descent.[77] A person born abroad may become a citizen of Malaysia who is not a citizen of Singapore if his father is a citizen of Malaysia and not a citizen of Singapore who meets certain requirements.[78]

A person born abroad after the effective date of the Union of South African Citizenship Act becomes a citizen if his father was a South African citizen at the time of the person's birth. However, such a father also must be either a South African by birth, registration, or naturalization, or a South African by descent born in South-West Africa, or have been in the service of the South African government at the time of the birth, or have been ordinarily resident in South Africa at the time of the birth. In all cases such an individual born abroad will not become a South African citizen if the birth is not registered within the specified time limit. Notwithstanding the foregoing provisions, an individual born in another Commonwealth country, under whose law he

76. Ghana Nationality Act, 1961, sec. 2.

77. Constitution of Nigeria, 1963, sec. 11; Constitution of Jamaica, 1962, sec. 6; Constitution of Sierra Leone, 1961, sec. 5; Constitution of Trinidad and Tobago, 1962, sec. 12(3) and Constitution of Uganda, 1962, sec. 10.

78. Any person born abroad after Aug. 31, 1947, and before Sept. 16, 1963, became a citizen of the Federation of Malaya if his father was a citizen at the time of the birth and was either born in the Federation or was in the service of the government of the Federation at such time. Constitution of the Federation of Malaya, art. 14. All persons who had gained such status prior to Sept. 16, 1963, became citizens of the Federation of Malaysia; however, after that date citizenship by birth abroad was regulated by the Constitution of Malaysia. Under the latter instrument every person born outside of the Federation whose father is a citizen of the Federation, but not a citizen of Singapore, at the time of the birth, becomes a citizen of Malaysia if his father were either born in the Federation or was in the service of the Federation or a State at such time. If such a person meets the above-mentioned requirements but his father was not born in the Federation or was not in the service at the time of the birth, he may still become a citizen if the birth is properly registered within a prescribed period of time. Constitution of Malaysia, Second Schedule.

becomes a citizen by birth, shall not become a citizen of the Union unless his father was in the service either of the government of the Union or "of a person or association of persons resident or established in the Union."[79]

Incorporation of territory.   The citizenship laws of a considerable number of Commonwealth countries make provisions for acquisition of citizenship in the event of incorporation of new territory. The governments concerned may under such conditions specify which of the inhabitants will become citizens by reason of their connection with said territory.[80] Such provisions are of necessity somewhat vague, for the acquisition of citizenship in such cases may be affected by international agreement, as was the case in the recent treaties concluded by India and France whereby the latter ceded certain French settlements in the subcontinent to India.[81]

4. Deprivation or Loss of Status

The citizenship enactments of all Commonwealth countries contain rather lengthy provisions on these matters. Indeed, the stipulations give the impression that it may at times be almost as difficult to retain citizenship as it is to acquire the status in the

79. South African Citizenship Act, sec. 6. If the child were illegitimate, the mother may be substituted for the father in transmitting status.

80. See, for example, British Nationality Act, sec. 11; Australia Citizenship Act, sec. 33; Indian Citizenship Act, sec. 7; New Zealand Citizenship Act, sec. 15; Pakistan Citizenship Act, sec. 13 and the provisions concerning the Northern Cameroons in the Constitution of Nigeria, 1963, sec. 10. See note 37, *supra*, for such provisions concerning Malaysia.

81. In Treaty of Cession of the Territory of the Free Town of Chandernagore, signed by India and France on Feb. 2, 1951, art. 2 provided that French subjects and citizens of the French Union domiciled in the territory when the treaty came into effect would become nationals and citizens of India. However, art. 3 of the agreement provided that such persons could opt for retention of their nationality within six months after the effective date of the treaty. 203 U.N.T.S. 55. Similar arrangements were made by the Treaty of Cession between India and France concerning the French Settlements of Pondicherry, Karaikal, Mahe, and Yanam concluded in 1956, but such provisions were only applicable to French nationals born in the territory and domiciled therein on the effective date of the treaty. Singh and Nawaz, *loc. cit. supra* note 57, at p. 186, citing Lok Sabha Secretariat, *Foreign Policy of India: Texts of Documents* (1958), pp. 211–220.

first place. The complicated and verbose provisions invite a general rather than an exhaustive treatment of the subject.

Plural citizenship. No Commonwealth country follows the doctrine of indissoluble allegiance at the present time, and all members except Pakistan have formal provisions in their citizenship enactments whereby citizenship may be renounced. Despite these provisions, plural citizenship or nationality is still one of the chronic problems of Commonwealth citizenship laws. It may be pertinent to recall the Naturalization Act Committee of 1901 which reported to the House of Commons in Great Britain that "To guard effectively against the occurrence of cases of double nationality would require the assimilation in this respect of all various systems of law prevailing in civilized communities, an ideal which, however desirable, is not likely to be realized."[82] The diversity of enactments in the separate Commonwealth countries did not improve the situation in the intervening years.

The United Kingdom, in keeping with her role as the mother country, has no regulations prohibiting plural citizenship. Although all other Commonwealth countries except Zambia have restrictions on plural citizenship, the provisions are sometimes worded in such a manner that the deprivation of citizenship is discretionary and not mandatory. In the case of some Commonwealth countries the exercise of certain obligations or rights in another foreign country may have the same effect on the operation of the law as if the person had voluntarily acquired citizenship in such a country. The laws of Sierra Leone are unique in that a person who holds Sierra Leonean citizenship on the basis of birth within Sierra Leone may maintain dual citizenship, but any other citizen may be deprived of his Sierra Leonean citizenship if he is a citizen of another country. The Constitution of Nigeria does not provide for deprivation of citizenship except in the case of a citizen who is also a citizen of another country and has not made a statement of renunciation of his other citizenship. The constitution stipulates that the government may not deprive a natural-

82. Cd. No. 723 (1901).

born Nigerian citizen of his citizenship for any reason other than the failure to make such a renunciation.[83]

Registered or naturalized citizens.   Again, as in the matter of acquisition of citizenship, the provisions for deprivation or loss of citizenship by registered or naturalized citizens, and in some cases by citizens by descent, make it strikingly clear that certain classes of citizens are more subject to disabilities than are others. The provisions for the loss of citizenship by naturalized citizens follow rather closely the provisions of the British Nationality and Status of Aliens Act of 1914;[84] however, in many cases such provisions are applicable to registered citizens as well as naturalized citizens. Registered citizens have on occasion referred to their status as that of "second class citizens." Since the registered citizen is very closely assimilated to the naturalized citizen in the matter of loss of citizenship in a number of the Commonwealth countries, it would perhaps be wiser in such cases to do away with the separate categories and to give both registered and naturalized citizens the same classification or status as has been done in the case of Ceylon and Canada. In all of the Commonwealth countries both registered and naturalized persons may be deprived of citizenship where a natural-born citizen (or a citizen by descent) would not lose citizenship under the same conditions. Malaysia has, however, protected both registered and naturalized citizens from deprivation of citizenship in certain cases where the government is satisfied that such deprivation of citizenship would make the person stateless.[85]

Dissatisfaction on the part of registered and naturalized citizens over laws concerning their loss of citizenship has been particularly chronic in Australia, Canada, and New Zealand, all of which have attempted to attract and assimilate large numbers of immigrants since World War II.[86] There has, therefore, been a

83. See for example, Constitution of Jamaica, 1962, sec. 8(2); Constitution of the Federation of Malaysia, 1963, art. 24; New Zealand Citizenship Act, sec. 22(2) (b); Constitution of Nigeria, 1963, secs. 13, 16(6); Sierra Leone Constitutional Amendment No. 10 of 1962, sec. 8.

84. Sec. 8, cited note 40, *supra.*

85. Constitution of Malaysia, 1963, sec. 26B.

86. See Appendix, *infra,* pp. 279–280.

general tendency in the three countries to bring the disabilities of registered and naturalized citizens more into line with those of natural-born citizens in the matter of loss of citizenship by major revisions in their laws since 1958.[87]

．　．　．　．　．

The movement after World War II to create a new type of status based on the British subject or Commonwealth citizen retained many of the common advantages from the time when there was but one status—that of British subject—for the whole empire. Under the new system a citizen of one Commonwealth country is not considered to be an alien in another Commonwealth country. The *inter se* doctrine has also continued in operation under the new common status. This has permitted certain legal practices, as for example, extradition between Commonwealth countries, the reciprocal enforcement of judgments, and certain jurisdictional arrangements to survive relatively intact despite the new citizenship laws. Commonwealth citizens or British subjects may still claim legal or civil rights or be held liable to legal or civil obligations although they are not citizens of the individual Commonwealth countries in which such rights or duties are exercised. In many instances the new common status has also proved advantageous in the matter of relations with non-Commonwealth states. This is especially true where treaty practices and the espousal of claims on behalf of British subjects are concerned.

The Commonwealth citizen may, however, be denied ingress to another Commonwealth country or after gaining entry into such a country may suffer discrimination based on ethnic origin or race rather than nationality. The new citizenship laws also introduced elements of exclusion which in many cases denied citizenship to inhabitants of individual Commonwealth countries despite birth, naturalization, or long domicile in such countries. The changed

87. See British Nationality and New Zealand Citizenship Amendment Act, *New Zealand Statutes, 1959*, Act No. 38; Canadian Citizenship Amendment Act, 7 Eliz. 2, c. 24; Australian Citizenship Amendment Act, *Commonwealth Acts, 1957*, Act No. 16; Australian Nationality and Citizenship Act, *ibid., 1959*, Act No. 78; and Australian Nationality and Citizenship Act, *ibid., 1960*, Act No. 82.

status is particularly evident in matters concerning the loss of citizenship as a result of exercising certain rights or acquiring citizenship in another Commonwealth country. Although the status of Commonwealth citizen or British subject offers many advantages, these are not as widespread or numerous as the perquisites of the status of British subject within the Common- wealth prior to World War II.

6

Domestic Jurisdiction

John M. Howell*

Members of the Commonwealth have exerted considerable influence upon the development and application of the concept of domestic jurisdiction. Commonwealth countries were active in the drafting of the domestic jurisdiction reservations at both the Paris Peace Conference following World War I and the San Francisco Conference of 1945. As members of both world organizations established at these conferences, Commonwealth nations have taken a lead in applying and interpreting the reservations drafted on each occasion. But Commonwealth countries have not followed a uniform approach to the concept of domestic jurisdiction, especially in the period since the founding of the United Nations. Indeed, within the ranks of the Commonwealth, a division of opinion has emerged clearly reflecting the two opposing approaches to domestic jurisdiction which have crystallized in the post-World War II era.

The more traditional of these approaches, the "international obligations" approach, has its roots in the language of the League of Nations Covenant. Consequently, the first portions of this chapter trace the role of Commonwealth members in drafting the League reservation on domestic jurisdiction and in interpreting the domestic jurisdiction concept in the interwar years. The newer approach, that of "international concern," springs from the United Nations Charter. The part played by Commonwealth countries in framing the language of the Charter on domestic jurisdiction and in projecting the "international concern" ap-

* Chairman, Department of Political Science, East Carolina College.

proach in the years since World War II provides the focus for the latter portions of this chapter.

1. Drafting the League Reservation

By the time of the Paris Peace Conference of 1919, clauses for restricting the obligation to arbitrate international disputes were already in common use.[1] The most widely copied reservation in the period from 1900 to 1919 was in the British-French Treaty of 1903.[2] Article 1 of that treaty referred to differences of a "legal nature," but excepted vital interests, independence, national honor, and interests of third parties. About eighty treaties based on this model were concluded before World War I;[3] Britain was a party to sixteen.[4] Thus, before the time came to draft the Covenant, Britain had developed a practice of protecting its domestic jurisdiction, although without employing the descriptive word "domestic."[5]

During the drafting of the Covenant, British support of domestic jurisdiction was indicated by a draft amendment which provided: "Nothing in this Covenant shall be deemed to limit the

1. See Hans Wehberg, "Restrictive Clauses in International Arbitration Treaties," 7 *Am. J. Int'l L.* 306 (1913), who listed the constitution, national honor, vital interests, sovereignty, and the rights of third states as the subjects of reservations. Amaro Cavalcanti, "Restrictive Clauses in International Arbitration Treaties," 8 *ibid.* 733 (1914), adopted the same list.

2. Robert R. Wilson, "Reservation Clauses in Agreements for Obligatory Arbitration," 23 *ibid.* 79 (1929). For text of the 1903 treaty, see 96 *Brit. & For. State Papers* 35 (1903).

3. Helen M. Cory, *Compulsory Arbitration of International Disputes* (1932), pp. 52–53.

4. Norman L. Hill, "British Arbitration Policies," *Int'l Conc.*, No. 257 (1930), pp. 89–92. The number sixteen includes the original. See also League of Nations, *Arbitration and Security: Systematic Survey of the Arbitration Conventions and Treaties of Mutual Security Deposited with the League of Nations* (1927), pp. 93, 95, 99, 112, 116, 118, 138, 140.

5. Since the domestic jurisdiction reservation in art. 15, para. 8, of the Covenant provided the pattern which replaced earlier reservations, the conclusion may be drawn that its relationship to them is conceptual. See Lawrence Preuss, "Article 2, Paragraph 7 of the Charter of the United Nations and Matters of Domestic Jurisdiction," 74 *Recueil des Cours* 558–559 (1949); Francis O. Wilcox, "The United States Accepts Compulsory Jurisdiction," 40 *Am. J. Int'l L.* 713 (1946); D. J. Llewelyn Davies, "Domestic Jurisdiction: A Limitation on International Law," 32 *Transact. Grot. Soc'y* 61 (1947).

sovereignty of the States members of the League or their right to decide their own domestic policy, except as herein expressly stated."[6] The decision not to introduce the British amendment in the twelfth meeting of the conference on March 24 has been attributed to the fact that the Wilson amendment, as proposed and adopted, covered somewhat the same ground.[7]

It has been suggested that the British amendment was drafted at a time when developments in the United States had begun to make themselves felt at Paris and that it did not "point to any anxiety on the part of the United Kingdom to protect the 'reserved domain' so much as a desire to find a compromise which would be acceptable to American opinion."[8] The force of this suggestion is somewhat weakened when it is recalled that the British were faced with a threat that the Irish might apply to the League for aid in obtaining their independence, as well as with rather strong expressions of nationalism from Canada and Australia.

Canadian and Australian expressions on domestic jurisdiction arose in connection with the Japanese proposal to add to the Covenant an endorsement of equality of nations and just treatment of their nationals. Canadian concern was expressed in a cable from the Canadian Privy Council to Sir Robert Borden, asking that all signatories to the Covenant clearly recognize that:

(1) The right of each nation to regulate and control the character of its own population by restriction of immigration is maintained unimpaired, and . . . such control is recognized as a matter of purely domestic concern and not one in which the League of Nations is concerned; (2) This Covenant does not in any way interfere with the

6. David Hunter Miller, *The Drafting of the Covenant* (1928), I, 332. As early as the Plenary Session of the conference on Feb. 14, Lord Robert Cecil expressed the British Empire view that "the League should not in any respect interfere with the internal affairs of any nation." *Ibid.*, II, 566. This preceded the development of general public opposition in the United States.

7. *Ibid.*, I, 332.

8. Charles B. H. Fincham, *Domestic Jurisdiction: The Exception of Domestic Jurisdiction as a Bar to Action by the League of Nations and the United Nations; A Contribution to the Study of Article 15, Paragraph 8, of the Covenant and Article 2, Paragraph 7, of the Charter* (1948), pp. 19–20.

fiscal freedom of Canada nor with the control or regulation of its own tariffs.[9]

The Canadians appeared to be willing to compromise with the Japanese on the racial amendment, but Hughes of Australia would accept nothing "unless it were balanced by specific protection of national control of immigration and naturalization."[10] Indeed, Hughes has been described as the "moving spirit of the Conference in opposition to the 'racial equality' clauses proposed by the Japanese which he feared might challenge the 'White Australia' principle."[11]

The United States representatives apparently opposed privately the Japanese amendment, but it was the British who presented public opposition. The British said that the amendment would encroach "upon the sovereignty of States members of the League" and that the Japanese proposal, if effective, would open the door to "serious controversy and to interference in the domestic affairs of States."[12]

In assessing the Commonwealth role in the authorship of the reservation in the Covenant, account should be taken of the fact that support of the protection of domestic jurisdiction may be evidenced in connection with matters other than the drafting of a reservation. What should be considered is a general sentiment for the idea expressed in the reservation. One writer has suggested that the Commonwealth showed a disposition to put safeguarding domestic jurisdiction higher than establishing an effective international organization.[13] Account should also be taken of the fact

9. Cited after G. P. deT. Glazebrook, *Canada at the Paris Peace Conference* (1942), pp. 69–70.

10. *Ibid.*, p. 72.

11. Gwendolyn M. Carter, *The British Commonwealth and International Security: The Role of the Dominions, 1919–1939* (1947), p. 7. Hughes pointed out that the Covenant protected domestic jurisdiction and suggested that the greatest thing which the delegation had achieved at the conference was the policy of White Australia. He boasted that "my colleagues and I have brought that great principle back to you from the Conference." Australia, *Parl. Deb.* (House), vol. 89 (1919), pp. 12172–12175. Lapradelle, in arguing the French side in the *Tunis-Morocco Nationality Decrees* case at a later date, referred to Hughes' objection to the League's interference in immigration, naturalization, and franchise laws and quoted him as saying, "No people could submit to such dictation; in such matters internal problems must remain within the domestic jurisdiction of each nation." P.C.I.J., ser. C, no. 2, at 76 (1923).

12. Miller, *op. cit. supra* note 6, at II, 389.

13. Carter, *op. cit. supra* note 11, at p. 7

that the peace conference marked an important step forward in dominion autonomy, and the delegates from the dominions were especially anxious to emphasize it by putting their imprint on the treaty.[14] Finally, it should be remembered that so far as the domestic question related to the racial equality rule, the Commonwealth voted as a unit.[15]

2. Interpreting the Concept: The Interwar Period

In the period between the two world wars, the Commonwealth generally stood as a unit in interpreting the concept of domestic jurisdiction, advocating by and large the "international obligations" approach. Positions of individual Commonwealth members emerged in the course of debate over a variety of proposed League of Nations activities. Another area in which Commonwealth views figured prominently was international adjudication, including the *Tunis-Morocco Nationality Decrees* case, the leading case on the subject of domestic jurisdiction during the era.

In the strictest sense, location of the domestic jurisdiction reservation in the League Covenant (art. 15, para. 8) limited its application to arbitration procedure. Otherwise the Council and the Assembly presumably might deal with matters of domestic jurisdiction: that is, "any matter within the sphere of action of the League or affecting the peace of the world" (arts. 3 and 4), any war or threat of war (art. 11), or economic matters and other questions generally regarded at the time as domestic. In League practice, however, members invoked the concept of domestic jurisdiction in questioning the League's competence to deal with a great variety of activities. The British Empire representative, strongly supported by the Australian and Canadian representatives, took the lead in the attempt to employ the concept to curtail the general activities of the League. The British opening attack was centered around opposition to a reference in

14. Glazebrook, *op. cit. supra* note 9, at p. v.
15. Carter, *op. cit. supra* note 11, at p. 10.

the report of the Child Welfare Committee to the need for providing "swimming baths" for children in future town planning. The British representative said that, although such subjects were of "high importance," there was a danger for the League in "thus invading the purely national sphere of its Member States lest these States should be indisposed by the interference or the real purpose of the League be obscured."[16] The discussions indicated that the Commonwealth members did not interpret the scope of article 15, paragraph 8, in a limited way.[17]

The British technique for dealing with the expansionist tendency of the League was to propose machinery to determine the question of jurisdiction in each instance. No machinery was created, but the Assembly expressed its agreement with the feelings which inspired the proposal and recognized that each body of the League should satisfy itself that proposals to it came within the scope of the League and were of real importance.[18] Incidental references implying limits on League activity continued to come from the Commonwealth, as well as other states, as the members of the League attempted to accomplish the British objective in day-to-day activities. Although reference to article 15, paragraph 8, in a narrow and legalistic way in no case served as a bar to international action, the more vague invocation of the concept, as instituted by the British, appears to have "operated as an effective brake whenever any considerable expansion of the sphere of activity of the League was proposed."[19]

16. *League of Nations Off. J.*, 7th yr., No. 7, 854–856 (1926). The British raised the same objection in the Assembly discussion; *ibid.*, 7th Ass., Spec. Supp. No. 44 at 46–48 (1926).

17. Earlier, during the discussion of the Geneva Protocol, the British representative accepted art. 5 with the statement that he did not believe it added to the powers of the League under art. 11 and suggested, somewhat enigmatically, that a cursory inspection of the Covenant might leave in some minds doubt as to the relationship of art. 15, para. 8, and the powers of the Council under art. 11. *Ibid.*, 5th Ass., Spec. Supp. No. 24, Minutes of the 1st Committee, pp. 87–88 (1924). In the Seventh Assembly discussions regarding the League's powers, the Australian delegate said that art. 15, para. 8, barred the League "even in the gravest questions—those in which the peace of the world was threatened," and that in questions which concerned only international co-operation, the League would certainly have no right to deal with domestic matters. *Ibid.*, 7th Ass., Spec. Supp. No. 45, Minutes of the 1st Committee, p. 22 (1926).

18. *Ibid.*, 7th Ass., Spec. Supp. No. 44, Plenary Meetings, pp. 46–48 (1926); *ibid.*, Spec. Supp. No. 45, Minutes of the 1st Committee, pp. 19–25, 50–51 (1926).

19. Preuss, *loc. cit. supra* note 5, at p. 570; Fincham, *op. cit. supra* note 8, at pp. 42, 70.

In the final years of the League, the British partially reversed their position in an attempt to revitalize the international organization by proposing, *inter alia*, that the Council be given power to take actions short of recommendations under article 11, paragraph 1 (threat to the peace) without the concurring votes of parties to the dispute. New Zealand, South Africa, and Canada spoke in support of the proposal.[20] If the proposal had been adopted, it would have made possible Council action in situations which, apparently, some members regarded as domestic.

Delegates to the League also attempted to define domestic jurisdiction by a process of enumerating specific matters which fell within the content of the concept. Commonwealth statements indicated that, in the opinion of some members at least, questions of slavery and minorities were not domestic. The British Empire representative said that slavery "by its very nature" must be treated as an international question.[21] On the other hand, individual members opposed League activities in such matters as child welfare,[22] unemployment,[23] tariffs,[24] status of women,[25] broadcasting,[26] exploitation of natural wealth,[27] penal administration,[28] and

20. *League of Nations Off. J.*, 19th Ass., Spec. Supp. No. 189, Minutes of the 6th Committee, pp. 20, 30, 36–37, 43–44, 46–47 (1938).
21. For examples, see *ibid.*, 6th Ass., Spec. Supp. No. 39, Minutes of the 6th Committee, p. 8; *ibid.*, 5th Ass., 359 (1924). The South African delegation was especially active in expanding the League's activities in the field of minorities. This apparently led the Indian delegate to ask them, as "the declared champions of the rights of minorities," to strive for a satisfactory settlement of the Indian problem in South Africa. League of Nations, *Records of the Third Assembly*, Plenary Meetings, I (1922), 174–176.
22. *League of Nations Off. J.*, 16th Ass., Spec. Supp. No. 142, Minutes of the 5th Committee, p. 24 (1935).
23. *Ibid.*, 7th Ass., Spec. Supp. No. 49, Minutes of the 5th Committee, p. 33 (1926).
24. *Ibid.*, 9th Ass., Spec. Supp. No. 64, Plenary Meetings, p. 42 (1928).
25. *Ibid.*, 4th Ass., Spec. Supp. No. 18, Minutes of the 5th Committee, pp. 14–15 (1923).
26. *Ibid.*, 9th Ass., Spec. Supp. No. 66, Minutes of the 2d Committee, p. 48 (1928).
27. League of Nations, *Records of the First Assembly*, Meetings of Committees, I, Minutes of the 2d Committee, p. 132.
28. Regarding a British resolution that would provide for the apointment of a committee to consider the best ways for the League to co-operate with the International Prison Commission, the Canadian delegate did not consider that the international aspect had been established. *League of Nations Off. J.*, 12th Ass., Spec. Supp. No. 98, Minutes of the 5th Committee, p. 29 (1931). India, interpreting the resolution as providing that if countries went so far wrong as to attract international attention they would not be allowed to take shelter behind the plea of nationality, was not ready to vote. New Zealand supported the resolution

amnesty.[29] League references to domestic jurisdiction in this incidental way were relatively common.[30] There was even a stimulating debate regarding alcoholic beverages, from which one might conclude that the Assembly decided that wine and beer were domestic while beverages with a higher alcoholic content were not![31]

In the interwar period, the Commonwealth made little contribution to domestic jurisdiction reservations in general arbitration treaties,[32] but in the pattern of the domestic jurisdiction reservations to the Optional Clause the Commonwealth countries took the lead. In 1929, the members of the Commonwealth, with the exception of the Irish Free State, deposited acceptances which excluded "questions which by international law fall exclusively within [their] jurisdiction." In 1945, fifteen of the acceptances of the court's jurisdiction contained similar reservations.[33]

The agency to determine whether a plea of domestic jurisdiction was justified was not named in any of the reservations. In view of the court's authority to determine its own jurisdiction under article 36, paragraph 4 (the Optional Clause article), it can be argued that the designation of the court (in the reservation) was unnecessary. One author, however, has argued that the United Kingdom, in omitting the name of the court at this point, did so in order to give itself the right to determine unilaterally whether the matter in dispute was within its domestic jurisdiction.[34]

---

since it asked only for information. The Irish Free State view was that the question might be "internal" but it constituted an international problem as well. *Ibid.*, 11th Ass., Spec. Supp. No. 89, Minutes of the 5th Committee, pp. 9–10, 13–14 (1930); *ibid.*, 16th Ass., Spec. Supp. No. 142, Minutes of the 5th Committee, p. 52 (1935).

29. *Ibid.*, 5th Yr., 386 (1927).

30. For references to many of these statements, see Walter Schiffer, *Répertoire des questions de droit international général posées devant la Societe des Nations 1920–1942* (1942).

31. *League of Nations Off. J.*, 8th Ass., Spec. Supp. No. 56, Minutes of the 2d Committee, pp. 29–32 (1927).

32. Of the sixteen new arbitration treaties from World War I to 1928, Britain was a party to only one; it retained the traditional reservations. Hill, *loc. cit. supra* note 4, at p. 93.

33. P.C.I.J., ser. D, No. 6, pp. 46–54 (1932); ser. E, No. 12, p. 335 (1935–36); ser. E, No. 15, pp. 215–216 (1938–39); ser. E, No. 16, p. 348 (1939–45).

34. H. Lauterpacht, "The British Reservations to the Optional Clause," 10 *Economica* 150–152 (1930). There is some evidence that the British, although

All the domestic jurisdiction reservations to the Optional Clause followed the Commonwealth and Covenant formulas in retaining the standard of international law to determine jurisdiction. It can be argued that the reservation of domestic jurisdiction in acceptance of Optional Clause jurisdiction was superfluous since the court was limited to the application of international law. The British themselves took the view that the reservation was "merely an explicit recognition of a limitation on the jurisdiction of the Permanent Court which results from international law itself."[35] This statement also implies the view that domestic jurisdiction will be determined by reference to legal obligations and, if that is the case, it gives further evidence of the legal emphasis during the interwar period on the concept of domestic jurisdiction. Nevertheless, it has been suggested that Australian, New Zealand, and South African officials believed the reservation necessary to protect national policies on immigration.[36]

Interwar Commonwealth acceptances of the Optional Clause referred to international law as the standard for determining domestic jurisdiction. In the *Tunis-Morocco Nationality Decrees* case, the question of the specific criteria to be applied in deciding on domestic jurisdiction arose. The British argument in the case advanced the "international obligations" approach to the problem of domestic jurisdiction. The British representative argued that, in the event of a dispute between two states in which a party relies on international treaty rights, the other party cannot make a unilateral finding that no such rights exist, and further that the mere fact that the parties to the dispute alleged international treaty rights removed not only the determination of the nature of the matter in dispute from domestic jurisdiction but also the

---

favorable to pacific settlement of disputes, were reluctant to commit themselves to submit to international tribunals in advance of the development of a dispute. Hill, *loc. cit. supra* note 4, at p. 95; Charles A. W. Manning, *The Policies of the British Dominions in the League of Nations* (1932), pp. 35–38. See also objections made by Commonwealth members to the obligatory jurisdiction of the Permanent Court of International Justice, League of Nations, *First Assembly Records* (1920), pp. 286–287, 293, 382, 496–498, 511–513.

35. Cmd. No. 3452, at p. 12 (1929).

36. Carter, *op. cit. supra* note 11, at p. 128; Lauterpacht, *loc. cit. supra* note 34, at pp. 150–151. The latter quotes a dispatch from New Zealand to the Home Government to that effect.

matter itself from domestic jurisdiction.[37] The emphasis in the British argument before the Permanent Court was that, in all its contentions, France had appealed to international law, therefore, the matter would not be within domestic jurisdiction. In all the international law relied on by the British, the intention had been only to show that the British case was also based on international law and not to present an argument on the merits of the case. The British argument ended with the statement that "whereas questions of Treaty obligations are by international law necessarily outside the exclusive domestic jurisdiction of any one state" the court should rule that the League Council had jurisdiction.[38] The court accepted the British contention that reliance on international law by the parties of itself removed a matter from domestic jurisdiction.

As previously indicated, the "international obligations" approach to domestic jurisdiction was rooted in the language of the League Covenant. The composition of the League and of the Commonwealth itself at that time also affected the interpretation of the concept. But all of these factors changed with the demise of the League and the advent of the United Nations.

3. Drafting the Charter Reservation

No one state can be confidently credited with originating the domestic jurisdiction reservation in the Charter of the United Nations. Although it has been reported that the British proposed the Dumbarton Oaks version,[39] authorship at San Francisco became somewhat hidden by the decision of the four sponsoring governments to propose a joint amendment regarding domestic jurisdiction. The role of Australia, however, in amending the proposal of the sponsoring governments is clear. The Australian representative, Herbert V. Evatt, was active in the debates

37. P.C.I.J., ser. C, No. 2 (1923).
38. *Ibid.*, pp. 193–211, 245.
39. See Cordell Hull, *Memoirs* (1948), II, 1705; Ruth B. Russell, *A History of the United Nations Charter: The Role of the United States 1940–1945* (1958), p. 463.

regarding the entire reservation, and he spoke strongly for the ambiguous language in the reservation (apparently with a view of expanding the effect of the reservation) that has been, along with the Australian-amended exception to the reservation, a factor in the postwar interpretive changes. Evatt opposed the proposal to make the organization the judge of its own activities. He favored the qualifying term "essentially" over "solely" (which had been used in the Covenant) because matters solely within domestic jurisdiction were constantly contracting. Nor did he see any need for expressly mentioning "international law" as the standard for determining domestic jurisdiction since there was no other possible standard.[40]

When the four sponsoring governments proposed the transfer of the domestic jurisdiction reservation to the second chapter of the Charter in order to give it general application, but excepted from that application Security Council action under what is now chapter 7, Australia pressed a proviso which would limit the exception to enforcement action (as distinguished from recommendation). The sponsoring governments at first opposed the change. But after "very heavy pressure"[41] had broken the solidarity of the sponsoring governments, the United Kingdom delegate agreed that the jealously guarded rights of national jurisdiction should not be infringed unless a dispute had become so serious that there was a threat of war. He announced that he saw "considerable force" in the Australian argument and would vote for the proposal.[42] It would appear in fact that there was never great reluctance on the part of the United Kingdom government to support the Australian position;[43] in the Australian House of Representatives a government spokesman paid tribute to the assistance given the Australian delegation by the United Kingdom on this change "which placed the power of the Australian Parliament in this matter beyond all question."[44] New Zealand

---

40. 6 *U.N. Conf. Int'l Org. Docs.* 511–512 (1945).
41. Herbert V. Evatt, *The United Nations* (1947), pp. 15–16.
42. 6 *U.N. Conf. Int'l Org. Docs.* 498 (1945).
43. Viscount Cranborne, a delegate to the conference, mentioned this action favorably in Parliament; 137 *H. L. Deb.* (5th ser.) col. 119 (1945).
44. Australia, *Parl. Deb.* (House), vol. 184 (1945), p. 5123.

official reports also establish that state's close support of the Australian position.[45]

Yet, despite the apparently broader language of the domestic jurisdiction reservation in the Charter, efforts to narrow the effect of the concept quickly appeared after the founding of the United Nations. Indeed, by a somewhat curious shift of circumstances, it fell to the Australian delegate to advance the "international concern" approach to domestic jurisdiction in the first important situation to come before the United Nations.

4. The Reservation and United Nations Action

Although the question of domestic jurisdiction arose in a wide variety of situations in the early years of the United Nations, the discussions of the problems of the relationships of member nations with the Franco regime in Spain and of the racial policies of the Union of South Africa dominated the postwar development of the concept. The Australian delegate, Herbert V. Evatt, assumed leadership in the clarification of the domestic jurisdiction reservation as it applied in the Spanish case. In doing so, he formulated the first clear statement of the doctrine of "international concern." The racial policies discussions were initiated by India, and the leading support for the opposing concepts of domestic jurisdiction came from the two Commonwealth countries most closely involved. South Africa strongly presented the legal concept of domestic jurisdiction in an effort to limit international competence. India, following Evatt's initial definition, elaborated again and again the political concept.

In neither of the two cases was the concept of domestic jurisdiction invoked to protect a popular cause. In the latter case, for example, the older members of the Commonwealth showed some dismay that a Commonwealth dispute was before the international organization and halfheartedly and sporadically

45. New Zealand, Dep't of External Affairs Pub. No. 11, *United Nations Conference on International Organization* (1945), p. 28; see also Eugene P. Chase, "Peter Fraser at San Francisco," 11 *Political Science* 17, at p. 20 (1959).

supported South Africa, but the overwhelming majorities in vote after vote followed the leadership of India in supporting the movement to end racial discrimination. Perhaps the most significant result was not the curtailment of unpopular actions but the revision of the domestic jurisdiction concept.

The way in which the Spanish case was introduced to the Security Council and the division it brought between the Soviet bloc and the free world, as well as the unpopularity of the Franco regime, influenced the situation in which the Australian delegation worked. Poland brought the case under articles 34 and 35 of the Charter (Pacific Settlement of Disputes) to which the domestic jurisdiction reservation in article 2, paragraph 7, applies.[46] Noting that the Polish delegate had not sought to establish a case under Chapter 7 and denying any advocacy on behalf of the Spanish government, the United Kingdom delegate raised the question of competence in view of the fact that the nature of the regime in any country is "indisputably a matter of domestic jurisdiction."[47] The Australian delegate agreed, but added in terms that were to recur: *"Prima facie,* then, this question is one of domestic jurisdiction. But the line between what is of international concern and what is domestic concern is not fixed, it is mutable."[48]

Standing between the United Kingdom doubts regarding competence and the Soviet bloc's insistence on immediate action, the Australian delegation proposed the establishment of a subcommittee to determine the issue of competence before taking action. Australia drafted two resolutions putting questions to the committee. The first asked if the Spanish situation was essentially within the jurisdiction of Spain,[49] and the second asked if the existence of the Franco regime was a matter of "international concern and not one essentially within the jurisdiction of Spain."[50] After Dutch objection to the introduction of "international concern," a concept which did "not find support in the Charter," the

46. The exception at the end of the paragraph refers to *enforcement* measures under chap. 7.

47. *U.N. Security Council Off. Rec.* 1st Yr., 1st ser., No. 2, 35th meeting 181 (1946).

48. *Ibid.,* p. 195.

49. *Ibid.,* p. 198.

50. *Ibid.,* 37th meeting 216.

Australians agreed to delete the term. The final compromise between Poland, Australia, and France simply asked the subcommittee to determine whether the situation in Spain had led to international friction and endangered international peace and security.[51] The United Kingdom supported the compromise resolution with the reservation that the Spanish government would have to be proved a threat to the peace before the Security Council could take any action.[52]

Evatt, reporting as chairman of the subcommittee which he appeared to influence strongly, said that although the group did not find that the activities of the Franco regime constituted an "existing threat to the peace, within the meaning of Article 39 of the Charter," it found that the activities did constitute a "situation which is a potential menace to international peace and security, and which is therefore a situation the continuation of which is likely to endanger the maintenance of international peace and security within the meaning of Article 34."[53] The subcommittee report blurred further the already hazy distinction between a dispute the continuance of which is likely to endanger the maintenance of international peace and security (article 33, to which the domestic jurisdiction reservation applies) and a threat to the peace (article 39, to which it does not apply regarding enforcement action).

The subcommittee's distinction was not as clear on the doctrine of international concern as was Evatt when he spoke to the Security Council. He disposed of the applicability of the domestic jurisdiction reservation to article 33 by saying:

Now, in *my* opinion, . . . it should be pointed out quite clearly that Article 2, paragraph 7 of the Charter does not say that the United Nations should not intervene in any matter which does not fall within Chapter VII. What it does say is that the United Nations shall not intervene in a matter essentially within the domestic jurisdiction of a State. . . . The facts are that there is a situation the continuance of which, in the finding of the Sub-Committee, is likely to endanger the maintenance of international peace and security. That situation has

51. *Ibid.*, pp. 225, 229, 239.
52. *Ibid.*, pp. 231–232.
53. *Ibid.*, 44th meeting 315.

already led to strong expressions of concern and disapproval by various Governments and to the closing of a frontier. There is a record of past participation in the Second World War and of recent action hindering the victorious Allies in removing the vestiges of Nazism. Various Governments, Members of the United Nations, have already broken off diplomatic relations and recognized a rival Government. All this is a matter of vital international concern. The situation, I submit, is the complete antithesis of an essentially domestic situation.[54]

Evatt's construction extended the exception of actions regarding a threat to the peace (or the assumption that a threat to the peace is not domestic) to cover less explosive situations under Chapter 6, and in so doing, he made the assumption that these less serious matters also ceased to be domestic.

On the basis of Evatt's construction, the General Assembly passed a resolution on Spain in 1947, thereby establishing that the doctrine would be used by that body as well as the Security Council even though at that time the General Assembly had not developed its authority to deal with a threat to the peace when the Security Council was stalemated by a veto. The concept of international concern has been used by other delegations in other situations,[55] but the issue between the legal and political concepts of domestic jurisdiction developed most fully in the questions regarding racial discrimination in the Union of South Africa.[56]

India brought the first racial discrimination case to the first session of the General Assembly under the heading of "Treatment of Indians in the Union of South Africa." A few years later India and other Asiatic countries brought an additional charge concerning the South African policy of *apartheid*. In the Seventeenth Session of the Assembly, the two were joined and debated together, and the attack on South Africa was led so aggressively by African states that the Asiatic position began to seem moderate. The cases have been perennial and the arguments of the two sides have been much duplicated, but the argument for interna-

54. *Ibid.*, pp. 317–318. Italics added.
55. For examples, *ibid.*, 2d year, 173d meeting 1684 (1947); *ibid.*, 4th year, 403d meeting 3 (No. 7) (1949); *ibid.*, 6th year, 563d meeting 1 (1951); *U.N. Gen. Ass. Off. Rec.* 1st Sess., pt. 2, 59th Plenary 1220 (1946); *ibid.*, 5th Sess., Ad Hoc Pol. Comm. 255 (1950), Vol. IV.
56. Herbert W. Briggs, "The United Nations and Political Decision of Legal Questions," *Proc. Am. Soc'y Int'l L. 1948*, pp. 42–53.

tional intervention has had a different emphasis in the two cases. In the Indian case, the emphasis has been on international obligations, some legal and some moral or political. In the *Apartheid* case, the emphasis has been on the international repercussions of the race conflict in South Africa. Opposition to international jurisdiction has been based on the contention that the matter would cease to be domestic only when regulated by binding, legal obligations.

South Africa has presented the legal argument in statements that have followed rather closely the construction developed during the League of Nations period. Starting from the premise that a binding legal obligation removes a matter from domestic jurisdiction, the South Africans argued the absence of such obligations. Regarding the bilateral agreements relied on by India, South Africa denied that they were true international agreements; regarding the Charter provisions on human rights, South Africa said they were too vague to be binding.[57]

In its application to the United Nations regarding the treatment of Indians, India pointed out that reactions in India to the South African policy had been "so serious" that India had to terminate trade arrangements and recall its high commissioner. The situation was "likely to impair friendly relations." Furthermore, the South African treatment violated fundamental principles of the Charter, and India had "moral and political obligations" toward the South Africans of Indian ancestry. Although India relied on the Capetown Agreement between India and South Africa, the Indian appeal said the question was "a political and not a legal one." Its "potential consequences" made it a world problem, and the United Nations must exercise its "moral sanction" to solve it.[58]

57. Noting that South Africa pleaded that the Capetown Agreement relied on by India could not remove the question from domestic jurisdiction because it was not an instrument creating international rights and obligations, R. Y. Jennings adds: "It is important to appreciate the true nature of the Union's argument. It is not that the matter being *inter se* is therefore domestic in the sense of international law. It is that the two agreements relied on by India, being *inter se* agreements and intended as such, were therefore not treaties, and therefore could not be said to take the issue out of the domestic sphere. . . ." "The Commonwealth and International Law," 30 *Brit. Yb. Int'l L.* 337 (1953).

58. *U.N. Gen. Ass. Off. Rec.* 1st Sess., pt. 2, Jt. Comm. of 1st and 6th Comms. 3, 52–53 (1946). See also *India and the United Nations* (1957), pp. 110, 113.

When reference was made to obligations on human rights, the Indians argued that such obligations did not have to be spelled out in detail and that South Africa was obligated by virtue of being "a party to the resolution protesting against racial persecution and discrimination recently adopted by the General Assembly."[59]

In 1947, newly admitted Pakistan joined India and injected more political argument. Ignoring the jurisdictional question entirely, the Pakistani delegate said that even if the International Court of Justice pronounced the question to be purely domestic, it would not hasten the solution of the problem, which, however, had to be solved.[60] In the Third Session of the General Assembly, the Indian delegate clearly added the repercussions argument to the other bases for international jurisdiction by referring to the "very tense situation" created by the African policy and the "gravest consequences" of it outside Africa.[61] If allowed to continue, he said, it "would become a potential threat to the peace."[62]

The United Kingdom delegate said that impairment of friendly relations did not give the United Nations the right to intervene and that it was very difficult to determine at what stage the impairment of friendly relations in a qualified fashion superseded article 2, paragraph 7.[63]

Thirteen Asiatic countries introduced the question of "Race Conflict in South Africa Resulting from the Policy of Apartheid" by saying that it was creating "a dangerous and explosive situation, which constitutes both a threat to international peace

---

59. *U.N. Gen. Ass. Off. Rec.* 1st Sess., pt. 2., Vol. IV, Jt. Comm. of 1st and 6th Comms. 10–12 (1946). When the Hyderabad case was before the Security Council, the delegate of Pakistan answered the Indian plea of domestic jurisdiction by saying that the question was just as political and humanitarian in nature as the South African case and took India to task for trying to argue two different ways in the two cases. *U.N. Security Council Off. Rec.* 4th year, 425th meeting 13–15 (1949). See Clyde Eagleton, "The Case of Hyderabad Before the Security Council," 44 *Am. J. Int'l L.* 277 (1950).

60. *U.N. Gen. Ass. Off. Rec.* 2d Sess., Vol. III, 1st Comm. 451 (1947). In the Thirteenth Session, the delegate of Pakistan distinguished between the two racial questions by saying the treatment of Indians case "hinges mainly on an international agreement and involves certain contractual obligations" between India and South Africa and involves basic principles of the United Nations. *Ibid.*, 13th Sess., Vol. II, Plenary 466–467 (1958).

61. *Ibid.*, 3rd Sess., pt. 2, 1st Comm. 256 (1949).

62. *Ibid.*, Vol. I, Plenary 438 (1949).

63. *Ibid.*, 2d Sess., Vol. IV, 1st Comm. 454 (1947).

and a flagrant violation of the basic principles of human rights and fundamental freedoms."[64] India made passing reference to obligations, but the emphasis clearly was on repercussions. India referred to "a dangerous tension . . . imperilling the entire continent of Africa" and "widespread indignation." In a rare attempt to define a potential threat to the peace, the Indian delegate said that:

The concept of a threat to peace was not confined to the case of a threat to the territorial integrity and political independence of a State. A threat to peace might assume various forms. A situation where there might be only a potential threat to peace was nonetheless likely to endanger the maintenance of international peace. Flagrant breaches of human rights by the government of a State would have serious repercussions outside that State and could affect international peace.[65]

During the same session, the United Kingdom delegate said that "tension" did not remove a matter from domestic jurisdiction.[66] Two years later, the Indian delegate said that questions "which would be subject only to domestic jurisdiction in periods of peace and stability were, in times of upheaval like the present, no longer essentially within that domestic jurisdiction."[67]

New members of the Commonwealth have joined the side of India and Pakistan. In the Eleventh and Twelfth Sessions of the General Assembly, the delegate of Ceylon denied that the racial problem in South Africa was domestic because it was a situation which was a source of tension and because it was covered by the human rights provisions of the Charter.[68] In the Twelfth Session Ghana's representative emphasized that the racial policies violated the Charter and that the domestic jurisdiction reservation should not be cited in a human rights case.[69] In the Thirteenth Session, Malaya joined in submitting a resolution on *apartheid,* and the Malayan delegate relied on the human rights provisions

64. *Ibid.,* 7th Sess., Vol. II, Annexes II, Agenda Item No. 66, at 2 (1952–53).
65. *Ibid.,* Vol. V, Ad Hoc Pol. Comm. 67–68, 96 (1952–53).
66. *Ibid.,* Vol. I, Plenary 62 (1952–53).
67. *Ibid.,* 9th Sess., Ad Hoc Pol. Comm. 204 (1954).
68. *Ibid.,* 11th Sess. Vol. VI, Spec. Pol. Comm. 35, 62 (1957); *ibid.,* 12th Sess. Vol. V, Spec. Pol. Comm. 87, 88 (1957).
69. *Ibid.,* pp. 52, 89.

and a claim that international peace was threatened to override the domestic jurisdiction plea.[70]

In the Thirteenth Session of the Assembly Ghana introduced the *apartheid* question by saying that since racialism was a threat to the very foundations of international peace and security, no member of the United Nations should be allowed to prevent discussion on the question on the pretext that it was domestic. He termed the South African policy an "affront to the conscience of the civilized world" that had "repercussions on race relations everywhere." He wondered if anyone could continue to doubt that the question of race conflict had become "such a threat to the peace as to constitute a matter of international concern."[71] In the following session, the delegate of Ghana increased the attack as he opened the debate again and assumed the role of spokesman for the oppressed groups. He said that the Africans in South Africa had had enough of *apartheid*. He reported that they were pleased with the affirmative votes of the United States, Canada, and New Zealand in the previous year and now appealed "through the delegation of Ghana" to the United Kingdom and Australia not to vote against the draft resolution.[72] In the general debate of the same session, the delegate of Ghana said that the independence of Ghana was meaningless unless it could be used to help other African peoples to be free and independent.[73] Other

70. *Ibid.*, 13th Sess. Vol. 2 Plenary 192 (1958); *ibid.*, Vol. 4, Spec. Pol. Comm. 31 (1958).

71. *Ibid.*, p. 7. The delegate of Ceylon said during the same meetings that the policies of racial discrimination, if allowed to continue, would create, "a situation which would be a threat to peace." *Ibid.*, p. 33. The newer Commonwealth members have made similar statements in other cases. The Indian delegate said that the dispute between Indonesia and the Netherlands was not a domestic issue because it had "forced 19 different countries in Asia and in the Pacific to meet at very short notice and to pass a unanimous resolution indicating the gravity of the situation." *U.N. Security Council Off. Rec.* 4th year, 403d meeting 3 (1949). Ghana's spokesman said that the Algerian question was not domestic because it was "of immediate and vital concern to every independent State." *U.N. Gen. Ass. Off. Rec.* 13th Sess., Vol. IV, 1st Comm. 350 (1958). Other delegations have implied that a matter is removed from domestic jurisdiction to international concern because of its "importance" or its "great importance." *U.N. Security Council Off. Rec.* 2d year, 172d meeting 1657 (1947); *ibid.*, 3d year, 392d meeting 10 (1948); *U.N. Gen. Ass. Off. Rec.* 5th Sess., Vol. IV Ad Hoc Pol. Comm. 256 (1950).

72. *Ibid.*, 14th Sess. Vol. IV, Spec. Pol. Comm. 67–68 (1959). In the vote, the United Kingdom voted against the resolution and Australia and Canada abstained. New Zealand joined the new members in voting for the resolution. *Ibid.*, p. 102.

73. *Ibid.*, Vol. 2 Plenary 162 (1959).

new members have joined Ghana in urging United Nations action to bring about independence of dependent peoples and have denied that such action violates domestic jurisdiction.[74] In the Fifteenth Session of the General Assembly, the Nigerian delegate said that the patience of his government was exhausted and that racial discrimination could never be regarded as being within domestic jurisdiction.[75]

When the United Kingdom delegate, followed by Australia, finally made the decision to vote for a resolution dealing with the racial situation in South Africa, he justified the change of position on the repercussions from the new developments in South Africa.[76] Since there was no new international obligation on this matter, that was the only explanation available for a change at that time.

Also, there have been occasions when Commonwealth proponents of the essentially legal "international obligations" approach have abandoned it in favor of "practical" arguments against United Nations action. For example, practical arguments were particularly outstanding in the Cyprus case. When the question was before the General Assembly in 1954, the United Kingdom delegate said that article 2, paragraph 7, "was applicable in its entirety," but he also argued that discussion would serve no useful purpose.[77] Apparently the latter argument carries some weight, for, after a discussion largely devoted to practicalities, the plenary session dropped the item by a vote of fifty to none with eight absentions.[78] The United Kingdom delegate interpreted this action as support of the view put forward that, legal considerations apart, discussion of the issue would acheive no useful purpose.[79]

74. *Ibid.*, 11th Sess. Vol. III, Plenary 1105 (1957); *ibid.*, 12th Sess., 1st Comm. 205, 229, 275–276, 303; *ibid.*, (1957) 13th Sess., 1st Comm. 368 (1958); *ibid.*, 14th Sess., 1st Comm. 277 (1959).
75. *Ibid.*, 15th Sess. Vol. 4, pt. 1, Spec. Pol. Comm., pt. 2, 41 (1961).
76. *Ibid.*, p. 77.
77. *Ibid.*, 9th Sess., Vol. 2, Gen. Comm. 8 (1954); *ibid.*, Plenary 53 (1954).
78. *Ibid.*, p. 539. The item had originally been placed on the agenda by a vote of thirty to nineteen (eleven abstentions). *Ibid.*, p. 60.
79. *Ibid.*, p. 539. Among other things, the Indian delegate claimed in the Hyderabad case that discussion could serve no useful purpose and would disrupt internal peace in India. *U.N. Security Council Off. Rec.*, 4th year, 425th meeting 7 (1949).

When the question of Cyprus was reintroduced in the 1955 session, the United Kingdom delegate hardly mentioned the domestic jurisdiction reservation.[80] The Greek delegate charged that this was an indication that the United Kingdom delegate had no conviction on that point and had put it forward merely to still "his colonial conscience."[81] In reply, the United Kingdom delegate said that the burden of his argument had rested not on article 2, paragraph 7, but on whether a settlement could not better be found by quiet diplomacy conducted in private.[82] This practical approach was supported by the Indian delegate, although he declared that the matter was not domestic.[83] It must have again found favor with the Assembly, for the plenary session decided not to include the item on the agenda.[84]

The older Commonwealth members also used the practical arguments in the West Irian dispute[85] and in the cases involving the French North African territories.[86]

5. The Reservation and the International Court of Justice

In regard to the International Court of Justice, the concept of domestic jurisdiction has figured prominently in reservations in acceptances of the Optional Clause and in a number of cases taken to the court. With respect to the Optional Clause, it was the United States and not a Commonwealth member that set the pace with its reservation of domestic jurisdiction "as determined by the

80. *U.N. Gen. Ass. Off. Rec.* 10th Sess., Vol. 3, Gen. Comm. 2–3 (1955).
81. *Ibid.*, Vol. 2, Plenary 54 (1955).
82. *Ibid.*, p. 56.
83. *Ibid.*, p. 62.
84. *Ibid.*, p. 65. The older Commonwealth members have made frequent references throughout the South African cases to the impracticality of United Nations discussion. During the Suez crisis references to "sovereignty" were more frequent than references to "domestic jurisdiction" John M. Howell, "The Application of Concepts of Domestic Jurisdiction and Aggression in the Suez Crisis," 4 *Tulane Studies in Pol. Sci.* 51–55 (1957).
85. *U.N. Gen. Ass. Off. Rec.* 9th Sess., Vol. 2, Gen. Comm. 3, 4 (1954); *ibid.*, Plenary 46–47 (1954); *ibid.*, Vol. 3, 1st Comm. 405, 417, 447, 453 (1954); *ibid.*, 10th Sess., Vol. 3, Gen. Comm. 16, 17 (1955); *ibid.*, Vol. 2, Plenary 229 (1955).
86. *Ibid.*, 10th Sess., Vol. 3; Gen. Comm. 12 (1955); *ibid.*, 7th Sess., Vol. 1, Plenary 279 (1952); *ibid.*, 8th Sess., Vol. 3, 1st Comm. 70 (1953).

United States" in its declaration of acceptance.[87] Of the Commonwealth members, South Africa (no longer in the Commonwealth), Pakistan, and India have deposited declarations with
reservations that follow closely the United States pattern of
matters "essentially within the domestic jurisdiction" as determined by the state concerned.[88] India replaced its Covenant-type
reservation with the broader reservation on January 9, 1956, after
Portugal initiated the *Right of Passage over Indian Territory* case.
A year later the Indian government terminated its acceptance of
Optional Clause jurisdiction and did not re-establish it until
January, 1960, at which time it reserved matters essentially within
the jurisdiction without claiming a right of unilateral determination.[89] By a new declaration of September 12, 1960, Pakistan
also returned to the original Commonwealth formula.[90] The
United Kingdom, apparently fearful that its nuclear testing
program might be involved in a case in which the court might
issue interim orders of protection pending the determination of
the jurisdictional question, deposited, in 1957, a national security
reservation which left the determination of national security to
the United Kingdom.[91] With some looseness of application, such a
national security reservation could accomplish the same protection as the United States reservation.[92] The United Kingdom
government rescinded the reservation in November, 1958,[93] and
returned to the form of domestic jurisdiction reservation devised
in 1929.

Following the use of the French reservation by Norway to
block a case brought to the court by France, the French government, in July, 1959, replaced its reservation with one on the

87. 1 U.N.T.S. 10; T.I.A.S. No. 1598.
88. [1958–1959] I.C.J.Y.B. 219, 224–225; [1955–56] *ibid.* 192.
89. [1959–1960] *ibid.* 241–242.
90. [1960–1961] *ibid.* 210–211.
91. [1957–1958] *ibid.* 211.
92. When asked during the debate on the Queen's speech whether he thought
the new British reservation would cover the same areas as the United States
reservation, the Foreign Secretary answered rather ambiguously, but later added:
"It seems to me . . . that one has to preserve the essential rights of this
country. . . . I maintain that if we exercise our rights, our proceedings should not
be subject to the jurisdiction of the International Court unless everybody accepts
the same jurisdiction." 577 *H.C.* Deb. (5th ser.) cols 475–476 (1957–58).
93. [1958–1959] I.C.J.Y.B. 225–226.

League and British pattern.[94] These developments cannot yet be taken as a trend to narrow the effect of the reservation, but the British reversal can perhaps be taken as a step in the direction of heading off a still broader expansion of the scope of the concept of domestic jurisdiction as used in acceptances of the Optional Clause.

In proceedings before the International Court, the point of domestic jurisdiction has been raised in several cases in which Commonwealth members have appeared. An early case was the Advisory Opinion on the *Interpretation of the Peace Treaties with Bulgaria, Hungary, and Romania.* The United Kingdom representative argued that the allegation of a treaty obligation removed the matter from domestic jurisdiction. He did not examine the content of the treaty to determine the degree of regulation. He argued that the "matter" before the court could not be domestic, for the proceedings were on a point of treaty interpretation or whether or not there had been a breach of a treaty. Such questions were "essentially and inherently matters of international jurisdiction."[95] The court decided upon its jurisdiction to give an Advisory Opinion on a limited examination of the law involved. The object of the request for an opinion had been solely that of obtaining from the court clarifications of a legal nature regarding the applicability of the procedure for the settlement of disputes under the peace treaty. "The interpretation of the terms of a treaty for this purpose could not be considered as a question essentially within the domestic jurisdiction of a State. It is a question of international law, which, by its very nature, lies within the competence of the Court."[96] This conclusion of the court followed the British reasoning, which in turn followed the *Tunis-Morocco* case precedent.

The United Kingdom also relied on the *Tunis-Morocco* precedent in an attempt to establish the jurisdiction of the International Court of Justice in the *Anglo-Iranian Oil Company* case in 1951. The United Kingdom agreed that the mere fact that a party

94. *Ibid.,* p. 212.
95. *I.C.J. Pleadings,* Interpretation of the Peace Treaties with Bulgaria, Hungary and Romania, pp. 315–324.
96. [1950] I.C.J. Rep. 70–71.

relied on international law was not enough to remove a matter from domestic jurisdiction, but that the grounds relied on must be of juridical importance. The United Kingdom delegate interpreted the nature of the domestic jurisdiction reservation in these words:

(*a*) An act is not within the "jurisdiction" . . . of a State if it relates to a matter as to which the discretionary power of the State is limited . . . by rules of international law or treaty obligation, and, in performing the act, the State infringes any of those rules or obligations.

(*b*) The question whether a matter is one as to which the discretionary power of the State is limited . . . can never be a question within the jurisdiction . . . of the State, but must be determined objectively.

(*c*) The question whether the State, when performing the act, did or did not infringe any rule of international law or treaty obligation cannot be a question within the "jurisdiction" . . . of the State, but must be determined objectively.[97]

Apparently the grounds were of juridical importance when it could be established (as of course it could) that international law, in principle, regulated the abrogation of foreign concessions.[98]

In the *Ambatielos* case (Obligation to Arbitrate) in 1952, the British were on the opposite side of the issue, and when the question of domestic jurisdiction arose the British representative asked for a *prima facie* finding that the claim of Greece was "based" on some provision of the treaty involved in the case. The Greeks would need to show that some provision of the treaty had been violated. Greece should prove "beyond all reasonable doubt" that the claim was based on the treaty; there must be "a *prima facie* connexity between the treaty and the Ambatielos claim."[99] This proof did not mean that Greece must show that the claim was "well founded" in the treaty, but that it was "founded."

Quoting with favor the British distinction between "founded" and "well founded," the court said that the Greek argument must be of "a sufficiently plausible character to warrant a conclusion

97. *ICJ, Pleadings, Anglo-Iranian Oil Company* case, pp. 353–354.
98. *Ibid.*, pp. 156, 159.
99. *ICJ, Pleadings, Ambatielos* case, pp. 378, 382, 383, 387.

that the claim is based on the treaty." It would not be necessary to show that an alleged treaty violation had an unassailable legal basis. The validity of the arguments presented would be determined by the Commission of Arbitration in passing upon the merits of the difference. If the interpretation given by the Hellenic government to any of the provisions relied upon appeared to be one of the possible interpretations that might be placed upon it, though not necessarily the correct one, the Ambatielos claim would be considered to be a claim based on the Treaty of 1886.[100]

Adopting the British construction, the International Court of Justice went much further in its general statement than the older court did in the *Tunis-Morocco* case. The provisional conclusion as it was applied in the *Tunis-Morocco* case called for a much more superficial examination than did the requirement of a *prima facie* case in the *Ambatielos* claim. But, though the court adopted the British construction, there did not appear to be a great difference in actual practice. Having regard for the contentions of the parties on the scope of the most-favored-nation clause, as well as the divergence of views concerning the meaning of the expression "free access to the Courts of Justice" contained in the treaty, and bearing in mind especially the interpretations of these provisions contended for by the Hellenic government, the court concluded that the case was based on the provisions of the treaty and that the United Kingdom had an obligation to submit to arbitration.[101]

When India claimed domestic jurisdiction in the *Right of Passage over Indian Territory* case in 1957, the conclusion of the court resulted in a Commonwealth member's failure to maintain a domestic jurisdiction plea. India argued that no part of the law relied on by the Portuguese justified the "provisional conclusion

100. [1953] I.C.J. Rep. 18–21. As in the case of the *Tunis-Morocco Nationality Decrees*, the court was faced with giving a decision on the jurisdiction of another body. The Greek claim was based on a Treaty of 1886 and a Declaration of 1926, under which the United Kingdom had obligations to submit to arbitration. The British defense before the court was that the claim was not related to the treaties. The court was not called upon to decide the merits of the case; that was for the Commission of Arbitration. The court was simply deciding whether the United Kingdom had an obligation to submit to arbitration.

101. [1953] *ibid.* 22.

that they are of real importance judicially for determining the legal position of the Parties with respect to the passage of Portuguese persons and goods."[102] Furthermore, the Portuguese claim was not reasonably arguable under international law unless based on express grant, for right to transit traditionally had been held to be within control of the territorial sovereign.[103] Again the court ruled that the facts were disputed by the parties and that it would not be possible to pronounce on India's domestic jurisdiction reservation without prejudging the merits. Accordingly, the court joined the objections to the merits.[104] Portugal, the other party, continued to argue on the merits that the fact that all parties relied on international law removed the matter from domestic jurisdiction. Although there was reference to the validity of these claims, the argument on the merits was not a principal one. The court, referring to India's domestic jurisdiction plea (then joined to the merits), said:

to claim that such an obligation is binding upon India, to invoke, *whether rightly or wrongly*, such principles is to place oneself on the plane of international law. Indeed, in the course of the proceedings both parties took their stand upon that ground and on occasion expressly said so. To decide upon the validity of those principles . . . , upon such obligation of India toward Portugal, and upon the alleged failure to fulfill that obligation, does not fall exclusively within the jurisdiction of India.[105]

Despite its rejection of India's plea of domestic jurisdiction, the International Court found that India had not acted contrary to her international obligations.

As the cases discussed above indicate, the record of the Commonwealth in using the concept of domestic jurisdiction before the International Court reveals some fluctuations. In the end, however, the "international obligations" approach expressed in the *Tunis-Morocco Nationality Decrees* case appears to have prevailed. Some wavering has also marked the record of Commonwealth nations in regard to the domestic jurisdiction reservation in acceptances of the Optional Clause. Several Common-

102. [1957] *ibid.* 131.
103. *Ibid.*, p. 149.
104. *Ibid.*, p. 150.
105. [1960] *ibid.* 33. Italics added.

wealth members adopted the "Connally" type of reservation first used by the United States, but they later returned to the form of reservation developed in the period between the two world wars.

6. The Changing Concept

The concept of domestic jurisdiction implies a sphere in which states may act with complete discretion and be held accountable neither by another state nor any international organization for actions taken within that sphere. The language of the League Covenant domestic jurisdiction reservation, article 15, paragraph 8, indicated that international law provided the standard for determining the extent and bounds of this discretionary, domestic sphere. Members of the Commonwealth took an active part in the framing of the Covenant provision on domestic jurisdiction.

In the interwar period, Commonwealth nations generally discouraged League activities in areas deemed to be domestic, at least in their eyes. By and large, Commonwealth members interpreted the concept of domestic jurisdiction from a legal point of view which stressed the "international obligations" approach to the concept. This approach marked the British argument and the Permanent Court of International Justice's opinion in the *Tunis-Morocco Nationality Decrees* case. The approach maintains that matters are domestic if a state has no international obligations regarding them, and, on the whole, it would retain a rather wide area for domestic jurisdiction. On the other hand, the "international obligations" approach rejects unilateral determination of the domestic sphere and confirms international law as the standard in this respect.

In the drafting of the domestic jurisdiction reservation in the United Nations Charter, article 2, paragraph 7, Commonwealth nations, especially Australia, again played an active role. In the main, their efforts were directed toward broadening the effects of the domestic jurisdiction provision in the Charter.

Since the founding of the United Nations, lack of uniformity among Commonwealth countries in their approach to the concept of domestic jurisdiction has been the case. During the League of Nations period, there was less open difference between members of the Commonwealth. In the United Nations period, the new Asiatic and African members have raised colonial and racial questions involving domestic jurisdiction. This difference has been a source of new developments in the concept, and leadership in this change has come from "new" Commonwealth members, notably India.

The "new" Commonwealth members have argued that matters are domestic only if they concern but one state or if they have no international repercussions. The "repercussions" approach has been developed in the doctrine of "international concern." Briefly stated, the doctrine holds that whenever a matter constitutes a *potential* threat to the peace, it ceases to be a matter of domestic jurisdiction and becomes a matter of concern of the international community. The "concern" justifies action in regard to the matter or establishes international jurisdiction.

Whether "new" Commonwealth members will consistently advocate the "international concern" doctrine in all cases, especially those in which it is invoked regarding events occurring within their own boundaries, remains to be seen. Experience before both the political and judicial organs of the United Nations suggests that a "new" Commonwealth member may abandon "international concern" for the "international obligations" approach when its own actions and policies are called into question. Conversely, the record indicates that "old" Commonwealth countries will at times embrace the "international concern" doctrine.

In sum, the Commonwealth has played a most influential role in the development and interpretation of the concept of domestic jurisdiction. On the whole, the position of the Commonwealth has supported the international law standard as the proper standard for delimitation of the sphere of domestic jurisdiction. At issue in the differences which have appeared among Commonwealth members is whether future development of the international law standard will result in reservation of a relatively wide area for domestic jurisdiction or in enlargement of the range of matters committed to international jurisdiction.

7

European Integration

*Herman Walker**

The juxtaposition of Commonwealth and Common Market evokes a picture of contrast. Communities both, they differ sharply in scope and composition, in character, in technique, and in tendency. The one is scattered, heterogeneous, loose-jointed, and moving away from union; the other, compact, relatively homogeneous, highly organized, and in the process of integration.

Contrast does not of itself imply opposition. The emergence in western Europe of the Common Market (European Economic Community or EEC) in face of the older Commonwealth, however, opened questions of rivalry, compatibility, and terms of co-existence. These come to a head in the much-publicized negotiation, in the early sixties, regarding entry of the United Kingdom into the EEC. That this negotiation could properly have occurred resulted from the legal nature of the Commonwealth and the wide latitude it allows for national policy-making within its framework. That it actually did occur bears witness to the underlying facts that condition the Commonwealth's existence as a commercial going concern and the nature of Britain's economic stake in the Commonwealth.

1. Regionalism, New Basis for Co-operation

A great deal was heard about Commonwealth versus Common Market during the course of 1961 and 1962 when consideration of

* Chairman, Division of History and Political Science, State University College, New Paltz, New York

British accession to the Common Market was in its most active phase. Nevertheless, the negotiations did not formally pit Commonwealth against Common Market. The EEC negotiated qua EEC, but not the Commonwealth; only one constituent of the Commonwealth sat at the table on its own account and not as Commonwealth agent. This implied no secession or intent to secede from the Commonwealth. The proceeding, throughout which this constituent consulted its Commonwealth partners and heeded their concerns, was consistent with the Commonwealth concept. Britain's right to join, notwithstanding Commonwealth membership and notwithstanding qualms in certain Commonwealth quarters, was conceded by the Commonwealth prime ministers in their September, 1962, meeting at London.[1]

While a British accession to EEC could conceivably have accelerated the weakening of Commonwealth ties, its failure leaves such a consequence entirely conjectural. What can be said is that it would have been in keeping with Commonwealth evolution. That evolution, so visibly characterized by centrifugality, has been attended by a flux of centripetal forces around poles located both within and without the Commonwealth. Apparently irreversible processes of segregation, to borrow Professor Scelle's terminology,[2] have not presaged utter fragmentation as the inevitable result, despite the split-ups of India and Rhodesia and Nyasaland, the successive split-offs of Ireland, Burma, and South Africa, and now the change in Singapore's relations. Rather, they have made place for new aggregations, both regional and international, in different forms and combinations responsive to changing circumstance, need, and aspiration.

Inside the Commonwealth, subcoalescences have occurred with the federation of the Canadian provinces, in Australia, in South Africa, in Malaysia, and with Tanzania. Each of these represents a comprehensive pooling of interest on a basis of geographical propinquity. Smaller bundles of regional interest have drawn together limited-purpose groupings that cut across

1. For text, see 183 *Board of Trade J.* 645–646 (1962).
2. Georges Scelle, *Précis de Droit des Gens* (1932), pp. 187–287.

and spill over Commonwealth bounds. Examples include the Colombo Plan (1950), which associates the United Kingdom, Canada, Pakistan, Ceylon, Malaya, New Zealand, and Australia with the United States, Japan, and various southeast Asian countries; ANZUS (1951), allying New Zealand and Australia with the United States; SEATO (1954) and its ancillary Pacific Charter, which join these three with the United Kingdom, Pakistan, the Philippines, Thailand, and France; CENTO (1955), which ties the United Kingdom and Pakistan with Iraq, Turkey, and Iran; NATO (1949), which allies the United Kingdom and Canada with the United States and certain European countries; and the OECD (1960), in which the same plus other non-Commonwealth countries collaborate in pursuit of a common purpose.

Ghana associated with Guinea and Mali in the Union of African States (1961), and with these plus Morocco and the U.A.R. in the Casablanca Group (also 1961). A free-trade arrangement called WAFTA, joining Ghana and Nigeria with Liberia and Cameroons, has subsequently been reported; Nigeria has since asked for terms of association with EEC; and further gropings for other partnerships and combinations may be expected. For her part, the United Kingdom has without any Commonwealth company joined in several regional ventures concerned variously with the military, political, and commerical interests of western Europe, notably, the Western European Union (1948), the Council of Europe (1949), and the European Free Trade Association (1960).

Accession of the United Kingdom to the EEC would simply have meant plunging deeper into such regionalism—to a greater degree and placing novel limitations upon Britain's intra-Commonwealth latitude, it is true, but in logic nonetheless a step (some would say a leap) farther down a road the United Kingdom was already traveling. The step was in fact not consummated owing to collapse of the accession negotiation at Brussels.[3]

3. General de Gaulle sounded the death knell in his press conference of Jan. 14, 1963, but adjournment of the negotiating sessions occurred on Jan. 29. For Prime Minister Macmillan's announcement, see text of his televised address in 29 *Vital Speeches* 332–333 (1963).

Whatever the cause and permanency of this collapse, however, the British government's decision to make the try reflected a studied conviction that it was the best alternative open, all things considered. The attempt having failed, there remains the problem for which membership in the EEC was to have been the solution.

2. The Common Market's Challenge

Although the nub of that problem is economic, British accession to the EEC would have been a political act carrying political implications. Hence, in the decisional process, British leadership faced a dilemma of the first water: whether the advantage of having a seat in the councils of a powerful incipient coalition across the Channel outweighed the cost of the accompanying entanglement, both the coalition and the entanglement being traditional aversions of British foreign policy. The decision to seek membership, consequently, was arrived at only in the summer of 1961, after the remarkably rapid development of the EEC had shown it unmistakably to be a going concern with a solid presumption of a successful future, and after preferred alternatives to membership had been found wanting.[4] This delayed decision was attended by implicit and explicit qualifications which, albeit well grounded in British thinking, inhibited prompt arrangement of entry and gave time for the mobilization of the obstacles that finally spelled rupture.[5]

4. For text of the prime minister's announcement of the decision on July 31, see 181 *Board of Trade J.* 245–246 (1961).

5. Prevailing opinion tends to blame General de Gaulle for the breakdown; see accounting given by Professor Hallstein, president of the EEC Commission, to the EEC Assembly on Feb. 5, 1963, *Bulletin from the European Community*, No. 60 (Washington, Feb., 1963), pp. 1–3, 6–8. The French claimed merely to be insisting that all face up to the demonstrable fact that "Britain is not yet in position to accept the disciplines of the [Rome] Treaty." See statement by the French foreign minister at the final session of the Brussels meeting, Jan. 29, 1963, text released by French Press and Information Service, New York, *Speeches and Press Conference*, No. 187; also his speech to the French Assembly, Jan. 24, 1963, text, *ibid.*, No. 186.

The position of the French and others of similar mind was that the integrity of the Rome treaty should be preserved, and there was suspicion about the wholeheartedness of British committal to membership, based on the following:

The United Kingdom very much favored, insofar as a choice might be open, a looser regional trading arrangement—one free of the "supra-nationality" and the many disciplines set up under the Common Market, but neatly contrived to secure the commercial advantages it held forth. An internationally approved formula for such an arrangement exists under the designation of "free-trade area."[6] Thereunder, it is permissible to dismantle trade barriers as between the constituent countries, while leaving each constituent in control of its tariff policy toward outside countries (e.g., the United Kingdom vis-à-vis the Commonwealth). Further, each constituent can be left in full control otherwise of its national policies, that is, with regard to all except the engagement to establish free trade with its constituent partners.[7] The United Kingdom's first response to the EEC, on the heels of its establishment, therefore, was a strenuous effort to merge it into such an arrangement with a much expanded membership.[8] When that

---

(a) earlier British aloofness to ECSC, EEC, and European integration generally, (b) the British-led attempt in 1958 to founder EEC aborning into a loose European-wide free-trade association, (c) the protracted haggling over terms at Brussels, and (d) toward the end, hostile rumblings from Labour party circles threatening the reopening of any accession agreement concluded by Macmillan. The increasing coalescence of EEC did not strengthen Britain's bargaining position, and the Bermuda meeting between Macmillan and Kennedy in Dec., 1962, evidently was final proof to de Gaulle of the ambivalence of British intentions. In *Europe Will Not Wait* (1960), Anthony Nutting had warned of the risks of a British failure to proceed promptly and decisively.

6. Art. 24 (8-b), General Agreement on Tariffs and Trade (GATT), T.I.A.S. No. 1700. For citations to later amendments, etc., of GATT, see the annual U. S. Dep't. of State publication, *Treaties in Force*.

7. Art. 24 (8-b) of GATT defines a "free-trade area" as simply "a group of two or more customs territories in which the duties and other restrictive regulations of commerce . . . are eliminated on substantially all of the trade between the constituent territories in products originating in such territories." There is no further requirement, except a ban on the immediate raising of the general level of pre-existing duties and other restrictions against outside countries; art. 24 (5-b).

8. The unsuccessful negotiation to this end (known as the "Maudling" negotiation after the Briton who chaired the meetings) was held in 1958 under the auspices of the Organization for European Economic Cooperation (OEEC). The attempt was supported by Austria, Switzerland, and the Scandinavians; the objective was an association including all seventeen of the OEEC's members (the six of the EEC, the seven later forming EFTA, and Greece, Turkey, Iceland, and Ireland). For a special pleading in favor of such an arrangement by an official in the OEEC Secretariat, see Marc Ouin, *The OEEC and the Common Market—15th April 1958* (1958). See also the Economist Intelligence Unit, *Britain and Europe* (1957), p. 60, for conclusion that a free-trade area would be advantageous to Britain, "while at the same time safeguarding the interests of the Commonwealth." For an account of the negotiation, see Emile Benoit, *Europe at Sixes and Sevens* (1961).

effort failed, the United Kingdom, as a fall-back position, banded with the other like-minded non-EEC European countries into a limited arrangement of the kind it had earlier proposed. The European Free Trade Association (EFTA).[9] With its fractional size and inadequately matched composition, the EFTA was never regarded as a substitute for an arrangement comprehending the Common Market countries;[10] and when the EEC persisted in its resistance to amalgamation with the EFTA group into a larger free-trade area, it became clear that the choice facing the United Kingdom was between joining and not joining EEC.[11]

9. Convention Establishing the European Free Trade Association, signed Jan. 4, 1960, in force May 3, 1960, between Austria, Denmark, Norway, Portugal, Sweden, Switzerland, and the United Kingdom. The free trade involves essentially industrial products. At first EFTA geared the progress of its own transitional period to that of the EEC, but at the Lisbon meeting, May, 1963, it fixed an independent schedule for the future. Finland has been brought in by a special agreement, dated March 27, 1961. The Secretariat of EFTA is in Geneva.

10. Nations in EFTA are dispersed geographically, do not include the Franco-German nexus of continental power, and do not furnish the market potential of EEC. As of 1955, the combined population of EFTA's major continental components (Austria, Switzerland, Denmark, Norway, Sweden) was about one-sixth of that of the EEC; their composite GNP, something under one-fifth and predicted to grow (up to 1970) less rapidly (by 51 per cent as compared with 60 per cent) assuming no trading arrangement comprehending the Six. The relative expansion of British exports, 1956–1961, was 25 per cent greater to EEC than to EFTA, though, since the tariff differential has begun to take hold, there has been growth in favor of EFTA; see note 31, *infra*. Moveover, the limited arrangement is not addressed to the paramount trade concern of certain EFTA countries, the two extreme cases being Austria and Switzerland. The EEC area was market for 50.7 per cent of the former's total exports in 1960–1961, and the EFTA area for only 13.4 per cent. For the latter the portions were 41 per cent and 16.3 per cent respectively. *Britain and Europe, op. cit. supra* note 8, at p. 10, table; EFTA Secretariat, *EFTA's Foreign Trade During the First Year of Operation* (1961), pp. 16, 20.

11. Although EEC could, under art. 238 of the Rome treaty, conclude with "a union of States or an international organisation," *inter alia*, "agreements creating an association embodying reciprocal rights and obligations, joint actions and special procedures," the EEC declined to negotiate with EFTA as a collectivity, but indicated willingness to entertain applications from each country separately either for associate status or for full membership. The ministerial meetings of EFTA in June and July, 1961, reached consensus that this approach was acceptable, subject to co-ordination within EFTA and terms that would permit all EFTA members "to participate from the same date" in an "integrated European market" (London communiqué of June 28 and Geneva declaration of July 31, 1963). The obligation thereby placed on the United Kingdom led to one of the issues remaining unresolved in the U.K.-EEC negotiation at the time of its break-off in Jan., 1963. The United Kingdom's decision to seek membership under art. 237 of the Rome treaty, as announced on July 31, was immediately followed on the same day by a like Danish decision. Thereafter, Norway applied for membership negotiations on April 30, 1962; and the others variously opted to seek associate status, Austria on Dec. 12, 1961, Sweden and Switzerland three days later, and Portugal on June 4, 1962. (Documentation supplied by the EFTA Information Office, Washington.)

In finally opting for membership, it was undoubtedly relevant to British policy calculations that the cost in political currency was minimized by the avowed limited purpose of the EEC.[12] As delineated in its charter (the Treaty of Rome of March 25, 1957),[13] the EEC is created to perform exclusively economic functions;[14] whatever its political potential, there is as yet no sign of its passing to political integration. It is first of all a customs union and constructed as such on the principle of free trade internally (that is, as among and between its constituents) and a common tariff and commercial policy externally (that is, between the union as a whole and the outside).[15] The commitments it otherwise provides concern economic matters ancillary to trade, with a view to harmonizing conditions of competition to the extent deemed essential to assure the achievement of a viable customs union.[16] That is the sum of it, on its face. Hence an

12. British public debate over the question of entry, however, tended to blur the limits in the commitments involved, leaving a residue of uninformed impression that membership would restrict British sovereignty in greater measure than the treaty's terms and the EEC's procedures (which stress community-wide consensus) actually entail. See John Starke Gordon, "The Development of the Position of the British Labour Party Regarding Britain's Entry into Europe" (Master's thesis, Duke University, 1963), p. 49.

13. The treaty entered into force Jan. 1, 1958, between Belgium, France, Federal Republic of Germany, Italy, Luxembourg, and the Netherlands. For tariff purposes, Belgium, Luxembourg, and the Netherlands, joined in the Benelux, are treated as a unit. Implementation began with the first step of "internal" tariff dismantling on Jan. 1, 1959.

14. The preamble to the treaty recites that the high contracting parties are ". . . *Decided* to ensure the economic and social progress of their countries, . . . *Anxious* to strengthen the unity of their economies and to ensure their harmonious development. . . . *Desirous* of contributing by means of a common commercial policy to the progressive abolition of restrictions on international trade. . . ." The long-range political implications of the EEC are, of course, significant. But this is a question of potential, for the future to answer; and if Britain were inside, she would be in strategic position to influence evolution. This opportunity, without doubt assessed by government leadership, tended to be lost sight of in the public forum, in subordination to a spate of fears about impairments of British political freedom.

15. The establishment of a single tariff structure vis-à-vis outside countries is what distinguishes a customs union from a free-trade area, in the definitions laid down in art. 24(8), of GATT.

16. These ancillary features are not required of a customs union, though in keeping with GATT's approval of "closer integration between the economies" of countries in customs unions; art. 24(4). On the probable necessity, under contemporary conditions, for co-ordination of economic policies by the countries composing a customs union, in conjunction with removal of trade barriers between them, see Jacob Viner, *The Customs Union Issue* (1950), p. 136. A partial listing of EEC's supplementary aspects, as set forth in the treaty, includes a common agricultural policy with a single price-support system (pt. 2, title 2); free move-

examination of the EEC-Commonwealth relationship focuses on economic facts and trends, especially those related to commerce.[17]

It may be generalized that the EEC's impact on Commonwealth trade is no different from that on other countries having like commodity interests, with the qualification that on the average the trade of Commonwealth countries has been less oriented to the Community area historically than that of others, implying at first blush a proportionately smaller effect one way or the other. In 1956, the year preceding signature of the Rome treaty and a "normal" postwar statistical year, under 15 per cent of all Commonwealth exports went to the Community area, as compared with the approximately 24 per cent that represented the share the EEC took of the exports of the rest of the world. About 45 per cent of the exportation of Commonwealth countries was to other Commonwealth countries; but a trend is under way marking a significant change in this pattern, as is indicated in Table 1.

From high-water mark in the postwar years, intra-area trade has been steadily declining in the share it claims of the area's total trade, back to the pre-1930 division, and more. In 1963, intra-

ment of persons, services, and capital (pt. 2, title 3); co-ordination of interstate transport policy (pt. 2, title 4); community anti-trust regulations and repeal of national laws that artificially distort trade (pt. 3, title 1); uniform minimal labor standards (pt. 3, title 3, and sec. 2 of appended Protocol relating to certain provisions of concern to France); a community Development Fund "for the promotion of the social and economic development" of overseas territories (art. 1 of the annexed Implementing Convention).

17. The question of monetary policy, the effect of the EEC on sterling and the Sterling Area, will not be gone into. In the absence of British accession, there is little to add to Brinley Thomas, "The Evolution of the Sterling Area and Its Prospects," in Nicholas Mansergh, *et al., Commonwealth Perspectives* (1958), pp. 175–207. Speculations about the EEC's possible interference with the Sterling Area system were highly conjectural. If anything, British membership would have contributed an element of strength, directly through making any sterling difficulties of the United Kingdom a matter of common interest calling for "mutual assistance" as appropriate (art. 108), as well as indirectly through the expected betterment of Britain's economic position. For the rest, the Rome treaty provisions on monetary policy are quite guarded; no common currency is presaged nor any Community central banking, nor is there any requirement for Community consent to alterations in the rate of exchange (arts. 103–109). Accordingly, no issue over the Sterling Area as such appears to have figured in the Brussels negotiations. See "Sterling Across the Channel," 2 *Common Market* 15–16 (1962).

Table 1. *Area Intratrade* (*exports, in percentage of total*)

	1928	1938	1948– 1949ª	1954	1958	1960	1962
Sterling Areaᵇ	40	50½	51½	53	48	43½	40
Commonwealthᶜ	41	52	51	46½	43	37	33

Note: The conspicuous diverging between lines 1 and 2 since the war is in part explainable by the departure of Ireland and South Africa from the Commonwealth, while remaining in the Sterling Area. It is also in part explainable by the permanent wrench done to Canada's trade pattern by the war and postwar restrictions applied against Canadian goods, Canada having a heavy statistical weight as the first trader of the Outer Commonwealth; in 1938, 40 per cent of Canada's exports went to Britain, but only 15–17 per cent since the war. A contrary influence in both lines has been the split of India and Pakistan, as their reciprocal trade adds a new intra-statistic.

ª The figure in line 1 is for 1948; in line 2 it is for 1949.

ᵇ For the Sterling Area, the *Board of Trade Journal* gives different figures, by calculating on a basis different from that used by Thorbecke and GATT (in common with the U.N.).

ᶜ Ireland is included as a unit of the Commonwealth for both prewar years; South Africa is dropped as from 1960. A computation omitting Ireland throughout, and South Africa in all postwar years, would give the following sequence in line 2: 39, 49, 46½, 42, 39, 37, 33.

Sources: Sterling Area: first three columns, Erik Thorbecke, *The Tendency towards Regionalization in International Trade 1928–1956* (1960), Table 48; last three columns, GATT, *International Trade 1962*; middle column (1964), both.

Commonwealth: League of Nations, *The Network of World Trade* (1942), Table 39 and Annex III, for the first two columns; for the third and fourth, Board of Trade, *The Commonwealth and the Sterling Area Statistical Abstract*, No. 73 (1949–52) and No. 76 (1955); fifth column, Commonwealth Economic Committee, *Commonwealth Trade 1959–60;* remaining columns, *ibid.* for 1963.

Commonwealth share was down to 31 per cent, and intra-Sterling was off another fraction of a percentage point.[18]

The shift to a much larger share for extra-area markets, however, has not been in the same geographical direction for the United Kingdom as for the other constituents. Western Europe has been the United Kingdom's great market-growth area. The decline of the Commonwealth as a customer since 1956 has been absolute as well as relative. Non-Commonwealth markets outside

18. The sterling statistic is derived from Board of Trade figures, as follows: 42.4 per cent (1961), 40.5 per cent (1962), 39.8 per cent (1963). One difference between sources in connection with "sterling" trade has to do with the handling of Persian Gulf oil; another, with whether Ireland and Iceland are counted as "overseas sterling."

western Europe have shown an average growth rate as a British outlet; expansion otherwise has been almost entirely in western Europe.[19] That area increased its take of British products by almost 50 per cent between 1957 and 1962. On the other hand, the conspicuous growth market for Outer Commonwealth and Overseas Sterling has been the world outside western Europe (including the United Kingdom). For them, as a group, the United Kingdom in 1957–1962 showed so little growth compared with its traditional role as to be classed as a more or less stagnant market.[20] The rest of western Europe has showed average growth, still absorbing in 1962 as in 1957 a sixth of their exports; the major growth has been in non-Commonwealth markets outside western Europe. Table 2 gives a detailed summation for the five-year period 1957–1962. The information presented in the table lends perspective to the varying Commonwealth interest in the British decision to seek entry into the EEC: the United Kingdom's urge to secure her trade future in western Europe and, on the other hand, the divers anxieties manifested in Outer Commonwealth quarters over possible prejudice to their exports resulting from the United Kingdom's moving behind the EEC customs frontier.

Outer Commonwealth anxieties, now being moot, may be passed over briefly. The United Kingdom has been the focal point

19. A major exception to the generalization in the first part of this sentence, however, would be the United States, as indicated by figures available at the end of 1965; these show also a tapering off of western Europe as a whole. Western Europe is defined as consisting of the thirteen countries of the EEC and the EFTA, plus Spain, Finland, Greece, Turkey, Iceland, and Ireland. This area, so defined, was for long an outlet for about 30 per cent of the United Kingdom's exports (the percentage consistently showing for each of the reference years 1928, 1938, 1953, and 1958); but from 1958, its share shifted markedly upward to 40 per cent in 1962 and 43 per cent in 1963–1964. In this period, the Commonwealth's share changed from 37 to 30 to 28, and "Others" from 33 to 30 to 29.

20. However, they shared (if less than *pro rata*) in the general British import boom that waxed during the course of 1963 and 1964. British imports during 1964, as compared with 1963, rose as follows (monthly averages, $ millions): 1286.5 *v.* 1124.7 (from all countries), and 389.5 *v.* 352.6 (from the Commonwealth). Thus the rise for the Commonwealth was about 10½ per cent as against just over 16 per cent for the rest of the world. (OECD source, with Commonwealth figures derived by adding Canada to Overseas Sterling, and subtracting South Africa, Libya, Kuwait, and Bahrein; thus a few minor non-Commonwealth countries are included.) When the full impact of the emergency import tax imposed late in 1964 for the purpose of curbing imports begins to show up in the trade statistics, however, the result could be less disadvantageous for the Commonwealth than the average of other countries, since many basic commodities such as Commonwealth countries mainly export are exempt.

Table 2. *The Commonwealth's Markets* (*exports, $ millions*)

	United Kingdom			Outer Commonwealth[a]		
	Commw.	W. Eur.[b]	Others	U.K.	W. Eur.[b]	Others
1957[c]	4,550	2,830	1,830	4,355	2,930	10,685
1962[d]	4,285	4,200	2,135	4,640	3,500	13,010
Growth	(− 265)	1,370	305	285	570	2,325

[a] The countries here covered under "Outer Commonwealth" are Canada plus those of the Overseas Sterling Area. Hence the term is employed loosely, and the picture given is indicative rather than exact in detail. Lack of comparability in statistical basis precluded the insertion of strictly Commonwealth figures from the *Commonwealth Trade* series into the framework of the present table.

[b] Western Europe is exclusive of the United Kingdom.

[c] Use of 1956 or 1958 as base would have shaved the decline shown in British exports to the Commonwealth by about one-half, as 1957 was a peak year for that trade. But these alternatives would also have added to the increase shown for Britain's extra-Commonwealth exports: by $420 million (using 1956) or by $320 million (using 1958).

[d] On the other hand, 1962 was perhaps depressed somewhat below cyclical by reason of the emergency import restrictions then in force in Canada, in face of which British exports to Canada dropped off $85 million from the 1960–1961 average. However, the revival of the Canadian market in 1963 meant no real arrest of the slippage trend; whereas 1963 was better than 1962 by some $60 million, it was yet under 1960–1961 average by some $270 million; *Commonwealth Trade 1963.*

Source: GATT table cited in note to Table 1, *supra,* as supplemented by other sources for break-out of Canada.

of the entire Commonwealth system; and, although its relative importance as outlet for Outer Commonwealth products is declining (one-fifth of their exports today, as against two-fifths before the war),[21] it has been and still is a substantial one. Its importance is especially great for certain members with an above-average reliance on the United Kingdom for their export earnings: e.g., New Zealand, Nigeria, Rhodesia, Cyprus, and British Honduras. The problem has been a mixed one, depending on the commodity and the country. The bulk of the trade probably never was in serious danger from the projected United Kingdom-EEC merger;[22] and the alarms sounded by anti-entry voices did not always judiciously distinguish the fancied from the real or take

21. On the other side of the equation, the Commonwealth took about one-half of Britain's exports just before the war, as compared with 30 per cent in 1962.

22. For example, many Outer Commonwealth products already have duty-free treatment in the EEC tariff: *inter alia,* wool (CXT No. 53.01), natural rubber (40.01), synthetic rubber (40.02), cotton (55.01), jute (57.03), certain wood

full account of the potential trade-generating effects of a merger.[23]
There were, nevertheless, some instances where the EEC's tariff,
if accepted unmodified, might be expected to burden trade in
a Commonwealth product significantly.[24] For these, the British
negotiators sought accommodations; and one unresolved category
of issues outstanding at the collapse of negotiations concerned a
residuum of vulnerable commodities for which concessions
deemed satisfactory by the British (and, indirectly, the Commonwealth) were still to be secured.[25]

As to her own export trade, the United Kingdom would appear
to have been entitled to at least as much concern over the future
of her western European market as the Outer Commonwealth
had over the fate of their British market. In fact, more; for

pulps (47.01), hides and skins (41.01). For textiles, there could hardly be
worsened treatment, and besides, cotton textiles are now regulated by the long-
term multilateral arrangement of 1962. For such a product as Canadian hard-
quality wheat, the EEC would continue to be dependent on the outside for its
requirements (for the EEC engagement regarding this commodity, see T.I.A.S.
No. 5035). On certain products, EEC was in course of ameliorating its tariff (e.g.,
cocoa); and it could be safely assumed that certain other ameliorations would
accompany British entry. Finally, actual experience was showing a satisfactory
Commonwealth access to the Common Market at a growth rate not being recorded
in the British market as things stood.

23. As envisaged by merger proponents, benefits would include increased British
capacity to absorb Commonwealth commodities, new opportunities for Commonwealth exporters to share in the growth of an enlarged market, and the prospect
that British participation in EEC policy-making would add a liberal influence
advantageous to Commonwealth trade.

24. R. W. G. Mackay, *Towards a United States of Europe* (1960), p. 131,
contends that "less than one-eighth" of Commonwealth trade would be affected by
British entry. The effects, however, would be unevenly distributed. Canada, the
biggest Commonwealth exporter to Britain, would on the whole not have basis to
anticipate disadvantage see S. F. Kaliski, "Canada, the United Kingdom and the
Common Market," 17 *Int'l J.* 17 (1961); G. L. Reuber, "Western Europe's
Demand for Canadian Industrial Materials," 28 *Can. J. Econ. & Pol. Sci.* 13
(1962); Roy A. Matthews, "Canada, Britain and the Common Market: A
Canadian View," 8 *World Today* 48 (1962). Other examples of countries with
little reason for apprehension are Ceylon, Malaysia, and Hong Kong (given the
1962 textile agreement, T.I.A.S. No. 5240). But in some cases, British entry
without appropriate adjustments could have serious adverse effects, e.g., West
Indies, New Zealand, Mauritius, British Guiana, and British Honduras.

25. Although the EEC was willing to suppress the duty on tea and to entertain
association for the dependencies and the Commonwealth countries of Africa and
the Caribbean, solutions had not been found regarding meat and butter (New
Zealand), soft wheat (Australia) and aluminium (Canada). Hallstein judged
solutions to be in sight for such issues (though not yet for the EFTA question);
de Murville held to the contrary, see note 5, *supra*. The technical problems
seemed soluble had there existed mutual political will. Mr. Heath, chief of the
British delegation to Brussels, attributed the lack of will to the French government in his report to Parliament; see 184 *Board of Trade J.* 303 (1963).

western Europe has now become twice as important for the United Kingdom as that country to the Outer Commonwealth, and the British export position in the Commonwealth has of late been suffering greater slippage than the Commonwealth's position in the British market. The heart of that western European market, and its most dynamic growth component, has been the EEC. Its commercial attraction, as compared with Commonwealth, consists not only in the fact that it is lucrative and thriving, but also in the accelerated rate with which it has overtaken the Commonwealth as Britain's leading market.

Table 3. *British Exports to Commonwealth and EEC, Compared* (*trade figures in £ millions*)

	1952–53	1956	1959	1961	1962–63	Growth
Commonwealth	1,125	1,276	1,246	1,292	1,192	67 (6%)
EEC countries	314	426	512	666	844	530 (169%)
Percentage (EEC of Commw.)	27½	33½	41	51½	70	790

Note: The 1952–53 column represents the average of the two years; 1962–63, the twelve months July through June. The OECD statistics used were those for U.K. "General Exports" (inclusive of re-exports); statistics compiled exclusive of re-exports would have given a different result in the third line of the column, 68 per cent rather than 70 per cent, as the U.K. did more re-export with the EEC in that period than with the Commonwealth. Computation involved subtraction of identifiable non-Commonwealth countries in the Overseas Sterling Area and conversion of monthly averages (rounded) in dollars to an annual pound sterling figure. For a forecast of the superior long-range attractions of EEC over Commonwealth preferences, based on 1953–1959 statistics, see Benoit, *op. cit. supra* note 8, at pp. 107–109. For later figures, see note 28, *infra.*

Sources: First column, *Commonwealth Trade, 1956–57;* second column, *ibid., 1959–60,* with subtraction of South Africa in each case; third and fourth columns, *ibid., 1961–62;* fifth column, OECD, *Foreign Commerce: Series A, Overall Trade by Countries* (1963).

Over this ten-year period, the ratio of EEC-destined to Commonwealth-destined British exports increased by an annual average of just under 2 percentage points in the first three and one half years, 2½ points in the next three, 5 points in the next two, and 12 in the latest year and one-half. At this galloping pace, the EEC seemed headed within a very short time to reach and pass beyond the Commonwealth as purchaser of British products. This has been possible because, notwithstanding that the Commonwealth contains 3½ times as many possible customers and affords the United Kingdom the advantages of privileged position and established business channels, the EEC area is characterized by a high and expanding purchasing power generating effective demand for goods such as the United Kingdom can furnish. How well the United Kingdom can continue to take advantage of the opportunity depends on the degree of facility of access henceforth, assuming price competitiveness.

As matters now stand, there is no assurance that the prospect for British exporters will continue to be so sanguine in the Common Market as in the past few years. The tariff regime ultimately envisaged for the EEC, when the step-by-step progressions scheduled during the current "transitional period" will have been completed,[26] has been only partially in effect up to the present.[27] In mid-1963, however, the progression passed the half-way mark; the dismantling of intra-Community industrial tariffs was then 60 per cent accomplished, and each of the Six was likewise 60 per cent of the way along in substituting the common external tariff for its pre-existing national tariff. The duty-rate differential which a Briton's competitor in any one of the Six enjoys in the rest of the Community, therefore, is beginning to become sizeable and will become increasingly so as the Community's tariff system progresses to its consummation a few years

26. The "transitional period" for attaining a full customs union was set at 12 to 15 years from Jan. 1, 1958, with "internal" tariffs to be dismantled in ten installments of 10 per cent each, grouped 3–3–4 in three successive "stages," and the "external" tariff to be approached in three steps, 30–30–40, synchronized with the accomplishment of each such "stage." The EEC is ahead of schedule in the "industrial sector," wherein British interest lies, having commenced the second "stage" on Jan. 1, 1962, and completed the tariff changes slated for that "stage" on July 1, 1963. Starting date for the "final stage" is Jan. 1, 1966; and the last evident obstacle to completion of the customs union has been finally removed by resolution of the issue precipitated in mid-1965 by the French government's rejection of certain policy proposals emanating from the EEC Commission.

27. The tariff impact of the EEC's first "stage" was ameliorated by a decision to "generalize" the first "internal" cut to outsiders, in the case of member rates above the common external tariff; and, in the first adjustment to the common external tariff in the industrial sector, each member proceeded as though the external tariff had been reduced by 20 per cent, except as this could carry a national rate below the common rate.

hence. In fact, a dampening effort is already evident. The momentum so long at work began exhausting itself in the closing months of 1963, and soon in 1964 signs of a leveling off were unmistakable.[28]

Joining the Common Market integrally, by putting the United Kingdom inside the EEC's tariff structure, would rectify the sharpening competitive disadvantage thus facing British exporters. Membership in EEC would have placed the United Kingdom, by the same token, fully in the stream of Community economic expansion. "Internal" trade, or that between the Community's members, almost doubled in annual volume in the first five years of the EEC's existence and seems headed for tripling by its eighth year.[29] Entry, conversely, would have subjected British industry at home to keener competition from continental producers—a "cost" carrying a compensating gain in the way of stimulating certain over-sheltered and laggard branches of British industry to greater efficiency (a benefit such as France, chronically in balance-of-payments difficulties before 1959, gained from EEC membership). A like stimulus of additional foreign competition

28. Deceleration of exportation to the EEC, in contrast with acceleration to the EFTA, illustrates how the diverging terms of market access are by now affecting trade. Monthly average British exports to the EEC and EFTA, respectively, have moved as follows ($ millions):

	1962	1963	1964	1965 (Jan.–May)
EEC	167.99	192.80	196.49	210.51
EFTA	108.03	117.07	129.15	141.84

From 1963, the increase to the EFTA was thus 24.77 (21 per cent); to the EEC, 17.71 (9 per cent). An added note to Table 3 above: the ratio of EEC to Commonwealth as British export outlet in calendar 1963 was 73½ per cent, above 75 per cent in the first half of 1964, and then back to 72½ per cent in 1964–1965 (twelve months, June-May). In the first nine months of 1965 exports to EEC were the same as in the same period of 1964, reflecting stoppage of growth, though Britain's exports overall were up 7 per cent.

29. In $ billions, "internal" trade rose from 6.8 in 1958, to 13.5 in 1962, to 15.7 in 1963, and an annual rate of about 18 in first-half 1964 (approximate import-export averages, derived from EEC's *General Statistical Bulletin*). Over-all, the EEC countries showed an increase of $11.5 billion (53 per cent) in their total annual export level between 1958 and 1962, whereas all other countries combined (exclusive of the Communist group) showed an increase in the same period of $16.5 billion (23 per cent). The 1962–1964 increases were, respectively, $8.37 billion (38 per cent) and $17.94 billion (22 per cent). For a table giving a detailed breakdown of the 1958–1962 increase pattern, based on GATT statistics, see Herman Walker, "Commonwealth and Common Market: Two Trading Systems," 63 *South Atlantic Q.* 295 (1964), Duke University Commonwealth-Studies Center Reprint No. 13, Table 4.

could, of course, be got through unilateral tariff reductions, but easing the access of foreigners to Britain's market is not the same as securing British access to foreign markets, the key concern.

3. The Commonwealth Preference System

The crucial importance of fostering export earnings loomed large in the background of the United Kingdom initiative to the EEC. The ratio of dense population to thin resources of raw materials, energy supplies, and arable land renders the United Kingdom extremely dependent upon foreign earnings for livelihood and prosperity. In decades past, she has been accustomed to financing excess import requirements, for which her exports were insufficient to pay, by net earnings from "invisible transactions" (e.g., dividends from foreign investments, shipping profits, international insurance, brokerage, etc.). In 1913, her investment income alone was £210 millions, more than enough to absorb the £158 million trade deficit of that year. In 1938, when times were harder and the British position was already weakened, investment income was still enough to pay over 23 per cent of the United Kingdom's total import bill and, added to other invisible earnings (primarily shipping), was almost enough to cover the deficit arising from excess of imports over exports.[30] But the war-caused need for heavy borrowing and liquidation of foreign holdings, together with the loss of primacy in such international services as shipping and insurance, has thrown the United Kingdom into heavier reliance today on trade than at any time since the mid-1800's—in face of a keener and more numerous competition. In the latter fifties, investments were yielding enough to cover only about 7 per cent of the import bill, on the average, and since 1959 less than 4½ per cent; moreover, the shipping account has been teetering between deficit and bare balance. The chronic fragility of Britain's balance of payments

30. Alfred E. Kahn, *Great Britain in the World Economy* (1946), tables on pp. 126–127. Other invisibles brought in £ 300 million (net basis, estimated).

has led to recurring financial crises since the war, the latest having erupted in the fall of 1964.[31]

Both before and since the frustration of Britain's entry into the EEC, there have been calls for a strengthening of the Commonwealth as the way of achieving the needed export expansion, or a significant part of it. The concrete means envisaged for pursuit of this objective, when a definite action program in terms of major policy re-orientation going beyond "promotion" is suggested, is a recasting and rejuvenation of the Commonwealth trade preference system—the system that has been the hallmark of the Commonwealth as a commercial concept and, indeed, a feature of the Commonwealth virtually since the Statute of Westminster (1931) created it as a legal concept. That the preference system as it now exists would require a major overhaul to make of it an efficacious instrument for rebuilding intra-Commonwealth trade seems to be generally accepted as axiomatic; what is yet to be so accepted is the feasibility, wisdom, and utility of such a course of action. In opting for EEC entry, the British government in effect rejected it as a preferred choice, and authoritative statements since the Brussels breakdown manifest no detectable intention on the part of the British government to espouse it as an alternative.[32]

31. Entries for all "invisible" transactions in the British balance-of-payments ledger for "current" transactions other than returns on investment canceled each other out over the period 1958–1962. It has been estimated that the United Kingdom needs to achieve an annual trade surplus of at least £ 70 millions, in the near term, if she is to be in a healthy economic position (see OECD economic survey of *United Kingdom 1963*, p. 25 and *passim*). But over the past decennium the trade balance has stubbornly fluctuated around an annual average deficit in the range of £ 140 to £ 150 million. A record deficit of £ 378 million in 1960 had been whittled to £ 44 million by 1963; but then came the swing back, with a deficit of £ 118 million in the first quarter of 1964, and £ 553 million for the year. By October, when emergency measures had to be imposed, it was reported that the total deficit on all counts (including debts falling due) had mounted to $1.8 billion. The credits of roughly $4.3 billion net (as of May, 1965), extended by the International Monetary Fund and friendly governments to help tide over the crisis, will in their turn give rise to further liabilities requiring the generation of a trade surplus higher than the £ 70 million previously estimated as needed. In 1965 the total payments deficit was £ 354 million ($991 million).

32. Prime Minister Macmillan and Mr. Heath, each implicitly, in speeches cited in notes 3 and 25, *supra;* Mr. Erroll, president of the Board of Trade, in speech, "Britain's Prospects of Trade Expansion in World Markets," 184 *Board of Trade J.* 695 (1963); Lord Drumbalbyn, minister of state, Board of Trade, 185 *ibid.* 1136 (1963); in similar vein, see speech by Mr. Redhead, succeeding Labour minister of state, Board of Trade, 187 *ibid.* 1050 (1964).

Why this should be so may be deduced from an examination of the system in the matrix of circumstance which surrounds it.

Although there are precedents for preferences in the history of British commercial policy, the modern version dates from the Ottawa Conference of August, 1932, and the agreements arising from it. This, it will be remembered, was in the depth of the Great Depression and a time of crisis measures. There had earlier been minor breaches[33] in the long-standing British policy of equal treatment for all supplier sources, and empire preferences of one sort or other had earlier been instituted in the dominions and colonies.[34] But the Ottawa Agreements signaled the common adoption of the preference principle and the United Kingdom's shift to privileged treatment of Commonwealth suppliers as a deliberate major policy. This was calculated to insulate, or largely insulate, Commonwealth trade from the impact of the master shift earlier in the year to tariff protectionism in the United Kingdom,[35] as well as to secure and improve favored access for British exports in protected Commonwealth markets.

The system was not designed to establish intra-Commonwealth free trade. Moreover, it has never been a coherent "system" proper, in the sense of a comprehensive, standardized, universally applicable formula or integral scheme. Its legal basis, aside from unilateral acts, is bilateral agreements; and the "system" rests on a network of such agreements, primarily between the United Kingdom (on her own behalf and on behalf of her dependencies)

33. The McKenna duties of 1919 and the key industry duties of 1921. Preferences as of 1929 covered 7 per cent of British imports from the Commonwealth, with an average margin on all Commonwealth-origin imports of 2 per cent to 3 per cent; see MacDougall and Hutt, "Imperial Preferences: A Quantitative Analysis," 64 *Economic J.* 233 at 237–244 (1954).

34. Started by Canada in 1898, followed by New Zealand and South Africa in 1903, and later by others. As of 1929, the United Kingdom was enjoying preferences in all the principal trading countries of the Commonwealth in varying degrees. The total of her Commonwealth exports so covered was about one-third, and the average margin on all her Commonwealth exports was estimated to be about 5 per cent. See *ibid.*

35. On the United Kingdom's side, there was mainly a guarantee to continue Commonwealth free entry as to commodities on which duties had been introduced in the Revenue Act of 1932 or on which the United Kingdom undertook to introduce or increase duties applicable to third countries. Kahn, *op. cit. supra* note 30, at p. 183. On the dominions' side, there were in existence high rates for which the Ottawa preferences meant reductions. For texts of Ottawa Agreements, see 135 *Brit. & For. State Papers* 151–264 (1932).

and various individual Commonwealth members (or former members), and secondarily between certain pairs of the latter. These agreements, the benefits of which have been largely though not entirely generalized within the Commonwealth, have been negotiated for an initial term (typically five years), subject to periodic revision and termination. The preferences accorded have been selective, rather than across the board, both as to the products affected and as to the margin of preference (i.e., the degree of tariff differential by which the product is favored). The extent to which the various parts and former parts of the Commonwealth have granted them has also varied. Some beneficiaries, indeed, grant only very limited ones or none at all; and although the United Kingdom prior to 1932 enjoyed in outlying parts certain unrequited preferences, it would appear that on the whole the United Kingdom has given more than she has received in benefits.[36]

Intra-Commonwealth trade grew after the Ottawa Agreements, in the sense of accounting for a materially enlarged portion of the total foreign trade of the countries and territories making up the Commonwealth. But it was merely a larger percentage of a smaller total; the Commonwealth's total exports in 1938 were approximately £1120 million (of a devalued currency, moreover) as contrasted with around £1750 million in 1928. The intra-Commonwealth portion fell off less than world trade at large (14 *v.* 30 per cent); but as against this, exports to third countries fell off even more, by a correspondingly sharper drop than world trade as a whole (46 *v.* 30 per cent). Whether this mixed result represented a blessing has been questioned by critics.[37] Actually,

36. For a recent analysis of the preference system, see Economist Intelligence Unit, *The Commonwealth and Europe* (1960), pp. 10–24. A PEP (Political and Economic Planning) study, *Britain and World Trade* (1947), pp. 24–25, concluded that the prewar balance of benefit had been much in favor of the Outer Commonwealth. The statistical showing is that the United Kingdom has been a more expansive customer for the Outer Commonwealth than the other way around.

37. The PEP study, *op. cit. supra* note 36, at p. 25, charges the system with having diverted trade at the expense of third countries and of British exports to third countries, and with contributing to the slow recovery of world trade after the Depression. According to Kahn, *op. cit. supra* note 30, at p. 184, the protective tariff to which the preferences were ancillary led to retaliation by third countries. Whether "internal" benefits were sufficient to offset external deficiencies has been

when the time came for renegotiation and renewal of the original agreements, in 1937, the occasion was not used as opportunity for generally widening the scope and intensity of the preferences; and beginning in 1938, the year of the celebrated Anglo-American trade agreement, the system has gradually decayed.

The decline may be seen in the subsiding of the general "incidence" of the preferences—that is, the composite percentage by which they favored Commonwealth sourcing, as measured by average margin times volume. The average margin of preference on goods imported into the United Kingdom in 1937–1938 (and vice versa) is estimated to have been somewhere between 10 and 12 per cent; in 1948, between 6 and 7 per cent; as of 1960, about 4 per cent and still subsiding; and a like erosion has been under way also where preferences have been significant in the Outer Commonwealth, especially Australia and New Zealand. The process has been less a deliberate removing of products from preferential schedules than allowing margins to be squeezed through a combination of the following: (*a*) price inflation, which has lowered the *ad valorem* equivalent of margins on goods subject to "specific" duties; (*b*) concessions granted to third countries in reciprocal trade-agreement negotiations;[38] and (*c*) shifts over time in the product composition of the trade, as between preference and non-preference items.

A factual analysis made in 1953 concluded that "the effect of preferences on our total trade cannot be more than marginal,"

---

questioned. Mackay, *op. cit. supra* note 24, at p. 57, finds that post-Ottawa intra-Commonwealth trade grew more in non-preference than in preference items. MacDougall and Hutt, *loc. cit. supra* note 33, at pp. 255–256, claim that the "shift in U. K. exports between Countries granting different margins of preference has on balance been of no importance."

38. For example, EFTA countries receive increasingly duty-free tariff treatment in derogation of Commonwealth preference commitments, and this obliged Britain to obtain releases from certain engagements in bilateral agreements with Australia, New Zealand, Union of South Africa, India, Pakistan, Ireland, Rhodesia, and Nyasaland. See 178 *Board of Trade J.* 779 (1960). Canada and the United Kingdom had already concluded a mutual release at the time of the negotiation of GATT in 1947. Again, Britain made concessions to the United States in the "fifth round" GATT tariff conference; see Annex A, Schedule 19, of the Protocol of July 16, 1962, T.I.A.S. No. 5253. "For most of the concession items (involving typically a 20% reduction), the margin of preference . . . have been automatically reduced, since most of such imports from the Commonwealth are free of duty." U. S. Dep't of State, Pub. No. 7349, *General Agreement on Tariffs and Trade: Analysis of United States Negotiations, 1960–61 Tariff Conference* (1962), I, 169.

and a subsequent study (1960) judged that "trade preferences for sterling goods" have by now been reduced "almost to the vanishing point," their remaining consequential impact being confined to a limited number of particular instances.[39] Another British author has ventured to predict their disappearance altogether by about 1970.[40]

4. Factors Affecting Preferences

As the tables above demonstrate, intra-Commonwealth trade nonetheless continued to be high long after the onset of the preference attrition. The trade pattern was thus also shaped by another factor: the policies and practices affecting the availability of the means of payment for imports. Consequent upon the abandonment of the gold standard in September, 1931, the United Kingdom established the Sterling Bloc (transformed in 1940 into the Sterling Area), a mechanism that permitted the members (all the Commonwealth, except Canada, plus several outside countries) to continue using sterling as a medium of exchange in their trade relations conveniently and freely. This undoubtedly served to facilitate intra-area trade in a period when so many countries, in an effort to bolster their currencies, were resorting to various trade-restricting devices.[41] The outbreak

39. Respectively, MacDougall, *loc. cit. supra* note 33, at p. 256; *The Commonwealth and Europe, op. cit. supra* note 36, at p. 25. Nonetheless, traders not entitled to preferences complain and those entitled continue to cherish them. Moreover, preferences are still vital for the trade of some Commonwealth parts; see note 24, *supra.*

40. Mackay, *op. cit. supra* note 24, at p. 131. A more prudent judgment is that they are a "waning asset." Yet, there is a vested interest in preferences that does not die easily. For example, the Conference of Commonwealth Ministers at Montreal in 1958, while urging trade expansion on the multilateral principle of non-discrimination, did not propose termination of existing Commonwealth preferences; see *Commonwealth Trade and Economic Conference, 1958.*

41. Evidence of the beneficial trade effect of the Sterling Bloc mechanism, as such, in the circumstances of the thirties, is afforded by statistics on British trade with the non-Commonwealth countries in the bloc (six Scandinavian and Baltic countries, Portugal, Siam, and Iraq). British trade with this group fared as well proportionately (exports-imports combined, 1929–1938) as that with the Outer Commonwealth. League of Nations, *Review of World Trade 1938* (1939). p. 35. Intra-Commonwealth trade, for its part, was helped also in some degree by various quotas and administrative controls applied by the United Kingdom; H. E. Friedlander and J. Oser, *Economic History of Modern Europe* (1953), pp. 438–439, 455–456.

of the war, of course, led to the imposition of strict controls. These controls were continued with severity in the period of disruption, stringency, and exhausted monetary reserves following the war by all except the few countries with "hard" currencies (notably, the United States, Canada, and Switzerland).[42] With the coming of recovery, aided by effective international collaboration,[43] these controls were progressively eased and dismantled in the fifties by the major nations having them; and so far as United Kingdom trade is concerned, they were abolished in principle with the restoration of "non-resident convertibility" of sterling at the end of 1958.[44]

Because preferences operated in a setting of abnormality in exchange management during the era in which intra-Commonwealth trade thrived most conspicuously in its share of total

42. Exchange controls, in their application to trade, typically go hand-in-hand with "quantitative restrictions" (administratively fixed quotas or ceilings on the amount of permitted imports). As a general rule, the GATT outlaws such restrictions (art. 11), especially those which discriminate (art. 13), but recognizes the legitimacy of certain necessary and defensible ones, notably those justified by serious "balance-of-payments" difficulties (arts. 12 and 14) or by the requirements of economic development in lesser developed countries (art. 18). By and large, the restrictions applied by Commonwealth countries since the war have been under the justification of these exceptions and have been liquidated in pace with the fading of the justification.

43. An outstanding regional example was the OEEC, created by convention signed April 16, 1948, between 17 countries of western Europe, in response to General Marshall's Harvard speech of June 5, 1947. (The U. S. and Canada became associate members in 1950, and Spain in 1958.) Among its functions was a systematic freeing of trade from the restrictions which had arisen out of the financial stringencies of the postwar years. Its major original missions were practically accomplished by the end of 1958, and it was shortly thereafter replaced by the OECD. A recapitulation of its work (and that of its adjunct, set up as a payments clearing-house and banker for payments deficits afflicting individual members, the European Payments Union) is contained in its Ninth Annual Report, *A Decade of Co-Operation—Achievements and Perspectives* (1958).

44. This, though symbolizing the restoration of freedom in the means of payment for imports into the United Kingdom, did not mean the end of restrictions throughout the Sterling Area, each member of which has its own trade regulations and, if independent, its own national currency and monetary policy. The list of GATT participants reporting restrictions "for balance-of-payments purposes" entailing "some degree of discrimination as between sources of supply" as of late 1959 included the following Commonwealth countries: India, New Zealand, Australia, Ghana, Malaya, Rhodesia and Nyasaland, and the United Kingdom. GATT, *Basic Instruments and Selected Documents*, 8th Supp. (1960), p. 67. During the following year great progress in liquidating them was recorded; *ibid.*, 9th Supp., pp. 66–68; and reports as of Dec., 1961, and July, 1962, mention only countries having non-discriminatory restrictions (New Zealand, Ceylon, India, and Pakistan, in the Commonwealth), *ibid.*, 10th Supp., p. 114, and *The Activities of the GATT, 1961/62*, p. 24.

Commonwealth foreign trade, it is impossible to say exactly what would have been the result on the basis of the preferences alone. International experience generally with the multifarious stratagems of trade restriction and trade diversion that have been tried in this generation, however, strongly suggests that financial controls tend to be more decisive than tariffs. For instance, the United Kingdom's share in Canada's postwar exports, when Canada was subject to the tight restrictions applied to goods of "dollar" origin, was drastically below prewar in the ratio of about 5:2. In any event, the declining importance of intra-Commonwealth trade latterly in evidence has paralleled, with a normal lag ascribable to momentum, the relaxation and removal of exchange controls. The degree to which an array of new and intensified preferences could be expected to reinvigorate intra-Commonwealth trade in the world of today, therefore, unless supported by restored administrative controls, cannot be judged by the statistical showing of Commonwealth trade in the years since the Ottawa Agreements.[45]

As the effect of the Commonwealth preference system has been obscured by this monetary factor, so its decay has undoubtedly been pushed, to an indeterminate extent, by the international opposition it encountered. From the standpoint of third countries, denied the benefit of the special tariff privileges enjoyed by the recipients of preferences, preferences discriminate against their trade.[46] So, from early days, the preferences inaugurated by the Ottawa Agreements provoked unfavorable reactions from other countries, for example, the United States.[47] American hostility

45. Re-imposition of the kind of administrative controls and restrictions needed to insure a major reshaping of the trade pattern, moreover, would violate art. 8 of the Articles of Agreement of the International Monetary Fund, T.I.A.S. No. 1501, as well as provisions of GATT—except as a temporary expedient to deal with a financial stringency in highly qualified conditions.

46. The United Kingdom contended that the preferences did not violate the principle of most-favored-nation treatment, on the argument that Commonwealth members were not "foreign countries." Other countries apparently acquiesced and the interpretation, though increasingly based on a fiction and no longer tenable in GATT theory, persists in Commonwealth commercial policy doctrine.

47. See the papers in preparation for the British trade agreement negotiation in U. S. *For. Rel.*, *1937*, II, 1–94, especially at pp. 11–14. Systematic opposition started with the advent of Mr. Cordell Hull as secretary of state; in the interval beforehand, the official stand was "no implication of acquiescence" and "reserves . . . position." *Ibid.*, 1933, II, 2, 4.

found a vehicle for effective expression in the 1938 Anglo-American Trade Agreement, in which in return for concessions obtained in United States duty rates the United Kingdom agreed to curbs on preferences.[48] Following that, the United States government, as occasion presented itself, obtained a succession of British assurances looking further to the negotiated circumscription, if not ultimate liquidation, of preferences: in the Atlantic Charter, the Lend-Lease Agreement of 1942, and the Financial Agreement of 1945.[49] Finally, the General Agreements on Tariffs and Trade (the GATT), to which the United Kingdom and other Commonwealth countries adhere, forbids new preferences.[50]

The latter interposes a special legal obstacle such as did not exist in 1932 to the revival of the preference system. Technically, a release from this GATT obligation forbidding new preferences is possible by means of a waiver approved by a special majority of the contracting parties to that instrument.[51] In several instances in the past, waivers affecting Commonwealth preferences have in fact been obtained.[52] But these have all been concerned with

48. Signed Nov. 17, 1938, E.A.S. No. 164. The conclusion of this agreement was facilitated by a feeling, on the British side, that the preference system needed to be modified in the interest of promoting international trade. The background of the agreement, from the British viewpoint, is summarized in RIIA, *Survey of International Affairs, 1937,* I, 102–104, and *ibid., 1938,* I, 19–27.

49. For texts of these documents, see *A Decade of American Foreign Policy, Basic Documents 1941–49,* S. Doc. No. 123, 81st Cong., 1st Sess., pp. 1, 3, and 739 respectively (1950). The latter is prefaced by a Joint Statement Regarding Commercial Policy (p. 737) relevant to the question in reference. For exchanges of views regarding the extent of the obligations imposed on the United Kingdom as to preferences by art. 7 of the 1942 Lend-Lease Agreement, see U. S., *For. Rel., 1942,* I, 525–537. Dismantling of preferences was correlated to satisfactory progress in the multilateral freeing of international trade more generally.

50. The following Commonwealth countries have been parties to GATT since the beginning (1947): Australia, Britain, Canada, Ceylon, India, New Zealand, Pakistan, Southern Rhodesia. The dependent territories have as a rule assumed membership in their own right, on attaining independence. The governing rule of GATT, as set forth in art. 1, is unconditional most-favored-nation treatment (para. 1); but theretofore existing preferences are tolerated as a special exception (para. 2), with the margins existing as of April 10, 1947, fixed as their ceiling (para. 4, but an earlier date in the case of Australia, Canada, and Southern Rhodesia, Annex G). The territorial ambit of the permissible existing Commonwealth preferences is specified in Annex A. Whether margins subsequently narrowed or cancelled can lawfully be put back to where they were on the cut-off date has not been authoritatively settled.

51. Art. 25(5). This provision is designed to apply "in exceptional circumstances." Approval by two-thirds of those voting is required, provided no less than an absolute majority of all members concur.

52. These waivers, through 1964, concern: (*a*) certain items traditionally entering the United Kingdom duty-free (Oct., 1953, March, 1955); (*b*) "special

relatively minor special cases, involving limited indulgences for which there has been exceptional justification and no jeopardizing of the GATT's integrity. The accommodations approved have been of a nature not intended or considered likely to divert trade in a way injurious to any third country; and, as a safeguard, each contracting party's rights under article 23 of GATT have been explicitly or implicitly reserved.[53] A major rejuvenation of the Commonwealth preference system would not square with the purposes for which the waiver procedure was designed and for which it has been used in practice. It is highly unlikely, therefore, that the non-Commonwealth contracting parties could be persuaded to accept a waiver of such far-reaching inconsistency with the objective of the GATT, the multilateral promotion of trade on a non-discriminatory basis. Nor does the Commonwealth, for its part, whether from the viewpoint of the United Kingdom or of Outer Commonwealth, have strong incentive to desire such a waiver. The general policy orientation set by the Commonwealth ministers in their Montreal meeting of September, 1958, internationalist and "outward-looking" rather than particularistic and "inward-looking" in emphasis,[54] remains grounded on a realistic appreciation of the directions in which the most fruitful cultivation of Commonwealth economic interests lie.

---

problems of dependent overseas territories" (March, 1955, Dec., 1960); (*c*) the special customs arrangement between South Africa and Rhodesia and Nyasaland (Dec., 1955, June, 1960, and Nov., 1960); (*d*) Australian favors to products of Papua-New Guinea (Oct., 1953, Nov., 1956, May, 1959). The "Decisions" granting the waivers and reciting their qualifications and justifiability are carried in the following annual additions to GATT's official register, *Basic Instruments and Selected Documents:* (*a*) 2d Supp. (1954), p. 20 and 3d Supp. (1955), p. 25; (*b*) 3d Supp., p. 21 and 9th Supp. (1961), p. 47; (*c*) 4th Supp. (1956), p. 17, and 9th Supp., pp. 46, 51; (*d*) 2d Supp., p. 18, 5th Supp. (1957), p. 34, and 8th Supp. (1960), p. 28. For complete list of waivers granted, and reports on them, see *ibid.*, 10th Supp. (1962), pp. 284–287; and indexes of subsequent volumes.

53. Art. 23 provides a recourse procedure, leading *in extremis* to retaliation, open to a contracting party aggrieved by the action of another contracting party; it is designed to insure that reciprocity of benefit is maintained.

54. See conference report, *op. cit. supra* note 40, particularly the following numbered paragraphs: 4 and 5 (that multilateral action is required to meet the trade problems of Commonwealth countries), 10 (calling for convertibility of sterling and removal of discrimination), 23–25 (noting with satisfaction the progress made in removing discrimination), 26 ("we cannot hope to flourish by developing trade between ourselves alone"). A different view, with proposal that a waiver be sought, is ventured by Sir Derek Walker-Smith and Peter Walker, "A Call to the Commonwealth," 9 *Commonwealth Development* 13 at 16 (1962).

5. Commonwealth Markets

The hub of the Commonwealth trading system is the United Kingdom, as already indicated. Trade between and among Outer Commonwealth countries has been secondary in importance. In 1938, approximately five-sixths of all intra-Commonwealth trade (export basis) was accounted for by the flow in and out of the United Kingdom; and in 1961–1963, that flow was still over three-fourths of the trade. Outer Commonwealth cross-trade, in over-all dimensions, is less than a twelfth of total Commonwealth trade; what it means to the Outer Commonwealth interrelationship itself is sketched in the following table.

Table 4. *Outer Commonwealth Countries: Exports to Each Other* (£ *millions; percentage of total*)

1928	1938	1954–56	1959–60	1961–62	1963
113	97	780	704	755	811
(11%)	(14%)	(16%)	(13%)	(13%)	(12½%)

Note: The third through fifth columns represent yearly averages. South Africa (as well as Ireland) is omitted in all postwar years shown. Inclusion of South Africa in 1954–1956 would have made the showing 18 per cent; subtraction of its trade for those years, for table purposes, entailed estimating "exports-to" from its import statistics.

Source: League of Nations, *Network of World Trade* (1942); *Commonwealth Trade, 1959–60,* for the third column; *ibid., 1963* for the other postwar columns. Table 2 of the latter substantially revises figures given in earlier editions.

It has been said that the cross-trade which does occur is only to a minor degree a Commonwealth-related phenomenon; it is primarily what neighborhood and other factors (especially, the commodities involved) would bring about in absence of the Commonwealth.[55] For that matter, as has been noted, a number of the

---

55. *The Commonwealth and Europe, op. cit. supra* note 39, at pp. 6–8; the general opinion expressed is that the "British connection is the sole unifying factor of the Commonwealth system" (p. 3).

Outer Commonwealth countries grant few if any preferences, and some of those granted are not available to all other Outer Commonwealth countries.

In an array, in order of importance, of the export markets of the Outer Commonwealth countries, the Outer Commonwealth will often be found to rank third or lower below some outside country or countries that with Britain rank ahead. For example, on the basis of a fairly recent statistical examination, each one of the Common Market countries (counting Belgo-Luxembourg as one) outranks the entire Outer Commonwealth, in the case of Nigeria; and the EEC is approximately double the Outer Commonwealth market for Rhodesia and Nyasaland, Canada, and New Zealand. The United States and the EEC each are quadruple for Ghana; and the United States, aside from taking 60 per cent of Canada's exports, is the first-ranking outlet also for Hong Kong and Jamaica. The United States and Japan each outrank any single Outer Commonwealth country for India, Pakistan, and New Zealand, as does Germany and the U. S. S. R. also for India.[56] This does not exhaust the list of examples of the sort.

The Outer Commonwealth evidently does not, in general, share more than a modest common denominator of the kind of economic interdependence and complementarity from which it is hoped the fabric of commercial integration can be woven. Such major expansion potential in Commonwealth cross-trade as does exist is undoubtedly conditioned by the same factors as are United Kingdom exports to the Commonwealth: economic development and overcoming the present lack of purchasing power. The advanced parts, with fairly high per capita incomes (Canada, Australia, New Zealand) contain less than 5 per cent of the Outer Commonwealth's population. Existing export channels become clogged and the opening of the new ones impeded, furthermore, by the tendency of countries wishing to industrialize

56. *Nigerian Trade Journal,* April/June, 1962; *Monthly Digest of Statistics* (Salisbury), April, 1963; *External Trade Statistics of Ghana* (Accra), Dec., 1962; *Commonwealth Trade 1960–1961; Commonwealth Development,* March/April, 1963; *EFTA Reporter,* No. 47, Oct. 2, 1962; U. N., *Year Book,* 1961. But in New Zealand's case, there is a developing trade with Australia which thrust that country in 1964 ahead of Japan as a market.

to place restraints upon the importation of consumer goods and to give special encouragement to the development of local production. The Commonwealth's hunger for capital goods, on the other hand, creates a vast potential for products that British industry can supply. However, the exploitation of this potential (whose realization bids in turn to generate a market for still other goods) involves financing and the furnishing of aid, discussed below.

Conversely, the Outer Commonwealth countries face limits on expansion of their market in the United Kingdom, measured by relative absorptive capacity. As of 1960, the Outer Commonwealth contained about one-fourth of the world's population as against the United Kingdom's 2 per cent; and the United Kingdom had only 8 per cent of the composite GNP's of the leading industrial nations of the world, not counting the Soviet area and all the other countries on five continents with their existing and growing demands. That is to say, the size of the Outer Commonwealth is extremely incommensurate with Britain's share of the world's potential consumers and purchasing power. Grouping on the part of Commonwealth countries for mutual commercial self-help would logically be fragmentary and tend to include non-Commonwealth countries of a given region.

Historically, the United Kingdom has been importer of raw materials and semi-finished commodities from the Commonwealth. As she imports from other countries types of products which the Commonwealth is in position to supply, there is room for larger Commonwealth trade in these;[57] but, except as any such increase represented an enlargement of British consumption, it could be achieved only through the self-defeating expedient of sacrificing trade with other countries. Because primary commodities are chronically plagued with erratic prices, cycles of overproduction, and laggard or fluctuating world demand, emphasis is being put on processing and manufacturing as offering the hope for a substantial share of the increases needed in the exports of the low-income countries for self-help financing

57. For relevant commodity-trade tables, see *Commonwealth Trade 1960–61*, p. 75 (U. K. imports); and *The Commonwealth and Europe 1962* (Council of Europe), p. 31 (Commonwealth exports).

of their development. Here there are displacement strains on British industry itself. The first major manufacture established in the Outer Commonwealth, low-grade textiles (and its predictable off-shoot, textiles of higher grade), prompted the putting into effect of *de facto* British import quotas for the protection of the Lancashire mills.[58] Britain's poor promise as an outlet for the more advanced manufactures of which the Outer Commonwealth may be capable is illustrated by the proportion of India's exports to Britain of leading categories of such products (i.e., other than grey goods and jute goods) in 1962–1963. Arrayed in order of over-all trade importance to India, the portions sold to Britain were: cotton fabrics, "other" (5 per cent); napery and the like, sec. 656.03 and 656.04 of the Customs nomenclature (30 per cent); hand tools and other hardware, sec. 699 (3 per cent); sewing machines and other miscellaneous machinery, sec. 716 (4 per cent); electrical apparatus, sec. 721 (2 per cent); all these categories combined (7½ per cent).[59]

The major growth potential thus lies elsewhere; and, as already pointed out, it is elsewhere that the recent growth has occurred. In terms of intensity and market-development need, the relative decline of the United Kingdom as purchaser of Commonwealth products has on the average fallen most heavily on the countries which have heretofore been most dependent on the United Kindgom for their export earnings. The following table shows this on the basis of dividing the Outer Commonwealth suppliers according to whether they have in the mid-fifties disposed of more than or less than 20 per cent of their exports in the United King-

58. The restriction took the form of a "voluntary agreement" in 1959 between the industries of the United Kingdom, India, Pakistan, and Hong Kong. In 1962–1963, the United Kingdom absorbed 46 per cent of India's exportation of cotton "grey goods," but under 5 per cent of jute goods; see note 63, *infra*. The latter product has recently been India's biggest export; moreover it accounted for better than half the over-all growth in India's exports during the last five years. *Reserve Bank of India Bulletin*, July, 1963, Table 45-B.

59. India, *Monthly Statistics of the Foreign Trade of India*, March, 1963, vol. I. The period covered is India's fiscal year, April-March. The percentages are rounded. The export valuation of each of these categories was approximately (in millions of rupees): 251, 40, 27, 17, and 14, respectively, for a total of 350 ($75 million), of which 27 were destined to the United Kingdom. By comparison, the United Kingdom took 24 per cent of India's total exports—mainly tea and other primary commodities—29 per cent, if jute goods (for which she has small use) are excluded.

dom (omitting minor suppliers which together account for less than 3 per cent of the total flow). Group I comprises Canada, Pakistan, and Malaya; Group II the rest.

Table 5. *Commonwealth Exports to the United Kingdom (percentage)*

	1954	1957	1960	1961
Group I (under 20%)	16.6	14.9	16.1	15.2
Group II (over 20%)	43.1	34.6	33.5	29.4

Source: Commonwealth Trade and U. N., *Yb. Int'l Trade Statistics*, various. The 1963 edition of the first-named source gives a year-by-year breakdown covering 1959–1963 (Table 18). The United Kingdom's share in Canadian exports was the same in 1963 as in 1959—15 per cent—but substantially declined in the case of Pakistan and Malaysia. Rises occured as to Ceylon and Hong Kong (2 and 4 percentage points); but declines occured for all the rest (by 10 percentage points each for Australia, New Zealand, and Nigeria, and 4 to 7 for Ghana, India, and Rhodesia and Nyasaland), except for the miscellaneous "Others" (unchanged as a group).

For the first group, the fractional change is of small consequence in their total trade picture. But for the second group, the repatterning is of major dimensions; in seven years, the United Kingdom market dropped away from a share of roughly 3 to 4 to one of roughly 3 to 7. A few examples of how the shift is occurring may be given. Before the war, Japan took only one-fifteenth as much as the United Kingdom from Australia; now Japan is rivaling the United Kingdom as Australia's first customer.[60] Japan has proved a fast-growing customer also for New Zealand and North

60. The following table from the *Australian Financial Review* (No. 614, Sept. 18, 1962, p. 10) shows the trend, in percentage of total exports:

	1937–38	1950–1955 avg.	1959–60	1961–62
U. K.	54.8	35.7	26.4	19.0
Japan	3.7	7.5	14.4	17.3

In 1963–1964, Japan almost overtook the U.K. (£A million 225 v. 232), but dropped back to about her 1961–1962 position in 1964–1965, relatively speaking (£A million 204 v. 238, for the first 11 months of the fiscal year). China has also become a substantial customer, to the point of taking about a third as much as Britain in 1963–1964 and a fourth as much in 1964–1965.

Borneo, as well as for Canada.[61] As regards India's exports, eastern Europe absorbed 17 per cent of the total in 1964–1965, 12 per cent in 1962 and 3 per cent in the mid-fifties.[62] Between 1957 and 1961, the sales of Ghana, Kenya, New Zealand, and Jamaica to the United States approximately doubled, British Guiana's quadrupled, and Hong Kong's expanded almost as much.[63]

In sum, the Commonwealth exists in a field of trade magnets tugging outward on the members. The EEC's attraction has been most pronounced vis-à-vis the United Kingdom. For the Outer Commonwealth, it has in its first five years been simply an average growth market, accounting for about one-eighth of Outer Commonwealth exports. For certain Outer Commonwealth countries, the performance has been above-average, for others less. As of 1962 the latter include, notably, Australia, New Zealand, India, and Pakistan, a quartet for which western Europe generally has been deteriorating as a market. Although statistics for fiscal 1963–1964 suggested a retrieval of market position for them, EEC imports from them were up about 15 per cent over 1962, a degree of gain which applied to the Outer Commonwealth generally in equal measure to the "Old Dominions" and the "less developed countries" (hereafter referred to as "LDC's").[64]

Two special anxieties have been awakened by the EEC's

61. North Borneo is a striking example. In 1956, Britain was its first customer, with a 23 per cent share, while Japan's was 10 per cent. As of 1960, the former's percentage had fallen to 9, and Japan's had risen to 43. As for New Zealand, its exports to Japan increased thirteen-fold from 1954 to 1964; during that ten years, the United Kingdom's share declined from 67 to 49 per cent while that of Japan plus the United States increased from 6 to 17½ per cent.

62. *The Economist* (London), June 1, 1963, p. 928. *Monthly Statistics of the Foreign Trade of India*, vol. I, March, 1965 (GOI, Calcutta). The figure for fiscal 1964–65 was 148.32 lakhs of rupees out of 835.24. (India's fiscal year ends March 31. To convert the figures to dollars, multiply by 2.1 million.)

63. The following figures show exports to the United States in 1957 and 1961, respectively, with total 1961 trade shown in parentheses. All figures are in millions. Ghana, £14.5 and 27.0 (102.4); Kenya, £2.5 and 5.0 (35.3); New Zealand, £22.1 and 40.8 (283.7); Jamaica, £11.2 and 21.8 (60.6); Guiana, BWI$ 7.7 and 30.7 (149); Hong Kong, HK$ 198 and 701 (3930).

64. Of the four, New Zealand recorded the best improvement, an increase of 20 per cent in calendar 1964 over 1963; and Pakistan the least, a scant improvement in the period cited in text, but a fall-off for the calendar year. But New Zealand's spurt was then offset by the largest decline of the four in early 1965 (Jan.-April), a drop of 22 per cent from the same period the previous year, while Pakistan was the only one to do so well as simply maintain position. OECD, *Overall Trade by Countries*, ser. A, EEC, *Foreign Trade Monthly Statistics*.

emergence. One of these, affecting especially the "Old Dominions," relates to the fate of temperate-zone agricultural products under the EEC's tortuously evolving Common Agricultural Policy. This is a subject as yet clouded in uncertainty and argument; and a review of it would require attention, beyond the scope of this study, to the more significant stake of the United States, Denmark, and southern Latin America. It may be passed over here with the observation that, in absence of a United Kingdom merger with the EEC, agricultural policy apparently impinges on established Commonwealth interests to a minor degree only; of the Commonwealth's major export-production, wool is duty-free, hard wheat probably has its future reasonably assured (*supra*, note 24), its tobacco enjoys a duty arrangement deemed to give it an advantage over its principal competitor (U. S. tobacco), its meat and butter have not heretofore been marketed in any quantity in the countries of the area, and the area has been only a sporadic customer for its soft wheat.

The second worry relates to commodities of special concern for certain tropical countries of the Commonwealth which, in company with those outside, have been apprehensive over the EEC's special relationship of association with ex-French and ex-Belgian Africa. As provided in article 133 of the Rome treaty, imports originating in the now-independent states of the territories in question, plus certain others of subordinate importance (Algeria, Somaliland, and France's Overseas Departments and Dependent Territories),[65] "shall on their entry into Member States benefit by the total abolition of customs duties" in pace with the scheduled abolition of duties among the Six themselves. They thus gain a competitive advantage in Germany and Italy, especially over other producers of the same tropical and subtropical commodities, since the outsiders will be subject to the EEC's common external tariff whereas all alike were previously subject to the tariffs of those two countries.[66] In compensation, however, the

65. The areas covered by art. 133 are listed in Annex IV of the treaty. The Overseas Departments are automatically covered as being integral parts of the French Republic, and as is Algeria (as of the time the treaty was signed); they are specifically provided for in art. 227(2).

66. The Benelux situation is generally analogous, as their previously low tariff structure is being raised. The pre-EEC rates of the several member states, and the

tariff wall of Italy is being lowered and easier access to France in competition with the previously privileged products of associated territories of "French expression" is being secured. Moreover, a considerable volume of LDC-interest commodities is free-listed.

So far, these apprehensions remain to be borne out in a hypothetical future—in the over-all, at least, and apart from special problem cases. The evidence of the first six years of experience under the Rome treaty suggests that the non-associated LDC's as a whole have been faring very well.

Table 6. *EEC Imports from Developing Countries* (*monthly averages, in $ millions*)

From	*1958*	*1961*	*1963*	*1964*	*Gain*
Associated territories	129	148	159	171	42
Others	440	483	577	648	208
All	569	631	736	819	250

Note: To get approximate annual figures, multiply by twelve. For definition of "developing countries," "developed" nations, and "LDC's," see *infra*.

Sources: EEC, *General Statistical Bulletin—1964*, No. 10 (Oct.), Tables 82 and 88; and *ibid., 1965*, No. 6, Tables 84 and 90.

On the basis of world statistics available through 1962, it appears that non-associated LDC exports to the EEC have been expanding faster than the exports of all LDC's to non-EEC "developed" nations: 80 per cent more gross increase in the former than in the latter in the four years following 1958. EEC continued its pace-setting role in 1962–1964, though with a shortened lead.

To alleviate some of the particular difficulties that might later arise, as the differential rates of the association arrangement take full effect, it was provided that the EEC external tariff be reduced on certain tropical products, having a varying interest to

common external tariff as originally fixed, are shown for certain products in Table 27 of the Report by a Panel of Experts (Haberler Report), GATT, *Trends in International Trade* (1958), and the preferences existing in 1962, in Table 4–17 of the document *World Economic Survey 1962*, vol. I, with accompanying text. For an airing of the issue, see these two generally (at pp. 115 *et. seq.* and 81 *et. seq.*, respectively).

Commonwealth producers, effective January 1, 1964. The vehicle for this measure was the new convention associating the African states and Madagascar with the EEC, signed at Yaounde July 20, 1963.[67] The list includes cocoa, from 9 to 5.4 per cent; tea, from 18 to 10.8 per cent, or duty free contingent upon like British action; tropical woods, some contingent free-listing; and several others.[68] Meanwhile, expansion has continued; in the first four months of 1965, imports from the associated areas averaged $8 million per month more than in the same period of 1964 and from the outside LDC's, $35 million more.[69]

6. Investment and Aid

A second important economic factor in the inter-linkage equation concerns investment and financial aid.[70] And here, as capital

67. The parties to it are the EEC, its six member states and the eighteen associated states. An English translation is carried in 2 *Int'l Legal Materials* 971–1008 (1963); and a summary and explanation may be found in "Information Memo," No. P-23/63 issued by the Official Spokesman of EEC (July, 1963). This instrument, initialed in Dec., 1962, replaces for another five-year period the "implementing Convention" relating to the Association of the Overseas Countries and Territories that was annexed to the Rome treaty.

68. The other reduced duties (with the previous rates in parentheses) are: coffee, 9.6 per cent (16 per cent); fresh pineapple, 9 per cent (12 per cent); cloves, 15 per cent (20 per cent); dried coconut, 4 per cent (5 per cent); nutmeg, 15 per cent (20 per cent); pepper, 17 per cent (20 per cent); vanilla, 11.5 per cent (15 per cent). Further see first sentence of note 25, *supra*. The West Indies are a major producer of nutmeg, and Zanzibar of cloves; some vanilla is produced in the Seychelles, and some dried coconut in Malaya. Commonwealth coffee production, though minor in comparison with South America, is in a comparable range with ex-French Africa; it is important in East Africa and significant in India. The Commonwealth produces about 60 per cent of the world's cocoa and pepper, or did recently. For coffee, cocoa, and pepper, the EEC has come to be a more important market than the United Kingdom for the Commonwealth.

69. If the heavy EEC imports of Libyan and Kuwait oil are excluded as a special distorting factor, the increase in EEC imports from LDC's may be said to have been shared roughly *pro rata* by the associated and the non-associated groups; the edge which the former should logically gain from existing tariff arrangements appears to require a considerable period of gestation, owing undoubtedly to the circumstances of their production potential.

70. A third factor, the international money and exchange system known as the Sterling Area, also affects Commonwealth relations, though to an extent qualified by the fact that certain non-Commonwealth countries are in the Sterling Area (e.g., Ireland and South Africa) whereas the most economically powerful Outer Commonwealth country (Canada) is not. One reason for its creation (non-convertibility) ended in the late fifties. It continues to be convenient as well as to enjoy a certain necessity by reason of the heavy claims that Overseas Sterling countries have accumulated against its central financial pool, the Sterling

fountainhead, the United Kingdom has been the Commonwealth's hub even more than in trade. The Outer Commonwealth
is variously capital deficient and must look abroad for investment
and development funds. Even the parts most advanced in capital
formation, the "Old Dominions," are still net capital importers, if
perhaps not in a necessitous plight in that regard.

Before World War II, aside from American participation in
investment in Canada, the United Kingdom supplied virtually all
outside capital received by the overseas Commonwealth countries. In the decennium following the war, she was able to
maintain a predominent, if no longer practically exclusive, role;
during 1946–1955, she was recorded as supplier of about 70 per
cent of the £2370 millions then placed in the overseas sterling
countries.[71] But a decline which set in with the war, has become
increasingly more pronounced in the years since the mid-fifties.[72]

Some impression of the shifting toward other capital suppliers
may be gotten by comparing prewar and recent sourcing, respectively, with the picture given in the following table which shows
the estimated current value of foreign holdings, by source, in
1957–1958 in principal areas of the Commonwealth as it then
stood.

Equalization Account maintained in London and underwritten by the British
government. Whereas the account was in equilibrium before World War II,
Britain has since become increasingly a heavy sterling debtor; her net sterling
liabilities stood at £3,543 millions in late 1962, for example, and £4,021 millions
in early 1965. Professor Thomas has estimated that if Great Britain, the system's
banker, "is to function properly as the head of the sterling system she must
generate . . . a surplus" of at least £350 million annually (*loc. cit. supra* note
17, pp. 206–207), a consummation that seems as remote today as when Professor
Thomas wrote in 1958. Further, see notes 17 and 31, *supra* and OECD's latest
Economic Survey of the United Kingdom (Paris: June, 1965).

71. For yearly breakdowns, see Table 33 in A. R. Conan, *The Rationale of the
Sterling Area* (1961), p. 96, who cautions that such figures are estimates. The
figures concern private investments, presumably those of the so-called direct
variety, and are on a gross outflow basis. In addition, the Conan table gives figures
for British "public" (governmental) foreign "investments" during the period
(£462 million, exclusive of subscriptions to international agencies).

72. This may be seen implicitly also in the relative decline of Britain as
furnisher of capital goods (as measured crudely by world trade statistics in
products covered by SITC class 7, machinery and transport equipment). In 1955,
the United Kingdom was the origin of approximately four-sevenths of the world
consignments of this category to the Sterling Area. In 1960, her proportion had
dropped to three-sevenths; and 89 per cent of the expansion that had occurred in
the interim had been taken up by other suppliers; U.N., *Commodity Trade
Statistics*.

Table 7. Foreign Holdings in the Outer Commonwealth (in £ millions)

	Australia	India-Pakistan	South Africa	Subtotal	Canada
United Kingdom	900	400	800	2,100	1,064
Other	400	700	400	1,500	5,177

Note: Mackay, *op. cit. supra* note 24, at p. 59. The showing is partly attributable to war sales of British assets and other wartime transactions. A breakdown given by Thorbecke, *op. cit. supra* Table 1 note, at p. 161, shows the British part (with total foreign investment given in parentheses) as follows (£ millions): Australia, 350 (600); South Africa, 500 (700); colonial territories, 450 (500); Rhodesia, 250 (300); India, 100 (250).

During 1958–1961, it is estimated that British private "direct" investment in the Sterling Area plus Canada averaged approximately £142 annually. The major portion of this flow, about £82 million of it, was into the "Old Dominions" (Australia, Canada, New Zealand, South Africa). By comparison, there was a like annual average flow into the same group in the same period of the equivalent of £123 million from the United States. In 1962, the flow into the "Old Dominions" from the United Kingdom remained at the 1958–1961 average, while that from the United States rose to £143 million and an important newcomer, Germany, supplied over £70 million.[73] In the case of Australia, the Sterling Area country most favored by British investors (about 30 per cent of their Sterling Area placements having been there in recent years), as against the 9:4 ratio of British-origin capital *in situ* a few years ago, the British-origin inflow rate was in the ratio 7:6 in fiscal biennium 1958–1960, and down to 3:4 in fiscal 1962–

73. *Board of Trade J.* for April 19 and Nov. 15, 1963 (184: 880, and 185: 1085); *Survey of Current Business* (U. S. Department of Commerce, annual review by Pizer and Cutler, August issues of 1961, 1962, and 1963); "Information Funk der Bundesregierung," March 23, 1963 (courtesy, Office of German Commercial Counselor, Washington). The £ figures given for the United States and Germany represent conversions from $ and DM respectively, and the British figures contain an upward adjustment to take *pro rata* account of estimated non-response to the questionnaire on which they are based. The British and American figures here are net of capital repatriation; moreover, identifiable oil investments are excluded. The German figure is not necessarily fully comparable, nor are figures quoted for previous years.

1963; now, for the first time, more capital came from the United States than from the United Kingdom.[74]

The diminishing British role as supplier of the Commonwealth's capital is partly attributable to the competing demands of Britain's own economy and partly, also, to the availability of more attractive alternatives outside the Commonwealth for Britishers able and willing to venture their money abroad. The United Kingdom is becoming less and less a net foreign investor in general; the average annual excess of exports over imports of long-term private capital, a rather modest £123 million during 1953–1955 and £141 million during 1956–1958, fell to £42 million in 1959–1961 and a mere £13 million during 1962–1963.[75] Of the gross outflow, the portion directed into non-Sterling countries has been growing as follows: 30 per cent (1945–1961 average), 38 per cent (1952–1957 average), 44 per cent (1958–1961 average), 47 per cent (1962 estimated); and western Europe has overtaken Canada as top-ranking placement area. In other words, in entrepreneurial investment is found the same general weakening of basic position compounded by increasing diffusion of interest that has characterized the trade complex.

In the matter of non-entrepreneural fund-supplying—the furnishing of assistance to the LDC's in this era of "rising expecta-

74. 4 *Commonwealth Digest* 201 (1963). The 1962–1963 figures were (in £ A millions): 55.6 (U.K.), 56.0 (U. S.) and 20.1 (others). The 1958–1960 statistics were supplied by the Office of the Australian Commercial Counselor, Washington. In the case of India, the largest of the Commonwealth but having a poor "investment climate," the private capital flow averaged £13 million from the United Kingdom and £7½ million from the United States in the triennium 1960–1962; and was £6 million approximately from Germany (same sources, note 73, *supra*). The enlarging role of the United States as capital source for the area is shown in the growth in the value of American-owned investments between 1950 and 1960 in various places (figures in $ millions): Australia, 201 to 856; West Africa, 42 to 290; Rhodesia and Nyasaland, 26 to 82; India, 38 to 159 (Joint Economic Committee, *Trade Restraints in the Western Community*, 87 Cong., 1st Sess., 1961, Table 11).

75. IMF, *International Financial Statistics, Supplement to 1964/65 Issues*. By contrast, in the years immediately prior to 1914, Britain was adding to her foreign investment holdings at an estimated annual rate of $900 million, or the equivalent of about £550 million in terms of present-day gold par values. This equivalent needs to be adjusted upwards considerably, moreover, for real comparative purposes, in order to take account of intervening rises in prices, population, and income. The balance-of-payments crisis of Oct., 1964, does not portend early firm reversal of present trend; the raising of the bank rate to an extraordinary 7 per cent, indeed, was calculated to discourage outflow and encourage inflow of money, and the April, 1965, budget imposed further inhibitions upon investing abroad.

tions"—Britain's relative potential in the Commonwealth framework may be inferred from the following simple datum. The United Kingdom has about one-twelfth of the composite GNP of the Western "developed" nations considered to have aid-giving capacity and responsibility, whereas the Commonwealth contains about one-half of the non-Communist world's LDC population considered to be in need of such aid (as of 1960). More precisely, according to the formula elaborated by Professor Rosenstein-Rodan for the determination of ability to give and of capacity to absorb, the United Kingdom's appropriate share of the aid-carrying burden would be 8.4 per cent and the Commonwealth's appropriate share on the aid-receiving side would be about 48 per cent during the period 1961–1966.[76]

If, therefore, the United Kingdom furnished her rightful share all to Commonwealth members, the latter would still have to find five-sixths of their imputed requirements elsewhere.[77] The United Kingdom has already been meeting the rule-of-thumb goal of according an annual assistance equalling 1 per cent of GNP and has been performing, in relation to capability, above the average of most countries attributed assistance-giving responsibilities in the OECD.[78] Intensified effort thought necessary to reach a higher flow of assistance is more the responsibility of others than the

76. P. N. Rosenstein-Rodan, "International Aid for Underdeveloped Countries," 43 *Rev. of Economics and Statistics* 107 (1961), Table 6 and derivation from Table 4-B, using India alternative I and excluding Communist countries and the LDC's in Europe. A computation made as of today would probably shave the cited British percentage.

77. This means almost entirely outside the Commonwealth, since the aid-giving potential of the other developed members is at best relatively small. Of these, only Canada has thus far participated in the Development Assistance Committee, the group organized under the OECD to promote optimum and orderly assistance to the LDC's. It consists of the United States, Portugal, Norway, Japan, Denmark, Canada, the United Kingdom, and the EEC countries other than Luxembourg. Canada's record for the triennium 1961–1963 is a total of approximately $268 million out of the $24,800 million reported for all DAC countries to all LDC's. Independently, Australia is reported to have given $174 million in development assistance and relief during biennium 1962–1964, representing about two-thirds of 1 per cent of her national income.

78. The British cumulative showing for triennium 1961–1963 was $2.2 billion. The country conspicuously exceeding the 1-per-cent-of-GNP goal has been France ($3.65 billion for the period). The figures given include both governmental and non-governmental funds. In the United Kingdom program, a greater share is attributable to private investment and lending (about two-fifths of her total showing) than is the case on the average with the other members of DAC (under one-fourth). Thus, she contributed about 7 per cent of the official grants and loans made by all DAC countries, but accounted for 16½ per cent of the amounts

United Kingdom, on this showing. The Colombo Plan, the best known Commonwealth-related venture set up for aid purposes, illustrates both the requisite multilateralization and the loose-jointed nature of the Commonwealth.

The British-sponsored Colombo Plan, which originated in a meeting of Commonwealth ministers in 1950, was conceived as a framework into which would fit also non-Commonwealth aid-suppliers and non-Commonwealth aid-recipients. So, the United States and Japan participate, as do Indonesia, the Philippines, Viet-Nam, Cambodia, Laos, and Burma, as well as India, Pakistan, Ceylon, and other Commonwealth countries. It is a "plan" in only an amorphous sense. Essentially, it is a forum for focusing attention on the needs of south and southeast Asia and for mutual consultation in responding to those needs, rather than an agency for allocating or managing aid from either the contributor or the recipient end. Its organ, consequently, is called the "Consultative Committee" and convoked in annual meetings in a circuit of places; its annual reports are principally vehicles for recording what each participant has gotten and given, country by country. During the first ten years, the cumulative record of contributions made to the countries of the region, by source (including loans of the IBRD and unexpended commitments) was as is indicated in Table 8.

With the region that includes the Commonwealth nations needing the heaviest assistance thus provided for,[79] the United Kingdom is able to direct a more telling share of its direct effort into selected areas where the need is more commensurate with British resources.[80] This means differentiating between Common-

---

recorded for private investment and lending (aside from guaranteed long-term export credits). Report of the Chairman of the DAC, OECD, *Development Assistance Efforts and Policies . . . 1964 Review* (1964), Table 1 headed "The Flow of Long-Term Financial Resources to Less-Developed Countries and Multilateral Agencies, by Major Categories, 1961–63 (Disbursements)."

79. This does not indicate all sources from which aid has come into the region. For example, in the "consortia" organized by the IBRD in support of the current five-year plans of India and Pakistan, the EEC countries are listed as down for about 17 per cent and Austria also for a share of the $4.9 billions subscribed up to mid-1963. 9 *Commonwealth Survey* 596 (1963).

80. Africa, where perhaps one-ninth of the Commonwealth's LDC population dwells, was recipient of almost three-fifths of British net official disbursements for LDC assistance in 1961: $232 million, as compared with $105 million spent in

Table 8. *Contributions to Colombo Plan, 1950–1960*

	$ millions	percentage
United Kingdom	724.1	6.5
Outer Commonwealth	448.7	4.1
(New Zealand)	(22.7)	
(Australia)	(95.0)	
(Canada)	(331.0)	
United States	8,309.0	74.9
Japan	299.8	2.7
IBRD	1,328.0	12.1

Note: The percentages do not add to an even 100 because of rounding. The figures other than for the United States and Canada represent conversions from the national currencies. Japan, in addition, reported an almost equal amount of reparations and about $35 million of private investment. The IBRD is a world agency with no particular connection with the Colombo Plan. For the text of the plan's basic instrument, see Ruth Lawson, *International Regional Organization: Constitutional Foundations* (1962), pp. 265–274.

Source: Tenth Annual Report of the Consultative Committee of the Colombo Plan for Co-Operative Development in South and South-east Asia (1961).

wealth members in aid-programming, but such differentiation comports with the dispersiveness of contemporary Commonwealth economic interrelationships already noted in other connections. The integration of the United Kingdom into the European Common Market could hardly have intensified the dispersive tendency in the aid field in a manner prejudicial to the aid aspirations of the Commonwealth LDC's. In this matter, they stood, if anything, to gain.[81]

Asia; OECD, *The Flow of Financial Resources to Developing Countries* (1963), Table 8. On motion of the Commonwealth prime ministers at their May, 1960, meeting, there has been organized a "Special Commonwealth African Assistance Plan" functioning under the Commonwealth Economic Council. In purpose and procedure, it resembles the Colombo Plan, but differs in being confined to Commonwealth countries. *Aid to Developing Countries*, Cmnd. No. 2147 (1963), pp. 23–24 (*q.v.* generally for postwar British record in the aid field, predominantly Commonwealth-oriented).

81. Aid-giving potential is, of course, generally enhanced by improved economic condition. France, EEC's major ex-imperial power, secured explicit Community support for African aid: a fund providing $581 million in 1958–1962 and an additional $800 million in 1963–1967. For an outline of the arrangement, see the association conventions cited in note 67, *supra;* for an accounting to Dec. 31, 1962, see *Journal Officiel des Communautés Européennes*, March 20, 1963, pp. 722–724.

7. Conclusion

On the evidence, it can hardly be said of Britain's non-entry into the EEC that Britain's loss was the Commonwealth's gain. Blurring of the Commonwealth's distinction as a trading system has not ceased, nor has the erosion of Britain's distinctive ability to sustain Commonwealth commerce, finance, and economic development. Western Europe's importance as a market for British products continued to grow, from the 40 per cent share to which it had risen in 1962 to 43 per cent in fiscal 1963–1964. With that growth now dampened by the intensified differentials hampering their competitive access to the EEC heart of that market, the Commonwealth will stand to derive small comfort from the denouement. Britain's economic advantage to the Outer Commonwealth is correlated to Britain's general economic health: the capacity to absorb imports and to generate capital.

Remedy for Britain's recurring financial difficulties is yet to be found. Neither the appropriate remedy, nor the better nourishment of the Commonwealth generally, is to be looked for in the kind of turning inward that was tried at Ottawa in the depths of the Depression. The opposite tack, rather, was taken by the British government in face of the crisis of October, 1964; the emergency import tax then imposed was made applicable to Commonwealth and non-Commonwealth suppliers alike. Still another blow to the Ottawa system is presaged by the British offer, made at the United Nations Conference on Trade and Development in April, 1964, to negotiate the extension to all LDC's of the preferences now reserved to Commonwealth countries; and removal of further vestiges of that system seems a likely consequence of the Kennedy round of tariff negotiations, which moved into an intensive stage in January, 1965, at Geneva.

If there was solid ground for General de Gaulle's charge, in his fateful press conference of January, 1963, that the United Kingdom had refused to "give up" the Commonwealth, the negotiation for the United Kingdom-EEC merger collapsed to that extent on a tenuous issue, economically as well as juridically speaking.

What was really "given up"—or, perhaps, just put off for a while —was Britain's chance to get fully into the mainstream of a vigorous regional undertaking and to gain Commonwealth-minded representation in its guidance. But this is undoubtedly not the end of Commonwealth venturings into the threshholds of regional commercial arrangements. For the increasing emphasis placed on multilateralism by Commonwealth countries in the pursuit of their interests does not rule out the supplementing attractions of well-conceived common markets. The EEC's example has strikingly demonstrated how a regionally integrated market can promote trade for its members and at the same time for non-members too.

8

Extradition

Robert E. Clute

Guidance of legal development in the British Commonwealth has been effected by the utilization of two systems of law touching affairs between states. One is a particular law regulating many aspects of the *inter se* relations of member states (sometimes former member states) and might be called "Commonwealth law." The other is international law, which increasingly governs relations between Commonwealth nations and normally operates between Commonwealth countries and foreign countries. The former usually is based on practice, customs, or imperial acts which regulated affairs between components of the British Empire prior to their attainment of independence and are in many instances still in force. Therefore, Commonwealth extradition *inter se* is usually conducted under the United Kingdom Fugitive Offenders Act, 1881,[1] and is not governed by the law of nations. Extradition between foreign states and Commonwealth members, however, is accomplished under treaty provisions in accordance with accepted rules of international law.

The present study is limited principally to an examination of those aspects of extradition which are *sui generis* in the Commonwealth due to the unique legal ties, constitutional position, and international status of its members.[2] Emphasis will thus be placed on extradition *inter se* rather than extradition between Common-

---

1. 44 & 45 Vict., c. 69. This act was extended to include protected states by the Fugitive Offenders Act, 1916, 5 & 6 Geo. 5, c. 39.
2. For additional discussions, see Paul O. Higgins, "Extradition within the Commonwealth," 9 *Int'l & Comp. L. Q.* 486 (1960); and Robert E. Clute, "Law and Practice in Commonwealth Extradition," 8 *Am. J. Comp. L.* 15 (1959).

wealth countries and foreign states. The problem of intrastate rendition within Commonwealth countries under a federal government is not treated. Nor is it intended to examine in detail Commonwealth extradition practice under the general rules of international law.

1. Extradition Under International Law

British treaty provisions as a whole reflect the gradual transition of the entities of the empire from colonial status to that of independent countries in the Commonwealth of Nations.[3] Extradition treaties likewise depict this trend but at a slower pace than in the case of treaties of commerce. As early as 1880 self-governing colonies were no longer automatically included under British commercial treaties unless such colonies so desired.[4] A similar development did not occur in extradition treaties until almost forty years later. Until World War I the provisions of United Kingdom extradition treaties were automatically applicable to the self-governing dominions, colonies, and possessions.[5] However, since that time Britain has provided for separate adherence to such treaties by individual entities of the Commonwealth and empire by means of notification through the proper diplomatic representatives in much the same manner that a country would notify a depository state of accession to a multilateral treaty.[6]

Attainment of Commonwealth status by former dependencies of the empire did not in any way alter the continued validity of British extradition agreements made applicable to such entities prior to the attainment of independence, as is illustrated by the *Ex parte O'Dell and Griffen* case. The applicants contended before the High Court of Ontario that

3. See Robert E. Clute and Robert R. Wilson, "The Commonwealth and Favored-Nation Usage," 52 *Am. J. Int'l L.* 455 (1958).

4. See Canada, *Sessional Papers, 1883*, vol. 14, No. 89, pp. 7–8; and Treaty of Commerce and Navigation of 1880 with Roumania, C. No. 2615 (1881).

5. See, for example, Extradition Treaty of 1910 between the United Kingdom and Greece, Cd. No. 6074 (1913).

6. See, for example, Extradition Treaty of 1924 between the United Kingdom and Finland; 34 L.N.T.S. 80.

the present relationship between the Crown and this country is completely different from the relationship which existed in 1842 when Canada was only a possession of Her Britannic Majesty in America and that subsequently the Ashburton Treaty, not being a treaty made by her Britannic Majesty on behalf of Canada as a self-governing and independent nation, no longer has any force and effect.

The court did not find this to be true and said in part:

There is nothing to prevent Canada from entering into a new treaty with the United States or substituting some other extradition arrangement for the one which is not embraced within the terms of the Ashburton Treaty, but until that is done the treaty remains in force and effect. . . .[7]

The partition of the Indian subcontinent caused the government of Pakistan to be particularly concerned over state succession in regard to the former treaties of India. Former Indian extradition treaties, however, did devolve upon the new state of Pakistan.[8] As a matter of fact, some independent states not members of the Commonwealth continue to adhere to extradition agreements concluded by the United Kingdom on their behalf prior to their separation from the empire and Commonwealth.[9]

Commonwealth members may now conclude their own extradition treaties. However, they seldom negotiate separate treaties; for example, in 1964 American extradition practice with all Commonwealth states except Canada was governed by treaties between the United Kingdom and the United States.[10] The United Kingdom continued to provide for separate accession to and termination of United Kingdom agreements by Common-

7. [1953] 3 D. L. R. 207.

8. See, for example, the exchange of notes between Pakistan and Belgium in regard to the continued validity of the Extradition Treaty of 1901 to which India had acceded; 133 U.N.T.S. 199. The United States also views such agreements as operative in regard to Pakistan; see *Treaties in Force, 1964,* p. 146.

9. See, for example, with respect to Burma, *ibid.*, p. 21, and to the Republic of South Africa, *ibid.*, p. 98, and South Africa, *Government Gazette*, vol. 4 (1962), p. 5. For a brief survey of Irish extradition practice, see A. G. Donaldson, *Some Comparative Aspects of Irish Law* (1957), pp. 105–106; and Andrew Phelan, "The Republic of Ireland and Extradition," 56 L. J. 39 (1956).

10. See U. S., *Treaties in Force, 1964,* pp. 28, 70. Canada's unique situation may be explained by her proximity and close ties with the United States. Canada is party to a number of extradition treaties which are confined in operation to the United States and Canada; for examples, the Supplementary Convention of Oct. 26, 1951, T.I.A.S. No. 2454, and the Supplementary Convention of May 15, 1922, T.S. No. 666.

wealth members even after the latter achieved independent status in the international community.[11]

Extradition procedures of the United Kingdom and Commonwealth countries are, however, divergent as a result of the alteration of treaties by separate Commonwealth entities and because of variations in the domestic laws, as in the case of double criminality. A Commonwealth country might refuse to extradite a criminal whereas the United Kingdom might not, given the same facts.

Extradition treaties of the United Kingdom have taken on a character analogous to that of multilateral extradition treaties because of the practice of a separate accession to and termination of such agreements by Commonwealth countries. The obligations of the signatories to such instruments may even vary in a manner similar to that of the signatories of a multilateral convention who have signed such an instrument with reservations. A Commonwealth entity may even amend a British extradition treaty by carrying out direct negotiations with the foreign state concerned without altering the obligations of other Commonwealth countries which have acceded to the treaty.[12] Thus, although the same extradition treaty may be in force in regard to a number of Commonwealth countries, its provisions may not be applicable to all in the same manner.

Although the statutory means of implementing extradition treaties is not the same in all Commonwealth countries, practice is fairly uniform. In the United Kingdom extradition treaties are not self-executing and must be implemented by municipal laws. Earlier practice in the United Kingdom required the enactment of separate legislation for each treaty,[13] but after the passage of

11. See, for example, the Supplementary Extradition Treaty of 1935 between the United Kingdom and Hungary; 181 L.N.T.S. 338.

12. See the exchange of notes between the Union of South Africa and Estonia, March 28, 30, 1938, amending the Extradition Convention of 1925; 196 L.N.T.S. 413. A Commonwealth country may also be a party to a supplementary convention which amends an original convention even though the original did not provide for separate accession by the self-governing dominions or colonies. See, for example, the Supplementary Treaty of 1937 with Luxembourg amending the Extradition Treaty of 1880; Cmd. No. 5811 (1937–1938).

13. See, for example, the act of 1862 for giving effect to the convention with Denmark for the mutual surrender of criminals; 25 & 26 Vict., c. 70.

the Extradition Act (Imperial) of 1870,[14] United Kingdom extradition treaties could be made applicable to foreign countries or entities of the empire by means of orders in council passed under the authority of the act. The Extradition Act of 1870 is in force in Eire and all Commonwealth countries except Canada, Ghana, India, and Sierra Leone.[15] Under the provisions of this act Great Britain continues to promulgate orders in council providing for Commonwealth accession to or termination of extradition treaties.[16]

United Kingdom extradition treaties have followed the general practice of international law in making double criminality one of the requirements for the extradition of a fugitive.[17] Since the local laws of Commonwealth countries vary considerably, problems have emerged in regard to double criminality which are similar to those faced by the states of the United States. Prior to the Extradition Act of 1870 the United Kingdom contended that the law under which criminality should be determined was the law of the entity in which the fugitive was apprehended.[18] The practice was retained in the First Schedule of the act of 1870, which states

14. 33 & 34 Vict., c. 52, as amended by the Extradition Act, 1873, 36 & 37 Vict., c. 60; the Extradition Act, 1895, 58 & 59 Vict., c. 33; the Extradition Act, 1906, 6 Edw. 7, c. 15; the Extradition Act, 1932, 22 & 23 Geo. 5, c. 39; the Counterfeit Currency (Convention) Act, 1935, 25 & 26 Geo. 5, c. 25.

15. Canada enacted its own extradition legislation, 40 Vict., c. 25 (1877), 45 Vict., c. 20 (1882), to replace the Imperial Extradition Act of 1870. India ceased to be covered by the imperial extradition acts or the Fugitive Offenders Act after passage of the Indian Extradition Act of 1962; however, sec. 2(c) of the Indian act retains in operation any extradition treaty applicable to India prior to its passage. For text of 1962 act, see 2 *Indian J. Int'l L.* 531 (1962). Ghana also passed its own extradition act in 1960, sec. 3 of which provides for the continued validity of all extradition treaties in force prior to the act's passage. Part 1 of the Fugitive Offenders Act continued to be applicable to Ghana. *Ordinances and Acts of Ghana, 1960,* Act No. 22. Sec. 2(3) of the Sierra Leone Extradition Act of 1962 also provides for the continued validity of all applicable extradition treaties; the entire Fugitive Offenders Act remained in force. *Supplement to the Sierra Leone Gazette* (1962), vol. 92, No. 25, Act No. 10.

16. With the assent of Australia, the Extradition Act of 1870 was made applicable to the Convention of Aug. 3, 1949, with Luxembourg; *Stat. Instr.* 1951, No. 1171. In 1953 Australia and New Zealand terminated the extradition treaty with Sweden in respect of the Extradition Act of 1870; *Stat. Instr.* 1953, Nos. 1220, 1221.

17. See, for example, art. 2 of the treaty of May 30, 1924, with Finland, 34 L.N.T.S. 80; and art. 3 of the treaty of Dec. 22, 1931, with the United States, T.S. No. 894. For discussion of double criminality with regard to Canada and the United Kingdom, see Manley O. Hudson, "The Factor Case and Double Criminality in Extradition," 28 *Am. J. Int'l L.* 274 (1934).

18. See extradition act in regard to Denmark, cited note 13, *supra.*

in part: "The following list of crimes is to be construed according to the law existing in England, or in a British Possession (as the case may be) at the date of the alleged crime. . . ."[19] Criminality is thus determined on the basis of local Commonwealth law and is not dependent on English law.[20] The local law concerned may be a form of common law akin to that of England, but there may also be considerable variation. This was particularly true of the Union of South Africa and India prior to 1962 when they ceased to be governed by the Imperial Extradition Act.[21] In South Africa the substantive criminal law is influenced by the Roman-Dutch law. In the case of India the penal code follows the nationality principle and permits jurisdiction to be exercised over crimes committed by nationals of India outside of India's territorial limits.[22]

The problem of which local law to apply in establishing double criminality is even more complicated in the case of federal

19. This practice has been reinforced in extradition treaties of the United Kingdom. For example, art. 8 of the treaty of 1924 with Finland provides that a request for extradition must be accompanied by "such evidence as, according to the laws of the place where he is found, would justify his arrest if the crime or offense had been committed there." 34 L.N.T.S. 80. Thus when Ghana, India, and Sierra Leone enumerated extraditable crimes in their new extradition acts, the continued operation of such provisions in United Kingdom treaties applicable to them was not altered.

20. An illustration is the *Curry* case, [1888] N.Z.L.R. 630, in which an applicant convicted of *banquerote frauduleuse* was released by the New Zealand Supreme Court. The offense was listed as an extraditable crime in the treaty of May 10, 1878, between France and the United Kingdom. By the Extradition Act, 1870, however, the list of crimes had to be construed according to the law of the British possession concerned. The court held that offenses under the generic term *banquerote frauduleuse* were different in New Zealand from such offenses under French law.

21. See note 15, *supra*. South Africa continued to be governed by the Fugitive Offenders Act, 1881, and the imperial extradition acts after she left the Commonwealth. However, these acts ceased to apply to the Republic after enactment of the South African Extradition Act of 1962. Nevertheless, under sec. 2(4) of the 1962 act, all extradition agreements applicable to the Union under the imperial extradition acts continued to be in force. Under the schedule of the 1962 act, sec. 24 of the Extradition Act, 1870, and sec. 5 of the Extradition Act, 1873, regarding the taking of evidence in criminal matters in the United Kingdom also remained in operation. South Africa, *Government Gazette*, vol. 4 (June 20, 1962), No. 264, p. 5. See also note 54, *infra*.

22. See M. K. Nawaz, "Criminal Jurisdiction and International Law," 1 *Indian Yb. Int'l Aff.* 212–213 (1953). The Indian Extradition Act of 1962 does not specifically include double criminality as a requisite for extradition. On this matter, and the act in general, see J. N. Saxena, "India—The Extradition Act of 1962," 13 *Int'l & Comp. L. Q.* 116 (1964). For the first case arising under the new Indian act, see the *Tarasov* case in 3 *Indian J. Int'l L.* 323 (1963).

Commonwealth governments in which the component states each have their own criminal law. This is not a problem in Canada, but represents a difficulty in Australia as the latter does not have a federal criminal code except in regard to the Australian Capital Territory. Soon after the creation of the Commonwealth of Australia it became obvious that the national extradition laws left something to be desired. In the case of *In re Gerhard,* the defense counsel contended that the police magistrate, who derived his authority from the state of Victoria, had no right to issue an extradition warrant under an order made by the governor-general of the Commonwealth of Australia. Justice Holroyd held that the word "Governor" as used in the Extradition Act of 1870 did not refer to the governor-general of Australia, because the national government had not enacted any laws on the subject of extradition. The court, therefore, found that the power of extradition had remained with the states after federation and that Gerhard should be released.[23] The situation was remedied by federal legislation in 1903 whereby the powers of the Extradition Act were vested in the governor-general or any deputy authorized by him. Consequently, the state governors were delegated as deputies.[24] In the following year an order in council was passed which permitted the exercise of the powers of extradition by both the national and state governments.[25] Thus the law of either the national government or the state governments could be exercised to determine criminality, and the proper law would depend on the part of Australia from which extradition was requested.

2. *Inter-Se* Extradition

The extradition of fugitives from justice within the Commonwealth of Nations or the British Empire is not usually governed

23. 27 Vict. L. R. 655 (1901). For an account of Australian extradition practice, see G. B. Castieau, "The Statutory Basis of Extradition in Australia," 1 *Proc. of the Australian and New Zealand Soc'y of Int'l L.* 122 (1935).

24. Order in Council of March 7, 1904; Australia, *Commonwealth Acts, 1901–1950,* II, 1853.

25. Australia, *Commonwealth Statutory Rules, 1907–1927,* IV, 3395. A similar problem arose in regard to the Fugitive Offenders Act; see notes 46–50, *infra.*

by extradition treaties or by the general rules of international law concerning extradition. Return of fugitives from one Commonwealth country to another or between parts of the empire is ordinarily carried out under the Fugitive Offenders Act, 1881.[26] The framers of this statute evidently regarded it as a purely administrative matter to be used within the empire and did not view the statute in the same manner as extradition under the law of nations.[27] However, when the empire evolved into a commonwealth of independent states, practice under the act took on more of the character of a particular international law of extradition which did not provide some of the rules normally utilized in general international law to safeguard the rights of a fugitive.

The *inter se* return of fugitives in general is covered by part 1 of the act which qualifies extraditable crimes by the eliminative method rather than following the enumerative method utilized in United Kingdom extradition treaties with foreign nations.[28] It is stipulated that the act applies to treason, piracy, or any "offense punishable in the part of His Majesty's Dominions in which committed for a term of twelve months or more with hard labour."[29]

26. See note 1, *supra*.

27. The lord chancellor stated that the act was designed to replace one of 1843 which governed only treason and felonies, noting that it would be a useful and necessary measure to provide more effective means for the arrest of fugitive criminals. See also, *infra*, note 51. Sir James Stephen, *A History of the Criminal Law of England* (1883), II, 74, also reflected this attitude, dismissing the act with the remark: "It is unnecessary to notice its provisions in detail; they are administrative and involve no principle of interest."

28. In the Asian African Legal Consultative Committee, of which Ceylon, India, and Pakistan are members, a majority went on record in 1961 as favoring the eliminative method which the committee considered to be the modern trend in extradition practice. However, Ceylon and India preferred the enumerative method. When India replaced the Fugitive Offenders Act, 1881, and the Extradition Act, 1870, with the Extradition Act of 1962, she utilized the enumerative method for extradition to Commonwealth countries and foreign countries with which she had no treaty arrangements. See *Asian African Legal Consultative Committee, Report of the Fourth Session, Tokyo, 1961*, pp. 24–26, and Indian Extradition Act, 1962 (*op. cit. supra* note 15), Second Schedule. The Ghana Extradition Act, 1962, Schedule I (*op. cit. supra* note 15) likewise adopted the enumerative method both in regard to the Fugitive Offenders Act and to normal extradition.

29. Imprisonment with hard labor was abolished by the United Kingdom in the Criminal Justice Act, 1948, 11 & 12 Geo. 6, c. 58, which brought this provision of the Fugitive Offenders Act into question. In Bailey v. Kelsey, 100 Commw. L.R. 352 (1959), the High Court of Australia found that, although the applicant would not be sentenced to hard labor if returned to the United Kingdom and convicted of a charge of false pretences, he would, according to the United Kingdom Prison Rules of 1949, be required to work while in prison. The court held that such work

If a warrant originates in one part of Her Majesty's Dominions issued by the governor of a "possession," a secretary of state of the United Kingdom, or by a judge of a superior court, a magistrate from any other part of Her Majesty's Dominions may issue a provisional warrant for the apprehension of the fugitive if the facts "would in his opinion justify the issue of a warrant if the offence of which the fugitive is accused had been committed within his jurisdiction." The magistrate is to hear the case in the same manner as if the offense had occurred in his jurisdiction. If the evidence "raises a strong or probable presumption that the fugitive committed the offence mentioned in the warrant and that the offence is one to which the part of the Act applies" the magistrate shall imprison the fugitive to await return. The prisoner "may" be returned after fifteen days have elapsed or if he has applied for a writ of habeas corpus after the court has rendered a decision on such an application.[30] If the prisoner is not returned within one month after commital, the court must show cause why he should not be released or the prisoner "may" be released.[31] If the prisoner is not tried within six months after his return, he will on request

---

was compatible with the Fugitive Offenders Act, sec. 9, which states that "any confinement in prison combined with labour, by whatever name it is called shall be deemed to be imprisonment with hard labour." In re Shuter [1959] 2 All. E. R. 782, the court found that the applicant had been committed without sufficient evidence that the offenses charged were offenses punishable under Kenya law by at least twelve months of hard labor. The case was remanded to the magistrate to take further evidence as to the law in Kenya.

30. Sec. 6 of the act provides that a secretary of state in the United Kingdom or a governor in a British possession "may if he thinks it just" issue a warrant for the return of a prisoner to the territory from which he is a fugitive. The home secretary used this section to refuse the return of Zacharia to Cyprus in 1962 even though the House of Lords had dismissed an appeal on the case; see, at note 56, *infra*. In R. v. Brixton Prison (Governor) and Another, Ex parte Enahoro, [1963] 2 All E. R. 477, the court held that "may" was permissive and was a matter of discretion for the home secretary. However, this provision applies only to part 1 of the act, and part 2 does not contain a similar provision.

31. Thus far only two cases have arisen under sec. 7, which provides that a secretary of state in the United Kingdom or a governor in a British possession "may unless sufficient cause is shown to the contrary" order a fugitive to be discharged if he is not returned within one month. In *re Shuter, op. cit. supra* note 29, the court held that the term "may" should be interpreted as mandatory in the absence of sufficient cause to the contrary and that reasonableness might be taken into account in determining whether sufficient cause existed; in the instant case, the arrangements were found reasonable and the application was refused. In the *Enahoro* case, *op. cit. infra* note 5, the court found that the delay was chiefly attributable to the applicant's supporters and had been to assist him in the case and was therefore not unreasonable. Enahoro's application was refused.

be returned free of cost to the place where he was apprehended.

Part 2 of the act is even more liberal and applies to British
possessions which are grouped together because of their contiguity. Under this part of the act a magistrate on receiving a
warrant from a proper authority in an area to which this section
applies may apprehend the fugitive merely by endorsing the warrant. If the magistrate is satisfied that the warrant is authentic,
he may extradite him without further proceedings. The magis-
rate does, however, under section 10 in regard to part 1 of the
act, or under section 19 in regard to part 2 of the act, have the
discretion to refuse to return the fugitive if the offense is too
trivial, or if the application is not made in good faith, or if he finds
that the punishment is unjust, oppressive, or overly severe.

It is to be noted that the return of a fugitive under part 1 is
more analogous to normal extradition procedure under the law of
nations than is part 2 of the act. However, the similarity between
this imperial act and normal extradition procedure between
foreign countries is far from complete. On occasion the courts
have noted these differences. One of the main differences lies in
the matter of proof of guilt. As can be seen from part 2 of the act,
the return of a fugitive offender to a contiguous territory is
extremely informal, with little concern over proof of guilt. Indeed, this caused the courts of India to declare the Fugitive
Offenders Act invalid.[32] However, the courts may expend considerable effort on proof of guilt before a fugitive is returned under
part 1 of the act, as is illustrated by the case of *R. v. Delisle*. The
judge, in speaking of the Fugitive Offenders Act, said in part:

The underlying principle of such legislation is the same which governs
in extradition matters. . . . Our Government will not surrender to a
foreign state, however friendly, any person . . . without first having
ascertained, by the proceedings and findings of the highest Courts of
Canada, that such a crime has really been committed by that person.
Likewise, Canada will not surrender to any Government of Her
Majesty's possessions any criminal fugitive without clear evidence of
guilt made and controlled under the authority of the Superior
Courts.[33]

32. See *Re C. G. Menon and Another, op. cit. infra* note 59.
33. 20 *Canadian Abridgement* (1940), col. 136.

Traditionally, however, the courts were less particular in this matter than would have been the case under an extradition treaty. For instance, in the Canadian case of *In re Harrison* the judge drew attention to the difference between practice under the Extradition Act and the Fugitive Offenders Act. He noted that under the latter the judge has discretion and may if he so desires "accept only the allegation of the complaint as the foundation for issuing the warrant." The judge continued:

It is quite obvious that some additional care ought to be taken in the case of extraditing persons to foreign countries than in facilitating criminal proceedings in the various parts of the Empire, to which alone the Fugitive Offenders Act applies.[34]

Recently the courts have shown an increased tendency to be more critical of the evidence before returning a fugitive. This may be due in part to the state of flux existent in some of the new Commonwealth countries. The new trend was evident in the case of *Re James*, handed down on November 28, 1961, in which the court held that James could not be returned to Southern Rhodesia as the evidence was not sufficient. The chief justice said, in part, that, if there were evidence on which a magistrate could find that a strong or probable presumption had been shown, the court would not interfere; the evidence before him, however, was not sufficient to set up a presumption.[35] The following month, the return of a fugitive from Cyprus was likewise refused because the evidence did not raise a "strong or probable presumption" of guilt as required by section 5 of the act.[36] Indeed, Chief Justice Parker, who had been presiding justice in the *Re James* and *Re Mourat Mehmet* cases, spoke to the matter in a dictum in his decision on a request for extradition of a fugitive to Israel under the Extradition Act. Lord Parker noted that although the formula regarding evidence under the Extradition Act was slightly different from

34. 25 B. C. 433 at 437 (1918). See also Ex parte Lilly White, [1901] N.Z.L.R. 502 at 505, in which it was said of the difference between the Extradition Act and the Fugitive Offenders Act: "At common law there was thought to be an asylum for foreign offenders; and it is only by virtue of treaties that foreign offenders are given up. The rendition of an offender against the Crown from one portion of the possessions of the Crown to another portion should, it seems to me, be differently viewed."

35. *The Times* (London), Nov. 29, 1961, p. 16.

36. Re Mourat Mehmet, [1962] 1 All E. R. 463.

that which appears in section 5 of the Fugitive Offenders Act, he was "prepared to accept that there is no real distinction between those two."[37] Recent decisions thus bring the practice of examination of evidence under part 1 of the Fugitive Offenders Act more in line with accepted practices in regard to extradition under general international law.

An examination of judicial decisions under section 10 of the act, which gives the magistrate discretionary power to refuse the return of a fugitive if it appears that the application was not made in good faith or the punishment would be unjust or severe, reveals a similar development to that under section 5. The courts rarely exercised their powers under section 10 and gave that section a very narrow interpretation until quite recently.[38]

A somewhat wider interpretation was given in *R. v. Governor of Brixton Prison, Ex parte McCheyne* (1951) in which Chief Justice Goddard ordered the discharge of a fugitive from South Africa under section 10 of the act; however, he warned that the jurisdiction to discharge a fugitive in such a case "ought to be seldom and carefully exercised."[39] Discharge was likewise ordered under section 10 in *R. v. Governor of Brixton Prison, Ex parte Campbell* (1956), but the case was not reported.[40] However, in *Re Shuter* (1) (1959) the applicant was unsuccessful in his claim that the application for his return to Kenya was not made in good faith and in the interests of justice.[41] In the case of *Governor of Brixton Prison, Ex parte Naranjan Singh* the applicant was charged with cheating under the Indian code in 1952 but was not arrested until 1961, despite the fact that he and his wife made no attempt to conceal their identity and had started a new life in the United Kingdom under their own names. Chief

37. Re Shalom Schtraks, [1962] 2 All E. R. 176 at 186.
38. For example, in Re Henderson, [1950] 1 All E. R. 283, counsel for the fugitive argued that under sec. 10 he should not be returned because he would not be able to defend himself properly, since he would not be able to see or hear the prosecution witnesses. The judge commented: "I think the kind of matters with regard to which this court would act would be where it appears that the contemplated proceedings, although perhaps lawful by the law of the country concerned, are really going to be conducted in a way contrary to natural justice or contrary to our ideas of it."
39. 211 T.L.R. 25 (1951).
40. *The Times* (London), July 12, 1956, p. 13.
41. [1959] 2 All E. R. 782.

Justice Goddard reviewed recent practice in regard to a wider construction of section 10 and found that the court did have a wide discretion under the section. Lord Goddard held that return of the applicant would be unjust and oppressive due to the delay involved and would present difficulties for the applicant in defending himself. Naranjan Singh was, therefore, discharged.[42] An applicant attempted to widen further the discretion of the courts under section 10 to include political offenses in the case of *Zacharia* v. *Republic of Cyprus*; however the House of Lords held that such offenses were not covered by section 10 of the act. The Lords declared that it must be assumed that the Cyprus court was competent to discriminate between fabricated and true evidence and that the proper precautions would be made to prevent the assassination of the applicant.[43]

Part 2 of the act also utilizes the eliminative method for qualifying extraditable crimes and there is, therefore, no specific list of crimes for which a person may be extradited from one entity of the Commonwealth to another. Any offense punishable by twelve months' hard labor and which the judge does not consider to be too trivial in nature is an extraditable offense. Under the international law of extradition a person once extradited may generally not be tried for an offense other than the one for which he is extradited;[44] however, under the act fugitives from justice may be tried for a crime other than the one listed in the extradition warrant.[45]

After the creation of the Commonwealth of Australia a problem arose under the Fugitive Offenders Act similar to the one which

42. [1962] 1 Q. B. 211. The Indian Extradition Act of 1962 governing extradition to both foreign and Commonwealth countries contains in sec. 29 a provision similar to sec. 10 of the Fugitive Offenders Act, but the authority to discharge the fugitive is vested in the central government rather than in the courts.

43. See at note 56, *infra*.

44. C. C. Hyde, *International Law Chiefly as Interpreted and Applied by the United States* (2d rev. ed., 1945), II, 1032–1034; *Oppenheim's International Law* (Lauterpacht, 8th ed., 1955), I, 702.

45. R. v. Phillips, [1858] 1 F & F 105; R. v. Esser, 9 N.L.R. 238 (1888); R. v. Cohen, 71 J.P. 190 (1907). However, under sec. 2(b) of the Ghana Extradition Act of 1962 (*op. cit. supra* note 15) a fugitive who has been extradited to any other country may not be tried for any offense other than the offense for which he was extradited.

arose under the Extradition Act due to Australia's new federal form of government. Prior to federation, jurisdiction under the Fugitive Offenders Act was exercised by the judges and magistrates of the various colonies in the Australian continent. Soon after the Commonwealth of Australia was established the supreme courts of Western Australia and Queensland held that Australia was a single entity in regard to the act of 1881 and found that the act no longer applied to the individual states.[46] In *McKelvey* v. *Meagher* the applicant's counsel maintained that a Victorian judge or magistrate did not have jurisdiction under the act after the federation of Australia because jurisdiction rested with the central government, as was the case in Canada after the latter's federation. However, the court noted that the national Parliament of Canada had jurisdiction over criminal matters, whereas there was no general criminal law applicable to the Commonwealth of Australia. It held that "The Central legislature referred to in the Fugitive Offenders Act 1881 is a central legislature which has the power to deal with criminal matters." The court therefore found that the Victorian judges and magistrates did in fact have jurisdiction.[47]

The problem arose again in the case of *Re Munro and Campbell* in which the Supreme Court of New Zealand held that a writ of habeas corpus should issue to the fugitives. The crime for which Australia had requested their return was found to be an offense committed and punishable by the law of the state of New South Wales, not that of the Commonwealth of Australia, which for the purposes of part 2 of the Fugitive Offenders Act was a single entity.[48] The following year in the case of *McArthur* v. *Williams* the High Court of Australia referred to *Re Munro and Campbell* and said in part, "We are respectively of the opinion that it does not give the true effect of the Australian political system." The High Court found that even though Australia was "one British possession" for the purposes of the act, the judicial officers of the individual states had authority under the law of that possession

46. In re Willis, 7 W. Austl. L. R. 249 (1905); R. v. Pierson, Ex parte Small, [1906] Queensl. St. 5.
47. 4 Commw. L.R. 265 (1906).
48. [1935] N.Z.L.R. 59.

and were therefore competent to assume jurisdiction under the provisions of the act.[49] The latter decision was reflected in New Zealand shortly thereafter when the Court of Appeals found that a fugitive could be returned to Australia for an offense "against the law obtaining in any part of the Commonwealth of Australia."[50]

The post-World War II growth of the Commonwealth has resulted in a wide variety of political systems in which there is sometimes considerable political friction between the entities. This situation has given rise to the question as to whether the generally accepted principle of international law that a person may not be extradited for a political offense should not also be applicable to the Fugitive Offenders Act. The act is silent on the matter, but the committee report on this act is rather revealing. The Member of Galaway, Mr. T. P. O'Conner, drew attention to the fact that it was not customary to extradite fugitives for political crimes and asked that the word "treason" be dropped from the enumerated offenses. He posed the question, "Why should a different practice be introduced in their relations with Colonial Governments to that which obtained in their relations with foreign nations?" The attorney general declared that "the Government could not possibly agree to this." He noted that

as regarded the Mother Country and her Colonies, the authority of the Crown extended over the whole. The result of allowing such an amendment would be that a person in this country might pass over to a Colony and yet be made answerable to a law general to both the Colony and the Mother Country.

Mr. O'Connor was assured that even though the word "treason" were dropped the general wording of the act would still cover such an offense, so the proposed amendment was dropped.[51]

A rather large number of cases touching on the return of fugitives for political offenses have arisen under the Fugitive Offenders Act in the past decade. In the case of *Re C. G. Menon and Another* the Madras High Court did not treat the question of

49. 55 Commw. L.R. 324 (1936).
50. Goodwin v. Walker, [1938] N.Z.L.R. 712.
51. 265 *H.C. Deb.* (3rd ser.) cols. 597–600 (1881).

Menon's allegation that he was a victim of political animosity, as Menon was released for other reasons.[52] However, in the case of *Re Government of India and Mubarak Ali Ahmed,* decided by the High Court of Justice in 1952, the court spoke to the problem. The applicant attempted to obtain a writ of habeas corpus to prevent his return to India for forgery. Counsel for the applicant claimed that the latter had been persecuted for political reasons by India and was considered to be a spy for Pakistan. Lord Chief Justice Goddard did not find that the applicant would be persecuted as a political offender and ordered his return. However, after citing *Re Castioni* he said in part:

I am quite sure that in a proper case the court would apply the same rules with regard to applications under the Fugitive Offenders Act, 1881, as it does under s. 3(1) of the Extradition Act, 1870. If it appeared that the offence with which the prisoner was charged was in effect a political offence, no doubt this court would refuse to return him.[53]

The case represented an attempt to draw on the law of extradition in order to give the Fugitive Offenders Act an interpretation more in agreement with accepted rules of international law regarding extradition and more suitable to modern conditions in the Commonwealth. However, this dictum could certainly not be justified by the letter of the act nor by the intent of its framers, as evidenced by the attorney general's statement quoted above.

The minister of state for commonwealth relations was questioned in Parliament during May of 1960 in regard to political offenses under the Fugitive Offenders Act. A member noted that South Africa had passed a Prohibition of Communism Act which made political offenses criminal offenses and asked if the United Kingdom had received requests to return persons to the Union from the protectorates of Swaziland, Basutoland, and Bechuanaland. The minister replied that the United Kingdom government would not require persons to be returned to the Union on political grounds but noted that it would be for the courts to decide whether a matter was a political or criminal one. The minister also

52. *Op. cit. infra* note 59.
53. [1952] 1 All E. R. 1060.

drew attention to section 19 of the act which permits the court to refuse to return a fugitive under certain conditions. In December of 1960 Ghana, perhaps motivated by these events, became the first Commonwealth country to revise its laws to prevent the return of political offenders to other Commonwealth countries and to forbid the trial of an extradited person for an offense other than the offense for which he was surrendered.[54] In contrast to the general trend among Commonwealth nations, Ceylon took the position at the 1960 session of the Asian African Legal Consultative Committee in Colombo that no distinction should be made in extradition between ordinary crimes and political crimes, whereas Burma, India, and Pakistan did not favor extradition for political offenses. Although the committee was treating the matter of general extradition under international law, it must be assumed that Ceylon would take the same stand in regard to the return of fugitives under the Fugitive Offenders Act.[55]

In the case of *Zacharia* v. *Republic of Cyprus* (1962) defense was based in part on the fact that the alleged offense was political, in view of Zacharia's activities against the EOKA during the struggle for independence in Cyprus. The House of Lords did not accept Lord Goddard's dictum and held that this portion of

54. 623 *H.C. Deb.* (5th ser.) cols. 1485–88 (1959–60). The Ghana Extradition Act, 1960, *op. cit. supra* note 15, under sec. 2 retained the operation of part 1 of the Fugitive Offenders Act and forbade extradition to either a Commonwealth or a foreign country for political offenses. Sec. 16(b) of the Sierra Leone Extradition Act, 1962, *op. cit. supra* note 15, does not permit extradition to foreign countries for political offenses but permits the continued operation of the Fugitive Offenders Act with no restriction on the return of political offenders. The Indian Extradition Act, 1962, *op. cit. supra* note 15, suspended the operation of the Fugitive Offenders Act and did not permit the return of political offenders to either Commonwealth or foreign countries. The United Kingdom was evidently not content to rely on sec. 19 of the Fugitive Offenders Act, for in the Third Schedule of the South Africa Act, 1962, 10 & 11 Eliz. 2, c. 23, the Fugitive Offenders Act was to continue in effect toward fugitives from South Africa as if the Republic were a part of Her Majesty's Dominions if a warrant had been issued, endorsed, or executed outside of the Republic prior to May 31, 1962. However, no person was to be returned to the Republic for an offense of a political character which was not an offense under the law of the territory in which the warrant was endorsed. Sec. 15 of the South African Extradition Act, 1962, *op. cit. supra* note 21, suspended the operation of the Fugitive Offenders Act and followed international practice regarding the extradition of political offenders. For a discussion of political offenses under the Fugitive Offenders Act, see Higgins, *loc. cit. supra* note 2, at pp. 486–491.

55. *Asian African Legal Consultative Committee, Report of the Third Session, Colombo, 1960* (1960), p. 216.

the defense was irrelevant since the Fugitive Offenders Act made no exception for political offenders. An attempt on the part of the appellants to avoid return under section 10 of the act was also rejected. Only the decision of the home secretary to exercise his discretion under section 6 of the act prevented the return of the offenders to Cyprus, which came as a disappointment to those who had believed that the courts would use their discretionary powers under the act to avoid the return of political offenders even though such offenses were not specifically covered by the act. The secretary announced his decision in the question period and one member asked whether it might not be possible to amend the act. The secretary replied that the government was bound by the terms of the act but would keep the question under review.[56]

The *Zacharia* case raised the possibility that the government would use its discretion to prevent the return of political offenders when the courts were unwilling to act. However, in the case of Chief Enahoro, Nigeria requested the return of the applicant to face charges of treason and conspiracy to effect an unlawful purpose. The applicant was refused appeal to the Divisional Court and the House of Lords on the basis of section 10 of the act, but later succeeded in an appeal to the Divisional Court under section 7 of the act on the ground that he had been detained in excess of one month. On March 14 the home secretary decided to issue the warrant for the fugitives but delayed action in order to consult Parliament. The House of Commons supported Secretary Butler's decision after assurances by the prime minister that Enahoro would not face the death penalty and would be allowed British counsel of his own choice. However, the usual Conservative majority of 100 votes fell to 56 votes and there was considerable criticism of the Fugitive Offenders Act. The opposition expressed the hope that Enahoro would be the last man to suffer under what was considered a bad law and the prime minister promised to consult the Commonwealth about amending the

56. [1962] 2 All E. R. 438; 658 *H.C. Deb.* (5th ser.) cols. 811–812 (1961–62).

Fugitive Offenders Act. The court refused Enahoro's application and the secretary endorsed the warrant for his return.[57]

The refusal of the Privy Council to review the *Enahoro* case was regrettable, for the provisions of the act were broad enough to invite adjustments to modern political realities and changed conditions within the Commonwealth through judicial interpretation. The *Enahoro* case not only revealed the inadequacy of the act in regard to political offenders but drew attention to the fact that neither the courts nor the government were willing to exercise the discretionary provisions of the act to avoid the obvious shortcomings that had emerged in its operation. It would doubtless be easier to handle such problems through judicial interpretation or through the administrative process than to obtain the consent of Commonwealth members to formal revisions of the existing act.

Although the application of the Fugitive Offenders Act is not questionable in the case of most Commonwealth countries, there appears to be some doubt as to the future of this act in some of the newer Commonwealth countries. The judicial decisions of India over the past decade gave clear warning that the Fugitive Offenders Act was not operating smoothly in that country. In the case of *Re Government of India and Mubarak Ali Ahmed*, it was held that the "Fugitive Offenders Act, 1881, is in full force and effect between this country and India."[58] The Madras High Court found that the act was in effect in India in the case of *Re C. G. Menon and Another*, but found that part 2 of the act could not be enforced by the court as it denied the equal protection of the laws and was repugnant to the Constitution of India. Menon was, therefore, not returned to Malaya. However, the case was appealed to the Supreme Court of India, which found that the Fugitive Offenders Act, 1881, was not in force in respect to India and raised some very serious questions as to India's position in regard to the surrender of fugitives to other Commonwealth

57. [1963] 2 All E. R. 477; 674 H.C. Deb (5th ser.) col. 43 (1962–63), written answers; *The Times* (London), April 11, 1963, p. 8; David Watt, "Brooke's Last Stand," *The Spectator*, May 31, 1963, p. 693.
58. [1952] 1 All E. R. 1060.

countries. In speaking of the Fugitive Offenders Act, 1881, the court said in part:

The situation completely changed when India became a Sovereign Democratic Republic. After the achievement of independence . . . by no stretch of the imagination could India be described as a British Possession and it could not be grouped by an Order-In-Council among those possessions. Truly speaking, it became a foreign territory so far as other British Possessions are concerned and the extradition of persons taking asylum in India, having committed offences in British Possessions could only be dealt with by an arrangement between the Sovereign Democratic Republic of India and the British Government and given effect by appropriate legislation. . . . The provisions of that Act could only be made applicable to India by incorporating them with appropriate changes into an Act of the Indian Parliament and by enacting an Indian Fugitive Offenders Act.[59]

Despite the fact that the Fugitive Offenders Act was not operative in India itself, the United Kingdom courts and orders in council continued to apply it to India as the latter did not formally suspend the act until the passage of the Indian Extradition Act of 1962. Through the various independence acts the Fugitive Offenders Act has continued to be applicable to Commonwealth members, but some of the newer Commonwealth countries have adopted provisions which alter the operation of the act in regard to such entities.[60] All Commonwealth countries are of course free to suspend the operation of the act in regard to their territories, although India is the only country that has taken such action.

The relation of Eire to the Commonwealth under the Fugitive Offenders Act is unique. Traditionally, the act has been applied between Ireland and England, Scotland, or Wales. In the case of the latter, the return of fugitives is governed by the reciprocal provisions of the Indictable Offenses Act, 1848, section 12,[61] and the Petty Session (Ireland) Act, 1851.[62] In *The King* v. *Commissioner of Metropolitan Police, Ex parte Nalder*, which came

59. 17 Sup. Ct. J. (India) 621 (1954).
60. See for example, the Nigeria Independence Act, 1960, sec. 3; Sierra Leone Independence Act, 1961, sec. 3; Malaysia Act, 1963, sec. 3; Zanzibar Act, 1963, sec. 1(2); acts cited chap. 5, *supra* note 4.
61. 11 & 12 Vict., c. 42.
62. 14 & 15 Vict., c. 93.

before the King's Bench Division of the High Court of Justice in 1948, the applicant claimed that proceedings ought to have been properly instituted under the Fugitive Offenders Act, 1881. Lord Chief Justice Goddard noted that in the Irish case, *The State, at the Prosecution of Michael Kennedy* v. *Edward J. Little* (1931), the court held that the Fugitive Offenders Act was considered to be in force between Canada and Ireland by the effect of section 73 of the Irish constitution of 1922. Lord Goddard found, however, that the proceedings had been properly instituted under the Petty Sessions (Ireland) Act, 1851, which was still in force on the basis of the Irish Free State (Consequental Provision) Act, 1922. He noted, "It is not necessary to express an opinion whether the Act (Fugitive Offenders Act) can apply at all between England and Eire, though the strong inclination of my opinion is that it cannot."[63] Although the validity of the Fugitive Offenders Act does not appear to have been contested by the courts since the 1931 case cited by Lord Goddard, it would appear that the act is still in effect; it rests on the same constitutional basis as the Petty Sessions (Ireland) Act and an examination of the Irish statutes does not reveal that Ireland has passed any legislation in regard to the Fugitive Offenders Act which could be taken as a basis for its repeal.[64]

．　．　．　．　．

Nearly a century has passed since the promulgation of the Extradition Act, 1870, and the Fugitive Offenders Act, 1881. The

63. [1948] 1 K. B. 251. As late as 1952, the High Court of the Republic of Ireland held that the Petty Sessions Act, 1851, was still in force in Ireland; see Donaldson, *op. cit. supra* note 9, at p. 120, citing The State (Duggan v. Topley), [1952] Ir. R. 62.

64. Phelan notes, *loc. cit. supra* note 9, at p. 57, that there is a rather serious gap in the extradition law of Ireland. The Indictable Offenses Act and Petty Sessions Act cover the whole island and are not applied as between Northern Ireland and the Republic. He writes: "At present a thief, for example, who flees across the border is apprehended and returned only by police cooperation in unlawful acts and his inability to make an habeas corpus application in time." The Republic of Ireland is evidently content with extradition machinery as it now stands. During the question period in the Dail Eireann on March 4, 1954, the minister of justice was asked if he would consider proposing legislation repealing the statutory law whereby citizens were arrested in the Republic and transferred to Great Britain. The minister replied: "I think we should be very slow to upset an arrangement which has stood the test of time and has given so little cause for complaint over so long a period." *Parl. Deb.*, vol. 144, col. 1285.

fact that these acts have operated so long and under such changed conditions is a credit to the law-makers who originated them, for they were wise enough to permit a rather high degree of local discretion. The transition from empire to Commonwealth has changed the circumstance in which these acts were created and the constitutional basis on which they formerly rested. The Extradition Act has presented few problems but the Fugitive Offenders Act is beginning to show signs of strain.

The latter act was passed at a time when the supreme legislative power for the empire rested in the Parliament at Westminister and the Judicial Committee of the Privy Council was the highest court of appeal for the empire. Provisions regarding proof of guilt, the return of a prisoner when the case is frivolous or return would be unjust, and the inadequacy of protection for political offenders hardly seem compatible with the independent legislative and judicial systems of the Commonwealth states. The act may prove to be particularly troublesome in view of possible political refugees from Commonwealth countries which have experienced a revolution or a coup, as is the case with Ghana, Nigeria, and Uganda. Considerable revision in these areas will be needed to bring the act into line with modern developments.

9

Enforcement of Foreign Judgments

Don C. Piper[*]

The legal arrangements fashioned to effect co-operation between the constitutent parts of the British Empire varied in scope
and in the nature of their subject matter. They were comple-
mented by the *inter se* doctrine, which provided that those
relations between parts of the empire that if subsisting between
other countries would be regarded as international relations and
governed by the rules and principles of international law, were
neither international relations nor governed by the rules and
principles of international law.[1] The statutory procedure for the
enforcement of judgments among the member states of the
Commonwealth is based upon a set of legal rules that was
intended initially to be applicable only to members of the
Commonwealth. Although these rules are operative in many parts
of the Commonwealth, there are also subsequent rules that make
it possible to extend on the basis of reciprocity a similar registration and enforcement system to Commonwealth and non-Commonwealth countries. The development of new legal rules of
broader application is an illustration of the continuing trend
within the Commonwealth of decreasing reliance on *inter se* legal
rules and the utilization of more general rules of public and
private international law applicable to the wider international
community. This chapter traces the general pattern and trend of
the enforcement procedure and the enlargement of this initially

* Department of Government and Politics, University of Maryland

1. J. E. S. Fawcett, *The Inter se Doctrine of Commonwealth Relations* (1958);
and R. Y. Jennings, "The Commonwealth and International Law," 30 *Brit. Yb.
Int'l L.* 320 (1953).

closed system into a broader system susceptible of world-wide application.

1. Imperial Background

This variety of co-operative legal arrangements, and especially the taking of appeals to the Judicial Committee, suggests that an imperial enforcement procedure might have been established so that a judicial decree issued by a colonial court would be automatically enforceable in the United Kingdom or in any other colonial court of the empire. This was not the case, however. Because of the diversity of the legal systems within the empire and the principle of the territoriality of law, which is fundamental to the common-law system, there was never fashioned for the entire empire an automatic and uniform judgments enforcement procedure. Furthermore, it seems clear that in matters of private international law the common status or allegiance to the Crown was insufficient to render a subject liable in one part of the empire for actions or procedures in another part.[2]

British courts consistently held that a judgment issued in one part of the empire which was presented for enforcement to a court in another part of the empire was a "foreign judgment." This was clearly stated in *Bank of Australasia* v. *Nias,* where the court said that "it has often been said, by Judges and judicial writers of great eminence, that the judgment of a colonial Court of the British Empire comes within the category of a foreign judgment, and that a foreign judgment is only prima facie evidence of a debt, being examinable in the Courts of this country."[3] The characterization of a colonial judgment as a "foreign judgment" did not mean that the judgment was issued

2. G. C. Cheshire, *Private International Law* (5th ed., 1957), p. 617. See also the comment of Berrierdale Keith, "Notes on Imperial Constitutional Law," 3 *J. Comp. Leg. & Int'l L.* (3d ser.) 310 (1921).

3. 16 Q.B. 717 (1851); see also Houlditch v. Donegall, 2 Cl. & Fin. 470 (1834). A basic work on this matter is H. E. Read, *Recognition and Enforcement of Foreign Judgments in the Common Law Units of the British Commonwealth* (1938).

from an alien court, but that it was issued in a legal system extraneous to the legal system of the court called upon to make the enforcement. It did mean, however, that under the common law the same enforcement procedure applied to both colonial judgments and alien judgments, the one distinction being that a decision of a colonial court might be taken on appeal to the Judicial Committee of the Privy Council.[4]

As a result of the courts' decisions regarding colonial judgments, some legal authorities and practitioners suggested that an imperial judgments extension law be enacted to facilitate the direct enforcement of colonial judgments. These proposals were not inspired by any legalistic view of imperial unity, but by the practical desire to facilitate commerce within the empire, specifically that between the mother country and the colonies.

The problem of enforcement of colonial judgments was discussed extensively at the Colonial Conference of 1887 where F. T. Piggott, the author of a leading text on the enforcement of foreign judgments, and others advocated imperial adoption of a uniform procedure similar to that incorporated in the British Judgments Extension Act of 1868. Although most of the conference participants favored a common imperial procedure, they recommended that the enforcement of judgments be predicated on the rule of reciprocity. Despite their common agreement, the practical utility of their deliberations and recommendations was mitigated by the lord chancellor's assertion that creation of an imperial federation was a prerequisite for direct registration and enforcement of colonial judgments. His precondition clearly doomed any immediate action by Westminster and forestalled any reciprocal enactments by the colonies.[5]

A quarter-century later the problem was again discussed at an imperial conference. The 1911 Imperial Conference recommended that the imperial government in consultation with the dominion governments consider whether it was practicable to

---

4. Francis Piggott, *Foreign Judgments and Jurisdiction* (3d ed., 1908), p. 6.
5. *Proceedings of the Colonial Conference, 1887*, C. No. 5091 (1887), pp. 51–75, 124–141, 446–460, 604–628.

enact mutual arrangements for the enforcement in one part of the empire of judgments obtained in another part of the empire.[6] Toward the end of the decade, a special committee appointed by the lord chancellor to consider legal matters within the Commonwealth recommended that progress toward an imperial judgments extension act, patterned along the lines of the 1868 act, proceed cautiously, since there was not unanimous support throughout the empire for such an act. The committee believed that the 1868 act, relating to judgments extension in the United Kingdom, was made possible by short distances and easy communications and a mutual confidence in the judgments of the superior courts. The slowness of communications and the differences in history, race, institutions, and traditions existing within the far-flung empire would make the enactment of an imperial judgments extension act difficult. The committee recommended that the colonies and dominions individually enter into such arrangements on the basis of reciprocity and that foreign judgments be registered and enforced only when the local court was satisfied that the extra-territorial enforcement of the judgment was just and convenient.[7]

Following the recommendations of the committee, the British Parliament enacted the Administration of Justice Act, 1920, which operated between the United Kingdom and the individual dominions. Since practice in the United Kingdom frequently provides the pattern for overseas practices, it is proposed to examine first the enforcement procedure in the mother country and then to examine the enforcement procedures that have been adopted by some of the other members of the Commonwealth.

2. United Kingdom

The enforcement of Commonwealth judgments in the United Kingdom is governed either by the provisions of the common law

6. *Minutes of the Proceedings of the Imperial Conference, 1911,* Cd. No. 5745 (1911), p. 425.

7. *British and Foreign Legal Procedure,* Cmd. No. 251 (1919), pp. 7–11.

or by one of three parliamentary statutes. All three statutes permit a more efficacious procedure than that provided under the common law, i.e., they authorize the direct registration and enforcement of certain types of judgments.[8]

The first act was the Judgments Extension Act, 1868, which established a simple registration procedure for various judgments of the superior courts in England, Ireland, and Scotland.[9] Under the provisions of the act, a judgment for a debt, damages, or costs obtained in a superior court in one part of the United Kingdom may be registered with and enforced by a superior court in another part of the United Kingdom. The act permits registration only of judgments involving the payment of money and thus excludes injunctions, judgments in actions for the recovery of land, and decrees of equity courts. In addition, the courts have held that a judgment registered in accordance with the act may not serve as the basis for bankruptcy proceedings.[10] A recent legislative enactment, however, authorizes institution of bankruptcy proceedings based upon a registered judgment.[11]

Under the provisions of the basic act, registration by the superior court is automatic upon the presentation by the judgment creditor of a certificate from the issuing court. The superior court to which the certificate is presented is not authorized to inquire into the validity or the merits of the original judgment. The act does not stipulate that there must be reciprocity of treatment between England, Ireland, and Scotland, but its terms insure reciprocity.

Initially the act applied to all of Ireland. In 1924, after the enactment of the Irish Free State (Consequential Provisions) Act, 1922, by the Parliament at Westminster, the English Court of

8. See Clive Parry, "Foreign Judgments," in *Dicey's Conflict of Laws* (7th ed., 1958), pp. 981–1055; and Hessel E. Yntema, "The Enforcement of Foreign Judgments in Anglo-American Law," 33 *Mich. L. Rev.* 1129 (1935).

9. 31 & 32 Vict., c. 54. The superior courts are the English High Court of Justice, the High Court of Justice of Northern Ireland, and the Scottish Court of Session. In 1882, the principles of the act were applied to judgments of certain inferior courts within the United Kingdom to provide a broader base for judgments extension. Inferior Courts Judgments Extension Act, 1882, 45 & 46 Vict., c. 37.

10. Re a Bankruptcy Notice, [1898] 1 Q.B. 383.

11. Administration of Justice Act, 1956, 4 & 5 Eliz. 2, c. 46, sec. 40.

Appeal held that the provisions of the 1868 act no longer applied to judgments obtained in the Irish Free State.[12] Nevertheless, the Free State High Court held in *Gieves* v. *O'Connor* that the act was still enforceable within the Irish Free State.[13]

The second statutory provision which relates to the registration and enforcement of judgments within the United Kingdom is part 2 of the Administration of Justice Act, 1920.[14] Its terms clearly embody the recommendations of the 1911 Imperial Conference and the lord chancellor's committee to consider legal matters within the Commonwealth. Although it was enacted by the imperial Parliament, the act provides only for the registration and enforcement of Commonwealth judgments within the United Kingdom and stipulates that such registration requires reciprocal treatment in the overseas dominions. Under the terms of the act a judgment for a sum of money obtained in a superior court in any of the overseas dominions to which the act has been extended[15] may be registered in a superior court in the United Kingdom if that court thinks it is "just and convenient that the judgment shall be enforced in the United Kingdom." Registration must occur within twelve months after the original judgment, unless the court allows a longer period. From the date of registration by the superior court, the judgment has the same force and effect as a local judgment, and proceedings may be taken against it as if it were a judgment of the territorial superior court.[16]

It should be emphasized that unlike the 1868 act, wherein registration and enforcement are automatic upon the presentation of a certificate, registration under the 1920 act is at the discretion of the superior court. If the court does not consider registration to be "just and convenient," it may refuse to register the judgment. In such an event, the judgment creditor may institute proceed-

12. Wakely v. The Triumph Cycle Company, [1924] 1 K. B. 214.
13. [1924] 2 Ir. R. 282.
14. 10 & 11 Geo. 5, c. 81.
15. The judgment may be one obtained in either civil or arbitral proceedings, if the latter awards are enforceable in the same manner as civil awards. The superior courts designated in this act are the same as the superior courts designated in the 1868 act. See note 9, *supra*.
16. A bankruptcy notice may be instituted upon the registered judgment. Administration of Justice Act, 1956, 4 & 5 Eliz. 2, c. 46, sec. 40.

ings for enforcement in accordance with the common-law rules. In fact, the judgment creditor has the option of seeking registration and enforcement through the procedure specified in the act or of seeking enforcement through the common law. The act discourages the use of the latter procedure, however, by stipulating that the judgment creditor instituting common-law action sacrifices his right to the costs of the action.

The act permits the judgment debtor to raise several defenses against the registration of the judgment that are similar to those permitted under the common law. A judgment will not be registered if the original court acted without the proper jurisdiction, the judgment debtor did not submit to the court's jurisdiction,[17] the judgment debtor was not properly served and did not appear, the judgment was obtained by fraud, the judgment debtor convinces the court that an appeal is pending or that he intends to make an appeal, or the cause of action leading to the judgment was such that the judgment should not be entertained in the superior court on the grounds of public policy.

During the twenties the act was extended by order in council to most of the overseas dominions following action by their legislatures to provide for reciprocal registration and enforcement of judgments obtained in the United Kingdom. The act was also extended to many British colonies, protectorates, and mandates. It was not, however, extended to the Irish Free State. Enactment of the Foreign Judgments (Reciprocal Enforcement) Act, 1933, precludes further extension of the act to any other part of the Commonwealth. As of 1964, the act applied to eleven members of the Commonwealth, two of the Canadian provinces,[18] the six Australian states and the Northern Territory, and a number of colonies, protectorates, and trust territories.[19]

17. The statute does not set forth the bases for proper jurisdiction of the original court that will be recognized by the English courts. This may be one reason why the British courts are to exercise their discretion in the registration process.

18. Members to which the act applies are: Malaya (now Malaysia), Ghana, Ceylon, Cyprus, Jamaica, New Zealand, Nigeria, Sierra Leone, Tanganyika (now united with Zanzibar as Tanzania), Trinidad and Tobago, Uganda, Kenya, Malawi, Zambia, Zanzibar, and Malta. The Canadian provinces to which the act applies are Newfoundland and Saskatchewan. See *Annual Practice, 1961*, p. 961.

19. These include, *inter alia*, British Honduras, Basutoland, the Falkland Islands, and Gambia.

The third act relating to the registration of foreign judgments in the United Kingdom is the Foreign Judgments (Reciprocal Enforcement) Act, 1933,[20] which sets forth identical procedures for the registration of judgments obtained in Commonwealth countries and in non-Commonwealth countries. One purpose of the act was to supplant the separate registration procedure applicable to Commonwealth countries that was created by the 1920 act. Abolition of the special procedure for Commonwealth countries was warranted in that there had not been many applications under the provisions of the 1920 act.[21]

Under the terms of the 1933 act, a judgment creditor may apply to any high court in the United Kingdom within six years after the date of a judgment and have it registered for enforcement by the local court. The judgment must, of course, be valid in accordance with the principles of private international law as applied by the English courts and as set forth in the statute. In this regard the act sets forth in detail the bases for the jurisdiction of the original court that the English courts will recognize. A foreign judgment based on jurisdiction that is not specified in the statute cannot be registered. Inclusion of such provisions gives greater assurance that "substantial reciprocity of treatment" will be accorded judgments from the United Kingdom. Similar provisions were not included in the 1920 act.[22]

Registration gives the judgment the same status and effect as a local judgment. The court has no criteria of convenience or justness to consider and must register the judgment unless it has been wholly satisfied or unless it could not be enforced by the courts of the original country. The judgment must be final and conclusive between the parties and for a sum of money awarded in either criminal or civil proceedings. The former condition may

20. 23 & 24 Geo. 5, c. 13.
21. See *Foreign Judgments (Reciprocal Enforcement) Committee Report,* Cmd. No. 4213 (1932); and Cheshire, *op. cit. supra* note 2, at p. 603.
22. Bases for the jurisdiction of the original court include, *inter alia:* voluntary submission by the defendant; the debtor was the plaintiff in the original action or offered a counterclaim; or the debtor, being the defendant, was a resident or, being a corporation, had a principal place of business within the foreign jurisdiction. In a recent case the court suggested that English courts must grant to foreign courts the same jurisdiction which they claim. Travers v. Holley, [1953] 2 All E. R. 794.

be met notwithstanding that an appeal may be pending against the judgment or that it may be subject to an appeal in the courts of the original country. At its discretion, the court may set aside the application for registration or adjourn the proceedings for a suitable time, if it is satisfied that an appeal on the judgment is pending or that the judgment debtor intends to make an appeal.

Unlike the 1920 act, which does not prohibit a judgment creditor's taking action under the provisions of the common law, the present act stipulates that in cases where registration is obtainable under the provisions of the act, the judgment creditor may not institute proceedings on the judgment at common law. This does not, however, debar the judgment creditor from suing at the common law on the original cause of action.

Because the act, while broadly phrased, does not permit any alternative procedure under the common law, the courts have held that a registered judgment may be the basis for the institution of bankruptcy proceedings.[23]

Although the courts exercise little discretion in the registration process, the act requires them to set aside an application for registration on certain grounds. These grounds include, *inter alia*, that the judgment was obtained by fraud, that enforcement would be contrary to public policy, or that the original court did not have jurisdiction in the circumstances of the case. The problem of fraud was examined by the Court of Appeals in *Syal* v. *Heyward*. In that case the court held that before an application for registration could be set aside for fraud the defendant must establish that there was fraud on the foreign court pronouncing the initial judgment. In such a case, the defendant might introduce evidence known at the time of the initial judgment.[24]

The act may be extended to Commonwealth or foreign countries by order in council when there is evidence of "substantial reciprocity of treatment." If the act is extended to any part of the Commonwealth to which the 1920 act has been extended, the

23. Re a Judgment Debtor, [1939] 1 All E. R. 1.
24. [1948] 2 K. B. 443. See also Zelman Cowen, "Foreign Judgments and the Defence of Fraud," 65 *L. Q. Rev.* 82 (1949); and R. H. Graveson, "Notes of Cases," 12 *Modern L. Rev.* 105 (1949).

latter act ceases to have effect. Further extension of the 1920 act
to any other areas of the Commonwealth is precluded by virtue of
a general order in council extending the 1933 act to His Majesty's
Dominions outside the United Kingdom.[25] This general order
does not, however, have the effect of applying the act to any
particular dominion. An additional specific order extending the
act to each dominion is necessary.[26] At the present time, the act
extends only to Pakistan, India, and the Australian Capital
Territory.[27] Although it was intended to supplant the 1920 act,
that goal has not been realized, and the first act remains undimin-
ished in its scope and importance.

Although the 1920 and 1933 acts apply to the majority of the
members of the Commonwealth and most of the British colonies,
there are some parts of Commonwealth countries to which neither
statute has been extended (for example the provinces of Ontario
and Quebec). Judgments issued by the courts in these areas or
those judgments which are unenforceable under the statutes may
be enforced in the United Kingdom through the common-law
procedure. The judgment creditor may either obtain a judgment
in a British court based on the original judgment or else institute
new proceedings on the original cause of action and introduce the
foreign judgment as evidence.[28]

The common-law requirements for the enforcement of foreign
judgments are basically the same as those set forth in the
previously examined statutes.[29] A judgment for which enforcement is sought must represent the result of an application of the
judicial method; it must have been given by a court of competent

25. Reciprocal Enforcement of Judgments (General Application) Order, 1933,
[1933] *Stat. Rules & Orders* (No. 1073).
26. Yukon Consolidated Gold Corporation, Ltd. v. Clark, [1938] All E. R.
366.
27. Non-Commonwealth states to which the act applies are Belgium, France,
Norway, and Austria.
28. The former alternative does not require the judgment creditor to start fresh
proceedings a second time. The continued existence of these alternative procedures
has been termed an "illogical anomaly." Parry, *loc. cit. supra* note 8, at p. 996.
29. Clive M. Schmitthoff, *The English Conflict of Laws* (3d ed., 1954), pp.
458–479; *Foreign Judgments (Reciprocal Enforcement) Committee Report,* Cmd.
No. 4213 (1932), pp. 6–9; Cheshire, *op. cit. supra* note 2, at pp. 599–636; Parry,
loc. cit. supra note 8, at pp. 983–1039; and Marussia Borm-Reid, "Recognition and
Enforcement of Foreign Judgments," 3 *Int'l & Comp. L. Q.* (4th ser.) 49
(1954).

jurisdiction; it must be final; and action must be brought within twelve years after the date of issuance.

In any action for enforcement, a basic question is whether the original court had proper jurisdiction in the circumstances of the case. In this regard, the important matter for the English courts is not whether the original court had jurisdiction under its municipal law but whether the original court had valid jurisdiction according to the English rules of conflict of laws. Under these rules, valid jurisdiction for actions *in personam* must be based on the principles of presence within the territory and submission to the jurisdiction of the court. In addition, a foreign court's competence over persons who may not have actually submitted to its jurisdiction but who were at the time of the commencement of the suit nationals of the country is recognized.[30] Valid jurisdiction for actions *in rem* requires that the *res* be situated within the territorial jurisdiction of the original court.

The criteria for the finality of a foreign judgment are that the judgment be unalterable, that it be *res judicata* in the court where it was pronounced, and that, if the action is *in personam,* the judgment be for a specific sum of money.[31]

The sole concern of the English courts is that the four requirements mentioned above be met. The courts will not consider the merits of the original decision and will not determine whether it was correct in law or in fact. Furthermore they will enforce a foreign judgment, even if it is evident that the foreign court misinterpreted British law.[32] They will not, however, enforce a judgment if it is proved that the judgment was obtained by fraud,[33] or that the enforcement of the judgment would violate English public policy.[34] In instances where fraud or violation of

30. Emanuel v. Symon. [1908] 1 K.B. 302.

31. A judgment may be final and conclusive, although it is subject to appeal or an appeal may actually be pending against it. Parry, *loc. cit. supra* note 2, at p. 1033.

32. Pemberton v. Hughes, [1899] 1 Ch. 781; and Godard v. Gray, 6 Q.B. 139 (1870).

33. Abouloff v. Oppenheimer, 10 Q.B. 295, 306 (1882).

34. This latter criterion would seem to prohibit the enforcement of judgments for the collection of taxes. It is an established principle of English law that the courts may not be used to collect taxes imposed by another country. The fact that the latter country may be a member of the Commonwealth is immaterial. Re Delhi Electric Supply and Traction Co. Ltd., [1953] 2 All E.R. 1452.

public policy is alleged, the courts will investigate the facts of the case so far as necessary to determine the validity of the allegations.

3. Canada

Enforcement of Commonwealth judgments within Canada is more varied than in the United Kingdom and some of the other Commonwealth countries because Canada is a federal state with twelve distinct judicial units. Enforcement of Commonwealth and foreign judgments is a matter of provincial law and not of federal law. Moreover the courts of one province are foreign courts in relation to the courts of another province, and one province's judgments are foreign judgments insofar as any other province is concerned.[35] It is not surprising then that the initial efforts of Canadian legal scholars and practitioners were directed toward the creation of a uniform judgments enforcement procedure that would bring about co-operation among the provinces.[36] Accordingly the Conference of Commissioners on Uniformity of Legislation in Canada prepared a draft statute to facilitate the reciprocal enforcement of provincial judgments within Canada. This draft was adopted by the provinces of Alberta, British Columbia, Manitoba, New Brunswick, Ontario, and Saskatchewan. Under the terms of the uniform act, as adopted by the mentioned provinces, a monetary judgment given by a court in a civil proceeding or an arbitral award (if it is enforceable in the same manner as a court award) may be registered by the courts of a reciprocating province within six years after the date of the original judgment. A foreign judgment registered in accordance with the act has the same force and effect as a local judgment. In contrast to the 1933 British act, the uniform act specifically

35. Brand v. National Life Assurance Co., [1918] 3 West. Weekly R. 858, 866.

36. See the *Proceedings of the Fourth Annual Meeting of the Conference of Commissioners on Uniformity of Legislation in Canada, 1921*, p. 17, and the view expressed there. See also Kurt H. Nadelmann, "Enforcement of Foreign Judgments in Canada," 38 *Can. B. Rev.* 68 (1960).

provides that the judgment creditor is not deprived of his option either to institute action for the recovery of the judgment or to proceed under the statute. The act also sets forth the grounds which the judgment debtor may plead to prevent the registration of the judgment. These include that the original court did not have jurisdiction; that the debtor, not being ordinarily resident within the jurisdiction of the original court, did not voluntarily appear or submit to the jurisdiction of the original court; that the debtor was not served with the process and did not appear, notwithstanding that he was ordinarily resident in the area or that he had agreed to submit to the jurisdiction of the court;[37] that the judgment was obtained by fraud; that an appeal is pending or that the debtor intends to make an appeal; that the judgment was in respect of a cause of action which on the grounds of public policy would not be entertained by the registering court; or that the debtor would have a good defense if an action were brought on the original judgment. With the exception of the last-mentioned defense (which appears to give the registering court wide discretion), the available defenses reflect the common-law rules and are similar to those set forth in the British statutes.[38]

It should be noted that unlike the 1933 British act, the provincial acts do not set forth the bases for the jurisdiction of the original court that will be recognized by the registering court. In this regard the question whether the original court had proper jurisdiction over the parties in the light of the circumstances of the case is determined by the registering court according to the provincial rules of the conflict of laws.[39] Consequently, although

37. In Wedlay v. Quist, [1953] 4 D. L. R. 620, the Supreme Court of Alberta refused to grant an *ex parte* order under the Alberta statute, because the defendant had been personally served in Alberta by a writ that was issued in British Columbia.

38. For the text of the uniform act, see *Proceedings of the Seventh Annual Meeting of the Conference of Commissioners on Uniformity of Legislation in Canada, 1924,* pp. 60–63. See also *Rev. Stat. of Sask.* c. 84 (1953); *Rev. Stat. of Man.* c. 221 (1954); *Rev. Stat. of Ont.* c. 345 (1960); *Rev. Stat. of New Brun.* c. 192 (1952).

39. In Marshall v. Houghton, [1923] 2 West. Weekly R. 553, the court declared that it would recognize and enforce a foreign judgment where the defendant was a subject of the foreign country in which the judgment was obtained. Application of this rule presented difficulties between parts of the dominions, since it was not possible to speak of a subject of England or of Manitoba. Such a person was a subject of the King and not of any particular portion of the King's

the acts provide for procedural uniformity, they do not insure that there will be substantive uniformity and reciprocal recognition of the bases for the jurisdiction of foreign courts.[40]

Since the purpose of the acts was merely to create procedural reciprocity within Canada and not to provide for the reciprocal enforcement of Commonwealth judgments, they did not meet the reciprocity requirements of either of the British statutes.

In 1927 the Province of Saskatchewan enacted a subsequent statute, the Judgments Extension Act, to apply on a reciprocal basis to any part of His Majesty's Dominions outside of Canada. With minor exceptions, the act's provisions are essentially the same as those of the uniform act mentioned above.[41] Because of the empire-wide reciprocal procedures incorporated in the act, the 1920 British act has been extended to Saskatchewan.

In 1958, after almost two decades of discussion and work, the Conference of Commissioners on Uniformity of Legislation in Canada adopted a new uniform reciprocal judgments enforcement act that could be extended on a reciprocal basis to any foreign jurisdiction (Commonwealth or otherwise). In matters of substance the 1958 statute is basically the same as the 1924 uniform statute. As of 1962 the new act had been adopted by the provinces of Alberta, British Columbia, and Manitoba.[42]

Unlike the 1933 British act, the present uniform statute does not set forth the bases for the jurisdiction of the original court that will be accepted by the provincial courts. In this regard, the act provides that the judgment debtor may plead as a defense to

Dominions. The true test was whether the defendant owed allegiance to the power which legislated within the jurisdiction. Allegiance might be owed through nationality, domicile, or residence. It is now, of course, possible to speak of Canadian citizens. See chap. 5, *supra*, p. 101.

40. On the matter of reciprocal recognition of jurisdiction, see Gilbert D. Kennedy, " 'Reciprocity' in the Recognition of Foreign Judgments," 32 *Can. B. Rev.* 359 (1954); and *idem*, "Recognition of Judgments in Personam: The Meaning of Reciprocity," 35 *ibid.* 123 (1957).

41. A judgment from a Commonwealth area must be registered within twelve months after the date of the original judgment, rather than within six years. The debtor may not offer as a defense the fact that he would have a good defense if action were brought on the original judgment. *Rev. Stat. of Sask.* c. 86 (1953).

42. See *Proceedings of the Fortieth Annual Meeting of the Conference of Commissioners on Uniformity of Legislation in Canada, 1958*, pp. 90–96, for the text of the statute as adopted by the conference. See also *Stat. of Al.* c. 33 (1958); *Man. Stat.* c. 30 (1961); and *Stat. of Brit. Col.* c. 70 (1959).

the registration process the claim that the original court acted without the proper jurisdiction as recognized by the provincial conflict-of-laws rules. This means that the criteria for determining whether the original court had proper jurisdiction are not spelled out in the statute, but are left to the discretion of the registering court. Consequently, although procedural uniformity may be guaranteed, there is no assurance of reciprocal recognition of the grounds for original jurisdiction, as there is in the 1933 British act. This fact should not, however, stand in the way of the act's extension to the mentioned provinces. The act has been extended to India and Pakistan, and, as will be seen below, the Civil Procedure Code does not set forth the jurisdictional grounds that will be recognized by the Indian or Pakistani courts.

The pattern among the remaining provinces regarding enforcement of Commonwealth judgments is more varied. Neither Prince Edward Island nor Nova Scotia has adopted statutory provisions for the enforcement of provincial or Commonwealth judgments. Apparently the common-law provisions apply, insofar as they have not been modified by the local legislature. The Province of Newfoundland has adopted a statute very similar to the British act of 1933. It states specifically that the registration procedure applies to the United Kingdom and may be extended on the basis of substantial reciprocity of treatment to other areas of the Commonwealth or to foreign countries. Although the statute is patterned along the lines of the 1933 British act, the 1920 British act rather than the later act has been extended to the province.[43]

The enforcement procedure in Quebec is unlike that in any of the other provinces: there is no direct registration procedure. Under the provisions of articles 211 and 212 of the Code of Civil Procedure, a judgment from another province is considered to be *res judicata* and may be enforced by a Quebec court if the defendant was personally served in the other province or appeared in the original action. Enforcement of a judgment obtained outside of Canada is more difficult. Under article 210 of the code, which dates back to the Code Michaud of 1629, a

---

43. Foreign Judgments (Enforcement) Act, *Rev. Stat. of New.* c. 130 (1952). Newfoundland adopted the act before it entered the Confederation.

foreign judgment is not regarded as *res judicata,* and the defendant may offer any defense that might have been pleaded in the original action. Consequently the Quebec courts, unlike the common-law courts, will consider the merits of the original judgment. So long as such a provision exists it will be difficult for Quebec to participate in the reciprocal enforcement procedure.[44]

4. Australia

Although Australia like Canada is a federal state, a greater degree of statutory uniformity in the enforcement of foreign judgments has been obtained there than in Canada. In their legislative enactments, the Australian states have adopted the substantive provisions of part 2 of the British Administration of Justice Act, 1920, which provides for the direct registration and enforcement of certain Commonwealth judgments.[45] (Since the acts contain provisions identical to those of the British act, a separate discussion of their provisions here is unnecessary. The discussion of the 1920 act above [p. 234] is pertinent for the Australian statutes.) Only monetary judgments obtained in civil proceedings or arbitral awards, if such awards are enforceable in the same manner as civil awards, may be registered for direct enforcement. A bankruptcy notice may not be registered.[46]

The acts apply directly to the United Kingdom and may be extended on the basis of reciprocity to other parts of Her Majesty's Dominions, protected territories, and trust territories.[47]

44. See Walter S. Johnson, "Foreign Judgments in Quebec," 35 *Can. B. Rev.* 911–949 (1957); and J. G. Castel, "Reciprocal Enforcement of Judgments in the Province of Quebec," 21 *Revue du Barreau de la Province de Quebec* 128–143 (1961). See also Orsi v. Irving Samuel Inc., [1957] Que. C.S. 209; and Canadian Conveyors Ltd. v. Heakes, [1955] Que. C.S. 416.

45. Administration of Justice Act, 1921–1926 (South Australia); Supreme Court Civil Procedure Act, 1932 (Tasmania); Reciprocal Enforcement of Judgments Act, 1927 (Queensland); Administration of Justice Act, 1924–1957 (New South Wales); Supreme Court Act, 1928 (Victoria); Supreme Court Act, 1935 (Western Australia).

46. Re Bassett; Ex parte Farrow Brothers, 16 A. B. C. 178 (1953). In the United Kingdom, a subsequent enactment permits registration of a bankruptcy notice under the terms of the 1920 act. See *supra*, p. 234, n. 16.

47. The South Australia Administration of Justice Act declares that full reciprocity is unnecessary and that "a substantial measure of reciprocity will suffice." This undoubtedly is implied in the other statutes.

Notwithstanding this procedural uniformity, there is no uniform pattern in the states' extension of the acts to the other members of the Commonwealth of Nations. New South Wales, for example, has extended its act to a substantial number of the members of the Commonwealth, but Queensland has apparently extended its act to only a few members.

In addition to this direct enforcement procedure, foreign judgments may be enforced at common law by the institution of a suit upon the original judgment.

A separate procedure has been established to facilitate the enforcement of state judgments within the Commonwealth of Australia itself. Under the Service and Execution of Process Act, 1901–1953 (enacted by the federal government), a judgment from any court of record in any part of the Commonwealth may be registered and enforced in a court of like jurisdiction in any other part of the Commonwealth. Registration is not limited to monetary judgments, but includes orders requiring performance or non-performance of certain acts. The registration procedure is automatic and not at the discretion of the local authorities.[48] The Australian Commonwealth and the territories of Papua and New Guinea and Norfolk Island compose the territorial reach of the act.

5. New Zealand

The registration and enforcement of Commonwealth judgments in New Zealand is a centralized procedure in contrast to the Canadian and Australian practice and is based substantially

48. Australia, *Commonwealth Acts, 1954,* pp. 455 ff. W. L. Morison argues that different principles apply under the act than apply under the common law. Under the latter, before a foreign judgment can be enforced it must be shown that the original court had the proper jurisdiction in the international sense; under the act a judgment to be enforced need only be conclusive in the state in which it was pronounced. A foreign judgment may be refused enforcement on the grounds of public policy or natural justice; under the act a judgment cannot be refused enforcement on either grounds. Furthermore, a foreign judgment may be refused enforcement on the ground of fraud; under the act a judgment can be refused enforcement only where it might be set aside in the state which originally pronounced the judgment. "Extra-territorial Enforcement of Judgments within the Commonwealth of Australia," 21 *Austl. L. J.* 298–302 (1947).

on the British practice. The Reciprocal Enforcement of Judgments Act, 1934, which is presently in force, reproduces in substance the provisions of the British act of 1933. It extends to the United Kingdom and may be extended to any Commonwealth country outside the United Kingdom or to any other foreign country that offers substantial reciprocity of treatment.[49] Like the British statute, the present act sets forth the bases for the jurisdiction of the original foreign court that will be recognized by the New Zealand courts. The importance of such provisions was clear in *Sharps Commercials, Limited* v. *Gas Turbines, Limited,* where the Supreme Court refused to register a judgment obtained by an English creditor against the New Zealand firm. The court found that since the judgment debtor had not taken part in the proceedings or submitted to the jurisdiction of the court, the English court did not have valid jurisdiction in the original cause of action according to the New Zealand statute.[50] The "jurisdiction" of the original court, as specified in the act, relates to jurisdiction that will permit extra-territorial validity to the foreign judgment and does not relate to domestic jurisdiction to hear and determine the matter.

New Zealand's adherence to the British practice was also evident in the Administration of Justice Act, 1922, which was essentially a reproduction of the provisions of the British act of 1920.[51] Earlier New Zealand statutes, however, were unique in their inclusiveness and represent the type of empire-wide enforcement procedure that was mentioned at the Colonial Conference of 1887. The provisions of the Supreme Court Act of 1882, which were subsequently incorporated in the Judicature Act of 1908, permitted any person who obtained a decree or judgment for a sum of money from any court in any of His Majesty's Dominions to present a memorial of the judgment to the Supreme Court and have the judgment enforced by that court. The inclusive scope of this provision to cover a judgment or decree of any court in the empire without the requirement of reciprocity is

49. 25 Geo. 5, pp. 49–60. See W. J. Sim, "Reciprocal Enforcement of Judgments," 16 *N. Z. L. J.* 190–191 (1940).

50. [1956] N.Z.L.R. 819.

51. The 1922 act was repealed by the 1934 act.

certainly much broader than subsequent New Zealand legislation or any legislation that Britain or other Commonwealth countries have enacted.

The status of this section of the Judicature Act of 1908 was in question after the enactment of the 1922 act, and in 1925 a court held that the 1922 act repealed it.[52] The 1934 act reactivates the section, but specifically limits its application to orders and judgments that are not enforceable in New Zealand under its provisions. The act also permits the governor-general to exclude the act's application to a particular country, if that country's courts give unfavorable treatment to New Zealand judgments. This would appear to limit substantially the use of section 56 and make reciprocity of treatment a condition for its use.

As of 1960 the act had been extended to the six Australian states (plus the Capital Territory and the Northern Territory), the Commonwealth countries of Malaya, Nigeria, India, Ceylon, and Pakistan, and a number of colonies and trust territories.[53] (In addition the act applies to the United Kingdom.)

Since the 1934 act duplicates the provisions of the 1933 British act, one would expect that the latter act has been extended to New Zealand. However, this is not the case; it is the 1920 act that has been extended by the United Kingdom to New Zealand. Furthermore, New Zealand has extended its act to many of the Commonwealth jurisdictions to which the British have not yet extended their 1933 act.

6. India and Pakistan

The enforcement of foreign judgments in India and Pakistan, as in New Zealand and other Commonwealth countries, is modeled after the British practice, with the opinions of the high courts citing numerous British decisions and authorities.[54] Enforcement

52. Corry and Co. v. Kelway and Son, [1925] N.Z.L.R. 93.
53. These include, *inter alia*, Hong Kong, North Borneo, Sarawak, Fiji, Bechuanaland, Basutoland, and Swaziland.
54. See the courts' statements in Abdul Wazid v. Viswanathan, [1953] All India Rep., Madras, 261; and in Fazal Ahmed v. Abdul Bari, [1952] P.L.D., Dacca, 155.

is accomplished either by the institution of a suit based on the original judgment or by direct registration of judgments from those countries that offer reciprocal treatment. Since the same basic rules and practices apply in both countries, the procedures will be examined together in this section.[55]

In the absence of direct enforcement, a judgment debtor seeking to enforce a monetary judgment in either an Indian or Pakistani court must institute a suit on the judgment and obtain a local judgment. This procedure does not require reciprocity and is basically the same procedure as that available under the common law. Under the provisions of section 13 of the Civil Procedure Code, a foreign judgment (with some exceptions) is regarded as conclusive in regard to any matter directly adjudicated between the parties.[56] Since the judgment is *res judicata,* it may be pleaded in the local court as ground for enforcement or as a defense against action by the judgment debtor.[57]

The exceptions to the conclusiveness of a foreign judgment mentioned above are specifically enumerated in section 13 and deserve brief consideration. A foreign judgment will not be regarded as conclusive: (*a*) where it has not been pronounced by a court of competent jurisdiction, (*b*) where it has not been given on the merits of the case, (*c*) where it appears on the face of the proceedings to be founded on an incorrect view of international law or a refusal to recognize the local law in cases in which such law is applicable, (*d*) where the proceedings in which the judgment was obtained are opposed to natural justice, (*e*) where it has been obtained by fraud, and (*f*) where it sustains a claim founded on a breach of municipal law.

As has been noted above, any question regarding the jurisdictional competence of the original court is determined by the local

55. For a general discussion of foreign judgments and private international law, see T. S. Rama Rao, "Private International Law in India," 4 *Indian Yb. Int'l Aff.* 219 (1955); and Paras Diwan, "Recognition and Enforcement of Foreign Judgments and Decrees," 19 *Supreme Court Journal* 122 (1956); and M. M. H. Nizami, *Code of Civil Procedure with Commentary* (2d ed., 1955).

56. Initially the code applied only to the states of British India. It has been extended, with few exceptions, to the whole of both India and Pakistan.

57. It is, of course, important that the original judgment indicate the amount at issue. Barket Lal v. Devidas, [1953] All India Rep., Hyderabad, 29.

courts according to the rules and principles of private international law. It is not surprising that many of the rules of private international law regarding jurisdiction applied by the Indian and Pakistani courts are drawn from English decisions and authorities. One of the most frequently cited cases is *Sirdar Gurdyal Singh* v. *Rajah of Faridkote* in which the House of Lords declared that, if the defendant was not present within the territory and had not submitted in any way to the jurisdiction of the original court, its judgment was "by international law an absolute nullity" and should not be enforced by a foreign court.[58] In a more recent decision, the High Court of Bombay enumerated several grounds for permitting extra-territorial effect of *in personam* actions. The original court's jurisdiction would be admitted and its judgments recognized if one of the following conditions were met: (*a*) the defendant was a subject of the foreign country, (*b*) the defendant was resident in the foreign country at the time when action was begun against him, (*c*) the defendant was served with the process while temporarily present in the foreign country, (*d*) the defendant, as plaintiff in the foreign action, selected the forum where judgment was given against him, (*e*) the defendant voluntarily appeared, and (*f*) the defendant had contracted to submit to the jurisdiction of the foreign court.[59]

With the exception of the first requirement, these rules appear to follow the English principles of presence and submission. That nationality is sufficient to warrant extra-territorial validity of a foreign judgment appears questionable. The High Court of Madras once suggested that nationality was sufficient to support the extra-territorial validity of a foreign judgment, but the present view seems to be to the contrary.[60]

58. [1894] A.C. 670. Speaking for the Law Lords, the Earl of Selborne declared that judgments of the Faridkote courts (a native state) were foreign judgments in the courts of British India.
59. Mallappa Yellappa Bennur v. Raghvendra Shamrao Deshpande, [1938] All India Rep., Bombay, 173. See also Chormal Balchand Firm of Chowrahat v. Kasturi Chand Seraoji and Another, 63 *Calcutta L. J.* 175 (1936); and Ghulam Ahmad v. Sarosh Rattanji Wadia, [1959] P.L.D., Karachi, 624.
60. See Ramalinga v. Swaminatha, [1941] Indian L.R., Madras Ser. 891. See the contrary view in I & G Investment Trust v. Raja of Khalikote, [1952] All India Rep., Calcutta, 508.

The second exception, that a foreign judgment will not be considered *res judicata* if it has not been given on the merits of the case, would seem to be directly contrary to the long-established English practice of not inquiring into the merits of the foreign judgment. This is not really the case, however. The Indian and Pakistani courts do not act as appeal courts, examining the original court's reasoning and weighing the merits of the pleadings; their concern is that the foreign court examined the evidence in the case and based its decision on that evidence.[61] An error by the original court is not a matter that can be examined by the Indian courts.[62] Accordingly an *ex parte* judgment given by default because of the non-appearance of the defendant is not one given on the merits and is not conclusive for the local courts. All *ex parte* decisions do not necessarily fall within this exception —only those in which it is clear that the plaintiff did not offer any evidence to support his claim or that the court did not consider the evidence.[63] Although Indian and Pakistani law appears to be more flexible than the English law, local practice does not appear to be unlike British practice.

In *Shah Kantilal* v. *Dominion of India,* the High Court of Calcutta refused to enforce a judgment against the Dominion of India, as owner of the East India Railway, because under the rules of public international law a suit against a foreign state may not be entertained without the consent of the state.[64] Since the government of India had not submitted to the jurisdiction of the Baroda court, its judgment could not be enforced. The question as to whether foreign proceedings are contrary to natural justice has also been considered by the courts. Although it is difficult to spell out in a positive way the essence of natural justice, proceed-

61. East India Trading Co. v. Badat Co., [1959] All India Rep., Bombay, 415; Firm J.H.F.J.K.D. Rajan Singh v. Parma Nand, [1959] All India Rep., Punjab, 306.

62. Manohar Lal v. Raghunath, [1957] All India Rep., M.B., 74. In this case the court held that the original court was the proper forum to correct any mistakes.

63. See especially the statement of the Karachi court in Abdul Ghani v. Saley Mohammad, [1960] P.L.D., Karachi, 594. See also Govindan v. Sankaran, [1958] All India Rep., Kerala, 203; Triloehan Choudhury v. Dayanidhi Patra, [1961] All India Rep., Orissa, 158; Sevagaminatha v. Nataraja, [1961] All India Rep., Madras, 385; and Fazal Ahmed v. Abdul Bari, [1952] P.L.D., Dacca, 155.

64. 92 *Calcutta L. J.* 24 (1953).

ings involving a failure to notify the interested parties or denial of the opportunity to be heard are apparently so repulsive to fundamental rights that they constitute a denial of natural justice.[65]

The procedure for the direct registration and enforcement of foreign judgments is set forth in section 44 A of the Civil Procedure Code. Under the provisions of that section, a monetary judgment from a superior court in any reciprocating territory may be filed in a district court and executed by that court as if it were a local judgment. This reciprocal procedure was incorporated into the Civil Procedure Code in 1937 and was applicable only to His Majesty's Dominions. In 1952 India amended the section to make it applicable to any foreign state that would offer reciprocal treatment; as of 1962, it did not appear that Pakistan had made such a change.[66] The district court may refuse execution if it is satisfied that the judgment falls within any of the exceptions in section 13 mentioned above. Accordingly, a judgment debtor may offer the same defenses as those pertinent in a suit on a foreign judgment. There is an advantage obtainable from the procedure under section 44 A in that it is simpler and more direct, since institution of a separate suit is unnecessary. The benefits can be applied only to judgments from those states that offer reciprocity.[67] The question of whether India and Pakistan are reciprocating territories under the terms of section 44 A is one that arose after partition. The Indian High Courts have consistently held that although the basic Civil Procedure Code applies in both India and Pakistan, they are not reciprocating territories, since no reciprocal arrangement has been concluded by their governments.[68]

65. Abdul Wazid v. Viswanathan, [1953] All India Rep., Madras, 261.
66. In 1938 the British Foreign Judgments (Reciprocal Enforcement) Act, 1933, was extended to British India. At the present time it applies with few exceptions to the whole of India and Pakistan.
67. Chunnilal v. Dundappa, [1951] All India Rep., Bombay, 190; I & G Investment Trust v. Raja of Khalikote, [1952] All India Rep., Calcutta, 508.
68. Dominion of India v. Hiralal Bothra, [1950] All India Rep., Calcutta, 13. See also Golden Knitting Co. v. Mural Traders, [1950] All India Rep., Madras, 293; Kamini Kiuar v. State of Assam, [1952] All India Rep., Assam, 138. The High Court of Madras in *Muthiah Chettiar* v. *Firm Shwebo* held that since Burma was no longer a reciprocating territory, a Burmese judgment could not be enforced under the provisions of sec. 44 A; [1957] All India Rep., Madras, 25.

One problem which has arisen since independence and the establishment of the Indian Union is the question of whether judgments of the former native states issued before the formation of the Union are enforceable in the local courts or whether the judgments retain their initial foreign character and are not enforceable notwithstanding the political changes. Apparently some of the High Courts have taken the view that the judgments retain their foreign character and are not enforceable, whereas other High Courts have taken the view that such judgments lost their foreign character with the formation of the Indian Union.[69]

7. Other Commonwealth Countries

With respect to the enforcement of Commonwealth judgments in other Commonwealth countries, a few guiding generalizations may be made. It appears to be an established principle that the common law followed British settlers and colonizers to the overseas areas and became part of the local law. So long as that law has not been modified by local statute, the common-law procedure for the enforcement of foreign judgments would appear to be operable. In such an event, the decisions of British courts will continue to be important precedents and the writings of British legal scholars will have persuasive force for local courts. This would not, however, appear to be the case where the civil or Roman-Dutch law is utilized, e.g., in Ceylon, Southern Rhodesia, or the Province of Quebec.[70]

It is also clear that the other members of the Commonwealth have enacted legislation providing for the direct registration and enforcement of Commonwealth judgments that is similar to part 2 of the Administration of Justice Act, 1920. That act has been extended by order in council to all of the other members of the Commonwealth, and such action is predicated on the existence of

69. See 6 *Indian Yb. Int'l Aff.* 320–321 (1957); and the note of T. S. Rama Rao in 9–10 *ibid.* 191 (1960).
70. Sir Maurice Sheldon Amos, "The Common Law and the Civil Law in the British Commonwealth of Nations," in *The Future of the Common Law* (1937), pp. 24, 40.

reciprocal arrangements. It is also likely that some of the other members have enacted legislation similar to the 1933 British act. This is the case in Cyprus and Jamaica.[71] Even though enforcement legislation would have been enacted prior to political independence,[72] it is doubtful that it would be repealed following independence.

8. Conclusions

A uniform procedure for the direct registration and enforcement of foreign judgments has been widely adopted throughout the Commonwealth. This practice, which is simpler and more direct than the common-law procedure, is predicated upon the rule of reciprocity. Reliance upon this rule means that the Commonwealth states have in reality followed established international practice instead of formulating a unique *inter se* practice.[73] What is unique is that the statutory system was first applied solely to Commonwealth states before it was applied to non-Commonwealth states.

Two British enactments, part 2 of the Administration of Justice Act, 1920, and the Foreign Judgments (Reciprocal Enforcement) Act, 1933, provide the basic pattern, with similar legislation in force throughout most of the Commonwealth. The main areas that are not participants in this uniform pattern are some of the Canadian provinces. Although the procedure has been fairly

71. The Cypriot laws are Civil Procedure (Reciprocal Enforcement of Judgments) Law, 1921, and the Foreign Judgments (Reciprocal Enforcement) Law, 1935. The Jamaican laws are the Judgments and Awards (Reciprocal Enforcement) Law, 1923, and the Judgments (Foreign) (Reciprocal Enforcement) Law, 1936.

72. Fiji and British Honduras have both enacted legislation that is identical in substance with part 2 of the Administration of Justice Act, 1920, and with the Foreign Judgments (Reciprocal Enforcement) Act. See the Reciprocal Enforcement of Judgments Ordinance (Fiji) and the Foreign Judgments (Reciprocal Enforcement) Ordinance (Fiji) and the Reciprocal Enforcement of Judgments Ordinance (British Honduras). Part 1 of the latter act is identical with part 2 of the 1920 act, and part 2 of the act is identical with the 1933 act. Bermuda has enacted legislation that is identical with part 2 of the British act of 1920. See Judgments Extension Act, 1923.

73. See Mr. Justice Gray's comments on this rule in Hilton v. Guyot, 159 U. S. 113 (1895).

uniformly adopted throughout most of the Commonwealth, its reciprocal application by each member to all other members has been uneven—it has not been applied by each member to every other member to make a neat and symmetrical system. Apparently the procedure is extended by one country to another on the basis of need and utility. It is impossible to know how many judgments have been enforced throughout the Commonwealth in accordance with this standard procedure.

It is also clear that the idea that such a uniform procedure should apply wholly within the empire is no longer valid. The United Kingdom has enacted legislation making the registration and enforcement process applicable to non-Commonwealth countries on a reciprocal basis, and other Commonwealth members have followed suit. It seems likely that this trend will continue. Extension of the procedure to non-Commonwealth countries certainly has not disrupted or compromised its operation within the Commonwealth. Furthermore, its extension to non-Commonwealth countries follows the broader trend within the Commonwealth toward decreasing reliance on *inter se* arrangements.

The existence of a direct registration and enforcement procedure within the Commonwealth undoubtedly plays a minor role from the standpoint of the legal, political, social, economic, and educational ties which hold together the loose association that is the Commonwealth. Nevertheless, as a procedure for fostering respect for the law among states and protecting the legitimate rights of foreign litigants, the procedure plays a role that should not be minimized.

10

Appraisal

Robert R. Wilson

International law has clearly been apparent in the transformation of the British Empire into the present Commonwealth of Nations. As the evolving British Empire extended limited autonomy to the dominions and eventually Commonwealth membership to fully independent states, legal ties between the constituent entities changed. Concepts of statehood found free expression and empire controls gave way to autonomy that rested upon conventional and statutory grants. As the momentum of change increased, some pattern of relationships between the constituent entities had to evolve if any distinctive grouping of these entities was to survive. There were efforts to design a pattern and operate a system of rules for application by Commonwealth states *inter se,* and such rules did have considerable utility. The centrifugal forces, however, proved to be too forceful for arrangements of this sort.

The international law standard was found to be adaptable to many areas where *inter se* rules proved to be inadequate in view of the changes taking place. The standard not only permitted autonomy to run its natural course to complete independence in the legal sense; it also provided an element of flexibility sufficient to permit special ties of many kinds to continue in effect. This flexibility has allowed the member states of the Commonwealth freely to recognize the ties that bind them, if somewhat loosely, in their unique association. These changes can be traced in various fields.

However, recognition of the peculiar ties of the associated

states has not prevented the advent of a kind of neo-nationalism in the Commonwealth. Nor has it precluded the utilization of distinctive methods of official representation within the system. In the very manner and method of acknowledging the existence and application of international law, the states have acclaimed their individual freedom of action. In associated effort for interpretation and adaptation of the law under changing conditions the states have demonstrated their autonomy as well as their propensity for consultation and group action. Problems of nationality and citizenship have provided occasion for some understandings between Commonwealth members as well as legislation by the respective states. Some Commonwealth states have taken a very active part in efforts to distinguish matters of domestic jurisdiction from the viewpoint of international law. Developing patterns of world trade have provided occasion for re-examination of the economic ties which have for some decades been a distinctive force holding these states in their peculiar association. In less controversial areas, such as that of judicial assistance involving processes of extradition and the enforcement of foreign judgments, there has been evidence of adjustment to new and changing conditions. In all these matters there were applications of international law or construction against a background of that law.

Had the facts of history in the twentieth century been substantially different, and had not world wars marked this period, the evolution from dominion status to separate statehood might have taken a different course. There developed, under the impetus provided by constructive statesmen, a concept of self-governing, but not completely independent, entities. This concept merited favorable as well as critical attention and led eventually to the "landmark" pronouncements by the Parliament at Westminster. The development did not come without serious questioning from the point of view of practicability as well as desirability. The mere attainment of independence could not in itself bring to the peoples of the dominions all that they sought. Nor could a sudden and complete break with the empire be rightfully viewed as a step that was not fraught with danger in an insecure world. The statesmen whose concepts of statehood came to be significant in the period from 1917 to 1939 were not mere visionaries. The realization of their dream of statehood involved a gradual adaptation of public law to a situation wherein the dominions were not to be immediately separate in all respects from Great Britain. The dominions, nevertheless, were increasingly viable communities in a dawning new world. While principal emphasis was not always upon the legal aspects of the changing situation, the traditional British regard for law made it natural that there should be continuing regard for the legalities. In the principal world organization the dominions had separate membership. Exercising a right commonly associated in international law with independent states, Canada led the way in the early twenties by signing its own treaties. By the time of the outbreak of World War II the dominions separately could assert their legal right to go to war or to remain at peace.

As compared with the course taken by the members of the old Commonwealth, the emergence in the post-World-War-II period of a new type of Commonwealth state was more precipitate. What had been a multiracial empire became with some suddenness a multiracial and multinational Commonwealth. Even the formal governmental pattern of these new states was not everywhere the same. Some had previously been colonies, some protectorates, some trust territories. Some, exercising their right in the sense of international law, chose presidential rather than monarchical forms of government. In at least two geographical areas unsuccessful efforts for federation marked the stage preliminary to full statehood and Commonwealth membership. Nor was there, on the part of all the newcomers, express and uncritical subscription to *all* the rules of international law that had come to be applied in practice before their assuming the new stations which the United Kingdom had authorized.

There was, however, no express rejection of that law or, for example, the elements of it relating to state succession, as the conclusion of the so-called inheritance agreements with Great Britain will illustrate. The new states in general were soon to adhere vigorously to a policy of opposition to anything identifiable with colonialism or racial discrimination. Their opportunity was frequently found through international organizations. They have had occasion to counsel with other new states of the Asian-African group on such matters as state responsibility and, in particular, on the question of national treatment as the maximum which might properly be demanded by a state for its nationals in the territory of another state.

Except in the area of law last suggested, there have not been serious challenges of the generally accepted rules of international law on the part of spokesmen for the newer members of the Commonwealth. A development which may have effect upon the capacity of the new states to make their interpretations of the existing law effective has been the strong emphasis by states of Africa upon possible African unity. It is conceivable that further movement in this direction might ultimately have fruition in a kind of particularist international law on the African continent. In the meantime, in a situation involving international legal as well as constitutional aspects, Commonwealth states in Africa have joined with other states of that continent in a strongly critical attitude toward the governing regime which in 1965 came to exist in Rhodesia. When the United Kingdom continued in its refusal to concede independence to the Rhodesian state without a liberalization of the franchise, Rhodesia's leaders declared that state's independence. Commonwealth member states have acknowledged no duty on their part to recognize the regime in power in Rhodesia. In another situation, that of Cyprus, operation of the ordinary rules of international law has continued although conditions of communal strife have led to the sending of a United Nations peace force to the island.

As the number of Commonwealth members has increased, new questions have arisen with respect to official representation. It was natural that high commissioners should continue to be used and that their status should eventually rest upon international law rather than empire law. At the political center of the Commonwealth, however, developments seemed to make some changes desirable. One of these was the amalgamation by Great Britain of its overseas service for more effective handling of interests in other Commonwealth states—although in London the Foreign Office and the Commonwealth Relations Office remained separate. With respect to new Commonwealth states' representation in world organizations, association of these states' representatives with those of older Commonwealth states has proved useful for the purpose of tutelage and of assisting toward effective discharge of international responsibilities. In 1965, by action of the Commonwealth prime ministers' conference of that year, there came into existence the Commonwealth Secretariat, headed by a Canadian, and with personnel from other Commonwealth states as well as Great Britain. This development, along with the move by the same prime ministers' conference to create a five-member mission to exercise good offices in Viet-Nam, would seem to indicate that the Commonwealth has become more obviously an instrument as well as a symbol. The move was made against a background of the international law of pacific settlement.

Aside from Commonwealth members' formal assumption and exercise of full rights and stations under international law, the very nature of the Commonwealth was such that there was no uniform procedure for implementation of norms. The assumption of statehood attested acceptance of rules. Long before this, however, there were bases for the law's application to British-controlled territory. Evidence included extensions of the common law to overseas territories. Whether based upon custom, judicial pronouncements, acceptance of the Blackstone doctrine that the law of nations comprises an element of the common law, or explicit constitutional provisions, there is evidence that Commonwealth states adhere to the body of rules comprising international law. Ascertainment and interpretation of rules continue, however, to present problems. Some of these have naturally come before municipal courts. Spokesmen for some of the new states of the Commonwealth have not always accepted uncritically what Western states have in the past acknowledged as law. Recently under discussion have been such matters as the duties of states with respect to resident aliens and the treatment of alien-owned property. On another question, the extent of new Commonwealth states' obligations under prior (British-made) treaties, there has been recourse to the so-called inheritance agreements.

There are continuing problems of interpreting both customary and conventional rules. In work of the Asian African Legal Consultative Committee certain Commonwealth states have had a prominent part. In this connection there have been moves to examine or re-examine some of the elements of international law, such as those recently under study by the International Law Commission, as they are seen from the point of view of the newly independent states. Illustrative is the question of status, with respect to jurisdiction, of state-owned economic enterprises. Prescriptive rights of European states to territory in Asia or Africa have been sharply questioned by spokesmen for some of the developing states. In situations wherein political implications are not so obvious, adherence to traditional standards has been the more general rule. In India, for example, where the reference in the national constitution to international law is in such form that there might be argument as to its specific force and effect for the purpose of the courts, British judicial precedent and Indian regard for orderly government under law have obviously influenced practice. In general, international law as interpreted and applied in the new states of the Commonwealth, through executive and judicial agencies, reflects both the legal heritage and the aspirations of these states.

Matters of nationality and citizenship are relatable to both national and international law. In this connection there has been a transition in the Commonwealth from the concept of common status, i.e., that of British subject under the empire, to that of Commonwealth citizen. The latter term applies to an individual who has the nationality of any Commonwealth state. Some variance has marked practice of the different states of the Commonwealth, but the classification of Commonwealth citizen has legal and practical effect for the individual in a Commonwealth state other than the one to which he owes allegiance. There is nothing in customary international law, or in the commitment of a Commonwealth state to co-operate with other

Commonwealth states, which precludes a Commonwealth state's according to persons from another Commonwealth state treatment more favorable than that accorded to other "foreigners." The fact that the concept of Commonwealth citizen has been retained suggests the feeling that it has utility as well as sentimental purpose. Retention of the concept has not prevented discrimination in the Commonwealth, such as that based upon race or religion. Nor has adherence to the concept precluded immigration restriction. Even the United Kingdom legislation, beginning with the Commonwealth Immigrants Act, 1962, has marked a departure from long-established policy. Disadvantages are conceivable for non-citizens domiciled in some of the newer Commonwealth states whose respective constitutions provide for protection of fundamental liberties of "citizens" rather than "persons" or "individuals." The designation of "citizens" of a particular Commonwealth state would presumably exclude citizens of other Commonwealth states, but the latter would continue to have rights as aliens under international law.

In a number of Commonwealth states an individual who is a citizen of some other Commonwealth state, or a British subject without citizenship, and in some cases even a British protected person may enjoy legal rights by reason of his Commonwealth ties, i.e., rights not possessed by an ordinary alien under international law. The rights may include voting or office holding, or licensing for the practice of professions. There may also be for such a person, by reason of his Commonwealth-citizen status, some correlative duties, such as those of jury or military service. There is no uniformity throughout the Commonwealth with respect to such matters. In some of the states reciprocity is a conditioning factor. In contrast to what a state might have done when there was no such category as Commonwealth citizen, a Commonwealth state may, as is consistent with customary international law, make use of a considerable amount of classification. The latter might come into question in relation to application of the most-favored-nation principle in establishment provisions of treaties. Viewed from another angle, retention of the classification of Commonwealth citizen has made it more natural for a Commonwealth state to exercise good offices or to carry on reclamations in behalf of citizens of other Commonwealth states.

A concept which relates especially to the competence of international organizations, and about which certain Commonwealth states have voiced special concern, is that of domestic jurisdiction. The concept has both legal and political implications. Policies concerning it have apparently been motivated in part by consideration of Commonwealth ties and geographic factors, as well as the proper limits of international law and of the jurisdiction of international tribunals. During the period of the League of Nations, Commonwealth states in general viewed the concept as protecting states against intervention although the Covenant wording, with its express mention of international law, related only to Council action on international disputes. Members invoked the language of the Covenant in attempts to limit the League, and not merely in relation to League efforts for pacific settlement. In the United Nations the older Commonwealth members, with the exception of India, have to a large extent appeared to look to a protective element in the comparable provision of the United Nations Charter. The United Kingdom, which in the *Tunis-Morocco* case advocated a legal definition of the concept, also sought in that instance a standard of reference that would be useful in establishing the international organ's competence to hear the case.

As is well known, Australian spokesmen have in the past expressed concern lest an international body should move to exercise jurisdiction so as to limit the White Australia policy. The state's unwillingness to have international organizations exercise control over internal matters was apparently intensified by Australia's membership in the Commonwealth of Nations. Somewhat in contrast to this, however, has been the same state's position in several other situations—for example, in the Spanish case, the Indonesian case, and the "Observance of Human Rights in Bulgaria, Hungary and Romania"; in these instances Australian spokesmen veered toward the political concept of domestic jurisdiction. The extent to which the motivation was security can only be surmised. Australia's position may be contrasted with that of New Zealand, which has evinced concern for Commonwealth unity in situations where Commonwealth interests were involved, but which has shown no comparable concern for protection of its own or other states' domestic jurisdiction. Ghana's position has been more of a middle one, with willingness to use international organs as devices for mediation and conciliation while not condoning inflammatory discussions. Canadian spokesmen have offered suggestions for moderate procedures both in Commonwealth-related and in non-Commonwealth-related situations in which the domestic jurisdiction reservation was invoked.

The former Commonwealth state of South Africa has maintained what is perhaps the most protective view of domestic jurisdiction—the view that a matter is not removed from the sphere of domestic jurisdiction unless there is an international legal obligation specifically covering it. There has possibly been some deviation from this position in situations involving Communist-bloc countries.

South Africa's views and practice have seemed to incite newer members of the Commonwealth to take an extremely broad view of international jurisdiction as contrasted with domestic. Acclaiming anti-colonialism, opposition to racial discrimination, and human rights, this group has sought to use international organization as a positive force to these ends. Ghana introduced the attack on South Africa at the Thirteenth General Assembly. Whereas India, Pakistan, and Ceylon were once in the forefront of states which attacked the concept of domestic jurisdiction as a legal barrier to international action, it seems likely that Commonwealth states in Africa will in the future direct sharp attacks upon any domestic arrangements which they identify with racial discrimination. These Commonwealth states have already had a considerable part in promoting the relatively new concept of international concern, with its implications affecting the traditional right of independence of states under international law.

In the sphere of international economic relations within the Commonwealth, factors obtain which are in contrast to the legalistic and more purely jurisdictional matters identifiable with domestic jurisdiction. While international trade is obviously distinguishable from international law, and while the law has traditionally allowed each state to decide for itself upon trade policies, it would be unrealistic to assume that agreements in this sphere have no significance for international legalism in the Commonwealth. From a practical point of view the integration of western Europe and its effect upon Commonwealth trading would appear to have more significance for the future of the Commonwealth than, for example, the judicial ties that still exist between the United Kingdom and some Commonwealth states. A similar significance can be ascribed to the diminishing role of Britain as supplier of capital for the Commonwealth.

A distinguishing factor in commercial relations between the United Kingdom and other countries has been the system of preferences inaugurated in the Ottawa agreements of 1932. The magnitude and impact of this factor have, however, been gradually declining since World War II. A salient reason for this has been Britain's and other Commonwealth states' participation in an international undertaking for the expansion of world trade, the General Agreement on Tariffs and Trade (GATT). The terms of the agreement, moreover, interpose legal barriers of a sort that did not exist in 1932 to the construction and readjustment of selective preference schemes such as those devised at Ottawa.

Soon after its inception the Common Market began to overtake the Commonwealth as Britain's leading market, despite Commonwealth preferences. This development poses in very concrete terms continuing questions as to comparative advantages of purely Commonwealth arrangements. Specifically, there remains open the question of whether, despite the breakdown of earlier negotiations looking to British entry into the Common Market, Great Britain may not be drawn increasingly into the integration of western Europe. The potentialities of co-operative arrangements involving Commonwealth as well as non-Commonwealth participation find illustration in the Colombo Plan, initiated in 1950. That continuing arrangements for intra-Commonwealth preferences do not preclude rearrangement is indicated by Britain's entry into the European Free Trade Association (EFTA) in 1960. Commonwealth members have been active participants in the tariff-reduction efforts carried out since 1947 under auspices of the GATT, including the "Kennedy round" of negotiations that opened at Geneva in 1965.

Co-operation of Commonwealth states in matters relating to criminal law has involved some processes that proceed upon the basis, not of ordinary international law, but of special rules which have been devised for application by Commonwealth states *inter se*. This has been the case with respect to rendition of persons accused of crime. An imperial statute provides the basis for procedures which have recently come under considerable discussion, particularly as they have been contrasted with procedures and practice under international law. Re-examination of the practice which has been in use for almost a century has apparently been occasioned in large part by the fact that entities involved, once parts of an empire, are now independent states. The growth of the Commonwealth has already been attended by some changes in the system of returning a person to the jurisdictional unit wherein he is accused of committing crime. Still other changes have become subjects of official discussion. While the United Kingdom's Extradition Act (1870) has had considerable utility, questions have arisen as to the desirability of its application to certain areas, such as Burma and Eire, that were formerly under British jurisdiction but are not now members of the Commonwealth. The Fugitive Offenders Act, 1881, embodies provisions that are different from the general principles of international law applicable to extradition. Under the act a magistrate has authority to order the return of an accused person, if the evidence raises a strong or probable presumption of guilt, and also has authority to endorse the warrant and establish the identity of the fugitive. India's termination of its commitments under the act appears to have been the result of Indian objections to these provisions. A matter that has received much more publicity in the recent past is that, under the 1881 act (in contrast to the plan of the usual type of extradition treaty), political offenders may be extradited. Application of this provision in the *Enahoro* case occasioned critical discussion. On still another point, revision of the act might lead to abandonment of the practice whereby an accused individual can be tried for an offense other than the one for which his return has been obtained. The practice is in contrast to the rule of specialty in international extradition practice.

Innovations in the present system could, of course, be effected through passage of new legislation in substantially the same form by law-making bodies in the various Commonwealth states. Alternatively, judicial interpretation could conceivably effect improvements. As to the latter means, however, the termination by some states of the Commonwealth of appeals from their respective tribunals to the Judicial Committee of the Privy Council has left no one authoritative judicial body to which all appeals might go. A shift from the traditional practice in the Commonwealth to a basis which would permit application of established rules of international law concerning extradition, perhaps as embodied in a multilateral agreement to which not only Commonwealth members but also such states as Burma and Eire might adhere, would not seem to be beyond the range of possibility.

In another area of judicial assistance, the recognition and enforcement of foreign judgments, Commonwealth states have utilized a system of registration and enforcement, but without restricting it to Commonwealth members. There have been, against a considerable common-law background, applications of statutory rules embodied in United Kingdom enactments of 1920 and 1933. A state of the Commonwealth, or a province of such a state, may avail itself of benefits to be had under the plan. In the absence of general acceptance of the plan, there is no uniform Commonwealth-wide system that is in operation in all of the areas. In this field of private international law, still wider adoption of the system of registration and enforcement that is in operation in the Commonwealth would appear to be desirable.

In connection with the actual recognition and enforcement of foreign judgments, there has sometimes been invocation of considerations of "natural justice," as, for example, in India. A simple rule of reciprocity with any other state or jurisdictional unit thereof falls short of an adequate formula in this field of judicial assistance. Aside from this, considerations which in the past have appeared to make judgments of a court in one part of the empire enforceable (for that reason alone) in any other part thereof have undergone change. Eventual substitution for older arrangements of Commonwealth units *inter se* of rules based upon experience and capable of application regardless of the Commonwealth status or non-Commonwealth status of the entities concerned would seem to be a logical development. If treaty based, such an arrangement would comprise rights and duties under public as well as under private international law.

The foregoing consideration of some of the areas in which international law has figured in Commonwealth relations has sought to emphasize some distinctive developments. Historically, communities that are now independent members of the Commonwealth have found it feasible and justifiable to continue, in their relations *inter se,* certain procedures and rules distinguishable from those ordinarily in operation between sovereign states. The Commonwealth states' shift to a basis for public relationships that commonly exists between fully independent states has been a gradual one and is still not complete. Yet the shift to that basis has been eased and made a more natural one by reason of the very nature of the international law standard. For, despite weaknesses in actual application, that standard provides viable patterns of relationship between communities so diverse in race, natural resources, and traditions as are those in the Commonwealth. In the course of recent developments in the Commonwealth, continuing invention in the adaptation to special relationships has not precluded respect for and adherence to the more universal rules. Nor has it precluded effort looking to the improvement or clarified interpretation of those rules. Development of public law for application within states or between states is consistent with traditional Commonwealth resourcefulness and development. With the emergence of additional independent states as members, the element of international law in the Commonwealth relationship has become more obvious.

Appendix

Naturalization and Registration

Robert E. Clute

There is considerable diversity in the Commonwealth with respect to voluntary acquisition of citizenship. Generally, registration is designed to allow certain categories of persons who are either non-aliens or have a close association with the country or its citizens to become citizens of a Commonwealth country, whereas the traditional method of naturalization is in most cases used to bestow citizenship on aliens or British protected persons. Although registration as a method for the acquisition of citizenship is new in the Commonwealth, naturalization has been employed in Great Britain and the empire for centuries.

1. Naturalization

With the passage of the British Nationality Act of 1948 the common status of the naturalized person within the empire and Commonwealth had come full circle.[1] In the eighteenth century the American colonies granted naturalization within their territories, a policy the effects of which were felt throughout the empire. For example, an act of 1740 provided that all foreigners who had resided for at least seven years in "any of His Majesty's colonies in America" without having absented themselves longer than two

1. For summaries of law and practice in regard to naturalization and denization within the British Empire, see: *Report of the Royal Commissioners for Inquiry into the Law of Naturalization and Allegiance, 1868–1869*, Command Paper No. 4109 (1868–1869); *Report of the Naturalization Acts Committee of Inquiry of 1901*, Cd. No. 723 (1901); J. Mervyn Jones, *British Nationality Law* (rev. ed., 1956), chap. 2; Clive Parry, *Nationality and Citizenship Laws of the Commonwealth and of the Republic of Ireland* (1957), chap. 2.

months at any time could be naturalized "on taking oaths, making declarations and receiving the sacrament as therein prescribed."[2] However, the colonists were evidently not content, officially, with subsequent acts, for in the American Declaration of Independence they complained that the king was "obstructing the Laws of Naturalization of Foreigners" and that he had refused to pass other laws to encourage migration.[3]

Prior to 1844 no general naturalization acts were passed in England. Bills granting naturalization were passed as early as the thirteenth century,[4] but such statutes were usually for the benefit of specific individuals or categories of individuals. Letters of denization were also issued by the Crown in much the same manner, with such a letter covering at most a few individuals. The Committee on Law Relating to Aliens examined the matter in 1843 and reported that the special acts and letters were most costly and time consuming.[5] As a consequence, the Aliens Act of 1844,[6] the first general comprehensive naturalization statute to be adopted in the British Empire, was passed.[7] The act called a halt to the general practice of issuing letters of denization and special acts except in unusual circumstances; however, the practice, although infrequently resorted to, continued long after the passage of the act.[8]

Local effect. The act of 1844 introduced an element of doubt which complicated the law of naturalization within the empire for

2. 13 Geo. 2, c. 7. Later acts, 20 Geo. 2, c. 44, and 2 Geo. 3, c. 25, also pertained to the American colonies. The Naturalization Acts Committee of 1901 (*Report, op. cit. supra* note 1) reported that "as early as the 35th year of Charles II, and perhaps earlier," legislatures of British possessions passed acts conferring naturalization on aliens.
3. Para. 9
4. Parry, *op. cit. supra* note 1, at pp. 34 ff.
5. See C. No. 4109, *op. cit. supra* note 1.
6. 7 & 8 Vict., c. 66.
7. The first general legislation in the dominions treating naturalization was the Canadian Naturalization Act, 1881, 44 Vict., c. 13.
8. See C. No. 4109 and Cd. No. 723, *op. cit. supra* note 1. Parry, *op. cit. supra* note 1, at p. 70, notes that the last special naturalization act is claimed to have been passed in 1911. A recent example of an individual's claiming to be a natural-born citizen on the basis of such an act is to be found in Attorney General v. H. R. H. Prince Ernest Augustus of Hanover, [1957] 1 All E. R. 49. The Prince was born in Hanover but successfully claimed to be a British subject under "An Act for the Naturalization of the Most Excellent Princess Sophia, Electress and Dutchess Dowager of Hanover and the Issue of Her Body" passed in 1705.

several decades thereafter. Doubts were expressed as to the effect of naturalization certificates issued in the colonies, which also had their own naturalization laws.[9] Consequently, the Aliens Act of 1847[10] provided that naturalization in the colonies did not provide status within the United Kingdom and vice versa. Thereafter any common status within the empire for naturalized subjects ceased to exist. Since naturalization in the colonies had no extra-territorial effect, it became known as local naturalization. A person thus naturalized was treated as a British protected person by other parts of the empire except when he returned to his country of origin.[11] The extreme divergencies of the colonial naturalization acts subsequent to 1847 did little to engender a concept of common status.[12] The United Kingdom Naturalization Act of 1870 took the same position on the matter as did the act of 1847[13] with the result that considerable numbers of locally naturalized citizens were to be found in the empire as a consequence of the large European migrations to the colonies prior to 1914.

The status of a person in a colony other than that in which he was naturalized is illustrated by the case of *Ex parte Lau You Fat*, 1888. The applicant, a person of Chinese origin, was naturalized in Victoria on January 19, 1886, and returned to China for a temporary visit. On returning he attempted to land at Sydney but was considered to be an alien in New South Wales.[14] The courts of the United Kingdom likewise held in the *Markwald* case that

9. See C. No. 4109, *op. cit. supra* note 1.

10. 10 & 11 Vict., c. 83.

11. See C. No. 4109, *op. cit. supra* note 1.

12. For example, a Canadian act of 1858, 22 Vict., c. 1, required three years' residence; however, a New Brunswick act of 1861, 24 Vict., c. 24, required only one year's residence. Queensland was most lenient to natives of North America or of friendly European powers who could become citizens by merely taking an oath; but Asian and African aliens had to reside in the colony for three years, be married, have a wife resident in Queensland, and take an oath; 31 Vict., Act of Dec. 28, 1867. For a collection of the texts of the laws of British colonies, possessions, and protectorates governing naturalization at the close of the nineteenth century, see Cd. No. 723, *op. cit. supra* note 1.

13. 33 Vict., c. 14, sec. 16.

14. The court commented: "It is no doubt clear that the Acts passed under the authority of the Imperial Act, 10 & 11 Vict. c. 83 and 34 Vict c. 14, gave power to these colonies to pass Acts of Parliament for the purposes of naturalising aliens, but the colonial Acts passed under the provisions of this Imperial Act have no extraterritorial validity, and their effect is limited to the colony in which they are passed. . . ." 9 N.S.W. 269 at 274 (1888). See also Lloyd v. Wallach, 20 Commw. L.R. 299 (1915).

an individual naturalized as a British subject under the Australian Naturalization Act of 1903, who subsequently came to reside in London, was an alien subject to the Aliens Restriction Order of 1916.[15]

However, the Alberta Supreme Court in the case of *Re Solvang* arrived at a somewhat different finding. Solvang, a Norwegian locally naturalized in Canada, was called for military service. His counsel contended that the applicant was only a British subject within Canada and that if he went overseas, he would no longer be subject to service on arrival as he would not have the status of a British subject. The argument relied rather heavily on the *Markwald* case. The court found that Solvang was a British subject. It was held that if such a narrow view were taken of the Canadian statute, the same view would have to be taken on the effect of the British statute, since section 24 of the former statute upon which the applicant had relied was a reproduction *ipsissimis verbis* of section 7 on the British Naturalization Act of 1870 except for the substitution of the word "Canada" for "Great Britain." This appears to be a rather weak argument on the part of the court for it was generally accepted that the British act did indeed impart such a narrow interpretation. The justice also noted that the facts were different in the *Markwald* case since the applicant was still residing in Canada whereas Markwald was resident outside of Australia. The justice concluded that in the latter case the court took "perhaps too narrow a view of the effect of the legislation there in question."[16] The judgment against Solvang was not too well founded and was probably not in agreement with the Canadian government's interpretation of the act.[17]

15. Of the Australian naturalization certificate, the court said: "Such certificates seem to me to confer rights and duties within the Commonwealth [of Australia] only. . . . Nothing but naturalization under powers conferred by Act of Parliament of the United Kingdom can make him other than an alien in the United Kingdom." The King v. Francis, Ex parte Markwald, [1918] 1 K. B. 617 at 624.

16. 43 D.L.R. 549 at 551 (1918).

17. The court also cited considerably from *obiter dictum* in Ah Sheung v. Lindberg, [1906] Vict. L.R. 323, to the effect that by common practice a person naturalized in one colony would receive British protection in another colony. (However, it is submitted that being recognized as a British protected person and as a British subject are two quite different matters.) The decision was hardly in the spirit of the prevailing interpretation of the Canadian Naturalization Act. For

Imperial effect. The difficulties of local naturalization which resulted from such divergence of practice throughout the empire were obvious. A report of the Inter-Departmental Committee on Acts Relating to Naturalization, published in 1901, drew attention to some of the difficulties resulting from local naturalization. The report suggested that some term other than naturalization might be more appropriate for describing the status conferred by local naturalization; however, it was not recommended that the practice be discontinued. The committee also recommended that arrangements be made whereby the governor of a British possession could grant naturalization papers to an individual "conferring the status of a British subject in all parts of the world."[18] The matter was also discussed at length by the Imperial Conference of 1911.[19]

The British Nationality and Status of Aliens Act, 1914,[20] provided that naturalization in the United Kingdom would give an individual the status of a British subject in any British possessions except the self-governing dominions, which then included Australia, Canada, Newfoundland, New Zealand, and the Union of South Africa. The act was not to apply to the latter until the legislature of such a dominion had adopted part 2 of the British act dealing with naturalization. The government of any British possession could likewise grant certificates of naturalization effective throughout the empire provided that in a British possession other than British India or the self-governing dominions such grants would be subject to the approval of the secretary of state. Section 6, part 2, of the act also improved the status of a person already naturalized by providing that an alien naturalized prior to the passage of the act might apply to the secretary of state for a

example, in 1914, Sir Wilfrid Laurier noted in regard to the act that "the existant difficulty is that a person naturalized in Canada would be considered a foreigner in another part of the Empire." Canada, *Parl. Deb.* (Commons), Sess. 1914, p. 4127. One writer in referring to this case declared that "it was only by the most ingenious juristic sophistry that the judges evaded the logic of the *Markwald* case and upheld the legality of the conscription." Norman Mackenzie, ed., *The Legal Status of Aliens in Pacific Countries* (1937), p. 91.

18. Cd. No. 723, *op. cit. supra* note 1.

19. Cd. No. 5745 (1911).

20. 4 & 5 Geo. 5, c. 17. For subsequent revisions, see 8 & 9 Geo. 5, c. 38; 12 & 13 Geo. 5, c. 44; 23 & 24 Geo. 5, c. 49; 6 & 7 Geo. 6, c. 14.

certificate of naturalization under the act of 1914. Naturalization granted under the provisions of the common scheme based on the 1914 act has generally been known as imperial naturalization to differentiate the latter process from that of local naturalization.

The subsequent re-enactment of part 2 of the British Nationality Act of 1914 or its equivalent by the self-governing dominions[21] ended the practice of local naturalization except in the cases of New Zealand, which granted local naturalization to residents of the Cook Islands and Western Samoa who could not speak English;[22] India, which made similar provisions for non-English speaking persons;[23] and the Union of South Africa, which granted local naturalization under a separate act to aliens, who were subjects of ex-enemy powers domiciled in South-West Africa.[24]

The new citizenship laws. Despite slight deviations, the common scheme of 1914 survived even after the enactment of the Statute of Westminster until the system fell with the passage of the British Nationality Act of 1948. The latter act declares that anyone locally naturalized within a colony or protectorate shall be deemed to have become a British subject immediately before the commencement of the act and a person naturalized in the United Kingdom.[25] The British act does not deal with the local status of persons who were locally naturalized in other Commonwealth countries, which was left to the acts of the individual

21. Australia, Naturalization Act, 1917, *Commonwealth Acts, 1917,* Act No. 25; Canada, Naturalization Act, 1914, *Can. Rev. Stat.* c. 138 (1927), as amended by 21 & 22 Geo. 5, c. 39; New Zealand, British Nationality and Status of Aliens (in New Zealand) Act, 1928, 19 Geo. 5, No. 58; Union of South Africa, British Nationality in the Union and Status of Aliens Act, 1926, *Statutes of the Union of South Africa, 1926,* Act No. 18, as amended by the British Naturalization and Status of Aliens Amendment Act, 1942, *ibid., 1942,* Act No. 35, and the Alien Affairs Amendment Act, 1946, *ibid., 1946,* Act No. 52.

22. British Nationality and Status of Aliens (in New Zealand) Act, 1928, sec. 8, *op. cit. supra* note 21.

23. Indian Naturalization Act, 1926, Government of India, *Unrepealed Central Acts, 1924–1930,* Act No. 7 of 1926.

24. South-West Africa Naturalization of Aliens Act, 1924, *Statutes of the Union of South Africa, 1924,* Act No. 30, and the Naturalization of Aliens (South-West Africa) Act, 1928, *ibid., 1928,* Act No. 270. However, local naturalization thus granted was taken away by the Naturalization and Status of Aliens Amendment Act of 1942, *op. cit. supra* note 21, unless a person were the widow, divorced wife, or minor child of a person who was a British subject by means other than Act No. 30 of 1924 or Act No. 270 of 1928.

25. Sec. 32.

countries. It does provide that such persons shall be deemed to be naturalized citizens of the United Kingdom and colonies under the British act if by the law of any colony or protectorate they enjoyed the privileges of naturalization within such an entity prior to the commencement of the British act. However, the transitional provisions of the act also provide that persons naturalized by the government of any Commonwealth country in which a citizenship act had not taken effect might become British subjects without citizenship until the local law came into force and their status as potential citizens in that country had ceased.[26]

However, the common clause,[27] insofar as it had been adopted by a Commonwealth country, would bind that country to respect the decision of another Commonwealth country that locally naturalized British subjects had become citizens and therefore were Commonwealth citizens. For instance, the New Zealand Citizenship Act provides that locally naturalized persons who enjoyed the privileges of naturalization only within New Zealand shall be deemed immediately before the commencement of the act to have become British subjects and persons naturalized in New Zealand.[28] Ghana would thus be bound to recognize the status of such an individual, for by section 13 of the Ghana Nationality Act, 1961, any person who is a citizen of a Commonwealth country is recognized as a Commonwealth citizen.

With the exception of Ceylon, Ghana, and Malaya, all Commonwealth countries which achieved independence prior to 1960 provided that persons who held imperial certificates of naturalization issued within the country passing a new citizenship enactment were entitled to be registered as citizens of that country. Neither the Federation of Malaya Agreement of 1948 nor the Federation of Malaya Constitution contained provisions granting automatic citizenship to naturalized British subjects. However, the Constitution of the Federation of Malaysia permits persons ordinarily resident in a Borneo State or Brunei and who had become United Kingdom citizens as a result of naturalization

26. Sec. 13.
27. See chap. 5.
28. Sec. 2(7).

there to become citizens of Malaysia.[29] Under the Ceylon Citizenship Act a British subject holding an imperial certificate of naturalization could apply to be registered as a citizen of Ceylon, but the number of persons so registered was limited to twenty-five per year.[30] In Ghana no British subject naturalized in the territory of which Ghana is composed became a citizen unless he had a parent born in Ghana, or in the case of a woman, her spouse either became or would but for his death have become a citizen of Ghana under the act.[31] However, since under British legislation[32] such an individual continued to be a citizen of the United Kingdom and Colonies, he was thus eligible to be registered not as a naturalized British subject, but under the provisions of the Ghana Citizenship Act for registering citizens of Commonwealth countries.[33]

Most of the Commonwealth countries include provisions in their acts concerning registration of persons who had been locally naturalized within their territorial jurisdiction. Since most of the Commonwealth countries were free to determine who their citizens were and since such individuals were considered to be British subjects within the countries concerned, it does not clearly appear why any such special provisions were deemed necessary. However, the New Zealand, South Africa, and Pakistan citizenship acts make provisions for the acquisition of their respective citizenships by locally naturalized persons.[34] The Republic of

29. See chap. 5, *supra,* note 37. Under clause 125 (g) of the Federation of Malaya Agreement of 1948 a person naturalized as a citizen of the United Kingdom and Colonies under the British Nationality Act of 1948 could become a citizen of the Federation, provided he had resided in the Settlements twelve years prior to the effective date of the agreement and in the Settlements two years immediately prior to his application and had taken his oath within the Settlements. Citizenship thus acquired prior to Aug. 31, 1957, was retained by the Constitution of Malaya, art. 14 (1) and the Constitution of Malaysia, Second Schedule.

30. Sec. 12; act *op. cit. supra* chap. 5, note 6.

31. Ghana Nationality Act, 1951, secs. 5 and 6; Ghana Nationality Act, 1961, sec. 20; *op. cit. supra* chap. 5, note 29.

32. British Nationality Act, 1958, sec. 2(2); *op. cit. supra* chap. 5, note 4.

33. Ghana Citizenship Act, 1957, sec. 11(1); Ghana Nationality Act, 1961, secs. 3 and 20.

34. New Zealand Citizenship Act, sec. 2(7), *op. cit. supra.* chap. 5, note 9; South African Naturalization Act, 1926, Act No. 7 of 1926; South African Citizenship Act, sec. 2, *op. cit. supra* chap. 5, note 7; Pakistan, *Unrepealed Central Acts, 1924–1933,* vol. 8, p. 296; Pakistan Citizenship Act No. 2 of 1951, sec. 9. For laws governing naturalization in Pakistan, see the Naturalization Act of 1926, as

Cyprus granted citizenship to any person who had been natural-ized by the governor of Cyprus, or any person descended in the male line from a person so naturalized, if application for Cyprus citizenship was made within twelve months of February 16, 1961.[35]

Beginning with the Nigeria and Cyprus independence acts of 1960 the independence acts have followed a common pattern in regard to persons naturalized, either imperially or locally, as subjects of the United Kingdom. They provide that such persons who are United Kingdom subjects shall remain so unless such naturalization has occurred within the territory of the Common-wealth country concerned prior to the effective date of the independence act of the particular country. In the latter case the naturalized person loses his United Kingdom citizenship and acquires the citizenship of the country in which he was natural-ized. In the case of Jamaica, Nigeria, Sierra Leone, Trinidad and Tobago, and Uganda the constitutions follow the Cyprus formula and require that such persons must be registered as citizens of their respective countries before a specified date.[36]

The naturalization provisions of the acts give rise to some intriguing questions of status. If a person has been locally naturalized in a colony or protectorate prior to the commence-ment date of the British Nationality Act, he is deemed by section 32(6) of the act to be a British subject and a person naturalized in the United Kingdom and Colonies. Could such an individual receive citizenship or exercise other rights such as voting in a Commonwealth country other than the United Kingdom if such a country wherein he resided granted such privileges to resident British subjects?

Although no case involving status between two Commonwealth

---

amended by the Naturalization (Amendment) Act, 1950, *Central Acts and Notifications, 1951,* Act No. 23, and Naturalization (Amendment) Act, 1957, *ibid., 1957,* Act. No. 44.

35. British Nationality (Cyprus) Order, 1960, sec. 2 and Schedule D, sec. 5.

36. Constitution of Jamaica, 1962, sec. 4; Constitution of Nigeria, 1963, sec. 9; Constitution of Sierra Leone, 1961, sec. 3; Constitution of Trinidad and Tobago, 1962, sec. 11; Constitution of Uganda, 1962, sec. 8.

countries has been found, the case of *Bulmer* v. *Attorney-General*, 1955, involved the identical point at issue. The case concerned British recognition of localized naturalization in Burma after the latter country chose independence outside of the Commonwealth of Nations. The plaintiff's father was locally naturalized at Rangoon in 1878. It was contended that according to the First Schedule of the Burma Independence Act of December 19, 1947, Bulmer remained a British subject, as the act excepted an individual from losing British nationality if his father or paternal grandfather "became a British subject by naturalization." The court found that plaintiff's contention was correct. Justice Vaisey noted, "I should have thought that in an Act concerning Burma, naturalization in and *quoad* Burma was just the kind of naturalization most likely to have been in the contemplation of the legislature."[37]

This case does not speak directly to the question whether a locally naturalized British subject in one Commonwealth country would be recognized as such in another Commonwealth country under the present laws. It is submitted, however, that the interpretation given by the court raises a strong presumption that a Commonwealth court would recognize status granted by local naturalization unless the acts of the Commonwealth country specifically provide otherwise.

Any individual who has been registered or naturalized (either locally or imperially) as a citizen of the United Kingdom and Colonies and who has made a renunciation of citizenship to meet the requirements for the acquisition of citizenship in another Commonwealth country may resume his United Kingdom citizen-

---

37. The judge declared that naturalization anywhere could have had the same effect but noted that the case might have been more difficult if it had involved Canada or Australia rather than Burma and England, as "it might well have been argued that the legislature could not be supposed to have been considering a naturalization which was effectual neither in this country nor in Burma." He also differentiated the case from the *Markwald* case in that all the latter decided was that an alien locally naturalized remained an alien outside of the locality. The justice called attention to the fact that within Burma the plaintiff was a British subject and if anyone asked him, "Did your father become a British subject by naturalization?" he would answer in the affirmative. [1955] 2 All E. R. 718 at 722.

ship under certain conditions. However, the entity in which he was naturalized may not be an independent Commonwealth country at the time of the application for resumption of citizenship. Thus a person naturalized in Ghana would not qualify, as Ghana would not be a colony or protectorate of the United Kingdom on the date of the individual's application. Presumably a person naturalized in the Union of South Africa would qualify even though he had made a renunciation of United Kingdom citizenship, South Africa being no longer a member of the Commonwealth. A person naturalized in the United Kingdom who lost his status because of citizenship or potential citizenship under the citizenship enactments of another Commonwealth country could also apply for registration as a citizen of the United Kingdom.[38]

The citizenship laws of all countries which had the status of independent Commonwealth countries prior to 1960 contain provisions for the granting of citizenship to aliens, but the term "naturalization" is no longer used in regard to the acquisition of such status in Canada and Ceylon. Acquisition of Ceylon citizenship by aliens is, however, extremely limited.[39] Canada does not distinguish in its requirements between Commonwealth citizens and aliens except that the former are not required to file declarations of intention. Both categories are issued "certificates of citizenship" and the term naturalization has been abandoned.[40] The laws of Malaysia are unique in that a person naturalized as a citizen of Malaysia and not a citizen of Singapore must have at least an elementary knowledge of the Malay language and must have resided in Malaysia outside of Singapore for a period of seven to ten years. Ghana likewise requires knowledge of a

---

38. See *infra*, p. 285.

39. Ceylon, presumably fearful that residents of Indian ethnic origin who had not gained citizenship would attempt to become citizens by naturalization, does not make use of the term "naturalization," but provides that a person not otherwise qualified to be a citizen by descent or registration may be registered as a citizen of Ceylon under certain conditions, and limits the number to twenty-five in any one year. Ceylon Citizenship Act, sec. 12. During passage of the Ceylon Citizenship Act, one member of the House of Representatives called the naturalization provisions a "joke" and claimed that they provided "for no naturalization at all." *Parl. Deb.* (House), vol. 4 (1948–49), col. 1691.

40. Canadian Citizenship Act, sec. 10.

language "indigenous to and in current use in Ghana" as a precondition of naturalization.[41] The language requirements in the mentioned countries would restrict naturalization to persons with a rather close connection; most Commonwealth countries require only a knowledge of English.

The constitutions of the Commonwealth countries which have attained independence since 1960, with the exception of Sierra Leone's, did not make provisions for naturalization. However, the citizenship provisions of such constitutions do provide that aliens with a close connection to citizens of the respective country, such as alien spouses of citizens, may be registered as citizens. Sierra Leone has amended its constitution to provide for naturalization and has not been as restrictive as Ghana in regard to language requirements. The applicant must have "a sufficient knowledge of a language in current use in Sierra Leone," which would include English.[42] However, the constitutions of these countries authorize the legislatures to make laws concerning naturalization. Presumably such laws will be forthcoming in the near future unless the new African states tend toward exclusiveness as did Ceylon.

Disabilities of naturalized persons. Naturalized citizens are, as in many countries, subject to loss of citizenship and possible deportation for acts or omissions which would not cause a natural-born citizen to lose his status. The naturalized citizen may also be subject to certain legal disabilities which are not applicable to the natural-born citizen. Illustrative examples of such disabilities are to be found in the laws of Australia, Malaysia, New Zealand, and South Africa.[43]

The legal disabilities of naturalized citizens have caused much concern and a demand for reform especially in the "old" Commonwealth countries which hope to encourage immigration and at the same time desire to assimilate such immigrants by means of

41. Constitution of Malaysia, Second Schedule; Ghana Nationality Act of 1961, sec. 6.

42. Sierra Leone Constitutional Amendment No. 10 of 1962, sec. 3.

43. For examples see Australia, Act No. 46 of 1920, Act No. 15 of 1939; New Zealand, Act No. 23 of 1920; South Africa, *Statutes of the Union of South Africa, 1910–1947*, vol. 7, p. 249; Constitution of Malaysia, chap. 2.

naturalization. The removal or lightening of provisions for acts or omissions causing a naturalized person to lose his citizenship where a natural-born citizen under the same circumstances would not suffer a loss of citizenship has been a subject of debate in the parliaments of Australia, Canada, and New Zealand.[44] All three countries have recently amended their citizenship laws so as to improve considerably the status of both naturalized and registered citizens.[45]

An increasing liberality in laws governing naturalization and naturalized persons is understandable in countries desiring to attract immigrants. However, in countries like Ceylon, which is concerned about migrants from her subcontinent neighbors; or Malaya, which would like to prevent a further influx of Chinese; and in over-populated countries such as India, it is understandable that a parallel development in the softening of naturalization laws is not likely to be forthcoming.

2. Registration

All members of the Commonwealth of Nations which achieved independent status have provided for the registration of certain categories of persons who have not automatically become citizens by birth or descent. Examples of such persons are Commonwealth or Irish citizens, the spouses of citizens, certain minor children of migrants in the case of India or Pakistan, and non-indigenous persons of long residence in the case of Ceylon and Malaya. It will be noted that although an individual might be registered as a citizen in one country, another country might require a person of the same status to be naturalized; for example, alien wives of citizens are registered as citizens under some citizenship laws but must be naturalized under other citizenship laws.

Commonwealth citizens. Probably the most publicized of the registration provisions are those dealing with the registration of

44. See, for examples, Australia, *Parl. Deb.* (House), Sess. 1956, p. 3419; *ibid.* Sess. 1958, p. 711; New Zealand, *Parl. Deb.* (House), vol. 311, p. 413; Canada, *Parl. Deb.* (Commons), Sess. 1958, p. 4760.
45. See chap. 5, *supra*, note 87.

Commonwealth citizens. Due to the fact that the latter are not considered to be aliens, the process by which such individuals effect a change of citizenship within the Commonwealth is known not as naturalization, but as registration. In all Commonwealth countries except the United Kingdom, the registration of Commonwealth citizens is at the discretion of the Commonwealth government concerned.[46] Also, in most instances, with the exception of the United Kingdom, the residence requirements for the registration of Commonwealth citizens vary little from those for naturalization of aliens, and often a five-year residence is required for both categories. Canada has abandoned the use of the term naturalization and issues "certificates of citizenship" to both aliens and Commonwealth citizens. About the only difference between the latter and the former in the Canadian requirements is that an alien applies for such a certificate, whereas a British subject declares that he desires such a certificate.[47] Although Cyprus provides for the granting of citizenship to certain aliens or British subjects with close connections to the territory of Cyprus, it does not have registration as such.[48]

The registration provisions also vary greatly among the Commonwealth countries. Provisions are made for the registration of Commonwealth citizens in all countries which had achieved Commonwealth status prior to 1960 except Ceylon and Malaya (subsequently Malaysia). All such countries except Ghana, India, and Pakistan treat citizens of Eire as Commonwealth citizens for purposes of registration. Since that date Sierra Leone has provided for the registration of Commonwealth citizens. However, the constitutions of Jamaica, Trinidad and Tobago, and Uganda do not have provisions for the registration of Commonwealth citizens in general. In the latter countries registration is restricted to persons with close local ties, such as

46. The New Zealand registration provisions were originally mandatory, but in 1959 a furor resulted over newspaper accounts that the parents of two brothers known to be dangerous criminals serving sentences in Great Britain planned to bring the brothers to New Zealand for resettlement on completion of their sentences. See New Zealand, *Parl. Deb.* (House), vol. 319, pp. 472–473; *ibid.*, vol. 320, pp. 1255–1257. The British Nationality and New Zealand Citizenship Amendment Act of 1959 made registration subject to the discretion of the minister under sec. 8 (1).
47. Canadian Citizenship Act, sec. 10.
48. See chap. 5, *supra,* note 36.

spouses of citizens, locally naturalized British subjects, or persons born in the territory whose parents were not born in that territory.[49]

Language requirements are prerequisites for the registration of Commonwealth citizens in Australia, Canada, Ghana, New Zealand, Sierra Leone, and South Africa. Since English has been the *lingua franca* of the Commonwealth, this works little hardship except in the case of Ghana where the registrant is required to have a sufficient knowledge of a language which is "indigenous to and in current use in Ghana." Such a language requirement would in most cases insure a close connection with the country.[50] Australia and in some cases New Zealand, evidently concerned with the problem of assimilating large numbers of immigrants, require some knowledge on the part of the registrant of the responsibilities of citizenship.[51]

India, as in the case of Commonwealth citizenship, has placed the registration of Commonwealth citizens or citizens of Eire on a reciprocal footing.[52] The details of the provisions for registration in Pakistan are unclear.[53] Sierra Leone, Trinidad and Tobago, and Uganda permit the registration of British protected persons on the same basis as Commonwealth citizens.[54]

Despite the publicity which the provisions for the registration

49. Constitution of Jamaica, 1962, sec. 4; Constitution of Trinidad and Tobago, 1962, sec. 10; Constitution of Uganda, 1962, sec. 8.

50. The language requirement, in sec. 11, Ghana Citizenship Act, 1957, and sec. 3, Ghana Citizenship Act, 1961, may account for the fact that Ghana registered only 36 persons by May, 1961, all of whom had been citizens of Commonwealth countries. Provisions of the 1961 act also allow citizens of approved neighboring African countries to be registered in the same manner as Commonwealth citizens. During passage of the 1961 act, the minister of interior, in commenting on these provisions, said: "Considerable changes have occurred, however, since 1957, and the concept of the Union of African States is a reality. We now have ties with certain African States as close, if not closer, than those which link the Commonwealth countries. Clearly, this visible orientation of our national outlook should be reflected in our nationality law. . . . " Ghana, *Parl. Deb.* (N.H.), vol. 23, col. 580.

51. Australian Citizenship Act, sec. 12; New Zealand Citizenship Act, sec. 8 (1d).

52. Indian Citizenship Act, sec. 5.

53. Sec. 20 of the Pakistan Citizenship Act provides: "The Central Government may, upon such terms and such conditions as it may by general or special orders specify, register a citizen of a commonwealth country as a citizen of Pakistan." It does not appear that orders implementing this section have been issued.

54. Sierra Leone Constitutional Amendment No. 10 of 1962, sec. 3; Constitution of Trinidad and Tobago, 1962, sec. 10; Constitution of Uganda, 1962, sec. 8.

of Commonwealth citizens have received, they do not allow a Commonwealth citizen to move about and acquire citizenship at will. In many cases the provisions for registration offer few advantages over those for naturalization. The registered citizen may be required to renounce his former citizenship as a condition of registration, thus making as definite a break with his past status as if he had been naturalized in a foreign country. Furthermore, the registered citizen in some Commonwealth countries has a status similar to that of the naturalized person in that he may lose his citizenship and be deported for actions which would not result in loss of citizenship for a natural-born citizen or a citizen by descent.[55] The prerequisites for registration do not vary greatly from those for naturalization.

In some instances where a resident British subject is allowed to exercise citizenship rights, provided he has been allowed legal entry for residence, it is highly doubtful that he will gain any advantage by registering as a citizen. Canada has faced this problem in that some Commonwealth citizens have been somewhat negligent in registering since they may vote and run for office at the end of one year's residence, whereas registration requires five years' residence.[56]

However, a mere examination of the provisions of Commonwealth citizenship laws is not a clear indication of the legal disabilities which a Commonwealth citizen must undergo in order to register as a citizen of a particular country. In order to utilize the registration provisions, the individual must in most cases gain entry into the country, and a Commonwealth citizen migrating to any country within the Commonwealth other than the United Kingdom is considered to be an immigrant. The entrance requirements for Commonwealth citizens may be more difficult than

---

55. See chap. 5, *supra*, p. 000.

56. A member of Parliament drew attention to this problem and suggested that it might be wise to register such individuals after one year of residence. Canada, *Parl. Deb.* (Commons), Sess. 1959, p. 1664. On another occasion an amendment was proposed, but not approved, to encourage Commonwealth citizens to register by providing that after five years' residence they would have an additional year to register. If they did not register within the additional year, they would have to begin their required five years' residence anew before being again eligible to register. *Ibid.*, Sess. 1956, pp. 1089–1090.

those for a foreigner entering the same country. Almost all Commonwealth countries have in some form or another imposed restrictions on the immigration of British subjects or Commonwealth citizens. This is particularly true in the case of the "old" Commonwealth countries which have long discriminated against so-called non-white immigrants. Such restrictions have possibly been one of the greatest sources of friction in Commonwealth relations.[57]

The United Kingdom. In keeping with her position as the mother country, the registration provisions of the United Kingdom are more far-reaching than those of any other country in the Commonwealth. A citizen of Eire or the Commonwealth of full age and capacity who is ordinarily resident in the United Kingdom and has been so resident throughout a period of twelve months is entitled to apply for registration as a citizen of the United Kingdom. A person who was a British subject before the commencement date of the 1948 act and would have been a citizen of the United Kingdom or Colonies but for his citizenship or potential citizenship in another Commonwealth country could apply for registration as a citizen of the United Kingdom until the end of 1962. This provision went far in eliminating statelessness in the case of British subjects who did not attain citizenship under the citizenship enactments of the Commonwealth countries in which they were domiciled.

Under the South Africa Act, 1962, any person who was a British

---

57. See chap. 5, *supra*, note 17. The matter was discussed, sometimes rather heatedly, at almost every Imperial Conference; see Cd. No. 5745 (1911), Cd. No. 5746–1 (1911), Cd. No. 9177 (1918), Cmd. No. 1474 (1921), and Cmd. No. 5482 (1936–37).

In *Re Munshi Singh*, 1914, a British Columbia court upheld the exclusion of a British subject from Canada. The chief justice averred: "That the King, with the advice and consent of the Imperial Parliament, had the power to make laws for the exclusion from British possessions of immigrants, whether British subjects or not, has not been questioned, as indeed it could not be doubted." Another justice declared that "it seems to me plain beyond question that Canada has a right to make laws for the exclusion and expulsion from Canada of British subjects . . . irrespective of whether they came from Calcutta or London." And another justice, after noting that the term "Asiatic race" included Hindus, declared that the better classes of Asiatic races do not leave their own countries. 20 B.C. 243 at 255, 286, 292 (1914). See also, Rex v. Padsha, [1923] So. Afr. L. R. (A. D.) 281.

subject by virtue only of his citizenship of South Africa ceased to be a British subject on May 31, 1962. However, such a person is deemed to be a British subject for registration purposes under the British Nationality Act if he applied for registration as a citizen of the United Kingdom before the end of 1965.

The British Nationality Act of 1964 makes it extremely easy for a person who has been a citizen of the United Kingdom and Colonies in an entity which does not have independent Commonwealth status at the time of his application to apply for a resumption of citizenship. Under the 1964 act a person who has ceased to be a citizen because of a declaration of renunciation made on the assumption that it was necessary because he was about to become a citizen of another Commonwealth country may register as a citizen of the United Kingdom. Such an individual must have been born, naturalized, or registered as a citizen of the United Kingdom and Colonies or have become a British subject by reason of annexation of territory included in such a colony. Such an individual may likewise register if he was born in a British protectorate or protected state or his father or paternal grandfather was so born and was a British subject. If a citizen of the United Kingdom and Colonies makes a declaration of renunciation of citizenship to become a citizen of another country, and the declarant does not attain citizenship of that country within six months, he is deemed to have remained a citizen of the United Kingdom and Colonies.[58]

India and Pakistan. The registration provisions of India and Pakistan are unique in that they attempt to deal with certain demographic problems peculiar to the area. The Indian subcontinent has for some time experienced a large-scale emigration which has resulted in a large number of migrants of Indian and Pakistani origin who have gone abroad but who have not been assimilated. The partition and subsequent mass migrations within the subcontinent have also made the determination of citizenship status a rather difficult problem in both countries.

58. British Nationality Act, 1948, part 2; South Africa Act, 1962; British Nationality Act, 1964, secs. 1, 2.

The Indian constitution (art. 6 [b] [ii]) provides that a person who has migrated to India on or after July 19, 1948, from territory now included in Pakistan and had been registered prior to the commencement of the constitution as a citizen of India by an officer appointed by the government of the Dominion of India shall be deemed to be a citizen of India. Article 8 of the constitution was designed to cover both migrants and persons of Indian ethnic origin living abroad. It provides that any person born, or whose parents or any of whose grandparents were born, in India as defined by the Government of India Act of 1935 and who resides in a territory outside of India as so defined shall be deemed an Indian citizen if he has been registered as a citizen by an Indian diplomatic or consular representative in the country where he is residing. A person who is not a citizen by any of the other provisions of the constitution or the Indian Citizenship Act may, subject to certain conditions and restrictions as prescribed, be registered. However, such an individual must be of Indian origin and be ordinarily resident in India. He must also have been so resident for six months or must be a person of Indian origin ordinarily resident in any place outside of undivided India.[59]

Pakistan's provisions are roughly similar to those of India. The central government of Pakistan may register as a citizen by migration a person who before the commencement of the Pakistan Citizenship Act migrated to the country from any other part of the Indo-Pakistan subcontinent with the intention of residing permanently in Pakistan. However, such a person must, unless exempt by special or general order of the government, have a certificate of domicile.[60] Moreover, if an individual migrated into India after March 1, 1947, from territory which now is part of Pakistan, he shall not be a citizen unless he has returned to Pakistan under a permit for his resettlement or permanent return.[61] Any person who was born or whose father or paternal grandfather was born in the Indian subcontinent and who was

59. Indian Citizenship Act, sec. 5.
60. Pakistan Citizenship Act. sec. 6 (1).
61. *Ibid.*, sec. 7.

ordinarily resident in a country outside of Pakistan at the commencement of the Pakistan Citizenship Act may also be registered as a citizen, provided that he has attained a certificate of domicile or been exempted from such certification.[62]

Federations of Malaya and Malaysia. The provisions for registration in the Federation of Malaya were rather stringent. This was due in part to the heavy influx of Chinese and Indians who could not be assimilated. To this must be added the fact that in the recent past there have been ten sovereigns in Malaya, i.e., the nine local rulers and Great Britain. The native Malay population was not too concerned with the influx of non-indigenous people until after World War II as the Chinese and Indians were often transients with no intention of residing permanently in Malaya. However, postwar developments in China hampered the return of many Chinese to that country with the result that their residence in Malaya became more or less permanent. Development of new citizenship laws in India also made the return of individuals of Indian origin to their homeland more difficult. The citizenship laws of the Federation of Malaya, therefore, attempted to maintain the indigenous Malay hegemony. This explains the lengthy residence requirements varying from seven to twelve years which were applicable to the Federation rather than to the geographic entity of Malaya. The large numbers of Chinese in Singapore were thus excluded from citizenship in the Federation of Malaya.

With the creation of the Federation of Malaysia and the inclusion of Singapore within the new Federation another dimension was raised in the problems of registering citizens. The constitution provided that citizens of Singapore, the Federation of Malaya, and the Borneo States were citizens of Malaysia. Citizenship of Singapore was not severable from citizenship in the Federation of Malaysia, and if such a person lost one of the citizenships he also lost the other. All citizens of the Federation of Malaya became citizens of Malaysia. However, persons who

62. *Ibid.*, sec. 7.

developed a close connection with a citizen of Malaysia who was not a citizen of Singapore, such as wives and minor children, could become citizens by registration. Any person over eighteen years of age born in the Federation of Malaya before August 31, 1957, or in a Borneo State could be registered as a citizen of Malaysia; a citizen of Malaysia was not a citizen of Singapore if he could satisfy certain requirements including a seven-year residence period in the Federation outside of Singapore. Singapore citizens over twenty-one years of age wishing to terminate their dual citizenship and become citizens of Malaysia but not citizens of Singapore could do so through so-called enrolment under the registration provisions. However, such persons had to meet the ten-year residence requirement just as if they were being naturalized.[63]

Ceylon. The provisions of the Ceylon Citizenship Act are quite simple and incomplete as the country had not faced the problems of registration at the time the act was drawn up. Registration has been a much greater problem in Ceylon than in any other part of the Commonwealth. The problem is concerned mainly with the large number of inhabitants from the Indian subcontinent who came to Ceylon under British rule to work the plantations. On gaining independence Ceylon immediately tightened its immigration laws to stop the influx, although the illicit entry of large numbers of Indians has allegedly continued. The Ceylon Citizenship Act of 1948 excluded large numbers of its inhabitants of Indian and Pakistani origin from the possibility of attaining citizenship.[64] The problem seems to have centered mainly on Indian residents, and the Pakistani are seldom mentioned in discussions of the subject. Parliamentary debate on the problem of Indian residents has probably consumed more time in Ceylon

63. Constitution of Malaysia, secs. 15–19. For background of the unique citizenship problems in Malaya, see F. G. Carnell, "Malayan Citizenship Legislation," 11 *Int'l & Comp. L. Q.* 504 (1952). See also note 70, *infra.*

64. Numerous unsuccessful attempts have been made by the Indian community to dispute the validity of Ceylon's new citizenship law; see Sudali Andy Asary, et al. v. Vanden Dressen, 54 C.N.L.R. 66 (1952); Pillai v. Mudanayake, [1953] A.C. 514 and 54 C.N.L.R. 433 (1953); Mudanayake, et al. v. Sivagnana-sunderam, 53 C.N.L.R. 25 (1951).

than any other subject.[65] Ceylon contains about 982,000 persons of Indian origin, and restrictive policy of Ceylon toward such individuals has resulted in considerable tension between that country and India.[66] Ceylon finally attempted to solve the problem by the passage of the Indian and Pakistani Residents (Citizenship) Act of 1949, which made concessions far beyond those desired by many supporters of the government, and the Kandyans in particular. The act as amended provides that, notwithstanding the provisions of the Ceylon Citizenship Act of 1948, certain residents in Ceylon of Indian and Pakistani origin will be permitted to register as citizens of Ceylon.[67] The residence requirements are extremely difficult to satisfy. The act also has very lengthy provisions on form and administration, providing the officialdom with endless opportunities for delay or rejection. The slowness with which registration progressed resulted in increased tension. The prime ministers of India and Ceylon therefore met in New Delhi from January 16 to 18 of 1954 to discuss the matter. The resultant Delhi Agreement provided in part that the two countries would co-operate to end illicit immigration and that Ceylon would expedite registration under the 1949 act. However, in the statement issued by the two prime ministers there was apparent disagreement as to the fate of persons who would not be registered as citizens of Ceylon. The

65. Thus, in the period 1948–1955, the *Parliamentary Debates* of the Ceylonese House of Representatives contain over 1,500 columns devoted to the subject. The prime minister of Ceylon once referred to the problem as the most important with which Ceylon had ever been faced; *Parl. Deb.* (House), vol. 16, col. 3200.

66. *Ibid.*, col. 3208. In Aug., 1963, Prime Minister Nehru declared that there were 950,000 persons of Indian origin in Ceylon; India, *Parl. Deb.* (Lok Sabha), 1953, vol. 3, col. 45.

67. Indian and Pakistani Residents (Citizenship) Act, 1949, Ceylon, *Acts of Parliament, 1949*, Act. No. 3; amended by the Indian and Pakistani Residents (Citizenship) Act, 1952, *ibid. 1952*, Act No. 45. The act, as amended, defines an eligible Indian or Pakistani as one who came from undivided India to reside permanently in Ceylon and does not require domicile as such. Tennekoon v. Duraisamy, [1958] A.C. 354; 59 C.N.L.R. 481 (1958), concerned a person who had come from India and resided in Ceylon since 1939. Due to currency controls in 1950, in order to send money to his mother in India, he signed a currency exchange form stating he was "temporarily resident in Ceylon." The commissioner refused his application for registration on the basis of his having signed the form. The Supreme Court of Ceylon reversed the commissioner's order. On appeal, the Privy Council held that, despite his signature on the exchange form, the applicant's conduct had pointed to an intent to reside permanently in Ceylon. See also Tennekoon v. Panjan, 59 C.N.L.R. 512 (1958).

Indian delegation maintained that only those holding Indian papers or those who were registered with the Indian high commissioner were Indian citizens, whereas the remainder would be stateless. However, Ceylon had hoped to return such individuals to their place of origin.[68]

The application of the law has proven to be extremely stringent and slow.[69] On November 1, 1956, almost two years after the Delhi Agreement, only 50,670 persons had been registered as citizens, and almost half of the applications had been rejected.[70] In December of 1957, Nehru declared that India would accept any such individuals from Ceylon who were eligible to become citizens but, with apparent reference to the stateless group, warned, "we do not accept any person who came under compulsion."[71] The impasse was finally resolved in December of 1964 when India and Ceylon signed an agreement whereby the former would accept 525,000 Ceylonese residents of Ceylon who were of Indian ethnic origin for repatriation in India. Ceylon agreed to confer citizenship on 300,000 other residents of Indian origin in Ceylon. Foreign Minister Swaran Singh of India termed the agreement the "best possible solution."[72] Had India not been willing to make such a compromise a rather large number of

68. See "Treaties," 4 *Indian Yb. Int'l Aff.* 325 (1955). In debate on the Delhi Agreement in the Ceylon House of Representatives, one member said that India "quite unjustifiably trotted out this stateless class." The Prime Minister concluded: "We have got about a million Indians in this country and we cannot afford to have them. We must, therefore, by love and affection send them away." Ceylon, *Parl. Deb.* (House), vol. 16, cols. 3208, 3271.

69. For a summary of judicial decisions under this act, see K. P. Krishna Shetty, "The Law of Citizenship for Indian and Pakistani Residents in Ceylon," 7 *Indian Yb. Int'l Aff.* 165 (1956). The author leaves the impression that the administrative authorities have attempted to make registration as difficult as possible within the letter of the law, while the judiciary has in many cases corrected errors or excesses of the administrators. See Abdul Cader, 56 C.N.L.R. 572 (1955); Pandoram v. Commissioner for Registration of Indian and Pakistani Residents, 58 C.N.L.R. 443 (1957); Chandiram v. Commissioner for Registration of Indian and Pakistani Residents, 59 C.N.L.R. 85 (1958).

70. Ceylon, *Parl. Deb.* (House), vol. 27, col. 866. Compare these figures with the registration of Indians in Malaya. In March, 1963, Prime Minister Nehru noted that as of Dec. 31, 1952, 200,000 Indians had attained citizenship in Malaya; India, *Parl. Deb.* (Lok Sabha), 1953, 3d Sess., vol. 1, col. 672. In May, 1954, the deputy minister of external affairs estimated that there were 615,000 Indians in Malaya; *ibid.*, 1954, 6th Sess., vol. 3, col. 2518.

71. *J. of the Parliaments of the Commonwealth* 90 (1958).

72. New York *Times*, Nov. 27, 1964, p. 63.

unregistered individuals might have been forced to linger on in Ceylon with the unenviable status of unwanted, second-class nationals. Registration practices in Ceylon serve as an excellent example of the insensitivity of governments to human considerations in the face of heavy economic and political pressures.

. . . . .

The provisions regarding the naturalization of citizens in Commonwealth countries show no startling innovations not to be found in the general practice of the international community, except for slight divergence in the matter of residence and the treatment of British protected persons. However, the question of the status of locally naturalized citizens is peculiar to the Commonwealth. The time which has elapsed since the new citizenship laws became effective has not been sufficient to provide the evidences of practice necessary to clarify completely the legal position of such locally naturalized persons.

The provisions for the registration of Commonwealth citizens are not as liberal as they would appear at first glance. The same disabilities exist in most cases which existed for British subjects prior to the passage of the new citizenship enactments and are in no way a product of the latter, but are the result of local discriminatory provisions, as in the case of immigration acts. Actually registration provisions in most cases work to the advantage of immigrants who are welcome in the host countries, such as white immigrants to Australia, Canada, New Zealand, and South Africa, but are still kept quite out of reach of unwelcome immigrants through local restrictive measures. Insofar as the registration of Commonwealth citizens is concerned, the procedure, the resultant effects, and the availability of the device do not in many cases differ greatly from the naturalization process.

Registration provisions for persons other than Commonwealth citizens have proved to be useful instruments for allowing certain persons to attain citizenship because of close connections with the country concerned without utilizing the traditional naturalization process. However, most of all, registration has been useful in the

Asian Commonwealth countries where the normal rules of *jus sanguinus* or *jus soli* would not have achieved the desired result of excluding certain inhabitants of the territories from becoming members of the citizen body because of their religious or ethnic backgrounds.

Index